Addresses and Papers
of
John R. Mott

GENERAL PREFACE

MANY FRIENDS in different parts of the world have during recent years expressed their desire that I write the story of my life and their conviction that I should do so. The preparation of an auto-biography has never appealed to me or to my family. However, the attention which I have devoted to the thorough examination of my somewhat voluminous archives has convinced me that it is my duty to make available invaluable source material bearing on the origin and development of the world-wide Christian movements which it has been my privilege to help establish and develop. The personal records of my extensive and repeated journeys to all parts of the world have added much that is essential. If advantage is ever to be taken of the light which such foundation records shed upon these significant ecumenical movements there is no time to be lost.

It has been my opportunity to be intimately related to the beginnings and development of the Student Volunteer Movement for Foreign Missions, the World's Student Christian Federation, the International Missionary Council, the Young Men's Christian Association, and the modern ecumenical movement, together with various auxiliary or tributary bodies. It has seemed wise, therefore, to devote much attention, in the unsettled period of the Second World War and its aftermath, to assembling and classifying the essential source data, much of which has long been out of print. It early became evident that at least one volume for each movement would be necessary. A final volume is devoted to my papers and addresses which served a wider range of interest than that of any one of the movements to which a full volume is devoted.

NEW YORK, 1946   JOHN R. MOTT

ADDRESSES AND PAPERS
OF
JOHN R. MOTT

The
Student Volunteer Movement
for
Foreign Missions

"The Mount Hermon One Hundred"

ADDRESSES AND PAPERS
OF
JOHN R. MOTT

Volume One

The
Student Volunteer Movement
for
Foreign Missions

NEW YORK
ASSOCIATION PRESS
1946

145

THIS VOLUME IS DEDICATED TO ROBERT P. WILDER,
PIONEER AND PATHFINDER OF THE STUDENT
VOLUNTEER MOVEMENT FOR FOREIGN MISSIONS;
TO FENNELL P. TURNER, ITS MASTER-BUILDER IN
THE MOST CRITICAL YEARS; AND TO ROBERT
E. SPEER, SPIRITUAL LEADER AND PROPHET
THROUGHOUT ITS ENTIRE HISTORY.

CONTENTS

✣✣

VOLUME ONE

THE STUDENT VOLUNTEER MOVEMENT

CONTENTS

PART THREE

PART FOUR

INTRODUCTION

✻✻

IT WAS MY PRIVILEGE to be a student delegate at the first International Christian Student Conference at Mount Hermon, Massachusetts, in the summer of 1886. This gathering will ever be memorable as the beginning of the Student Volunteer Movement for Foreign Missions. Later, I had a responsible part in the organization of this Movement, and then for thirty-two years served as its chairman. It has been a sacred trust to assemble and place on permanent record in the present volume invaluable source material in the form of the official quadrennial reports, all of which it fell to my lot to write, and likewise, certain addresses and articles which my colleagues have felt to be of permanent value. It has seemed best to print all this material without change, although it has involved a certain amount of repetition.

While these documents and papers are of historical value, it is believed that they likewise include vital experiences of significance for the coming day. Knowledge and experience are still our chief and most reliable teachers. The record of this greatest dedication of chosen personalities to the missionary program of the Christian Church constitutes both an apologetic and a challenge to successive generations of youth, as well as to trainers of youth. Every stage in the evolution of the world mission has its vital lessons and incitements for subsequent generations.

While without doubt we shall be dominated chiefly by the forward view, we should not overlook the fact that there are priceless advantages in taking backward glances, and at times making penetrating studies with reference to significant uprisings of dedicated lives.

The study of these records should, and one believes will, throw a flood of light on the qualifications of leaders needed by the world mission in the present most demanding period, likewise on the most rewarding processes and experiences in the preparation of workers and in the successful meeting of the perils in the pathway of those aspiring to leadership.

It is hoped that this assembling of materials bearing on the expansion of Christianity will stimulate interest, concern, and action with reference to the spread of the Christian faith to the totally unoccupied parts of the non-Christian world. When we ponder afresh the unmistakable desires and designs of Christ it is nothing short of alarming that not less than 250,000,000 people are in fields still unoccupied by missionaries. The period of higher specialization on which the missionary movement has entered likewise accentuates the importance of the widening of the appeal for life service.

Influential among the leaders of the significant, modern, ecumenical movement have been former members of the Student Volunteer Movement and the related and more comprehensive Christian Student Movements. Among them are not a few moving spirits in the current program to bring into being a World Council of Churches. All this lends added significance to the foundation-laying, the unifying, and the prophetic aspects of the student missionary uprising.

NEW YORK, 1946   JOHN R. MOTT

PART ONE

EARLY HISTORY OF THE STUDENT VOLUNTEER MOVEMENT FOR FOREIGN MISSIONS

The Haystack Monument at Williams College

EARLY HISTORY OF THE STUDENT VOLUNTEER MOVEMENT FOR FOREIGN MISSIONS[1]

✣✣

I. ORIGIN

IN THE EARLY DAYS of this century, partly as a result of the wonderful spirit of revival which was then sweeping through the Eastern colleges, and partly as a result of reading the record of the heroism and sacrifice of the pioneer representatives of the first missionary societies of England, a deep interest in foreign missions began to develop among the students of New England. It first assumed a practical form in 1808 when Samuel J. Mills and a little group of his fellow students secretly organized at Williams College the Society of Brethren. "The object of this society," in the words of its constitution, "shall be to effect in the persons of its members a mission or missions to the heathen." The main reason for secrecy, doubtless, was the possibility of failure, because in those days there was comparatively no sentiment in favor of such an enterprise. It will be remembered that there was then no missionary society on this continent which had a station on a foreign field. Obviously one great problem which confronted these students was so to affect public opinion as to lead to the formation of an aggressive foreign missionary society. By publication and circulation of two strong addresses on missions, by correspondence with leading clergymen, and by personal work with them during vacations, much was accomplished. The center of activity was then transferred to Andover Seminary. Here some of the men who had come from Williams were joined by Nott, Judson, and others, whom they were surprised to find filled with the same idea and spirit. As a result of their combined labor and influence in the seminary, in the colleges, and in the churches, wherever they spoke, they achieved their purpose; for this missionary movement led by students of the New England colleges furnished the occasion for the formation of the American Board of Commissioners for Foreign Missions.

The leaders in this student missionary movement were anxious to

---

[1] Prepared in 1892, one of the first pamphlets written by Dr. Mott.

accomplish another important object. Not only did they recognize the importance of educating and arousing the Church to send forth and sustain missionaries, but they also clearly discerned that something must be done to awaken and maintain an active interest in missions among college men, in order that there might be a sufficient and constant number of candidates for foreign service. To make this possible they sought by correspondence and visitation to have missionary societies formed in the different colleges. So much in earnest were they that, it is said, some of the members of the parent society at Williams left that institution and entered other colleges, in order to spread the missionary spirit. Their strong desire was to bind the colleges together in an intercollegiate missionary movement. While their labors resulted, in a few years, in planting societies in several institutions, and in raising up a considerable number of missionaries (including some of the most distinguished who have gone out from America), they failed to realize their chief aim—the formation of a widespread, permanent student missionary movement. Their failure in this respect appears to have been due to lack of organization, and more especially to the low spiritual condition of many of the colleges at that time, notwithstanding the fact that in others there had recently been marked revivals of religion. To the American and Canadian students, nearly three quarters of a century later, was left the realization of this hope and purpose.

A memorable conference of college men was held from July 6 to August 1, 1886, at Mount Hermon, overlooking the Connecticut River, in the state of Massachusetts. Two hundred and fifty-one students from eighty-seven colleges, representing all parts of the United States and Canada, had come together at the invitation of Mr. Moody to spend several weeks in Bible study. Ten days passed before the subject of missions was even mentioned in the sessions of the Conference. A few young men, however, like Wilder of Princeton, Tewkesbury of Harvard, and Clark of Oberlin, had come with the deep conviction that God would call from that large gathering of college men a number who would consecrate themselves to foreign missions. They called together all who were thinking seriously of spending their lives on the foreign field. Although several of them had not definitely decided the question, twenty-one students answered this call. This little band of consecrated men began to pray that the spirit of missions might pervade the Conference, and that the Lord would separate many of the delegates unto this great work. In a few days they were to see their faith rewarded far beyond what they had dared to claim.

On the evening of July 16, Dr. Arthur T. Pierson gave a thrilling address on missions. He supported by the most convincing arguments the proposition: "All should go, and go to all." He pressed upon the consciences of his hearers that their relation to missions was after all "only a matter of supreme loyalty to Jesus Christ." He sounded the keynote which set many men to thinking and praying.

A week passed. On Friday night, July 23, a meeting was held which may occupy as significant a place in the history of the Christian Church as the Williams Haystack Prayer-meeting. It is known as the "Meeting of the Ten Nations." It was addressed by sons of missionaries in China, India, and Persia, and by seven other young men of different nationalities—an American, a Japanese, a Siamese, a German, a Dane, a Norwegian, and an American Indian. These men in pithy, burning, three-minute speeches each made one dominant point, namely, the need in his country of more workers from the body of students assembled in that Conference. After the appeals were given, each speaker, during a most impressive silence, repeated in the language of the country which he represented the words, "God is love." Dr. Ashmore, after a few sentences, left with the students the searching challenge, "Show, if you can, why you should not obey the last command of Jesus Christ." The meeting closed with a season of silent and audible prayer, which will never be forgotten by those who were present. The people left the hall in silence. That night was preeminently a night of prayer.

On Tuesday morning, July 27, Dr. William Ashmore of China (who had, as soon as he learned of this Conference on arriving in the country, canceled his engagements for over a week in order that he might attend and lay upon the students the claims of China) added fuel to the flame. He made a ringing appeal to Christians to "look no longer upon missions as a mere wrecking expedition, but as a war of conquest." Mr. Sankey sang with spirit and thrilling fervor, "Tell It Out Among the Nations That the Lord Is King." Mr. Moody prayed earnestly that the missionary spirit might fall upon those present.

By this time the number of volunteers had increased from twenty-one to nearly fifty. During the remaining five days of the Conference the interest became more and more intense. Meetings of the volunteers and those specially interested were held each day. Possibly the most sacred of these was the one held in the parlor of Crossley Hall, from twilight until midnight, on Friday, July 30. Missions became the absorbing topic of conversation wherever the students gathered—in the rooms, in the dining hall, at the swimming wharf, and on the athletic field. Each volunteer became an enlister of others. But the large majority of the decisions were not reached in the presence of others. One by one, the men, alone in the woods or in their rooms with their

Bibles and God, fought out the battle with self, and became obedient to the heavenly vision. Late in the afternoon of the last day the number of volunteers had reached ninety-nine. They assembled for a farewell meeting, during which a man came in and volunteered, making the number at the close of the Conference an even one hundred.

At this final meeting there was a unanimous expression that the missionary spirit, which had manifested itself with such power at Mount Hermon, should be communicated, in some degree at least, to the thousands of students in the colleges and seminaries who had not been privileged to come in contact with it at its source. It was the conviction of the volunteers that the reasons which had led them to decide would influence hundreds of other students, if those reasons were once presented to them in a practical, intelligent, faithful, and prayerful manner. Two days before this the suggestion had come to a few of the volunteers and leaders of the Conference, while on a tramp over the hills near the Vermont border, that a deputation, something like the Cambridge Band, be sent among the colleges. This famous band was composed of seven Cambridge students noted for their scholarship, their prominence in athletics, and above all, their consecration and spirituality. Before going out to China they made a memorable tour among the British universities, creating a great missionary revival among the students—felt also more or less by the entire Church. When this plan was mentioned to the volunteers it was heartily and prayerfully adopted; and a deputation of four students was selected to represent the Mount Hermon Conference and to visit during the year as many institutions as possible.

II. DEVELOPMENT

Of the four men selected for this important mission among the colleges, only one, Mr. Robert P. Wilder, was able to go. After much prayer, Mr. John N. Forman, also of Princeton, was induced to become a member of the deputation. A prominent layman of one of the eastern cities, who was at Mount Hermon during the impressive, closing days, generously offered to bear the expenses involved in the tour, and ever since he has sustained a most helpful relation to the Movement. It would be impossible to estimate the manifold fruitage which has been gathered by the Church as a result of this one man's consecrated giving. Messrs. Wishard and Ober, at that time the international college secretaries of the Young Men's Christian Association, who had selected the members of the deputation, also assumed the responsible duty of facilitating their tour. This first year (1886-1887) may properly be characterized as the year of rapid and wide extension. Messrs. Wilder and Forman visited 176 institutions, including nearly all the leading colleges and divinity schools of Canada and the United States. As a rule they traveled together, but now and then separated in order that they might touch more institutions. Their speeches packed with fresh and telling facts, their arguments firmly anchored in the Scriptures, their unwavering faith in the possibility of evangelizing the world in their generation if the students would but rally around the idea, above all the prayerfulness of their lives, made a lasting impression wherever they went. As a result of their labors the number of volunteers passed from 100 to 2,200 during the year. Even Dr. Pierson in his most sanguine moments had not dared to predict that the Movement would, in so short a time, reach beyond a thousand.

During the second year (1887-1888) the Movement was left to itself. It was unorganized, and had no leadership or oversight whatever. Notwithstanding this fact, and as a result of its inherent life and acquired momentum it continued to expand. The volunteers themselves, by personal work, swelled their number to nearly 3,000. But, on the other hand, like any other vigorous movement left without a guiding hand, it began to manifest certain dangerous tendencies. No particular notice of these was taken until the summer of 1888, when about fifty volunteers from different sections came together at the World's Student Conference at Northfield, and reported the condition of the Movement in their respective institutions. It was then found that there was: (1) A tendency in the Movement at some points to lose its unity. All sorts of missionary societies and bands—with different purposes, methods of work, and forms of constitution—were springing up. It was plain that it would lose much of its power should its unity be destroyed. (2) A tendency to decline in some colleges, because not carefully supervised. (3) A disposition to conflict with existing religious societies appeared in a very few places. All these tendencies were decidedly out of harmony with the original spirit and purpose of the Movement; accordingly it was decided that immediate steps should be taken toward a wise organization. Another consideration helped to influence this decision, and that was a desire to extend the Movement. Thus far it had not touched more than one fifth of the institutions of higher learning on this continent. It was a very critical time in the history of the Volunteer Movement. To Mr. C. K. Ober is due in large measure the credit of safely passing the crisis. He recognized clearly the possibilities of this Movement if properly guarded, developed, and extended; and firmly believed that all the dangerous tendencies would be checked by judicious organization. As chairman of the committee appointed by the volunteers at Northfield for that purpose he suggested, in the main, the flexible yet comprehensive scheme of organization under which the Movement has since been working. Had the counsels of some prevailed at this time, in all human probability the Movement would have disintegrated, and much of the interest have passed away, just as the British delegates at Northfield reported had been the case in their universities after the members of the Cambridge Band and a majority of the men whom they enlisted had gone to the foreign field, and just as the missionary interest waned among the students of New England not long after the pioneer student missionaries had entered upon their lifework in foreign lands. In this connection it is interesting to consider the conditions confronting the Volunteer Movement in the last decade, which differed from those which existed in the colleges in the first decade of the century when the students of Williams College were seeking to form an intercollegiate missionary movement. We have seen that they failed in the effort to accomplish this aim largely because of the lack of Christian organization among the students then, and also because of the low state of spiritual life in many of the colleges. The Volunteer Movement entered a field in which a much larger majority of the students than ever before were Christians. Moreover, it found those Christians peculiarly susceptible to the missionary appeal because of the preparation their minds and hearts had received in Bible classes, in personal work, in country and city missions, and, to a limited extent, in the study of missions, in connection with their Christian Associations. The presence of large intercollegiate Christian organizations not only rendered the spread of the Volunteer Movement a comparatively easy thing, but they also afforded the conditions for making it permanent.

The third year of the history of the Movement (1888-1889) may be called the year of organization. The committee appointed to take this matter in charge decided that the Movement should be confined to students. It was therefore named the Student Volunteer Movement for Foreign Missions. It was noted that practically all the volunteers were members of some one of the four great interdenominational student organizations: the College Young Men's Christian Association, the College Young Women's Christian Association, the American Interseminary Missionary Alliance, and the Canadian Intercollegiate Missionary Alliance. This suggested the plan of placing at the head of the Movement a permanent executive committee composed of one representative appointed by each of these organizations. Thus far the last two organizations named have appointed the same man. This committee is to develop and facilitate the Movement in accord with the spirit and constitutions of the organizations which they represent, and as an organic department of them—thus obviating a new and an unnecessary organization. The plan was first submitted to the College

Committee of the International Committee of the Young Men's Christian Associations, and was heartily approved. They appointed Mr. John R. Mott as their representative. He has held this position ever since. The plan was fully endorsed by the International Committee of the Young Women's Christian Associations, and Miss Nettie Dunn was chosen to represent them. In 1891 she was succeeded by Miss Corabel Tarr. The two Missionary Alliances also favored the plan and named Mr. Robert P. Wilder as their representative. He occupied the position until 1891, when he was followed by Mr. Robert E. Speer, who was succeeded in turn in the spring of 1892 by Mr. D. Willard Lyon. (Mr. Mott was chosen to serve as chairman of the Movement and held that position for over thirty years.) The Executive Committee as first constituted began its work in January, 1889, and soon completed the work of organization. This may be briefly outlined as follows:

The Executive Committee (composed as above) has general supervision and direction of the Movement. It meets on an average of once each month.

The Committee has the following secretaries: (1) A traveling secretary (at times there have been two), whose work consists in organizing, educating, quickening, and setting to work the volunteers in the different institutions and in extending the Movement, not only among previously visited institutions, but also among those as yet untouched. (2) A corresponding secretary, who enrolls and classifies the names of volunteers, tabulates statistics, prepares and distributes printed matter, conducts an extensive correspondence with several hundreds of institutions, and renders such aid to the missionary boards as may be within his power. He also acts as treasurer. Mr. William H. Hannum held this position until shortly before he sailed for India in 1890. Since then Mr. Walter J. Clark has filled the office. (3) An editorial secretary, who aims to keep the Movement before the Church and volunteers. Messrs. R. S. Miller, Jr., E. W. Rand, and Max Wood Moorhead have in turn held this position. Since 1891 it has been unoccupied.

There is an Advisory Committee, with whom the Executive Committee confers about any especially important step in the development of the Movement. It has been composed from the beginning of the following: The Reverend A. J. Gordon, D. D., Bishop M. S. Baldwin, D. D., Miss Abbie B. Child, President Merrill E. Gates, The Reverend George Alexander, D. D., The Reverend A. T. Pierson, D. D.

The Executive Committee, through its traveling secretary, is unable to touch more than one-fifth of the colleges and theological seminaries during the year. It therefore aims to have a corresponding member (or Corresponding Committee) in every state and province in which the extent and condition of the Movement demands it. His work is to carry out the policy of the Committee in his particular field.

In each institution the volunteers are united in what is known as the Volunteer Band. In the colleges this is organized as the missionary department of the College Association. In theological seminaries it is a part of the regular missionary society. These bands hold regular meetings for prayer and for systematic study of missions. Moreover, they seek to spread missionary intelligence, to secure new volunteers, to stimulate systematic giving, and to kindle the missionary spirit in young people's societies and in churches.

While the third year in the life of the Movement has been called the year of organization, it was by no means limited to that. Mr. Wilder was induced to devote this, a second year to work in the field. During that time he touched ninety-three institutions, twenty-five of which had been previously visited, and enrolled 600 new recruits. The larger part of his time, however, he spent in reorganizing the volunteers secured by Mr. Forman and himself on the first tour. During their first year in the work they had favored letting the volunteers form bands independent of the existing religious societies. It was impossible at that time to foresee the result. Two years' observation of the working of these independent bands, however, had completely convinced Mr. Wilder (Mr. Forman in the meantime had gone to India) that it would be far better from every consideration for the volunteers to group themselves together as a part of the missionary department of the existing associations and societies. Within this year, and the one following it, over sixty—or nearly all—of the independent bands merged themselves into these organizations.

The year 1889-1890 will always stand out prominently in the history of the Volunteer Movement as the year of the deepening of its inner life. Mr. Robert E. Speer, of Princeton, 1889, touched 110 institutions, or a larger number than have ever been touched in one year by any other man in the college field. He reached many new colleges, especially in the South and Southwest. Now that the track on which the Movement was to run had been laid down, in the form of wise organization, Mr. Speer saw that its power and efficiency depended on the spiritual life of the individual bands; and so he sought incessantly to bring these groups of volunteers to the great sources of spiritual life and light. Along the pathway of his tour he also gathered 1,100 new volunteers.

The Movement with its principles, purposes, and possibilities was first brought before the Church in a public and an official manner in the year 1890-1891. That was the year of its First International Convention, held from February 26 to March 1, 1891, at Cleveland, Ohio. It constituted the largest student convention ever held, there being about 600 volunteers present from 159 institutions, representing all parts of the United States and Canada east of the Rocky Mountains. In addition to the students there were thirty-three representatives of the leading missionary societies of the United States and Canada, over thirty returned missionaries representing every quarter of the globe, and over fifty other Christian workers. This Convention gave the Movement standing in the eyes of the leaders of the missionary work of the Church. The most conservative among them as they came to understand its methods and spirit gave it the weight of their unqualified approval. During this year the Movement was represented in the field by Mr. W. H. Cossum, of Colgate University, who is now at work in China. Several hundreds of volunteers were added to the roll, and much was done toward making the bands studying and working centers. Miss Lucy E. Guinness, of England, spent nearly three months among the women of our colleges, both in co-educational institutions and in distinctively women's colleges, and enrolled at least 240 volunteers. This tour marked a very successful beginning of special efforts for this class—a phase of work very much neglected up to that time.

The past year (1891-1892) has been a year of education. Mr. J. Campbell White, of the College of Wooster, as traveling secretary, has devoted much of his time, in the 100 institutions which he visited, to the much-needed work of marking out courses of study and lines of work for the volunteer bands. Miss Eloise Mayham has pursued a similar policy in her thorough work among the young women in thirty-five additional institutions. They have been supplemented in this by Mr. Clark, at the office, who has also developed the publication department. Moreover, at the student summer schools, missionary institutes have been established for training leaders of the various volunteer bands. The inauguration of these institutes marked the greatest advance of the year in the development of the Movement. The life and efficiency of the Movement depend chiefly on the life and efficiency of the individual bands; and that in turn depends principally upon the life and efficiency of the leaders of the bands. There was also carried on during the year a thorough investigation into the exact condition and problems of the Movement. This involved a complete examination of the records of all the volunteers as filed in the office, and a careful inquiry into the status of the bands themselves. As the result of a better understanding of the tendencies of the Movement several changes in its methods and policy were made.

The most important of these possibly was the change in the wording of the volunteer pledge or, as it is better called in Great Britain, the volunteer declaration. This was effected on July 14, 1892, at the close of the World's Student Conference at Northfield in a joint meeting of members of the Executive Committees of the Volunteer Movement in Great Britain, and in the United States and Canada. The old wording was: "I am willing and desirous, God permitting, to become a foreign missionary." As changed, it reads: "It is my purpose, if God permit, to become a foreign missionary." The former wording has, as a rule, where it has been carefully explained, been understood to mean simply purpose. At the same time experience had proved that it had been difficult for some men who had employed the old declaration to make its real meaning clear, and moreover, that in some cases, even when clearly presented, it had been misunderstood. It was believed by the two Committees that the new form of declaration would be much more easily explained, and, therefore, much less likely to be misinterpreted. It was decided that the new declaration should be signed only by students who might volunteer after its adoption.

III. Achievements

Several thousands of students have been led by the Volunteer Movement to take the advanced step of consecration involved in forming the purpose to become foreign missionaries. In the large majority of instances this decision has been formed in the spirit of prayer, and solely as unto God. The Biblical argument has influenced far more men than even the vivid presentation of the needs of the fields. The most powerful consideration has been the thought of loyalty to Jesus Christ by obedience to His last command. Well might Dr. McCosh ask before the Movement was two years old: "Has any such offering of living young men and women been presented in our age, in our country, in any age, or in any country, since the day of Pentecost?"

Over 500 volunteers have already gone to the foreign field under the various missionary agencies, and fully 100 more are under appointment. A noted foreign missionary, while at a conference in this country three years ago, said that not more than 2 per cent of those who volunteered in a missionary revival ever sailed. But already, 7 per cent of the members of this Movement have sailed, and fully 10 per cent of the Canadian contingent. Moreover, a large majority of the volunteers are still in the various stages of preparation. The following list of countries in which volunteers are already working indicates their wide distribution: North, East, West, and South Africa; Arabia, Burma, China, Korea, India, Japan, Persia, Siam, and Laos; Syria and Turkey; Bulgaria and Italy; Central America and Mexico; Brazil, Chile, and the United States of Colombia; and the South Sea Islands.

By means of this Movement, missionary intelligence, methods, enthusiasm, and consecration have been carried into 300 colleges on this continent. In 1885, there was comparatively no interest in missions, save in a few of these institutions. Now the missionary department of the College Young Men's and Young Women's Christian Associations is probably the best developed and certainly one of the most influential departments in their entire scheme of work. Today there are nearly six times as many students in these colleges who expect to be foreign missionaries as there were at the inception of the Movement. At least one fifth of the officers of the Christian Associations are volunteers, although the volunteers constitute but one fifteenth of the active membership. Another important fact should not be lost sight of, and that is that every volunteer who sails means more than one missionary. He stands for a large constituency who are interested in the work because he goes. Who can measure the importance of thus enlisting the intelligent sympathy and co-operation of thousands who are to remain at home, in the great missionary undertakings of the Church?

Missionary interest has also been intensified in forty-five theological seminaries. Special missionary statistics concerning the seminaries show that the number of prospective missionaries has been greatly increased during the past few years. Before 1886, it has been stated that one ordained minister out of seventy-seven had gone into the foreign field. Since then, over 11 per cent of the seminary undergraduates have volunteered for foreign service. A more comprehensive study of missions is being carried on by seminary men. As a result of such study, and of the object lesson of so many devoting their lives to the cause of missions, the men who are to enter the home pastorate are realizing as never before their special responsibility to the world field. The Movement is thus rendering an invaluable service. One of the veteran missionary secretaries of America recently said that the great need today is that of a generation of missionary pastors to supplement the missionary volunteers by spreading missionary intelligence and keeping the conscience of the Church sensitive on the subject of the divine claims of foreign missions.

When this Movement began its work in the institutions of higher learning it found fewer than a dozen collections of missionary books which were abreast of the times. Extended search now and then revealed a few of the old class of missionary biographies and broken files of missionary society reports. In very few cases could there have been found in the reading room a missionary periodical. For seven years the representatives of the Movement have been emphasizing in season and out of season the importance of continued study of the best and latest missionary books and papers. Through their influence carefully selected missionary libraries have been introduced into fully seventy-five institutions; and, in the aggregate, several thousands of dollars' worth of the most helpful and stimulating books have been scattered throughout the student field. It would be difficult now to find an institution where there are not now two or more missionary periodicals on file. Some of the best missionary works of Great Britain have, through the influence of the Movement, been introduced into wide and general circulation.

The plan for colleges and theological seminaries to support their own missionaries under their respective boards has been promoted. The seminaries have been led to treble their contributions, and the colleges, which before 1886 were giving practically nothing to missionary work, have for several years been giving over $10,000 each year. It should be stated that this amount comes from only about one tenth of the institutions. The importance of having students acquire the habit of giving systematically to the cause of missions cannot be overestimated. They will not abandon it after they leave the college and the seminary, but as leaders in their churches they will do much to solve the financial problem of missions.

It may truthfully be said that the Volunteer Movement has done more than all other agencies combined to emphasize the idea that each church should support its own missionary. Volunteers have elaborated the plan and have also printed and circulated a pamphlet clearly setting it forth. Moreover, they have actually introduced it in many churches of different denominations with the most gratifying results. A large number of strong testimonials have been collected. The following given by the secretaries of the Foreign Mission Board of the Presbyterian Church, U.S.A., is a striking recognition of the importance of this work:

> We have before us a long list of testimonials from pastors who have tried the experiment with most gratifying results; and we are assured that if this method should become general throughout the churches, it would mark a new era of progress in foreign missions, while, by its reflex influence at home, it would bring one of the greatest blessings that the Church has experienced in a generation.
>
> . . . We gladly recognize the influence which has been exerted along these lines by the Student Volunteer Movement in our colleges and theological seminaries. . . . And we recognize with equal clearness and satisfaction the large part which this Movement has had in arousing churches, Young Men's Christian Associations, Christian Endeavor Societies, etc., to a new interest and to a more adequate contribution of means. . . . The interest which they (the volunteers) create and the funds which they raise are a clear gain. . . .
>
> So far as the Presbyterian churches are concerned, we most heartily commend the work.

F. F. ELLINWOOD,
ARTHUR MITCHELL, } *Secretaries*
JOHN GILLESPIE,

NEW YORK, November 6, 1890   WILLIAM DULLES, *Treasurer*

The success of the Volunteer Movement in the United States and Canada has been so marked that its influence has already been strongly felt in British and Continental universities. The delegates who have come from these insitutions from year to year, have been particularly impressed by this student missionary uprising, and have done much to carry back its methods and spirit. Messrs. Forman, Reynolds, Wishard, and McConaughy have also at different times done not a little toward bringing its principles to the attention of European students. To Mr. Wilder is due in large part the credit of actually organizing the Movement in Great Britain and Scandinavia. For two years students from these countries had urged the Executive Committee to send some representative to Europe. Mr. Wilder was induced to undertake this mission while on his way to India in 1892. An organization to direct the work among the universities of Great Britain was perfected in April, at Edinburgh. It was modeled very closely after the organization which has worked so successfully on this side. The organization of the Movement in Scandinavia is just now taking definite shape. A striking fact is the recent introduction of the Movement in three institutions of South Africa. This resulted from reading accounts of the Movement in this country. Miss Rose J. Sears, a Wellesley volunteer, teaching in the Huguenot Seminary at Wellington, Cape Colony, united and organized the three groups of volunteers.

Another thing achieved by the Movement, while not as tangible as some of the other points named, has been nevertheless just as real and important, and that is the emphasis which it has constantly given to the idea of *the evangelization of the world in this generation.* In over 400 centers of learning this keynote has been sounded year after year in the ears of those who are soon to be the leaders of the different evangelical church agencies. At hundreds of conventions, in all parts of Canada and the United States, it has been proclaimed with convincing power. In thousands of churches it has appealed to the loyalty of Christians, and evoked a sympathetic response. It has differentiated the Volunteer Movement from every other missionary movement undertaken by students. It constitutes at once its ultimate purpose and its inspiration. More and more as the volunteers prayerfully look through the doors of faith opening today unto every nation, ponder the last command of Jesus Christ, and consider the resources of His Church, they are convinced of the necessity, duty, possibility, and probability of realizing their watchcry.

IV. PRESENT STATUS

During the past year an extensive correspondence has been instituted with the volunteers for the purpose of receiving information for statistics. A large proportion of the volunteers have responded, and the following figures, based upon the returns, all are considered safe estimates.

Distribution of volunteers, according to section where enrolled:

CANADA,			480
New Brunswick	15	Ontario	325
Nova Scotia	45	Quebec	95

NEW ENGLAND STATES,			650
Connecticut	95	New Hampshire	25
Maine	60	Rhode Island	25
Massachusetts	430	Vermont	15

MIDDLE ATLANTIC STATES,			1440
Maryland	45	New York	630
New Jersey	340	Pennsylvania	425

SOUTHERN STATES,			845
Alabama	10	South Carolina	25
Arkansas	15	Tennessee	190
Georgia	25	Texas	45
Kentucky	140	Virginia	270
North Carolina	80	West Virginia	45

CENTRAL STATES,			2345
Illinois	805	Michigan	390
Indiana	185	Ohio	740
Wisconsin	225		

WESTERN STATES,			1680
Iowa	460	Missouri	315
Kansas	450	Nebraska	255
Minnesota	185	South Dakota	15

PACIFIC STATES,			60
California	35	Oregon	20
Washington	5		

Total number of volunteers 7500

Distribution of volunteers according to stages of preparation:

IN INSTITUTIONS OF LEARNING,			2900
Academies	540	Colleges	1600
Normal schools	125	Medical colleges	110
Theological seminaries	425	Training schools	100

Out of Institutions (because of state of health, insufficient means, etc.)	950
Graduates (postgraduates, special students, etc.)	500
Ready to go	125

Acceptable by some Foreign Missionary Society.. 100
Hindered by outward surroundings or health, but still wanting to go... 625
Unknown or lost (a majority of them lost track of before Movement
    was organized) 775
Rejected by some Foreign Missionary Society.. 75
Renounced—would not go if conditions were favorable............................ 650
Deceased during preparation... 90
Sailed to engage in foreign missionary work.. 510
Non-students affiliated with voluntary bands.. 200

Distribution of volunteers according to age:

Under 20 years...	10 per cent.
Over 20 years and under 25 years............................	48 " "
Over 25 years and under 30 years............................	31 " "
Over 30 years..	11 " "

Distribution of volunteers according to sex:

Male, 4875	65 per cent.
Female, 2625	35 " "

Distribution of volunteers according to denomination:

Presbyterian, (8 branches).................................	28 per cent.
Methodist, (10 branches)..................................	27 " "
Baptist, (3 branches)......................................	18 " "
Congregational	15 " "
Other denominations	12 " "

V. PURPOSE

The Student Volunteer Movement seeks to enroll volunteers in the colleges and theological seminaries in numbers sufficient to meet all the demands made upon it by the foreign missionary agencies on this continent.

This Movement aims to carry the missionary spirit into every institution of higher learning in the United States and Canada, and to co-operate with similar movements in other lands. The power which will thus come from uniting the Christian students of the world to carry out the last command of Jesus Christ will be irresistible.

Not only does the Movement plan to enlist volunteers, but also to guard and develop them until they pass beyond its proper sphere of influence. This involves the organizing of the volunteers into bands; outlining courses of study for them; enlisting them in active work for missions on educational, financial, and spiritual lines; making the bands praying and self-perpetuating centers; and, finally, helping to bring the volunteers into touch with the various missionary societies or boards.

Since the financial problem is one of the most serious which today confronts every missionary agency, the volunteers propose to do all within their power to hasten its solution. An effort is being made to have each volunteer before sailing secure a financial constituency, and so to cultivate it as to ensure his support on the field. The plan of having each church support its own missionary will be introduced as widely as possible. Moreover, recognizing the wonderful possibilities of the various young people's societies of the day, the Volunteer Movement is making a special effort to secure their active co-operation. These two great movements, called into being during the same decade, are destined to supplement each other in their service to world-wide evangelization.

By far the greatest need of modern missions is that of united, definite, importunate prayer. This alone will lead the Church in this time of times to lift up her eyes and behold the fields. Moreover, the Christians of the two wealthiest nations on the face of the earth will never give as they should until selfishness and practical unbelief in the great designs of God are swept away by the prayers of men who believe in God. And beyond all this, the thousands of consecrated students who have given themselves to this work will never reach the great harvest fields of the world until there is absolute compliance with the human condition laid down by the Lord in His command: "Pray ye, therefore, the Lord of the harvest that He send forth laborers into His harvest." Each volunteer band, therefore, is urged to become a "school of prayer"; and each volunteer wherever he goes should have as his greatest burden the deepening of the prayer life of the Church.

Underlying all these forms of purpose is that ultimate and fundamental object of the Student Volunteer Movement—the evangelization of the world in this generation. This is the watchcry of the volunteers. What does it mean? It does not mean the conversion, or the Christianization, or the civilization of the world, no matter how much the volunteers may believe in each of these. It does mean that the Christians of this generation are to give every person of this age an opportunity to accept Jesus Christ. The volunteers believe that this is an awful necessity, because without it millions will perish. They believe that it is a solemn duty because Christ has commanded it. They believe that it is a possibility because of the inspired object lesson of its achievement by the early Christian Church under far more adverse circumstances than those which confront the Church of the nineteenth century. They believe that it is a probability because of the reasonableness of the demands made by the missionaries themselves that this may be accomplished. Within the last few years, in the two most densely populated and in many respects most difficult fields in the world, large conferences of missionaries have declared with confidence that this can be done. The volunteers say, if they at the front sound the battle cry, should we at the rear beat a retreat? The convocation of missionaries in India, whose estimate corresponds with that of the conference in China, maintained that at least one foreign missionary would be needed for every 50,000 people in unevangelized lands. This means then that 20,000 missionaries are needed in order to "preach the gospel to every creature" within this generation. To say nothing of the great student centers of Great Britain and Scandinavia, is that too large a number to ask for and to expect from the colleges and seminaries of the United States and Canada? There are two states in this country each of which has in its institutions of higher learning more than 20,000 students. Over 2,000,000 young men and women will go out from the institutions of Canada and America within this generation. The foreign field calls for only *one one-hundredth* of them. But where will the money come from to send and support them? It would take less than one six-hundredth of the present wealth of the Christians of America. Stated in another form, it would easily be secured should each of the over two millions of members of our many young people's Christian organizations raise but three cents each day.

There are men and women enough to spare for this grandest mission of the ages. There is money enough to spare to send them. May the spirit of Christ lead His Church to pray the prayer of faith, and to consecrate her men and money to the carrying out of His last command!

PART TWO

REPORTS OF THE EXECUTIVE COMMITTEE OF THE STUDENT VOLUNTEER MOVEMENT FOR FOREIGN MISSIONS

✿✿

REPORTS OF THE EXECUTIVE COMMITTEE OF THE STUDENT VOLUNTEER MOVEMENT FOR FOREIGN MISSIONS [1]

✠✠✠

REPORT PRESENTED AT
THE FIRST INTERNATIONAL CONVENTION
CLEVELAND, OHIO, FEBRUARY 26 - MARCH 1, 1891

INASMUCH as this is the first Convention of the Student Volunteer Movement for Foreign Missions, it seems best to review its history and to set forth its present condition.

I. ORIGIN OF THE MOVEMENT

In July, 1886, a memorable conference of college students was held at Mount Hermon, Massachusetts. Two hundred and fifty-one young men from eighty-seven colleges of the United States and Canada had come together at the invitation of Mr. D. L. Moody to spend four weeks in Bible study. Nearly two weeks passed before the subject of missions was even mentioned in the sessions of the Conference. But one of the young men from Princeton College had come, after weeks of prayer, with the deep conviction that God would call from that large gathering of college men, a few, at least, who would consecrate themselves to the foreign mission service. At an early day he called together all the young men who were thinking seriously of spending their lives in the foreign field. Twenty-one students responded to this call, although several of them had not definitely decided the question. This little group of consecrated men began to pray that the spirit of missions might pervade the Conference, and that the Lord would separate many men unto this great work. In a few days they were to see their faith rewarded far more than they had dared to claim. On the evening of July 16 a special mass meeting was held, at which Dr. Arthur T. Pierson gave a thrilling address on missions. He supported, by the most convincing arguments, the proposition that "all should go and go to all." This was the keynote which set many men to thinking and praying.

---

[1] The eight reports of this series were all prepared by the chairman, John R. Mott.

A week passed. On Saturday night, July 24, another meeting was held, which may occupy as significant a place in the history of the Christian Church as the Williams Haystack Meeting. It is known as the Meeting of the Ten Nations. It was addressed by sons of missionaries in China, India, and Persia, and by seven young men of different nationalities—an Armenian, a Japanese, a Siamese, a German, a Dane, a Norwegian, and an American Indian. The addresses were not more than three minutes in length, and consisted of appeals for more workers. Near the close, each speaker repeated in the language of his country the words, "God is Love." Then came a season of silent and audible prayer, which will never be forgotten by those present. The burning appeals of this meeting came with peculiar force to all.

From this night on to the close of the Conference the missionary interest became more and more intense. One by one the men, alone in the woods and rooms with their Bibles and God, fought out the battle with self, and were led by the Spirit to decide to forsake all and carry the gospel "unto the uttermost part of the earth." Dr. Ashmore, who had just returned from China, added fuel to the flame by his ringing appeal to Christians to look upon "missions as a war of conquest, and not as a mere wrecking expedition."

Only eight days elapsed between the Meeting of the Ten Nations and the closing session of the Conference. During that time the number of volunteers increased from twenty-one to exactly 100, who signified that they were "willing and desirous, God permitting, to become foreign missionaries." Several of the remaining 151 delegates became volunteers later after months of study and prayer.

II. EXTENSION

On the last day of the Conference the volunteers held a meeting, in which there was a unanimous expression that the missionary spirit, which had manifested itself with such power at Mount Hermon, should be communicated in some way to thousands of students throughout the country who had not been privileged to come in contact with it at its source. It was their conviction that the reasons which had led the Mount Hermon hundred to decide would influence hundreds of other college men, if those reasons were once presented to them in a faithful, intelligent, and prayerful manner. Naturally, they thought of the Cambridge Band and its wonderful influence among the universities of Great Britain and decided to adopt a similar plan. Accordingly, a deputation of four students were selected to represent the Mount Hermon Conference, and to visit during the year as many institutions as possible. Of the four selected, only one was able to undertake the mission, Mr. Robert P. Wilder, of Princeton College. Mr. John N. Forman, a graduate of the same institution, was induced to join Mr. Wilder in his tour.

During the year 167 institutions were visited. They touched many of the leading colleges and seminaries in the United States and Canada. Sometimes they would visit a college together; again, in order to reach more institutions, they would separate. Wherever they went their straightforward, forcible, scriptural presentation came with convincing power to the minds and hearts of the students. In some colleges as many as sixty volunteers were secured. Not an institution was visited in which they did not quicken the missionary interest. By the close of the year 2,200 young men and women had taken the volunteer pledge.

During the college year 1887-1888 the Movement was left without any particular leadership and oversight. Notwithstanding this fact, over 600 new volunteers were added during the year, very largely the result of the personal work of the old volunteers.

In the following year, 1888-1889, Mr. Wilder, on his second tour, enrolled 600 volunteers in ninety-three institutions. At least twenty-five of these institutions had not been touched previously by the Movement.

Mr. R. E. Speer, also a graduate of Princeton, during the year 1889-1890 visited 110 institutions, adding 1,100 volunteers to the Movement. He reached many new institutions, especially in the South and Southeast.

Thus far in the year 1890-1891 Mr. W. H. Cossum of Colgate University has added nearly 300 to the roll of volunteers and has extended the Movement to the Maritime Provinces. Miss Lucy E. Guinness of London, England, has spent nearly three months among the women of our colleges. The outcome of her work was at least 240 volunteers. Other volunteers have added several hundreds to those secured by regular workers. The number of names on the volunteer roll now stands at 6,200 scattered throughout the United States and Canada in 350 institutions.

III. ORGANIZATION

About fifty volunteers came together at the Northfield Conference in July, 1888, to pray and plan for the Movement. When the reports were presented, showing the condition of the Movement in all parts of the country, it was found that three dangerous tendencies were beginning to manifest themselves: (1) A tendency in the Movement at some points to lose its unity. All sorts of missionary societies and bands—with different purposes, methods of work, and forms of pledge and constitution—were springing up. It was plain that it would lose much of its power should its unity be destroyed. (2) A tendency to a decline in some colleges. Because not properly guarded and developed, some bands of volunteers had grown cold. (3) A tendency to conflict with existing agencies appeared in a very few places. All these tendencies were decidedly out of harmony with the original spirit and purpose of the Volunteer Movement; accordingly, the volunteers at Northfield decided that immediate steps should be taken toward a wise organization.

Another consideration helped to influence them in this decision, and that was a desire to extend the Movement. Not more than one fifth of the higher educational institutions of America had been touched thus far.

A committee was appointed to organize the Volunteer Movement. That committee, after long and prayerful consideration, decided that the Movement should be confined to students. It was, therefore, named the Student Volunteer Movement for Foreign Missions. It was also noted that practically all the volunteers were members of some one of the four great interdenominational student organizations: namely, the College Young Men's Christian Association, the College Young Women's Christian Association, the Interseminary Missionary Alliance, and the Canadian Intercollegiate Missionary Alliance. This suggested the plan of placing at the head of the Movement a permanent Executive Committee, one to be appointed by each of the organizations, which should have power to develop and facilitate the Movement in harmony with the spirit and constitutions of these organizations. The plan was first submitted to the College Committee of the International Committee of the Young Men's Christian Association, and was heartily approved. They appointed as their representative Mr. J. R. Mott. The plan was also fully approved by the International Committee of the Young Women's Christian Association, and Miss Nettie Dunn was chosen to represent them. The Executive Committee of the Interseminary Missionary Alliance endorsed the plan, and named Mr. Wilder as their representative. The Canadian Intercollegiate Missionary Alliance have also authorized Mr. Wilder to represent them.

The new Executive Committee began its work in January, 1889. They soon perfected a plan of organization which has commended itself to leading men of the different denominations to whom it has been submitted. The plan of organization may be briefly outlined as follows:

> The Executive Committee (described above) has general supervision and direction of the Movement. It has met on an average of once each month.
>
> The committee has three regular secretaries: traveling, corresponding, and editorial.

(1) The work of the traveling secretary consists in organizing, educating, developing, quickening, and setting at work the volunteers in the different institutions, and in extending the Movement, not only among previously visited institutions, but also among those as yet untouched.

The first traveling secretary appointed by the Committee was Mr. R. E. Speer, who held the position for one year. Mr. W. H. Cossum holds this office at present. During a part of this year Miss Lucy E. Guinness traveled in the interest of the Movement.

(2) The corresponding secretary has charge of all the office work of the Movement. He also acts as treasurer.

The work of the office embraces the enrollment and classification of volunteers, the tabulation of statistics, the distribution of printed matter, and an extensive correspondence with several hundred institutions.

Mr. William H. Hannum held this position until shortly before he sailed for India in 1890. Since then Mr. Walter J. Clark has filled this office.

(3) The editorial secretary aims to keep the movement before the churches and the volunteers. He corresponds regularly with the *Missionary Review of the World, The Intercollegian, The Evangel,* and *The Missionary Echo.* Occasional articles are sent to the denominational papers. Messrs. R. S. Miller, Jr., and E. W. Rand have each held the position. Mr. Max Wood Moorhead now occupies it.

There is an Advisory Committee composed at present of the following:— The Reverend Geo. Alexander, D. D., Bishop M. S. Baldwin, D. D., Miss Abbie B. Child, President Merrill E. Gates, The Reverend A. J. Gordon, D. D., The Reverend A. T. Pierson, D. D.

The Executive Committee is to confer with them about every important step in the development of the Movement, in order that nothing may be done which shall justify unfavorable criticism.

The Executive Committee, through their traveling secretary, are unable to touch more than one fifth of the colleges and theological seminaries during the year. They therefore aim to have a corresponding member in every state and province in which the extent and condition of the Movement demand it. This corresponding member carries out their policy, viz., to conserve and extend the Movement in that state or province. In states where it is thought to be advisable there is a corresponding committee instead of a corresponding member. The following states have corresponding members: Maine, Southern New England, New Jersey, Virginia, North Carolina, Ohio, Michigan, Wisconsin, and Missouri. In New York and Illinois there are corresponding committees.

In each institution the volunteers are united in what is known as the Volunteer Band. In the colleges this is organized as the Missionary Department of the college Association. In theological seminaries the band is made a part of the regular missionary society. These bands hold regular meetings for prayer and for systematic study of missions. Moreover, they seek to spread missionary intelligence, to secure new volunteers, to kindle missionary spirit in churches and young people's societies, and to stimulate intelligent and systematic giving to the cause of missions.

IV. ACHIEVEMENTS

The Holy Spirit has worked mightily both in and through this Movement during its short history of less than five years. Among the many things which have been accomplished under His guidance and in His strength, we gratefully record the following.

Fully 6,000 young men and women have been led to take the advanced step of consecration expressed in these words: "We are willing and desirous, God permitting, to become foreign missionaries." It is firmly believed that this step has been taken conscientiously and intelligently in the vast majority of cases.

At least 320 of these volunteers have already gone to the foreign field under the various missionary agencies. A noted foreign missionary recently said that not more than 2 per cent of those who volunteered in a missionary revival ever sailed. But already over 5 per cent of the members of this Movement have sailed; and fully 10 per cent of the Canadian contingent. A very large majority of the volunteers are still in the various stages of preparation.

This Movement has promoted the plan for colleges and theological seminaries to support their own missionaries under their respective boards. At least forty colleges and thirty-two seminaries have adopted the plan either wholly or in part, and in a majority of instances are pushing it with a high degree of success. It is estimated that at least $30,000 have been contributed within the last two years by institutions over and above what they were previously giving.

It may be truthfully said that the Volunteer Movement has done more than all other agencies combined to emphasize the idea that each church should support its own missionary. Volunteers have elaborated the plan and have also printed and circulated a pamphlet clearly setting it forth. Moreover, they have actually introduced it in many churches of different denominations with the most gratifying results. A large number of strong testimonials have been collected. The following given by the secretaries of the Foreign Mission Board of the Presbyterian church, U.S.A., is a striking recognition of the importance of this work:

> We have before us a long list of testimonials from pastors who have tried the experiment with most gratifying results; and we are assured that if this method should become general throughout the churches, it would mark a new era of progress in foreign missions, while, by its reflex influence at home, it would bring one of the greatest blessings that the church has experienced in a generation.
> ... We gladly recognize the influence which has been exerted along these lines by the Student Volunteer Movement in our colleges and theological

seminaries. . . . And we recognize with equal clearness and satisfaction the large part which this Movement has had in arousing churches, Young Men's Christian Associations, Christian Endeavor Societies, etc., to a new interest and to a more adequate contribution of means. . . . The interest which they, (the volunteers) create and the funds which they raise are a clear gain. . . .

So far as Presbyterian churches are concerned, we must heartily commend the work.

F. F. ELLINWOOD,
ARTHUR MITCHELL, } *Secretaries*
JNO. GILLESPIE,

WILLIAM DULLES, JR., *Treasurer*

NEW YORK, November 6, 1890

By means of this Movement, missionary intelligence, enthusiasm, and consecration have been carried into over 200 colleges on this continent in which there was comparatively no interest in missions five years ago. It has made the missionary department of the College Young Men's and Young Women's Christian Associations one of the most advanced and influential departments in their entire scheme of work. At least one fifth of the officers of these associations are volunteers. Moreover, it should not be forgotten that every volunteer won means more than simply one missionary. He stands for a large constituency who are interested in the work because he goes. Who can measure the importance of thus enlisting the intelligent sympathy and co-operation of thousands who are to remain at home in the great missionary operations of the Church?

The missionary interest has been intensified in the theological seminaries. Exhaustive study of the seminary problem has been made, and invaluable statistics have been compiled. These show that the number of prospective missionaries has been greatly increased during the past few years over any previous period. Over 11 per cent of the undergraduates have volunteered for foreign service. The amount of money contributed has been more than trebled; and a more comprehensive study of missions is being undertaken by seminary men. During the past year, especially, the Movement has endeavored to strengthen the missionary spirit in divinity schools by recommending the formation of five district alliances, and the inauguration of deputation work. The American Interseminary Missionary Alliance, at its last convention (October, 1890), passed resolutions favoring our recommendations. Many seminary volunteers have been led to urge systematically upon home churches a more intelligent interest in missions, and far more generous contributions. It is also a striking fact that the men in these seminaries who are to enter the home pastorate are realizing as never before their special responsibility to the world field.

The success of the Volunteer Movement in the United States and Canada has been so marked that its influence has already been strongly felt in British and Continental universities through the representatives of these institutions who have come from year to year to the intercollegiate meetings at Northfield.

Taking as its keynote *the evangelization of the world in this generation,* the Movement has emphasized the apostolic idea, so that thousands of Christians have realized its significance as never before. They not only find it suggested throughout the New Testament but also hear it from the lips of missionaries of all evangelical denominations today. The volunteers ask the question: If they at the front, bearing the brunt of the conflict, sound the battle cry, ought not we to re-echo it with equal conviction and enthusiasm?

V. PRESENT STATUS

During the past six months an extensive correspondence has been instituted with the volunteers for the purpose of receiving information for statistics. A large proportion of the volunteers have responded, and the following figures are based upon the returns, and are considered safe estimates.

Distribution of volunteers, according to section where enrolled:

CANADA,			335
New Brunswick,	10	Nova Scotia,	25
Ontario,	210	Quebec,	90
NEW ENGLAND STATES,			570
Connectiuct,	100	Maine,	65
Massachusetts,	340	New Hampshire,	25
Rhode Island,	25	Vermont,	15
MIDDLE ATLANTIC STATES,			1260
Maryland,	50	New Jersey,	340
New York,	560	Pennsylvania,	310
SOUTHERN STATES,			695
Georgia,	20	Kentucky,	150
North Carolina,	70	South Carolina,	30
Tennessee,	140	Texas,	15
Virginia,	240	West Virginia,	30
CENTRAL STATES,			1975
Illinois,	600	Indiana,	175
Michigan,	340	Ohio,	660
	Wisconsin,	200	

WESTERN STATES, ... 1365

Iowa,	375	Kansas,	375
Minnesota,	175	Missouri,	275
Nebraska,	150	South Dakota	15

Total number of volunteers 6200

Distribution of volunteers according to stages of preparation:

IN INSTITUTIONS OF LEARNING, ... 2600

Academies,	500	Colleges,	1200
Normal Schools,	175	Medical Colleges,	125
Theological Seminaries,	500	Training Schools,	100

Out of institutions, (owing to state of health, insufficient means, etc.) ... 700
Graduates, (postgraduates, special students, etc.) 600
Ready to go, ... 100
Appointed, (not including class of 1891) 20
Hindered, ... 250
Unknown, (large majority of these lost trace of before the Movement
    was organized) 450
Rejected by Boards, ... 50
Renounced, ... 450
Deceased, ... 60
Sailed, ... 320
Not students when enrolled, ... 600

Distribution of volunteers according to age:

Under 20 years,	14	per cent.
Over 20 years and under 25 years,	46	" "
Over 25 years and under 30 years,	29	" "
Over 30 years,	11	" "

Distribution of volunteers according to sex:

Male, 4340,	70	per cent.
Female, 1860,	30	" "

Distribution of volunteers according to denomination:

Presbyterian,	27	per cent.
Methodist,	24	" "
Baptist,	17	" "
Congregational,	17	" "
Lutheran,	3	" "
Episcopal,	2	" "
Friends,	1½	" "
Other Denominations,	8½	" "

Distribution of volunteers who have sailed according to fields:

AFRICA, ... 33

East Africa,	2	North Africa,	2
South Africa,	3	West Africa,	22

Unlocated, ... 4

ASIA, ... 229

Arabia,	1	Burma,	18
China,	69	Korea,	7
India,	49	Japan,	46
Persia,	9	Siam and Laos,	7
Syria,	8	Turkey,	15

EUROPE, ... 5

Bulgaria,	4	Italy,	1

NORTH AMERICA, ... 13

Central America,	2	Mexico,	11

SOUTH AMERICA, ... 12

Brazil,	10	Chile,	1

United States of Colombia, ... 1

SOUTH SEA ISLANDS, ... 6

MISCELLANEOUS, ... 7

LOCATION NOT DEFINITELY KNOWN, ... 16

Total, ... 321

VI. FINANCIAL STATEMENT

During the first three years the expenses were borne entirely by a friend of the Movement. Since then $4,852 have been received from individuals, parlor conferences, Young Men's Christian Associations, and churches, and from the sale of volunteer pamphlets. Of these amounts, $4,651 have been expended. This includes the expenses of traveling, corresponding, and editorial secretaries, printing, office furniture, etc. There are at present $201 in the treasury. Since the inception of this Movement no salaries have been paid. Over $10,000 would have been expended in salaries had the secretaries of the Committee received what is usually paid to men of their ability. At the lowest estimate, $3,000 will be needed during the coming year to meet the increasing demands made upon the Committee by the growth of the Movement.

VII. Policy

The Executive Committee have marked out the following policy, concerning which they invite the friendly criticism and counsel, and the earnest prayers of the members of this convention.

This Movement seeks to enroll volunteers in sufficient numbers to meet all the demands made upon it by the different missionary agencies of the day; and, more than that, sufficient to make possible the evangelization of the world in this generation.

The Movement should be judiciously extended to those institutions which have not yet felt its touch. Among them we would especially note the colleges of the South and Southwest; the colleges of Colorado and the Pacific slope; and the medical schools of our great cities.

It is our duty to guard and develop the volunteers as long as they are connected with our institutions. To this end there must be more and better state organizations; more studying, praying, and working on the part of volunteer bands; closer ties established between the volunteers and their respective church boards. In view of the importance and critical position held by the theological seminaries it is urgent that far more attention be given to establishing and developing the Movement in them. The Executive Committee realize the futility of securing volunteers in colleges unless we succeed in holding them in theological seminaries, because a large number of them must pass through divinity schools before sailing. No one can overestimate the importance of influencing the divinity men who are to become the leaders of the Church at home and abroad.

It is our aim to do all within our power to assist the missionary societies and boards in securing candidates, in raising money, and in other ways suggested to us. To accomplish this better it is proposed to come into more intimate and frequent contact with the secretaries of the societies. We shall also try to induce many more capable volunteers to work among the churches during their vacations. Wherever possible—in colleges, seminaries, churches, young people's societies—we shall continue to urge the introduction of the plan for supporting their own missionary.

Recognizing the wonderful possibilities of the various young people's societies of the day, the Volunteer Movement shall seek to spread the missionary spirit among them. It is believed that these two movements are destined to sustain a very important relation to each other.

During the coming year the Committee propose to employ a corresponding secretary who shall give his entire time to the work which centers at the office. This office will to a limited extent, at least, become a clearing house between the volunteers and the societies. A bureau of information will be established. The best missionary books, tracts, periodicals, maps, and charts will also be supplied to volunteers at cost. It shall be our endeavor to introduce a missionary library into every institution where there are volunteers. Additions will be made to the volunteer series of pamphlets as occasion demands.

Invitation has repeatedly come to the Committee from students in Great Britain and Scandinavia, requesting us to send a representative to introduce and organize the Movement among their universities. It is hoped that during the present year we shall be able to enter this most important door. If the students of the Protestant world are linked together by the power of the Spirit in this Movement it will greatly hasten the establishment of Christ's Kingdom throughout the world.

> JOHN R. MOTT, Intercollegiate Y.M.C.A., *Chairman*
> MISS NETTIE DUNN, Intercollegiate Y.W.C.A.
> R. P. WILDER, American Interseminary Missionary Alliance
> and Canadian Intercollegiate Missionary Alliance
> *Executive Committee*

REPORT PRESENTED AT
THE SECOND INTERNATIONAL CONVENTION
DETROIT, MICHIGAN, FEBRUARY 28 - MARCH 4, 1894

I. THE PURPOSE OF THE MOVEMENT

It is taken for granted by the Executive Committee that all the members of this convention are familiar with the origin, history, and progress of the Student Volunteer Movement down to the time of the First International Convention, held at Cleveland just three years ago this week. Before reviewing its development for the last three years, or considering its present condition, let us fix clearly in mind the main objects of this Movement. They may be stated as follows:

To lead students to a thorough consideration of the claims upon them of foreign missions as a lifework.

To foster this purpose, and to guide and stimulate such students in their missionary study and work until they pass under the immediate direction of the missionary societies.

To unite all the volunteers in a common, organized, aggressive movement.

The ultimate, yet central purpose, is to secure a sufficient number of volunteers, having the right qualifications, to meet the demands of the various mission boards—and even more, if necessary—in order to evangelize the world in the present generation.

Essentially involved in all this is the further object of the Movement—to create and maintain an intelligent, sympathetic, active interest in foreign missions among the students who are to remain on the home field, in order to secure the strong backing of this great enterprise by prayer and money.

Such are the positive objects of the Movement. It is hardly necessary, therefore, on the other hand, to add that it is not an organization to send out missionaries. Its members all go to the fields through the regular missionary societies. Moreover, the Movement does not usurp the functions of any other missionary agency; it simply seeks to supplement helpfully all existing missionary organizations. That such is the case is shown by the increasing number of endorsements which the Movement has received from those missionary secretaries and missionaries who are most familiar with its work.

II. The Field and its Cultivation

This is a student movement. The universities, colleges, theological seminaries, medical schools, normal schools, training schools—in short, all institutions of higher learning in the United States and Canada—constitute its field. It is true that individual volunteers are doing a great deal of work in churches and in Christian organizations among young people; but the field for the cultivation of which the Movement holds itself in a special sense responsible is the student class of North America. It alone among misionary agencies has complete access to this peculiarly important class.

This Movement was made possible by the preparatory work and influence of the four great student organizations of this continent: the Intercollegiate Young Men's Christian Association, the Intercollegiate Young Women's Christian Association, the American Interseminary Missionary Alliance, and the Canadian Intercollegiate Missionary Alliance. The Volunteer Movement is an organic department of these agencies. In this way it has a far more direct and favorable approach to the great body of students than it could possibly have in any other.

Since the Cleveland Convention the field has been cultivated more thoroughly than during the early years of the history of the Movement. This has been made possible by multiplying the agencies of supervision. The following constitute the principal means employed for the cultivation of the field:

The traveling secretary. This agency is the most potent because the traveling secretary comes in personal contact with the field. It has been employed since the inception of the Movement in 1886. The position is usually held for one year only, and by some student volunteer who is nearly ready to go to the foreign field. Mr. W. H. Cossum, of Colgate University, continued in the work after the last convention until the close of that college year, and then sailed to China, where he is doing a strong work. The year following, Mr. J. C. White, of Wooster College, held this position, and is now in India opening up a promising work among the 15,000 students at Calcutta. Mr. F. A. Keller, of Yale, was traveling secretary in 1893-1894. He devoted a part of his time during the same year to office work. He is now completing his studies preparatory to entering the foreign field. Mr. D. W. Lyon, of the McCormick Theological Seminary, at present occupies the important post of traveling secretary.

The corresponding secretary is also an important factor in the cultivation of the field. By correspondence and special reports he is able to keep in helpful touch with all the institutions having volunteers. Mr. Walter J. Clark, of Union Theological Seminary, was the first man called to give his entire time to this work. This appointment marked one of the advanced steps made possible by the Cleveland Convention. Mr. Clark filled the position over a year, and then went to India, where he is already carrying on a successful work. During the few months in which Mr. Keller succeeded him he introduced a number of advanced features suggested by his study of the Movement in the colleges. Mr. J. W. Angell, of Wooster College, rendered special and helpful assistance for a few months. Mr. H. B. Sharman of Toronto University has been corresponding secretary since last summer, and has brought the office department to an even higher state of efficiency.

Corresponding members and other special visitors have rendered exceedingly valuable service by visiting colleges or representing the Movement at conventions. It will be impossible even to summarize all of this work, for it has not all been reported. The list, however, should include among others the following: Miss Eloise Mayham, who made a tour among the women of a number of colleges of the North; Mr. James Edward Adams, who made a special tour among the colleges of Iowa and Indiana; Messrs. Horace Tracy Pitkin, Sherwood Eddy, and Henry Luce, who have carried on a thorough and extensive visitation among the institutions of New England, New York, and New Jersey; Messrs. Lyon, Tomlinson, Mitchell, and Kennedy in Illinois; Mr. Binkhorst in Michigan; Mr. Hotton in Wisconsin; Mr. Marshall in Nebraska; Mr. Strong in Kansas; Mr. Hill in Kentucky; Dr. Drew in Virginia; Mr. Kinsinger in Ohio; and Mr. Moore in Pennsylvania.

Secretaries in connection with the college department of the Young Men's and Young Women's Christian Associations—international, state, and metropolitan—have given a great deal of time and thought (in the aggregate more than any other agency) to the planting and developing of this movement.

The monthly organ of the Movement, *The Student Volunteer,* although only recently entering upon its second year, has become one of the most useful agencies employed by the Committee to keep in touch with the volunteers, and to keep the aims and methods and results of the Movement before the Church. The first suggestion of such a paper came from a minister in Cleveland who attended the sessions of the Convention; but it is due to Mr. Keller that the idea was carried into execution.

In connection with the college students' summer conferences during the last two years, there has been developed another plan for promoting a more thorough cultivation of the field. Missionary institutes designed to train volunteers for the leadership of the missionary interests of their respective institutions have been held. By this plan men who are authorities on the most approved methods of developing missionary interest have been scattered abroad over the college field.

The international conventions of the Movement, though very infrequent, are destined, if we may judge at all by the influence of the Cleveland Convention, to do incalculable good not only in establishing the Movement in institutions of learning, but also in defining its relation to the various missionary activities of the Church.

III. PROBLEMS

Although some of the most difficult problems which confronted the Movement three years ago have been solved, we are brought face to face with a few which remain. These can also be solved if the delegates of this Convention set themselves resolutely and prayerfully to the task.

A close and constant supervision of all the volunteer bands of the United States and Canada is absolutely essential if this Movement is to be a permanent, a growing, and a fruitful one. Over the larger part of the field which has been entered, such supervision has not been maintained. This is due to the fact that the supervising force has not been large enough to cover the entire field in any given year. Such supervision is rendered necessary by the constantly and rapidly shifting character of the student population of our institutions. As a result of our inability to cultivate the whole field each year, it has been necessary to work one year in one section and the next year in another. In some instances we have been obliged to leave whole groups of colleges for as long as three years without a visit. The natural result must necessarily be disastrous.

Closely akin to the problem of securing a more thorough supervision of the bands is that of keeping in closer touch with isolated volunteers, and helping to maintain and increase their interest. This includes that large class of volunteers who are obliged to stay out of college or seminary for months or years at a time, for financial, or other reasons. Cut off from the volunteer band and the missionary library, and surrounded often by influences which are calculated to deaden his interest in missions, the volunteer is in great danger of having his missionary purpose weakened and diverted.

Another problem confronts us in some quarters, and that is the difficulty of holding volunteers after they enter the theological seminaries. If they leave college with a strong purpose and are thoroughly grounded in missions, the question of holding them does not present insuperable difficulties. But even in such cases it is a real problem to preserve the faith and enthusiasm of volunteers who enter institutions where, to quote a prominent board secretary, "from the beginning to the end of the course the whole presumption in the teaching and attitude of the faculty is that the men are all going to stay at home." Add to this the constant pressure brought to bear upon them by home churches, and the solution of the problem is not simplified. In medical schools the difficulty is indeed more serious owing to the crush of work, their absence of missionary, and often even of religious spirit, and a lack of strong Christian student organizations.

How to bring the volunteers into closer touch with the missionary societies is another unsolved question. That there has been an increase in applications to the societies during the last few years, taking them as a whole, is very clear. The increase has been marked in the case of some denominations, and yet it is by no means what it should be when we consider the number of volunteers. The responsibility of the Movement does not cease until the volunteers are brought into direct communication with their respective boards. Nor does it cease entirely then. This suggests yet another difficulty.

The financial obstacle is today one of the greatest in the pathway of many volunteers. Within the last few weeks several missionary societies have indicated to us that they have more men who want to go abroad than they have money with which to send them. There are, it is true, other boards which are in greater need of men than of money. Then, again, we have heard that there are at least one or two boards, which, while they have no surplus of money, yet state that they will let the financial barrier stand in the way of no suitable candidates who are anxious to go. But even where the financial problem is the thing which prevents volunteers hastening to the fields, the Movement cannot free itself entirely from responsibility. It is our duty as volunteers to co-operate with the missionary boards in every way within our power in a determined effort to remove this hindrance.

It has been our purpose in this connection simply to state the most serious problems that stand before the Movement. Our object has been to stimulate thought among the delegates of this convention who, we repeat, are in a position to do more towards solving them than any others can possibly do. Further on we shall indicate some lines of policy which, properly carried out will greatly hasten their solution.

IV. PERILS

There are perils as well as problems attending the advance of the Student Volunteer Movement. This is true of every organization which is new, aggressive, and full of life. These perils should be clearly apprehended, and a united effort made by the volunteers to guard against them.

In the beginning, notice the perils with reference to the volunteer declaration. First among them is the peril due to misunderstanding the meaning of the volunteer declaration. For several years what now corresponds to the declaration was known as the volunteer pledge. It read: "I am willing and desirous, God permitting, to become a foreign missionary." The first traveling secretaries who used the so-called pledge interpreted its meaning in these words: "I am fully determined to become a foreign missionary, unless God blocks the way." All the other regular secretaries who subsequently employed it interpreted it in the same way. Notwithstanding the clear interpretation of the official representatives of the Movement, some others who used it unofficially gave it a different meaning. Moreover, some who heard it rightly interpreted were still confused by its statement. After the Cleveland Convention, the Executive Committee, for a full year, carried on through its members and the traveling secretary an examination in all parts of the field. As a result they reached the conclusion that the wording of the original so-called pledge could be changed to great advantage. Accordingly, the members of the Executive Committees of the Student Volunteer Movement for Foreign Missions, and of the newly organized Student Volunteer Missionary Union of Great Britain, met at Northfield in the summer of 1892 and, after exhaustive discussion, unanimously agreed to change the wording from "I am willing and desirous, God permitting, to become a foreign missionary," to "It is my purpose, if God permit, to become a foreign missionary." Moreover, they decided to abandon the use of the expression *volunteer pledge,* and adopted in its place the expression *volunteer declaration.* This change was made because the phrase "If God permit" renders it impossible to characterize the declaration as a pledge according to the common and accurate use of the word pledge. A man who signs the volunteer declaration signifies by the act that with the light that he then has he forms the definite and clear-cut decision that he will be a foreign missionary. To this end, he turns his face in that direction. He not only decides, and turns his face, but he begins to adapt his course of study and special outside work to his newly chosen lifework. He not only begins to do this, but he continues steadfastly in that direction. At the proper time, he applies to the missionary agency under which he desires to go to the field. This is stating the man side exclusively. It is working out these words of the declaration: "It is my purpose to be a foreign missionary." But there is another side which is involved in the words "If God permit." This phrase precludes the volunteer's taking his life into his own control. He is still under the direction of God; for he will not become a foreign missionary unless God permits. The Holy Spirit may delay him, may turn him aside, may temporarily, or even permanently, block his way. While it may be true that some volunteers have abandoned their original purpose for other than providential reasons, it is obviously wrong to subject volunteers who have been providentially kept from going to the field, to the charge of having broken a vow. Is it not simply maintaining that when a man signs the volunteer declaration he cannot expect any further leadings of the Holy Spirit concerning his lifework? It is impossible to read any such meaning into the volunteer declaration. Let us guard therefore, against the peril of having the declaration misunderstood. It is not, on the one hand, simply an expression of willingness to go anywhere for Christ; and, on the other hand, it is not an iron-clad pledge or vow to go to the foreign field whether God wants us there or not. It means what it says: "It is my purpose, if God permit, to become a foreign missionary." I begin and continue steadfastly to carry out that purpose formed in His presence and for His glory. If by walking in this path of duty the Holy Spirit leads me unmistakably into another path I shall leave the present one—and not till then.

The second peril in connection with the volunteer declaration comes from the wrong use of it. We must guard against its use by men who misunderstand it, or who cannot make its meaning clear. We must guard against its being used with those who for one reason or another are not in a position to understand its full significance, or are obviously unfitted for foreign service. We must guard against its being used at the wrong time, in the wrong place, or under wrong circumstances. All experience in connection with this Movement shows that the declaration should be used only under the manifest guidance of the Spirit.

Before leaving this matter of the declaration the Committee wish to record once more their firm belief in it. The fact that it has been misunderstood at times, or that it has been wrongly used, does not shake their confidence in it; for the fact still remains that without it there could have been no Movement. Beyond this, the Committee believe in the declaration because it leads men to make a definite decision; because it helps to hold men who have decided; because it puts a man in a position to do more for missions while he is securing his preparation than he possibly would or could do otherwise; because it puts a deep central purpose into his life which means greater power; and because it is the testimony of secretaries and missionaries that men who by this means were led to reach their decision early are, as a rule, more settled in their convictions, and better prepared when the time comes, to go abroad than the men who do not decide until about the close of their professional course of study.

There is also a peril in connection with the number of volunteers. The number of students who have volunteered at one time and another is indeed remarkably large. This fact has often led members of the Movement to boast, and to depend more upon the numbers than upon the Holy Spirit's power. This peril has been aggravated by an unwise and misleading use of the numbers. Unconsciously, our friends have been our worst enemies in this respect. How many noted speakers and editors have stated time after time that there are five, six, or seven thousand men and women in this Movement who are ready to go to the field at once if the Church could send them? This is not true. While there may have been many thousands who have signed the declaration, the Executive Committee has within the last year decided not to count as members of the Movement those of whom it has and can obtain no trace. The Committee has been unable to get accurate record of more than 3,200 volunteers. The large untraced contingent comprises chiefly those who volunteered within the first two years and a half of the life of the Movement, during which period it was not organized and had no oversight. Quite a number have been lost trace of since in sections or colleges which have had little or no supervision and band organization. Moreover, it must still be kept in mind that a majority of the volunteers of whom the Movement has record have not completed their courses of study. A recent investigation has made this circumstance very plain. To avoid creating further misunderstanding it is earnestly recommended that all friends of the Movement in their statements concerning it dwell not so much on the numbers who have taken the initial step (unless it be made very clear what those numbers mean) as upon those facts which show the fruitage made possible by those who have made the decision. In saying this the Committee would not give a discouraging impression. True, there has been a shrinkage in the number who have volunteered, but it is due not to the principles and methods of the Movement, but to a lack of clear emphasis of those principles, and to a failure to employ those methods; and this is due in turn to inadequate supervision, and also to the fact stated before, that the Movement was not organized for nearly three years. There has been very little shrinkage indeed among the men enrolled during the last few years, much less, in fact, than might be reasonably expected. But after all, the greatest cause for gratitude in connection with such a Movement is not so much the fact that so many have enrolled, as the facts showing what those who have volunteered have achieved under the Spirit in their colleges, in the home churches, and on the foreign field.

Some members of the Movement have been providentially prevented from going to the foreign field, it may be temporarily, or it may be permanently. These have often been characterized as hindered volunteers. There is a decided peril with reference to this class. The volunteer who considers himself hindered should be very sure that he has been hindered by the Holy Spirit, and not by friends, or self, or sin, or Satan. It is not an easy gauntlet that the volunteer must run in order to get away from a land where he is needed into the one where he is needed most. Let no volunteer mistake the logical results of ignorance and indolence for the staying hand of God's Spirit. We mean simply this—that it is a comparatively easy matter for a man to regard himself providentially hindered if he does not keep adding fuel to the missionary flame. In this connection the question is now and then asked: Why has such a volunteer abandoned his purpose to be a missionary? A number of such persons have been interviewed. In some cases the way had been obviously blocked by God. In all other cases the giving up of the missionary purpose could be traced directly to neglect on the part of the volunteers to study missions, to pray for missions, and to work for missions. To any volunteer, then, who may consider himself hindered, we would say: Be very careful not to miss God's plan. Test your sincerity most thoroughly. Keep the missionary fires buring by every possible means. In addition to this, apply to a missionary society. The examinations are very thorough. Counsel with the secretaries about personal difficulties and doubts. They will not let you make a mistake. If after applying these and other tests the volunteer is led to see that he is for the time being hindered, let him not be depressed. Rather than lose his interest in the Movement let him redouble his efforts and devote his life on the home field to backing up this mighty missionary enterprise as singly and earnestly as he would have done had he been privileged to hasten to the front. Above all, let him never wholly abandon the hope that some day the way will be opened to him to preach the gospel where Christ has not been named.

A fourth peril is seen in the tendency in some places to form a breach between the students who are volunteers and those who are not. In a majority of such instances the volunteers have been chiefly responsible. This peril has already manifested itself in connection with the Movement in Great Britain; and we can do no better than to quote from the last report of their Executive the following recommendation: "That whilst the zeal of volunteers be encouraged, care be taken that no tone of superiority be assumed over those who are not volunteers." The men who consider it their duty to spend their lives on the home fields have as much responsibility resting upon them for the world's evangelization as those who go abroad. If the message about Jesus Christ is to be taken all over the earth in our lifetime, it is absolutely imperative that the entire body of Christian students of this generation see eye to eye and work as one mind. United we stand and succeed, divided we fall and fail.

V. RESULTS

It is right that record be made of what the Spirit hath wrought both in and through the Movement. Among a multitude of definite things which have been accomplished, brief reference is made to the following.

Since the Cleveland Convention the Movement has been extended to the colleges of the Pacific Coast and of parts of the Southern States; also to some new colleges of Canada. Up to the present time we have record of 477 different institutions in which volunteers have been enrolled. It is safe to state that this Movement has entered more institutions than any other student organization.

Not only has the Movement entered the colleges and professional schools, but in them it has exerted a remarkable influence. Unquestionably it has deepened the spiritual life of the institutions. Those who have traveled most among students bear testimony that the most spiritual colleges they visit are those which have been most intimately touched by this Movement. But the most distinctive influence has naturally been on missionary lines. In hundreds of institutions the Movement has reiterated the last command of Christ; it has vividly set forth the awful need of the world, and proclaimed with conviction the responsibility resting upon this generation of students for the evangelization of the world. The words *missionary* and *missions* mean something entirely different to the student mind from what they meant eight years ago, even in a majority of the denominational colleges and divinity schools of the United States and Canada. Narrow and contracted ideas are fast giving way to new and enlarged conceptions of the grandeur, the transcendent possibilities, and the divinity of this greatest work which confronts the Church of God. Through the influence of this Movement, the missionary department of the College Young Men's and Young Women's Christian Associations has been carried from comparative weakness to as high a state of efficiency as that of any other department.

There has been a striking increase in the number of students who expect to be missionaries. Take the young men of the colleges for example. Accurate reports show that there were over three times as many men in the colleges last year who were expecting to be foreign missionaries as there were in 1885-1886, the year before this Movement started. If the comparison were restricted to that portion of the college field which has received most attention from the Movement, the increase in number of candidates would have been over fivefold. In the light of facts covering our leading seminaries, it is safely estimated that there are now over 50 per cent more theological students who plan to be missionaries than there were ten years ago. In several seminaries the increase has been far greater.

The Movement has inaugurated and is earnestly prosecuting an educational campaign on missions among the colleges and seminaries. It has been the chief factor in starting a series of regular monthly missionary meetings in about 200 institutions which did not have them before. Furthermore, it has very greatly improved the character of such meetings in institutions where they were already being held. More important still, in some respects, are the weekly band meetings for a systematic and thorough study of missions. When this agency entered the field there were less than ten such study groups in the United States and Canada. Now there are at least 136. In connection with these band meetings the Movement has prepared and introduced several courses of progressive missionary studies. These are being successfully used by a larger number of bands each year. It is interesting to note that the three series of missionary Bible studies have been used more widely than all others combined. All this marks a great advance; for over four years ago there was not in existence any specially adapted outline courses of study for a mission band. Another and a most fundamental feature of the educational work of the Movement has been the planting and enriching of missionary libraries in our institutions. In over 100 institutions which had practically no missionary books three or four years ago, there are now good working collections. Some of the leading theological seminaries of the United States had no modern missionary works whatever until they were secured through the influence of the volunteer band. The same thing is also true of a large number of the colleges. In the aggregate, thousands of dollars' worth of missionary literature has been placed within reach of students within the last three years. It would be difficult to overstate the importance of the service the Movement has rendered to missions on these practical educational lines.

At the Cleveland Convention it was reported that the colleges and seminaries combined had contributed during the preceding year about $15,000 to foreign missions over and above what they had previously given. Under the influence of the Movement this amount has been steadily increasing, until last year the colleges alone gave over $25,000 more than they had given before the Movement was started. The returns from the seminaries are not sufficiently full to enable us to give exact figures. It is a conservative estimate to say that the colleges and seminaries combined gave to foreign missions over $40,000 last year. This came almost entirely from between eighty and ninety institutions which are each supporting, or helping to support a missionary. This sum, considered in itself, does not mean much; but its influence on two lines means a great deal. In the first place, when churches learn that such a college or seminary is supporting a missionary, it will lead them to see the possibility of their doing even more than the students. A number of churches have been influenced to do this on learning these facts about the sacrifice of students. A more important influence, however, is that coming from educating the students themselves in habits of systematic and proportionate giving. The colleges and seminaries have in them the ministry of the future. They will not forget the object lesson of the support of a missionary, but will reproduce it in their churches and young people's societies.

How many volunteers have sailed is a question which should be answered in the record of the results of this Movement. We have the names of 630 who are now in mission lands. In all probability there are a number who have gone out that we know nothing about, because of the poor reports rendered by some institutions. It is a striking yet natural fact that more have sailed during the last two and one-half years than during the preceding five and one-half years. It shows conclusively that the movement is increasing in volume and momentum. The question is often asked whether the leaders are pressing toward the field. In answer, it may be stated that every volunteer who has ever served as a member of the Executive Committee, or as traveling or corresponding secretary, since the Movement was organized, is either on the foreign field, or under appointment, or has applied. The same might be said of nearly all the volunteers who have been the moving spirits in the various states or sections.

On lines parallel with its efforts to secure volunteers for foreign service, the Movement has enlisted the active interest of thousands of students who are to remain at home. Where this work is properly developed each volunteer stands for more than one volunteer. He represents a number of his student friends and classmates who, because of his offering himself to the foreign cause, and better still, because of the reasons which influenced his decision, will stand back of him and the missionary enterprise on the home field. The honorary secretary of one of our greatest missionary boards voices a conviction shared by many other secretaries in maintaining that one of the things most needed now in order to make possible the going forth of larger numbers of volunteers is more "missionary pastors—pastors of churches that will simply do their duty, that will lead their churches in the way they ought to go and are waiting to be led, some of them longing to be led." One of the ambitions of the Movement is to help meet this fundamental need.

Though absorbed principally in cultivating the student field, the volunteers have nevertheless made their influence felt in the churches. We know of a number of bands the members of which have, during the past year, made stirring appeals in from twenty-five to over 100 churches. Their work has been practical as well, for often it has resulted in a very considerable increase in the amount contributed to missions. Some volunteers have been enabled to secure pledges covering all or a part of their support as missionaries. As a rule, the most successful and hopeful work in the churches has been among the young people especially in promoting the study of missions and in enlisting financial co-operation. The volunteers have found this field to be peculiarly accessible.

In the report rendered at the convention three years ago it was stated that the Committee had been invited to send a representative to help introduce and organize the Movement among the universities of Great Britain and Scandinavia; and the hope was expressed that we might soon be enabled to enter that most important door. It is, therefore, with special gratitude that we record the fact that Mr. Wilder, on his way to India, found it possible to spend a year among the students of these countries, and to spread the principles and methods of the Student Volunteer Movement. As a result, largely of this work, the missionary interest of the British universities assumed organized form in the Student Volunteer Missionary Union. This organization, though less than two years old, has had a truly remarkable growth and influence. Missionary fires were also kindled by Mr. Wilder and Mr. Moorhead in the universities of Scandinavia, al-

though no definite intercollegiate organization has as yet been perfected. A volunteer who went out from Wellesley College to work in
South Africa has succeeded in raising groups of volunteers in some
of the institutions there, and has united them—forming a branch of
our Movement. It would be impossible to measure the extension of
the influence of the Movement through the hundreds of volunteers
who are touching the student life of scores of mission lands.

VI. Other Facts Showing the Influence of the Movement

We have reviewed some of the general results of the work of the
Movement. Its influence can be seen also by looking at what it has
actually accomplished in a few institutions, and by making a few contrasts. For obvious reasons we do not give names of institutions,
states, or sections.

One little denominational college with fewer than seventy-five students was touched by this Movement. At that time it had no foreign
missionary interest or work whatever. One man was led to volunteer.
He was thoroughly grounded and instructed in the spiritual principles
of the Movement. A missionary department was added to the religious organization of the college. Regular missionary meetings were
held which were regarded as the strongest and most popular meetings
in the institution. Four other men were led to volunteer. One of the
volunteers after graduating went at once to the foreign field, and the
students and faculty pay over $600 a year to support him. This whole
development took place within two years, and the students of that
institution trace it directly to the Student Volunteer Movement.

Take a state university. There is one which a few years ago had
about 1,000 students. Although it had one of the largest Christian
Associations in the country it had during a period of over two years
not a single missionary meeting; it had no missionary books; not a
student in the whole university was expecting to be a missionary; worse
than that, its long line of alumni, numbering thousands, included not
a single missionary; not a dollar was being given to missions; the word
missionary, to use Mr. Wilder's expression, meant *miserere*. This picture is strictly accurate. The Volunteer Movement entered that university and has kept fairly in touch with it since. Note the change.
Today the missionary meetings are among those most largely attended.
There is a band of sixteen students who expect to be missionaries.
They are carrying on a very thorough study of missions. A carefully
selected missionary library has been planted and additions are made
to it each year. Two or three of the volunteers have already sailed,
others have applied, and at least one is under appointment. One of

those on the field is largely supported by the students, who give annually for this purpose nearly $500. This complete change is due solely to the Volunteer Movement.

Now look at a theological seminary which today has very little active missionary interest because of the fact that the Movement has been unable to touch it for three years. During that time the volunteers have graduated. Prior to this period the Movement did a very thorough work in the institution. During the last year that the Movement was in contact with that seminary regular missionary meetings were held not only each month, but also each week. A volunteer band numbering eighteen was making a special study of missions. An alcove containing the best missionary literature was established. The churches in the vicinity of the seminary were divided up among the members of the band and special missionary addresses given in them. Over $700 was given to support a missionary. That year out of a graduating class of seven students, four sailed before fall to the foreign field. This varied and fruitful activity was due almost entirely to the Volunteer Movement.

It will be suggestive to contrast the condition of the missionary life in two theological seminaries. In one the Student Volunteer Movement was never permitted to have a foot-hold; in the other the Movement has for several years had right of way. Their general situation and conditions are practically the same. Viewed apart from this Movement, the one which might naturally be expected to be the more potent in all foreign missionary work is the one which, as a matter of fact, is the weaker. A careful examination shows that the only factor which enters into one which does not enter into the other is the unrestricted work of the Volunteer Movement. Keep in mind that the one having the poorer missionary showing is the larger institution. The seminary which does not favor the Movement has fourteen men who expect to be missionaries, a majority of whom became volunteers under the influence of the Movement in college before entering the seminary. In the other seminary there are nearly fifty volunteers. In one seminary the men who expect to be missionaries are carrying on no course of study on missions. In the other the volunteers are engaged in a most thorough and advanced series of studies. In one seminary fewer than thirty modern missionary books are within reach of the men; in the other over 200 have been secured under the influence of the volunteers. One gives less than $200 a year to foreign missions; the other gives over $1,000. The missionary students of one have carried on no aggressive work for foreign missions in the surrounding churches, whereas the volunteers in the other have made thirty-eight important missionary visits within the last five months.

During the past year a representative of the Movement visited a number of denominational colleges which had never come under the Movement's influence. He collected exact facts about the missionary status of each institution. We summarize the facts about eight of these colleges which make the best missionary showing. In contrast with these summaries we place the summaries of statistics gathered in connection with eight denominational colleges of the same rank and size, and in the same section, which had not been cultivated even partially by the Volunteer Movement. In the eight institutions untouched by the Movement, there were seven students who expected to be missionaries, and none of them had made their purpose known. In the eight colleges touched by the Movement there were sixty-eight volunteers who had declared their purpose. In the first group two of the eight were having regular missionary meetings; in the second all eight had such meetings. In the first group not a college had a class for the study of missions; four colleges in the second had such classes. The first group gave less than $90 to missions last year; the second group gave $460. In the first group only one college had missionary books; in the other group three colleges had such collections. The contrast might be made still more striking in favor of the influence of the Movement if we note the summaries of eight denominational colleges in a state where the Movement has been at work for several years. Those eight colleges last year had 142 volunteers; all of the eight had regular missionary meetings; six of the eight had mission band classes; six had large collections of modern missionary books; all contributed to missions in the aggregate $2,890.

Another interesting contrast is afforded by the state universities. Let us take five of them which have received special attention from the Movement for several years, and place against them five which have been practically untouched by the Movement. The five which have been untouched have the largest proportion of Christian students. In the five neglected universities there were last year only four volunteers, and three of them came as a result of the influence of the Movement at the summer schools. Only one of the five had missionary meetings. None of them had missionary books. Not a dollar was given to missions. In the five universities which have been quite frequently visited by the secretary of the Movement, there were last year seventy-three volunteers. Four of the five held strong missionary meetings. All five had collections of missionary books. Four contributed $1,238 to missions.

These comparisons and contrasts might be multiplied indefinitely, and some even more favorable to the Movement might have been given.

VII. POLICY

As the Executive Committee study the needs of this Movement, and consider the unexampled opportunities before it, they are led to outline several points of policy which the volunteers should seek to emphasize as never before.

We should strive to establish the Movement more widely and firmly in certain sections and among certain classes of students. At present the largest number of volunteers and highest development of missionary interest is to be found in the colleges between New England and Colorado, and north of the Ohio River. Of course there are a number of institutions within these limits which are greatly lacking in missionary spirit, but viewed as a section it is in advance of any other. The colleges of the South should receive special attention during the near future. The missionary record of certain southern institutions shows what splendid possibilities there are in this important section. The Maritime Provinces and Manitoba have been less cultivated on missionary lines than Upper Canada, but the little which has been done shows that a disproportionately low number of strong missionaries may be expected from these sections. Even an indirect touching of the colleges of the Pacific Coast has called forth such a response as to give us reason to believe that special efforts put forth in that section would bring a rich fruitage. Accurate reports show that there has been a falling off in the missionary interest and activity in the institutions of New England taken as a whole, although there are still some very bright exceptions. This is due primarily to lack of supervision. It is firmly believed that, with wise and continuous effort, the institutions of this section, which in the early days of this century, gave birth to American missions, and later to the Student Volunteer Movement, will furnish one of the largest contingents for the foreign field. A field second in importance to none, and in the light of the actual needs of the world possibly more important just now than any other, is that of the medical schools of North America. It is the unmistakable duty of the Movement to address itself at once, and with faithfulness, to the cultivation of this field. There is also real need of a special work among the college young women. This is seen at a glance from the fact that not more than one-third of volunteers are women. This is not due to any lack of willingness on their part to offer themselves, because the list of missionaries shows that more women by far have gone to the field than men. The small proportion of young women is due chiefly to the fact that while the women in co-educational institutions have come largely under the influence of the Movement, those in the distinctively women's colleges have not. If there could be a woman constantly at work among the tens of thousands of young women in our colleges, she could accomplish a work of untold importance. To summarize this point of policy, then, we would state that this Movement should keep in mind all classes of students in all sections of the student field. And this not alone for the sake of the Movement, but for the sake of the deeper spiritual life of the institutions themselves.

Let us reiterate what has been stated and implied over and over again in this report, that even more important than the work of extension is that of supervision. The largest, richest, and most permanent results have been found invariably along the pathway of constant supervision. Let us in a deeper sense than ever guard that which has been committed unto us. To this end we should increase the number and efficiency of the agencies of supervision. May not interested and influential professors be found in our institutions who will make the matter of foreign missions their outside specialty—as so many of them do with reference to Bible study today—and by their watchfulness and special counsel render an incalculable service in insuring the strength and permanency of this Movement? Out of this may we not expect eventually in many institutions that chairs and special lectureships on missions will be established as has been so successfully done already in a few places? Shall we not plan to have the chairmen of more volunteer bands and missionary committees attend the summer schools in order that in the special missionary institutes they may become better equipped to lead the volunteer and missionary activities of their respective institutions? Shall not more of the State Committees of the Young Men's and Young Women's Christian Associations co-operate with the Executive Committee in having state corresponding members appointed to look after this peculiarly important department of the Associations? Shall not one of the achievements of this Convention be that the Holy Spirit will lead us to make possible an enlargement of the secretarial force of the Student Volunteer Movement itself?

As during the past, so in the future, let us press with tactfulness and prayerfulness the claims of the unevangelized world upon the students of our generation, and help to lead them to a clear and glad decision to fling their lives into this greatest enterprise of the Lord Jesus Christ. Our numbers are large. They are not large enough. Let us not forget the words of a secretary of one of our greatest missionary societies: "The Volunteer Movement should be putting its men into our seminaries by the hundred and the thousand every year." Let us ring into the ears of the students of America the words of that splendid volunteer, Keith-Falconer, who in speaking to the students of Cambridge said: "While vast continents are shrouded in almost

utter darkness, and hundreds of millions suffer the horrors of heathenism and Islam, the burden of proof lies upon you to show that the circumstances in which God has placed you were meant by Him to keep
you out of the foreign field." Yes, the world need is great. The crisis
is on. The time is short. The students of our day must know their
duty before it is too late. Ours is the responsibility to make that duty
known.

Another aim should be to make possible a deeper, more comprehensive, more progressive, and more practical study of missions.
Therefore authorities on missions should be invited to elaborate
courses of study adapted to the needs and conditions of the volunteer
bands. Here is an almost uncultivated, and a most fascinating field.
Leaders to guide in such study must be enlisted and, in many instances,
trained. The use of these courses of study should not be limited to
volunteers but should be extended to students who are not volunteers.
To supply the necessary means or facilities for careful study an effort
should be put forth to establish an alcove of the best available missionary literature in every institution. Each student delegation at this
Convention should make a careful inspection of the educational exhibit
with reference to improving greatly the collection of missionary books
in their institution. This exhibit is the most complete of its kind which
has ever been made. A close study of it should lead within a year to
placing modern missionary libraries in at least 100 institutions where
they do not now exist. This is a fundamental condition of all solid
and growing and productive missionary interest.

The time has come when the volunteers must grapple with the
financial problem with greater wisdom and persistence. What good
reason is there that the volunteer who takes hold of this matter in the
right manner and spirit and keeps at it cannot, before he sails, increase
the annual contributions to his church board sufficiently to cover his
support on the foreign field? What individual volunteers, whom we
know, have done in this direction gives us confidence to believe that
hundreds or thousands of volunteers can do the same thing. The possibilities of raising up a vast constituency of new, systematic, and proportionate givers among the millions of members of the various young
people's movements are practically limitless. This field is peculiarly
accessible to students. It opens up to them on every hand, not only
while in college, but also during vacations. And why should not a great
many students who cannot yet see their way clear to offer themselves
for foreign service give themselves to this practical financial work,
and thus make possible the sending of their classmates as substitutes?

The Movement should seek to keep in touch with those of its
members who have sailed and are at the front. Every volunteer should

recognize that his responsibility to the Movement is not discharged when he sails. If anything, it is greatly increased, because the fact that he has sailed increases his influence immensely. He is in a position to do far more for the Movement than before he went abroad. His counsel concerning its problems and opportunities, as he views them from the field, will be especially valuable. His appeals for laborers will have an added force in the institution from which he came and wherever his name is known. His prayers, stimulated by actual contact with the awful need of the world, will yet become the greatest motive power in this Movement. And as the years pass, and larger numbers of the volunteers return for a brief sojourn in their native land, they can and will stir the colleges and seminaries as no other messengers possibly can. As the number of our members in the dark continents of the world increases, so will increase the clearness and persuasiveness of the Macedonian call. We appeal to the volunteers in other countries to do what the volunteers of India have done, namely, to perfect an auxiliary organization of their members, not only to help one another in the great work to which they have given themselves, but also to influence aright the volunteers at home, and to aid in realizing the central purpose of the Movement. The enterprise upon which all the volunteers have embarked, whether they are on the field, in an institution securing their preparation, or providentially hindered, is not a four-, or seven-, or ten-year effort; it is, if need be, to span our generation. Let us stand together, no matter where we are, until it is carried to a successful issue.

Let us preserve a close union with the Student Volunteer Missionary Union of Great Britain. Although their organization is comparatively young, it has made most remarkable progress; and a close study of its life and workings would abound in suggestion and inspiration to the American volunteer. This movement and our own have, as a common rallying point, the same declaration and, as a common inspiration, the same watchcry. For the first time the students of the Anglo-Saxon world are united in a mighty enterprise. Made one by the Holy Spirit of missions, who can measure the power of this Christian federation for a world's evangelization? With deep sincerity and gratitude we welcome to our convention and institutions Mr. Donald Fraser, the traveling secretary of the British movement, who comes to us as their fraternal delegate.

Let us keep to the front and ever before us as our hope and inspiration the watchcry of the Movement, "The Evangelization of the World in this Generation." This idea has passed from the region of mere conjecture into the realm of the actual faith and convictions of a rapidly increasing number of men and women. The Student Volunteer

Movement stands pre-eminently for the emphasis on the belief, that by an enlargement of the agencies employed by the missionary societies today, the gospel can be and should be fully preached to every creature during this generation. The volunteers believe that this is an absolute necessity, because without it millions will perish. They believe it is a duty because Christ has commanded it. They believe it is a privilege because it will hasten the appearance of Jesus Christ. They believe it is a possibility because of what the early Christian Church achieved under far more adverse circumstances than those which confront the Church of the nineteenth century. When this idea is firmly anchored in the consciousness of this Movement it will give it an irresistible power.

As this Movement advances in years, and in numbers, and in influence, there is need of recognizing with increasing faithfulness our absolute dependence upon the Holy Ghost. He furnished its kindling spark at Mount Hermon, and lighted its fires all over the North American student field. He called its secretaries and sent them up and down the land with a power not their own—touching and deepening and enriching the lives and purposes of thousands of students. From Him the generous gifts of money came which have made possible such far-reaching achievements. He spoke to the volunteers with that voice which His sheep always know, for a stranger they will not follow. He it is that must energize them and thrust them forth. It is He who will give them enduring fruits. He inspired our watchcry, and He alone can and will enable us to carry it to a full realization.

VIII. WHAT THE MOVEMENT NEEDS

To carry out with thoroughness these far-reaching aims, and to realize in any measure the possibilities wrapped up in this Movement, its members and friends must give it their unreserved co-operation.

It needs their intelligent and sympathetic counsel. The experience and convictions of secretaries and missionaries, in particular, will do much to confirm and guide the volunteers.

Money is needed in order to enable the Executive Committee to enter doors of unparalleled opportunity which open on every hand. From its inception God has never let this Movement suffer for want of money. He always increased the number of contributors to keep pace with its steady expansion. At least $6,000 a year are needed during the next three years.

There is need of an unwavering and enthusiastic belief on the part of each volunteer in the providential origin of this Movement, its deep scriptural basis, and its God-given purpose. Such a confidence will inspire a larger enterprise, a deeper sacrifice, a sublimer heroism, a more Christlike obedience. This faith, indeed, must necessarily be the victory which overcomes the world.

Beyond all else, the deepest need of the Volunteer Movement is definite, united, importunate prayer. This is imperative in order that volunteers may be recruited, not by men, but by God Himself. Prayer is needed still more during the long years of preparation, that the volunteer having put his hand to the plow may keep it there, and that he may be possessed by the Holy Spirit. Even then the thousands of students who have thus given themselves to this work, will never reach the great harvest fields of the world until there is a more absolute compliance with that wonderful condition laid down by Jesus Christ, "Pray ye, therefore, the Lord of the harvest, that He send forth laborers into His harvest." This has been strikingly illustrated at times in the history of the great Church Missionary Society of England. At one time in 1872, it is said, a day was spent in prayer offered distinctly and definitely for more men. It was followed by more offers for service than had ever been received. In the five years following it sent out 112 men, whereas in the five years preceding it had sent out fifty-one men. Again, in the latter part of 1884, men were sorely needed, and a day was appointed to pray for them. The previous evening Mr. Wigram was summoned to Cambridge to see a number of graduates and undergraduates who desired to dedicate themselves to the Lord's work abroad. More than 100 university men met him, and he returned to the prayer meeting next day to prove to his colleagues the promise, "Before they call I will answer." With deep conviction we reiterate, here lies at once our greatest need, our most solemn duty, and our most inspiring opportunity. "Lord, teach us to pray."

"Lord, it is nothing with Thee to help, whether with many, or with them that have no power. Help us, O Lord, our God; for we rest on Thee, and in Thy name we go against the multitude."

JOHN R. MOTT, *Chairman*
JAMES EDWARD ADAMS
MISS EFFIE K. PRICE

Executive Committee

REPORT PRESENTED AT
THE THIRD INTERNATIONAL CONVENTION
CLEVELAND, OHIO, FEBRUARY 23-27, 1898

I. THE PURPOSE OF THE MOVEMENT

The Student Volunteer Movement had its rise in the summer of 1886 at Mount Hermon, Massachusetts, in connection with the first international Christian student conference ever held. The Movement assumed organized form in 1888, just ten years ago, and has already become a recognized and influential factor in the missionary life of the Church.

The fourfold purpose of this organization is, (1) to awaken and maintain among all Christian students of the United States and Canada intelligent and active interest in foreign missions; (2) to enroll a sufficient number of properly qualified student volunteers to meet the successive demands of the various missionary boards of North America; (3) to help all such intending missionaries to prepare for their lifework, and to enlist their co-operation in developing the missionary life of the home churches; (4) to lay an equal burden of responsibility on all students who are to remain as ministers and lay workers at home, that they may actively promote the missionary enterprise by their intelligent advocacy, by their gifts and by their prayers.

The Volunteer Movement is in no sense a missionary board. It never has sent out a missionary and never will. It is simply a recruiting agency. It does not usurp or encroach upon the functions of any other missionary organization. It is unswervingly loyal to the Church; it is the servant of all the foreign missionary societies, and has received the endorsement of every leading board on this continent.

II. The Field and its Cultivation

This Movement is a student movement, and is the only organization which has shown itself fully adapted to cultivate the student field for missions. From the beginning it has restricted its operations to the institutions of higher learning in the United States and Canada. This field comprises not fewer than 400 universities and colleges, 100 theological seminaries, nearly 200 medical schools, and over 300 normal, missionary, and other institutions. While the Movement believes in awakening missionary interest in preparatory schools, it does not encourage the enrollment of volunteers among them. In a word, the field for the cultivation of which we hold ourselves primarily responsible is the 1,000 institutions of higher learning of these two countries.

Since the Detroit Convention, the Movement has cultivated its field more thoroughly than during any preceding period. The chief agencies of supervision and cultivation employed have been as follows.

There is an Executive Committee composed of official representatives of the four great student organizations of North America, namely, the Intercollegiate Young Men's Christian Association, the Intercollegiate Young Women's Christian Association, the American Interseminary Missionary Alliance, and the Canadian Intercollegiate Missionary Alliance. This Committee has the general direction of the Movement. During the two years' absence of the chairman from the country, Mr. F. S. Brockman served with devotion and efficiency as acting chairman. Much help has been rendered the Movement by an Advisory Committee consisting of secretaries and members of eight leading mission Boards.

The traveling secretaries are the most effective agents in the cultivation of the field because of the fact that they come into immediate contact with the students. The traveling secretaries for the past four years have been as follows: 1894-1895, Messrs. Sherwood Eddy, H. W. Luce, and H. T. Pitkin, and Misses Agnes G. Hill and Abbie M. Lyon; 1895-1896, W. J. Wanless, M.D., Messrs, John L. Marshall, Jr., and J. M. Brodnax, and Miss Clarissa H. Spencer; 1896-1897, Messrs. R. E. Lewis, and H. W. Luce, and Miss Nellie J. Allen; and this year Messrs. F. S. Brockman, R. P. Wilder, R. E. Lewis, and R. R. Gailey, and Miss Ruth Rouse. No Movement has ever been served by workers who have labored with greater self-sacrifice, or whose work has been characterized by greater faithfulness or followed by more enduring spiritual results. At the present time, one secretary devotes all her time to women's colleges, another works in the theological seminaries, a third gives the largest part of his time to professional and other institutions in the large cities, and the remaining two are engaged in visiting other colleges.

The general secretary, F. P. Turner, and assistant general secretary, J. E. Knotts, are stationed at the office of the Movement, and do much to facilitate, unify, and conserve all the work done in the field. Mr. H. B. Sharman, for the four years preceding this college year, occupied with marked ability the position of general secretary.

The educational secretaryship is an office which was created in the year following the Detroit Convention. It was held the first year by Mr. D. Willard Lyon, who with great wisdom marked out the lines on which this department has since been developed by Mr. Harlan P. Beach with ever increasing fruitfulness.

State and international secretaries of the Young Men's and Young Women's Christian Associations and the leaders of the two movements among theological institutions have been a great factor in promoting the work of the Student Volunteer Movement. Each year demonstrates anew the wisdom shown in making the volunteer work an organic department of these organizations. This relationship ensures its permanence; affords it larger, more direct, and more influential access to Christian students; and supplies it with favorable conditions for fostering the spiritual life of volunteers and for training them in Christian work.

The *Student Volunteer,* the official organ of the Movement, has become indispensable as an agency in the cultivation of the field. Going as it does nine times each year to thousands of students all over the continent, it serves not only as a unifying force but also as a constant guide and inspiration to the entire membership of the Movement and to the still larger number of students interested in Christian missions.

In connection with each of the eight student summer conferences, held from year to year in different parts of the continent, the Movement conducts a missionary institute. The object is to train leaders for volunteer bands, missionary study classes, and other missionary activities in the various institutions. The metropolitan unions of volunteers by similar training conferences and by other means are doing much to advance the Movement in institutions in and near our large cities.

Once in each student generation, it is the policy of the Movement to hold an international convention like the one in which we are assembled. These conventions have become noted not only as the most representative and fruitful missionary conferences of North America, but also as the largest student gatherings of the world. A Roman Catholic monthly in a discriminating article on the Detroit Convention says, "By no flight of the imagination could we hope to see at a congress assembled in the interest of Catholic foreign missions so large, or even proportionately so large, a representation of Catholic colleges. Nor could we expect to see as large a number of representative men, bishops, priests, and laity prepare papers and make speeches."

III.   INFLUENCE AND RESULTS

In order to understand the practical working and power of this Movement, it is necessary to consider some of the facts showing its influence and results. These facts afford abundant justification for the existence of the Movement, and give impressive evidence of the hand of God in its development.

The Movement has already touched 839 institutions. In a majority of these (including chiefly state, professional, and independent institutions) the Movement has presented the subject of foreign missions for the first time. Even in places where the subject had been presented before, professors and others bear testimony that this Movement has made the missionary appeal more attractive and impressive. Today probably a score of students are brought face to face with the claims of the world field to one who confronted it before the existence of the Movement. The student attitude toward missions in many colleges both denominational and state has been completely changed. No other subject has taken such deep hold of the convictions of college men or called forth from them such unselfish devotion. The fact that the interest of the student class, from whose ranks are to come the leaders of thought and action, has been enlisted in behalf of the evangelization of the world is of the largest possible significance.

Four years ago the Movement began to promote the systematic and progressive study of missions. At that time there were fewer than thirty classes carrying on such study in all the institutions of North America. The first year the Movement organized 144 classes with an average attendance of 1400. The next year the number of classes increased to 217 with an attendance of 2,156. Last year the number of classes reached 267, having in them 2,361 students. From present indications this year bids fair to witness a still larger enrollment. It should be noted that these classes are composed about equally of volunteers and non-volunteers. Largely in connection with the educational department, the Volunteer Movement during the past four years has placed in the colleges and seminaries fully $20,000 worth of missionary literature. Under the influence of the Movement the number of missionary libraries in our institutions of learning has been increased over tenfold within the past eight years, and in institutions which eight years ago had such collections of books the number of volumes has been increased considerably over threefold. It means much that the greatest readers of missionary literature today are the students. This educational work of the Volunteer Movement affords the true and safe basis for volunteering, and helps in a marked way to prepare the volunteer for his lifework. Moreover, it is raising up an intelligent missionary pastorate. Under its influence two conferences of professors have been called to consider the subject of missionary instruction in colleges and seminaries. The agitation carried on in connection with this work has led several institutions to introduce the study of missions into the regular curriculum. It has influenced one of the largest denominations to appeal to its colleges to make missions a part of their curriculum. It has also done much to stimulate some of the great organizations at work among the young to promote the study of missions, which after all underlies all permanent and growing missionary interest in the Church.

The Movement has influenced an exceptionally large number of students to decide to become foreign missionaries. It came into being at a time when few students were offering themselves for foreign service. The Boards then told us that they were greatly in need of men, and expressed their deep gratitude that God had called into existence a student movement to sound out the call for volunteers. The prayer for men has been answered. Today nearly every Board testifies that the Movement has greatly increased the number of applicants. Some prominent men continue to overstate the number of volunteers without any basis whatever for their statements, and thus do the Movement injury. For example, at a large meeting of ministers in New York a few weeks ago, it was emphatically said by an eminent preacher that there are 10,000 student volunteers who are ready to go at once. The fact of the case is that the number of volunteers on the roll of the Movement today is not many over 4,000. Of this number a great many have dropped out of college temporarily or permanently for financial or other reasons. It is almost impossible for the Movement to keep trace of this class. One-third of the volunteers now in institutions of learning are women, and two-thirds are men. The number of denominations represented is forty-eight. Notwithstanding the ultra-conservative policy which the Movement has followed for seven years in securing volunteers, the number of students who are expecting to become missionaries in the colleges is five times as great and in the seminaries is over two times as great as it was before the Movement started.

We have the names of 1173 volunteers who before the first of January had gone to the mission field. They have gone out under forty-six missionary societies, and are distributed through fifty-three countries in all parts of the world. Some have raised the question whether the Volunteer Movement has been an essential factor in leading these students to go to the foreign field. A somewhat extended investigation on the foreign field leads us to state that a very large majority of them were directly influenced by the Movement to decide for foreign missions; and most of the others have testified that the Movement greatly strengthened their missionary purpose, helped them in their preparation, and hastened their going to the field. In view of the requirements of most of the mission boards, in view of their conservative policy about sending out new missionaries during the years of financial depression, and in view of the fact that the great body of the volunteers have not completed their preparation, the number who have sailed is most encouraging. It is interesting to see that the leaders or recruiting officers of the Movement are pressing to the field. Of the twenty-six different volunteers who have been members of the Executive Committee or traveling secretaries from the beginning of the Movement, including this year's force, fourteen have sailed, four are under appointment to sail within eight months, three have applied to the boards and at the request of these boards are giving their time to foreign missionary work at home and the remaining five are still preparing themselves for foreign service.

Not only has the Movement greatly increased the number of missionary candidates and thus afforded the boards a larger basis of selection, but it has also improved the average quality of missionary applicants. All but two or three of the boards of North America have borne emphatic testimony to this effect. It should be so. It stands to reason that the thorough study of missions under the direction of the Volunteer Movement, the constant emphasis placed on daily devotional Bible study and secret prayer by the volunteer bands, and the practical training afforded in methods of organized Christian work, must necessarily improve the general quality of intending missionaries. The Movement by the conservative practice of its secretaries, and by its testing, training, and sifting processes, shows that it is more concerned about the quality of candidates than about their number. We believe that the need of the foreign field is not so much that of more men as of more man—above all more of God in man. That the Movement is not only aiming to secure strong men but is succeeding is shown by the following fact: of forty-four men who have held positions as intercollegiate secretaries in the international and state Christian Association work during the past ten years, thirty, or two-thirds of them, have been volunteers, although the volunteers have constituted less than one-twentieth of the Christian students of the continent.

The Volunteer Movement is rendering substantial help in the solution of the money problem. At its inception, the colleges and seminaries were giving about $5,000 a year to foreign missions; whereas, last year they gave probably not less than $40,000. Over 100 institutions now support a missionary either entirely or in large part. If the churches were giving proportionately as much as the colleges, there would be no money problem in missions. The object-lesson afforded to coming pastors and laymen of a group of Christians supporting a missionary, not to mention the training in systematic giving, is a result of far-reaching influence. Several volunteers before sailing have secured their own support. The volunteers have done more than any other one agency to lead individual churches each to support its own missionary under the boards. The work of hundreds of volunteers in societies among the young people as well as in the churches has resulted in spreading a vast amount of missionary information, and has without doubt considerably increased contributions to missions. During the recent years of financial stringency, the Volunteer Movement has afforded the boards one of their strongest and most persuasive appeals for giving on the part of the churches. In a time when doubt has been widely expressed as to the absolutely unique supremacy of the Christian religion, when missions have been insidiously assailed, and when

severe financial stress has been upon us, this student uprising has done
not a little to help hold the Church to the standard of her duty and
to inspire her with new hope.

The reflex influence of this foreign movement on the colleges and
seminaries of the home lands has been simply incalculable. For every
student who has been led to offer himself for Christ's service abroad,
we have reason to believe that more than one have been influenced to
give themselves to earnest Christian work at home, either as ministers
or laymen. Moreover, by interesting students in the world-wide purposes of Christ, the Movement has done much to free them from pride,
selfishness, and cant. It has led to spiritual awakenings in scores of
institutions, some of which have been completely transformed. Should
we eliminate its work from the religious life of the colleges, what a
different showing would be presented in connection with Bible study.
And who can measure what a factor the Movement has been within
the past few years by the use of its prayer cycle, and by emphasizing
the practice of the morning watch, in deepening the prayer life of the
colleges and seminaries?

Beyond question, the largest result of the Movement has been the
direct and indirect effect on the students of other lands. Nine years
ago the Volunteer Movement of the United States and Canada was
the only student movement in the world employing the volunteer methods, organization, declaration, and watchword. Today there are Student Volunteer Movements in Great Britain, Scandinavia, Germany,
French-speaking Europe, Australasia, South Africa, China, India, and
Ceylon; and all of them have expressed gratitude to the American
Movement for the helpful, practical influence it has exerted in the formative period of their work. With thankful and expectant hearts we
welcome to the Convention, Mr. Douglas M. Thornton, the fraternal
delegate of the Student Volunteer Missionary Union of Great Britain
and Ireland; and we record with gratitude to God the fact that from
the beginning there have been the most cordial, intimate, and mutually
helpful relations between that movement and our own. In our report
at the Cleveland Convention seven years ago occur these words: "If
the students of the Protestant world are linked together by the power
of the Spirit in this Movement, it will greatly strengthen the establish-
men of Christ's kingdom throughout the world." In the report presented at the Detroit Convention, four years ago, we announced
that "for the first time the students of the Anglo-Saxon world are
united in a mighty enterprise." Today we are able to state that the
prophecy of seven years ago has become inspiring history. Through
the World's Student Christian Federation, the Christian students of
the lands of Protestant Christendom have been united by the Spirit

of Almighty God. Still more, and a most significant fact in the judgment of missionary leaders, the students of mission lands have joined hands with those of Christian lands in a determined effort "to make Jesus King" among all races of mankind. In the history of the Church there has been nothing like this Federation which has made one in Christ the tens of thousands of Christian students scattered throughout five continents. It would seem that such an alignment of the forces must be a preparation for a larger work in the world.

IV. EXAMPLES OF THE INFLUENCE OF THE MOVEMENT

One of the best ways to see the practical influence of the Movement is to look at what it has actually done in definite institutions. We will call attention to a few such examples.

When one of our greatest universities was first touched by the Movement a few years ago, there was not even a missionary department in its Christian Association. Four men were expecting to be missionaries. There were no classes for the study of missions and no missionary meetings. Three missionary magazines constituted all the missionary literature accessible to students. Not a dollar was being given to foreign missions. This institution has since received a visit from our secretary each year. Their last report states that they have seventeen volunteers, conduct large missionary meetings, have a class of thirty students carrying on missionary study, have a collection of 176 missionary books, and support a representative on the foreign field at an expense of over $1,000 a year. This marked development is traceable directly to the Movement.

Eight years ago, the Movement sent a secretary for the first time to one of the largest of the ladies' seminaries. At that time it was reported that there were no volunteers there. Occasional missionary meetings were being held, but there was no systematic study of missions, and there was no collection of missionary books. No money was being given to missions. The latest report shows that there are now twenty-seven volunteers, that there are two missionary classes with a membership of sixty-four, that they have a missionary library numbering 260 books, and that $235 is being given to foreign missions.

Nearly eight years ago we obtained access to a prominent denominational college. Since then it has had the benefit of all our agencies of supervision and cultivation. At the time of our first contact with this field there were but two intending missionaries, and very little missionary interest. There were no students studying missions. There were no missionary books within reach, and no financial contributions were being made to missions. Today there are forty volunteers in that institution. Eight others have sailed within the last two years. They have regular missionary meetings, and twenty-five students in a missionary class. They have a modern missionary library of seventy volumes or more. Last year they gave $400 toward the support of a missionary. Within the past sixteen months, the volunteers of this institution have given missionary addresses in 135 churches.

It will be suggestive to contrast the missionary life in two sections of the field. In one section the Movement began its work this year, in the other it has been carrying on its work for years. Let us in each section take five institutions, two state universities, one denominational college, and two theological seminaries. In the five institutions formerly untouched by our secretaries, our representative this year found only eleven men intending to be missionaries. In the other group there are sixty-eight. In the uncultivated group there were no men studying missions. In the cultivated group there are eighty-eight men in five classes. In the first five institutions there were but 163 missionary books. In the second five, there are 2,054. In the first group the students were giving but $71 to missions, whereas in the second group they last year gave $732.

The power of the Movement will be seen more strikingly by contrasting one Canadian university and its affiliated colleges situated in the same city, with all the universities, theological seminaries, and colleges of Australia, Tasmania, and New Zealand, numbering some thirty in all. The group of institutions in this Canadian city have felt the favorable influence of the Movement for over ten years through visitation, conferences, publications, and correspondence. The institutions of Australasia were first touched by the Movement year before last. At that time, in all Australasia we found less than a score of students purposing to be missionaries. In the Canadian university there are sixty-six volunteers. In Australasia we found no class for the progressive study of missions. In the Canadian university there are five such classes, with sixty-six members. In all the institutions of Australasia we found fewer than 200 missionary books, whereas in the Canadian university there are 1,050. In Australasia the students were giving less than $300 to missions. In the Canadian university last year, the students gave to missions $1,025. We were told that fewer than a dozen of the 3,000 graduates of the five universities of Australasia had become foreign missionaries, whereas not less than seventy graduates of this Canadian university and its affiliated colleges have gone to the foreign field since the inception of the Volunteer Movement. The presence and work of the Volunteer Movement has been not the only, but the main factor which has made possible the markedly more favorable showing in the one case than in the other. It is interesting and to the point to add that although the Movement has been at work in Australasia less than two years the number of volunteers has increased from less than a score to seventy-one, of whom five have already sailed; and that a splendid scheme for the promotion of missionary study in all leading institutions has been adopted. One of the strongest contingents for the evangelization of the world is destined to come from the universities of Australasia.

V. The Movement Needed More Today than Ever

Great as has been the work of the Volunteer Movement in the first decade of its organized life, it has by no means accomplished its mission. It is even more needed today than ever before. Why? The world is better known, more accessible, and its need more articulate than ever. Therefore, the Movement is indispensable to enable the Church to meet this need. The generations of students touched by the Movement in the past have largely gone out of the institutions of learning into fields from which most of them cannot be called to missionary work. Therefore, reinforcements must come from students now in the colleges and seminaries, and from their successors. Thus the Movement will be needed as a recruiting force until the work is done. Foreign missions have begun to yield on a large scale. Surely this is not the time for the Church to hesitate and hold back. The Movement is needed to enable the Church to make the most of her present unparalleled advantage. As one great Christian statesman has said, if the Church fails to improve her present opportunity, the evangelization of the world may be delayed hundreds of years. The missionary enterprise has reached a stage which demands more of the best prepared missionaries than ever. What agency could do more to help supply this preparation than the Volunteer Movement? The Movement is needed for the sake of our colleges and seminaries; for it will do much to counteract the dangerous tendencies to materialism, skepticism, selfishness, pride, and ease, which result from the mind being shut in upon itself and losing the true objective of human existence—to fill the world with the knowledge of Christ. The Movement is needed as an outlet for the energies of the North American Church. Think of the energy resulting from her scores of missionary organizations and from nearly a century of missionary experience. Think of the energy in numbers, as we note the fact that her membership is increasing more rapidly than the population of the two countries. Think of the energy in wealth as we recall the statement of Dr. Strong that during this century each generation has handed down to the succeeding generation four or five times as much wealth as it received from the preceding generation. The great menace of the United States and Canada is materialism, and the peril of becoming self-centered. The spirit of the Volunteer Movement is in harmony, therefore, with the highest patriotism. Nothing better could befall these two great countries than to send forth to far more needy lands 10,000 of their choicest students with all the sacrifice, sympathy, and prayer, that this would call forth from the Church. The financial depression will be followed, as in similar periods in our history, by a time of great prosperity; with this difference, that the period of prosperity right before us will be characterized by the greatest missionary opportunities of the ages. Where can the Church look unless it be to the Volunteer Movement, to find the men and women to enable her to meet these opportunities? And let us not forget our watchword. If the world is to be evangelized in this generation, it will be necessary for our Movement to raise up an army of Spirit-filled volunteers. In a word, the Volunteer Movement is needed so long as there are one thousand millions of human beings in non-Christian lands, and so long as the last commission of Jesus Christ remains unfulfilled.

VI. REGIONS BEYOND FOR THE MOVEMENT

The Student Volunteer Movement should in no respect count itself as having already attained. Its undeveloped possibilities are simply limitless. As we view them, we are humbled with the thought of how little comparatively, after all, has been accomplished, and are led to resolve with God's help that the second decade in the life of the Movement shall be made more acceptable to Him than the first.

Notice the regions beyond in the realm of cultivating the student field of North America. Of the 1,000 institutions of higher learning in the United States and Canada, we are able to visit thoroughly only about 300 in a year, even with a force as large as we have at present. In view of the strategic importance of the theological seminaries which are to furnish so largely the leadership of the church at home and abroad, much more attention should be paid to them. Thus far we have barely touched the medical colleges of the continent. When we remember how the work of the medical missionary was honored by the life of Christ; when we see that in many fields today the medical missionary has the most influential access to the people, and that in spite of this fact the medical missionary force is comparatively the smallest; when we observe that the conditions in our medical colleges today are the most unfavorable for the promotion of strong spiritual life and activity; we are convinced that at least one man should give his entire time to work among medical students. Miss Rouse, who has had such wide and successful experience in promoting missionary interest among women's colleges in Europe, and more recently in these countries, has expressed her conviction that the women's colleges of North America need the entire time of two women. As one half the unevangelized world, and that by far the most neglected half, are women, and as but one-third of our volunteers are women, there can be no question about the great need of enlarged effort in this direction. When we remember that the results which have been outlined have come from such a small part of our student field, what might we not expect from a continuous and thorough cultivation of all the higher institutions of North America?

The educational work of the Movement has an unlimited horizon. It is encouraging to know that over 2,000 students are making a careful study of missions, and yet there are not less than 10,000 theological students on the continent, 25,000 active members in the College Young Men's Christian Associations, and over 10,000 active members in the College Young Women's Christian Associations, which means that but one in fifteen in the best prepared part of the student field is in mission classes. Every reason which has influenced the 2,000 to undertake the study of missions applies equally to the rest of these as well as to all other Christian students. Students must be led to recognize that to be abreast of the times, to be truly educated, indeed to be real Christians, they must be intelligent concerning the Kingdom of Christ in the world—its field, its progress, its present day triumphs, its problems, its resources.

There is still need for thousands of thoroughly qualified volunteers. Let us reiterate that the great majority of our volunteers have not yet finished their preparation. While it is true in the case of some boards that the supply of candidates exceeds the present ability to send, it is not probable that the conditions which obtain at present will continue much longer. This Movement must build for the future. It is never too early to begin to prepare for a great work. The chairman of the Committee, on his recent tour in mission fields, met some 1,300 missionaries, representing some seventy missionary societies, and they presented to him one unbroken appeal for more men and women. One of the oldest and most experienced board secretaries on this continent says that in view of the work before the Movement, it should be sending its men from the colleges into the seminaries by the hundred and by the thousand every year. The practical question is, should the Volunteer Movement take as the ideal governing its policy the practice of the home church as to giving, or the actual need and crisis in every mission field, the clear command of Jesus Christ, and the unquestioned missionary practice of the early Christian church? The concern of the Volunteer Movement in this connection should be to emphasize the highest qualifications, to appeal only to spiritual motives, and to make sure that the Holy Spirit is separating men unto the work whereunto God Himself has called them.

The volunteer should never lose sight of those great regions beyond where Christ has not been named. There is need among many of more determination to press to the front. Some have apparently dropped from the ranks of the volunteers and have joined those who will go when drafted. The spirit and meaning of the volunteer declaration might be well expressed in the language of the constitution of the first band of student volunteers in America, the Society of Brethren at Williams College, namely, "To effect in the persons of its members a mission or missions to the heathen." Nothing but the clear will of God should be allowed to keep permanently any volunteer from pressing to the front. To reiterate the language of the Detroit Report, "the volunteer who considers himself hindered should be very sure that he has been hindered by the Holy Spirit, and not by friends, or self, or sin, or Satan. It is not an easy gauntlet that the volunteer must run in order to get away from a land where he is needed into the one where he is needed most." Every volunteer who is worthy of a place on the foreign field will have obstacles placed in his path; and the stronger he is in Christian work, the more he will be pressed to stay at home to work. Obstacles are made, as Carey said, to be overcome. Most men who have done a great work in the world have had to fight their way through ranks of difficulties. The financial depression has been a good thing for the Volunteer Movement in that it has tested the largeness of our faith and the strength of our purpose. Unless a volunteer is rejected by the board for other than financial reasons, there is peril in letting himself believe that if the board does not send him his purpose is fulfilled. This cannot be true, if God called him. It is incumbent on him to do everything within his power to help the board remove this hindrance. The Church needs men with this kind of determination; or as Mr. Brockman well says, "In the beginning of the Movement the Church needed men who were willing to go; now she needs men unwilling to stay."

The Volunteer Movement has a great work to do in getting Christian students who are to remain at home to recognize that they are just as responsible for the evangelization of the world as are those who go to the front. There is a tendency among many Christian students to look upon the active promotion of the missionary movement as something quite outside the ordinary Christian life. They assume that to help extend Christ's Kingdom is purely an optional matter, and not obligatory. It must be pressed upon them that an active missionary spirit is inseparable from a real Christian life, and that a man may well question whether he is living the Christian life (i.e. having Christ live in him) if he is indifferent to the needs of half of the human race. It is clearly his duty to keep himself informed on missions, to spread missionary intelligence, to render financial assistance, to pray for the extension of Christ's Kingdom, and to enlist others in the work of the world's evangelization. The chief consideration which should keep a man at home today should be to work for the extension of the Kingdom of God throughout the whole world. Henry Venn, secretary of the Church Missionary Society, was wont to urge that a strong base of operations at home is indispensable for the aggressive prosecution of missions abroad. Every Christian man who is called of God to stay at home should help to develop on this continent a base adequate to the work providentially before us in mission lands. Young men should enter the ministry not so much with the idea of cultivating a parish as of world conquest; and should look upon their parish not alone as a field but as a force to be wielded on behalf of the whole world.

The opportunities in the realm of the financial problem are among the greatest which at this time confront the Volunteer Movement. Never have there been such appeals from the field. Never have there been so many worthy applicants refused by the boards. Never, probably, has there been such serious retrenchment in missionary operations. The prayer for men has given way to the prayer for money. We believe that the volunteers and their Christian fellow students constitute one of the largest latent forces to be used in the solution of the financial problem. Why cannot students in hundreds of colleges and seminaries do what has been done by the Methodist students in Canada, and by little bands of students in several institutions in the United States? The board secretaries of North America in their conference last year made this recommendation, "We suggest that wider use may profitably be made of the volunteer bands by our boards, as a valuable and efficient agency in quickening the zeal of our churches in this service, and leading them to recognize in the Movement, as they appear to have failed to do as yet, God's answer to their own prayer for laborers for the world's great harvest field, and His challenge to their greatest faith and consecration, and their enlarged and self-sacrificing liberality." We should heed the caution of the board secretaries also, that there ought to be careful conference and perfect understanding between the boards and the volunteers in this work. The usual plan followed is for students to devote the larger part of the long vacation to a missionary campaign in the churches. One denomination has appealed to its colleges for 100 students to engage in the work during the coming summer. Why should not hundreds of students give from thirty to sixty days to field work, and thousands

of others influence their home churches and societies among the young
people? We would call special attention to the field presented by the
nearly 5,000,000 members of the Christian Endeavor movement, the
Epworth League, the Baptist Young People's Union, and similar
movements. Without doubt there has been a marked providence in
calling into existence at the same time the Volunteer Movement and
these great organizations among the young. May it not be in order
that the millions may send the thousands? If this great army of young
people can be interested in missions, and led to form the habit of systematic and proportionate giving, it will afford an adequate outlet
for the volunteers of all branches of the Church. Although responsibility rests on all Christian students to assist in this work of arousing
interest in the churches and among the young people, we would especially appeal to volunteers. The best life of the volunteer depends on
active work for missions. He has been called of God to be a missionary. When and where does his missionary career begin? Six years
later in India or China, or now in the home land? Dr. George Smith,
Secretary of the Missionary Society of the Free Church of Scotland,
urges that "each volunteer should summon to his or her support abroad
the Christians of the congregation, community, or district around, in
a way that will not only not interfere with the church's or society's central fund, but must in the end stimulate its increase." American and
Canadian volunteers can not do better than to imitate Samuel Mills,
that first student volunteer of this continent to go to a foreign field,
of whom it is said, "When not ready to go to the foreign field he could
not wait in idleness. No dreams of a field more to his liking kept him
from tilling the field at his feet. He waited not for an opportunity to
turn up; he made the opportunity. He made himself master of facts
and used them as shot and shell to beat down the walls of carelessness
and indifference."

Let us never lose sight of the vast regions beyond in the realm of
the fulfillment of the watchword of the Movement—"The Evangelization of the World in This Generation." What is the meaning of the
watchword? It means to bring Christ within the reach of every person in the world that he may have the opportunity of intelligently accepting Him as a personal Savior. It does not mean the conversion of
the world, because the acceptance of Christ rests with the hearer, and
not with the speaker. It does not imply a superficial or hasty preaching of the gospel, or present any new or peculiar theory of missionary
work. It does not disparage any other form of missionary work, for
it may be questioned whether any other agency is today emphasizing
educational missions more, or doing more to promote medical missions than the Student Volunteer Movement. The Movement stands

pre-eminently for the emphasis of the belief that by a great enlargement of all agencies employed by the missionary societies, the gospel
can and should be brought within the reach of every creature within
this generation. Nor should the watchword be interpreted as a sure
word of prophecy. It calls attention to what may and ought to be done,
not necessarily to what is actually going to occur. The evangelization
of the world in this generation is a necessity, because one-half of the
inhabitants of the world have never heard of Christ. If we know that
He is necessary for us, have we a right to assume that others do not
need Him? The Christians of today are the only ones to whom the
heathen of this generation can look for the gospel. It is our duty to
evangelize the world, because Christ has commanded it. His command
to us applies to this, the one generation in all eternity for which we
are responsible. Without doubt it is entirely possible to evangelize
the world in this generation. We need only recall the achievements
of the Apostolic Church and then, in contrast, consider the extent and
resources of the Church today—her membership, her wealth, her organizations, her accumulated experience, her access to the world field,
the wonderful facilities at her disposal, the power of the native church,
bearing ever in mind the fact that the Church today can avail herself
of the same divine equipment which made possible the mighty works
of the early Christians, namely, the Word of God, the mountain-
moving force of prayer, and the power of the Holy Ghost. It should
greatly encourage us in working for the realization of our watchword
to know that it has been sounded out by the missionaries from their
largest conferences in India, China, and the Hawaiian Islands, and
that within the last year it has called forth resolutions of approval
from the Lambeth Conference of Bishops and from missionary societies of Great Britain, as well as from missionary leaders in America.
The more the watchword takes hold of the consciousness of the volunteers, the more apparent become its advantages. It is a great unifying
force in a Movement which has become world-wide. It gives to the
volunteer a mighty motive and a controlling purpose. It lends intensity to his life. It calls out the heroic and self-sacrificing in his nature.
It drives him to God. It must inevitably stir the life of the Church.

After all, the great region beyond is that within our own lives.
The ultimate success of the Movement depends not so much on the
number of men who go out as upon the spiritual quality of those who
do go. A spiritual work cannot be done by other than spiritual men.
To do the work of God we must have the power of God. The energy
of the flesh, or of the trained intellect, or of the moral earnestness
must not be allowed to take the place of the Holy Spirit. We can do
man's work without Him; but why be satisfied with having man work

when we may have the mighty God working through us? Only by having the unoccupied places in our lives filled with His Spirit can we fight the battle against sin within us and opposition and evil around us. Only as we are clothed with His power have we the right or the preparation to preach Christ where He has not been named. "Tarry ye in the city, until ye be clothed with power from on high. . . . Ye shall receive power when the Holy Ghost is come upon you; and ye shall be witnesses unto me."

VII. THE NEEDS OF THE MOVEMENT

The Volunteer Movement has needs which must be supplied if it is to fulfil its mission in the world.

It needs the continued helpful counsel of board secretaries and missionaries as to how it can most effectively promote the missionary enterprise.

There is need that the volunteer bands in the colleges and seminaries be more progressive and purposeful. We know of no better model at the present time than the band at Northwestern University.

In each institution we need the influential and intelligent co-operation of sympathetic professors in order that conditions may be made favorable for the best development of the missionary spirit.

The Movement needs not less than $16,000 a year during the next four years in order that it may cultivate this field of such marvelous possibilities—the student field of the North American continent.

Let it be reiterated that there is need that the volunteers and the students who are not volunteers work with one mind and with like determination and self-denial for the evangelization of the world and the establishment of the Messiah's reign.

There is need of a recognition on the part of the entire Church of Christ of the divine significance of this Movement and of the call of God through it to greater faith and more self-sacrificing liberality.

Above all needs, yes, comprising all our needs, is the need of prayer. Everything vital to the Movement or essential to its progress hinges on prayer—separating of men unto the work whereunto God has called them, thrusting them forth with that irresistible energy which characterizes God-sent as contrasted with man-sent men, supplying adequate money given with purity of motive and real sacrifice of self, overcoming of superhuman obstacles, commanding the power of the unseen world to come upon the workmen in the far-off fields, and crowning their labors with large and enduring fruitage. Few Christians indeed realize the scope and meaning of the common petition, "Thy Kingdom come." And the Church has not yet touched the fringe of the possibilities of intercessory prayer. Her largest triumphs will not be witnessed until individual Christians everywhere come to recognize their priesthood unto God, and day by day wield the omnipotent forces of the prayer kingdom.

> JOHN R. MOTT, *Chairman*
> J. ROSS STEVENSON
> PAULINE ROOT
> *Executive Committee*

REPORT PRESENTED AT
THE FOURTH INTERNATIONAL CONVENTION
TORONTO, CANADA, FEBRUARY 26 - MARCH 2, 1902

I. THE AIM OF THE MOVEMENT

The Student Volunteer Movement for Foreign Missions was called into being in 1886, primarily to raise up among the students of North America a sufficient number of capable missionary candidates to meet the requirements of the various missionary societies or boards. To help these candidates or student volunteers in their preparation for their lifework has been recognized from the beginning as falling within the purpose of the Movement. Another object is to develop among students who are to spend their lives in Christian lands, either as pastors or as laymen, a sense of responsibility to sustain and reinforce the foreign missionary enterprise by intelligent sympathy, by the giving of money, by prayer, and by aggressive effort on behalf of the world's evangelization.

The field for the cultivation of which the Movement considers itself responsible embraces all colleges, universities, and other institutions of higher learning in the United States and Canada. There are fully 1,000 such institutions, with an aggregate of over 200,000 students. From the college halls come the leaders in all the influential walks of life. No work, therefore, can be more important than that of making the student communities strongholds and propagating centres of missionary intelligence, enthusiasm, and activity.

II. AGENCIES OF SUPERVISION AND CULTIVATION

For several years the Movement was guided by an Executive Committee of three members, representing the three great interdenominational student organizations of North America. The work having assumed so much larger proportions it was found desirable not long after the Cleveland Convention in 1898 to enlarge the membership of the Committee, so that it now consists of six members: John R. Mott and H. P. Andersen representing the college department of the

Young Men's Christian Association; J. Ross Stevenson the theological section, and W. Harley Smith the medical college section of the same organization; and Miss Pauline Root and Miss Bertha Condé representing the Student Young Women's Christian Association. John R. Mott is the chairman, J. Ross Stevenson the vice-chairman, and F. P. Turner the recording secretary and treasurer. In order to transact the ordinary business of such an organization it is incorporated under the laws of the State of New York. There is a Board of Trustees consisting of the following: W. D. Murray, James A. Beaver, W. F. McDowell, N. Tooker, C. W. McAlpin, S. H. Blake, and John R. Mott, *ex officio*.

At the annual meeting of the Executive Committee following the quadrennial conventions, an Advisory Committee is selected. For the period September 1898 to September 1902 the members of the Advisory Committee have been: The Reverend Judson Smith, D.D., Mr. Robert E. Speer, The Reverend S. L. Baldwin, D.D., The Reverend H. C. Mabie, D.D., the Right Reverend M. S. Baldwin, the Bishop of Huron, The Reverend A. McLean, D.D., Professor E. C. Dargan, D.D., and Miss Abbie B. Child. The members of this committee have rendered from time to time invaluable aid by personal advice and counsel.

The secretaries of the Movement are a general secretary, an assistant general secretary, an educational secretary, and the traveling secretaries.

The position of traveling secretary is usually held for one year by some student volunteer who is nearly ready to go to the mission field, but occasionally a returned missionary has been employed. In a few instances secretaries have held the position two years. The size of the staff of traveling secretaries is determined by the funds at the disposal of the Executive Committee and by the number of available candidates.

During the period under review F. P. Turner has served as general secretary, J. E. Knotts as assistant general secretary, and Harlan P. Beach as educational secretary.

The traveling secretaries since the last Convention have been as follows:

1898-1899.—For theological colleges, Robert P. Wilder (one-half of his time); for colleges and universities, Sumner R. Vinton, Burton St. John, and S. Earl Taylor (two months); for medical colleges, John Rutter Williamson; and for women's colleges, Miss Constance MacCorkle, Miss Elizabeth Prentiss (two months), and Miss Elizabeth Ross (five months).

1899-1900.—For theological colleges, S. Earl Taylor (one-half of his time) ; for medical colleges, C. W. Ottley; for colleges and universities, V. W. Helm (two months), F. W. Anderson (two months), F. M. Gilbert (five months) ; for women's colleges, Miss Elizabeth Ross (four months), Miss Sophia B. Lyon, and Miss Angie Martin Myers (two months).

1900-1901.—For theological colleges, S. Earl Taylor (three months) and A. H. Ewing (three months) ; for colleges and universities, F. M. Gilbert, G. W. Leavitt, F. W. Anderson; for medical colleges, C. W. Roys, F. Howard Taylor (four months) ; for women's colleges, Miss Sophia B. Lyon, Miss Mabel Milham, Mrs. F. Howard Taylor (four months), and Miss Margaret H. Shearman (two months).

1901-1902.—For theological colleges, John N. Forman; for colleges and universities, D. Brewer Eddy, E. J. Lee (four months), W. B. Pettus (four months) ; for women's colleges, Miss Mabel Milham and Miss Sarah L. De Forest.

Each year in the month of September the Executive Committee conducts a conference for the purpose of training the new secretaries and also to discuss the work and problems of the Movement with the national student secretaries of the Young Men's and Young Women's Christian Associations.

The Intercollegian. In 1898 the monthly organ of the Movement, *The Student Volunteer,* which for six years had been a useful agency in keeping the volunteers in touch with the aims, methods and results of the Movement, and in keeping the Movement before the Church, was united with *The Intercollegian,* which magazine is now published jointly by the Student Department of the Young Men's Christian Association and the Student Volunteer Movement. By this arrangement not only have all the advantages of a distinctly missionary periodical been preserved, but access has been secured to a larger number of Christian students. For three years Charles H. Fahs served as managing editor. At present the magazine is in charge of an editorial committee composed of Harlan P. Beach, H. W. Hicks, and Thornton B. Penfield.

Secretaries of the Young Men's and Young Women's Christian Associations, especially those in traveling work, have been a great factor in promoting the interests of the Student Volunteer Movement. Several of these secretaries are volunteers. Each year demonstrates the wisdom shown in making the volunteer work an organic department of these organizations. This relationship insures permanence, affords larger, more direct, and more influential access to Christian students, and supplies favorable conditions for fostering the spiritual life of volunteers and for training them in Christian work.

At each of the student conferences held in different parts of the continent by the International Committee of Young Men's Christian Associations, and by the American Committee of Young Women's Christian Associations, missionary institutes are conducted by secretaries of the Student Volunteer Movement. During the four years under review, thirty-two of these conferences have been held as follows: For the colleges of Canada and the East, at East Northfield, Massachusetts; for the colleges of the South, at Asheville, North Carolina; for the colleges of the Central West, at Lake Geneva, Wisconsin; for the colleges on the Pacific Coast, at Pacific Grove and at Capitola, California. The object of these institutes is to train leaders for Volunteer Bands, for mission study classes, and for other missionary activities of the institutions represented. At the conferences of the theological section of Young Men's Christian Associations, special attention was given to missionary interests by the members and secretaries of the Executive Committee of the Movement.

There are volunteer unions in the large student centers of Toronto, Montreal, Boston, New York, Philadelphia, Baltimore, Nashville, Chicago, Denver, and San Francisco; also in several states where there are groups of colleges, as in Western Massachusetts, in Connecticut, and in Minnesota. The monthly meetings of these unions do much to advance the Movement in the institutions which are in touch with them.

It is the policy of the Movement to hold once in a student generation an international convention like the one now assembled.

The first, held in Cleveland in 1891, was attended by 680 delegates, representing 151 institutions, all the leading mission boards of North America, and nearly every mission field. At the second, held in Detroit in 1894, there were present 1,325 delegates, including students and professors from 294 institutions, the representatives of fifty-four American and Canadian mission boards, missionaries from all the great mission fields, and the national leaders of the various organizations that work among young people.

In 1898, the third convention met at Cleveland, with an attendance of 2,221 delegates. Of these, 1,598 students and 119 professors came from 461 institutions. There were eighty-nine returned missionaries, eighty national and state officers of Young Men's and Young Women's Christian Associations, twenty national and state officers of young people's societies, and eleven editors of religious papers. The general interest in this convention is indicated by the fact that 6,000 copies of the official report, *The Student Missionary Appeal,* have been sold.

III. What the Movement Has Accomplished

The work of the Movement through visitation, summer conferences, and correspondence has touched nearly, if not quite, 800 institutions. In more than one-half of these institutions nothing was being
done in the interest of foreign missions prior to the efforts put forth
by this Movement or, at its initiative, by the Christian Associations.
In many other colleges where there had been for years more or less
missionary interest, it has been the testimony of professors and of
others who are in a position to know that the Movement has greatly
increased that interest. It is significant that this missionary movement
has brought within the range of its plan and helpful influence more
colleges than has any other student movement save the World's Student Christian Federation.

The educational work carried on by the Movement has continued
to grow. Each year our traveling secretaries bring to the attention of
tens of thousands of students the needs of the non-Christian world
and the claims of missionary service. The regular missionary meetings
of the Christian Associations have under the influence of the Movement become far more popular and effective than in former years.

The most valuable educational work has been the promotion of
mission study. Without question the Volunteer Movement has been
the principal factor in the recent remarkable development in the scientific study of missions in the colleges and theological seminaries. In
its early years the Movement simply recommended subjects and books
for study. Later it outlined courses of study. Nearly eight years ago
the Educational Department was organized and an educational secretary appointed. At that time there were only about a score of mission
study classes in all the colleges and seminaries of North America.
These were isolated and their work in no way co-ordinated. At the
time of the Cleveland Convention, four years ago, the number of
classes had increased to 267, having in them 2,361 students, and the
work of these classes was being prosecuted on a unified and progressive
plan. During the past year the number of classes has reached 325,
with an enrolment of 4,797 students. Thus the number of students in
such classes has doubled within four years. It is an interesting fact
that over half the members of these classes are not volunteers. This
means much for the future leadership of the Church at home. Rochester Theological Seminary has the largest number of students in voluntary mission study classes among the seminaries, and among the colleges Hiram has enrolled the greatest number.

Even more important than the increase in numbers has been the
marked improvement in the quality of the educational work. This is

due to the wise direction of the department by the educational secretary, to the well adapted series of textbooks which have been specially prepared, and to the increased number of trained leaders of mission classes. The first cycle of mission study, covering a period of four years, has been completed and the second cycle has just been started. Since the last Convention, sixteen different mission textbooks have been issued by the Movement, all but four of which were specially prepared for its use. An immense service to the cause of missions has been rendered in the preparation of these textbooks.

Since January 1898, the following publications have been issued by the Movement (the last three being reprinted):

Africa Waiting, D. M. Thornton
St. Paul and the Gentile World, H. P. Beach
Dawn on the Hills of T'ang, or Missions in China, H. P. Beach
Japan and Its Regeneration, Otis Cary
New Testament Studies in Missions, H. P. Beach
Modern Apostles in Missionary Byways, several writers
The Healing of the Nations, J. Rutter Williamson
The Evangelization of the World in this Generation, J. R. Mott
Protestant Missions in South America, several writers
The Call, Qualifications, and Preparation of Missionary Candidates, Papers by missionaries and other authorities
Geography and Atlas of Protestant Missions, Volume I, H. P. Beach
The Student Missionary Appeal, (Report of Student Volunteer Convention at Cleveland, 1898)
Social Evils of the Non-Christian World, James S. Dennis
Introduction to the Study of Foreign Missions, E. A. Lawrence
The Cycle of Prayer
Money, Its Nature and Power, A. F. Schauffler
The Planting and Development of Missionary Churches, J. L. Nevius
A Hand Book of Comparative Religion, S. H. Kellogg
The Medical Mission, W. J. Wanless

Within these four years the sales of our textbooks and other publications have amounted to more than 100,000 copies. The secretaries of the Movement have continued to plant and build up missionary libraries. Before the Movement began, the students of but few colleges and seminaries had access to the best missionary literature. Now as a result of its work, well-furnished missionary libraries are to be found in a large majority of the institutions of higher learning. The fact that the students are the principal purchasers of missionary literature is another indication of the real strength of the interest of the colleges and seminaries in the cause of missions.

Since its inception the Volunteer Movement has pressed upon four successive student generations the claims of foreign missionary service as a lifework. In contrast with any time before the Movement began its work, few students leave college today without having heard this appeal. Formerly missionary candidates came from a comparatively small number of institutions. Volunteers are now being raised up in hundreds of institutions where, in the past, few students even considered the claims of missions. Even in colleges, which in the early days furnished the largest number of missionaries, the proportion of students offering themselves for such work during the period covered by the Volunteer Movement has been greater than ever, with the exception of possibly two institutions. Making all allowance for the present lack of candidates in connection with certain missionary societies, nearly all the boards have borne testimony that the Movement has greatly increased the number of intending missionaries. Several boards also testify that the work of the Movement has enabled them to raise their standard of qualifications. This has been made possible by affording them a larger number of candidates from which to choose their workers. The valuable preparation afforded by mission study, by cultivating right habits of Bible study and prayer, and by training in Christian work, has also helped to make this possible.

We have the names of 1,953 volunteers who, up to the present year, have sailed. They have gone out in connection with about fifty different missionary societies, and are scattered throughout all parts of the non-Christian world. Doubtless other volunteers, of whom we have no record, are at work on the mission field. During the four years which have elapsed since the Cleveland Convention, 60 per cent more volunteers have gone to the mission field than during the four years preceding that gathering. Taking the whole life of the Volunteer Movement into consideration, nearly 100 per cent more volunteers have sailed during the last eight years than during the first eight years.

The question from time to time recurs: Are the leaders of the Movement going out to the field? Of the forty-six volunteers who have served the Movement as members or secretaries of the Executive Committee, twenty-seven have sailed, and nine are either under appointment or have applied to the boards. Of the remainder, five have been prevented from going by ill health and four are still in preparation. This statement does not include missionaries who have served the Movement.

According to the latest reports received, the colleges and theological seminaries of the United States and Canada gave last year a little over $40,000 towards foreign missions. Several institutions are supporting wholly or in large part their own missionary. This represents in not a few cases much self-sacrifice. If the same spirit possessed the churches, the money problem of missions would be solved. The largest contributions, in proportion to the number of students, have been made by theological colleges. While the amount given by students is encouraging, when the number from whom it comes and the sacrifice are considered, this is not the principal benefit resulting from the financial co-operation of the students. Thousands of these young men are to become pastors of churches. If as students they adopt the habit of systematic and proportionate giving, and have before them the object lesson of their own college undertaking to support a missionary, is it not probable that in afterlife they will be more likely to lead their churches to do likewise? The indirect influence of the Movement on the giving of the churches, both as a result of the work of hundreds of students in the churches, and as a result of the powerful challenge which the Movement in itself presents to the liberality of Christians, has been very great indeed. We need only call attention to the student campaign work in the churches and to the Forward Movement of the American Board as illustrations.

The Volunteer Movement has exerted a mighty reflex influence on the religious life of the colleges and theological seminaries. If the volunteers and all that pertains to the work of the Movement were taken from our institutions, what loss these institutions would suffer. Think of the spiritual influence exercised by the traveling secretaries through their addresses and conversations. Consider how the missionary idea as emphasized in meetings and in mission classes has widened the horizon, enriched the sympathies, and stimulated the zeal of students. What a large part missions have had in developing the spirit of brotherhood, of self-denial, and of real service, and in promoting definiteness and unselfishness in prayer. Who can measure the effect on the lives of their fellow-students of the object-lesson of volunteers giving up all and going forth to preach Christ where He has not been named? Moreover, missionary intelligence, missionary activity, and the missionary spirit have done far more than is generally realized to counteract the evil and subtle influences of pride, selfishness, and rationalism as manifested in different student communities. Those who have traveled among the colleges have frequently observed that the greatest manifestation of the presence and work of the Holy Spirit has been in those places where there has also been the largest obedience to the missionary purposes of God.

During the last four years the Movement has been a greater factor than ever in promoting the missionary life of the churches. It has confined its activities chiefly to work among the young people. Volunteer bands and volunteer unions in all parts of the continent have taken a leading part in the work of the local societies of young people in their vicinity.

The principal result in this direction, however, has been the organization of the student campaign in connection with different Christian denominations. By student campaign is meant an organized effort of students, both volunteers and non-volunteers, to communicate to the churches through the young people's societies their missionary knowledge, enthusiasm, and consecration, as well as their practical plans of organization. The first and most successful effort of this kind was made by the Methodist Church in Canada. Within the past four years the students of twelve other denominations have inaugurated similar movements with varying degrees of success. The leaders of the Volunteer Movement have helped by counsel at every stage of this development. The leaders of all but one of these campaigns have been volunteers, several of whom have already gone to the mission field. Much of the success of this work depends on making the students themselves largely responsible for the campaign. Generally speaking it may be said that wherever suitable campaigners have been available, and wherever the plan has been wisely directed, the results have been noteworthy. Many hundreds of volunteers and other students have received valuable training while carrying on this useful work. In one denomination alone 325 students have engaged in campaign work during the last four years. In the pathway of the work of student campaigners thousands of young people's societies have been stirred with the missionary spirit, missionary committees have been organized, missionary libraries have been established, mission study classes and reading circles have been instituted, the young people have been influenced to form the habit of systematic giving, many churches have been led to support their own missionary, intercession on behalf of missions has been greatly promoted, and the spiritual life of the young people's societies has been quickened and strengthened.

A good example of the possibilities of such effort is seen in the work accomplished by the Yale band. This band, composed of five Yale students, devoted a year to traveling and working among young people's societies. During that time they visited seventy cities, addressed 884 meetings, and held 364 missionary conferences, at which some 2,000 young people's societies were represented. They influenced 241 of these societies to organize missionary committees, 579 to secure a collection of missionary books, 392 to undertake missionary study, 518 to adopt a plan of systematic giving, and 757 to use a missionary prayer cycle.

One of the principal contributions of the Movement to the Church has been the emphasis of its watchword, "The Evangelization of the World in This Generation." Although this watchword was first adopted by the North American Movement, it was until recently more earnestly advocated and pressed by the British Movement. Within the past two or three years it has been given large prominence in our plans and activities. The book entitled, *The Evangelization of the World in this Generation,* prepared at the request of the North American and British Movements, was published simultaneously in New York and London in August 1900. It has since been translated into German, Norwegian, and Swedish, and will soon be translated into Japanese and French. It is also being reprinted in India. It has been used as a textbook among students in many countries and has also been given a wide general circulation.

The watchword, which was so severely criticized in the early days of the Movement, has won its way to a very general acceptance, not only among students, but also among leaders of the missionary enterprise. The advantages of this watchword have become more and more apparent. It has exerted a great unifying influence among volunteers and other Christian students throughout the world. It has helped to hold volunteers true to their life purpose. It has arrested the attention and stimulated the thought of a multitude of Christians on the subject of missions. It has presented a powerful appeal to some men to become missionaries, and to others to make their lives in Christian lands tell for the world's evangelization. It has placed a much-needed emphasis on the urgency or immediacy of our missionary obligation. In the case of a large and increasing number of Christians who have taken it as their personal watchword, it has enlarged vision, strengthened purpose, augmented faith, inspired hopefulness, intensified zeal, driven to God in prayer, and developed the spirit of heroism and self-sacrifice.

The Volunteer Movement, which first assumed organized form in North America, has, under different names, become world-wide. Because of the intimate and responsible relation which our own Movement has sustained to the organization and development of the Volunteer Movement in other lands, and because of the importance and significance of these unions, attention is called to their progress. The Volunteer Union of Great Britain is firmly anchored in the British colleges, and commands the confidence of the British missionary societies. Over one-third of their volunteers have already sailed—an even larger proportion than have gone out from North America. The London Convention, held in January 1900, was the largest and most notable student convention ever held in Europe.

The Volunteer Movement in Germany, and also the one in Scandinavia, in the face of far greater difficulties than those which confront the Movement in Anglo-Saxon lands, have made most encouraging progress. They have materially increased the number of missionary candidates and have done much to promote the scientific study of missions. The Conference of the German Movement, held at Halle in April 1901, was the most remarkable student missionary convention ever held on the continent. Professor Warneck, the eminent missionary scholar and authority, has spoken most appreciatively of this Movement. While, because of its still greater difficulties, the Movement in France and French-speaking Switzerland has not made such marked progress as the other European Movements, it has nevertheless accomplished a useful work. Since the last report was rendered, the Volunteer Movement has been organized in Holland, the last unorganized Protestant country. In view of the strength of the Dutch students, and in view of the relation of their country to vast numbers of unevangelized people, the possibilities of this new Movement are very great. Notwithstanding their isolation, the Volunteer Movements in Australasia and South Africa are doing excellent work, especially in promoting mission study and in thrusting forth into unevangelized lands so many of their volunteers. The Student Volunteer Movement of India and Ceylon has recently entered upon a new regime which has much of promise for the cause of missions in India, and which will help greatly to guide in the development of similar movements in China and Japan.

The World's Student Christian Federation, which unites all the Christian Student Movements of the world, including the various organizations of student volunteers of all lands and races, has continued to go from strength to strength. One of its three main objects is "to enlist students in the work of extending the Kingdom of Christ throughout the whole world." The Federation embraces over 1,500 student Christian organizations, with a total membership of 70,000. It would be difficult to overstate the tremendous importance of such a union of volunteers and non-volunteers of both Christian and non-Christian lands for the world-wide extension of the kingdom of Jesus Christ.

IV. AN EIGHT YEAR CONTRAST—1894-1902

Thus far attention has been called to the developments of the last four years. It will be suggestive to contrast the Volunteer Movement of today with what it was eight years ago, at the time of the Detroit Convention. In 1894 the Movement had touched by its traveling secretaries 256 institutions; since then the number visited by them has increased to 798. Then the Movement had three secretaries; now it has eight. That year it rallied to the Detroit Convention 1,325 delegates; in this convention we have fully twice that number. Then the Movement had issued eight pamphlets; now its list of publications includes thirteen pamphlets and eighteen textbooks. Then there were fewer than thirty mission study classes, with but 200 members; during the past year there have been over ten times as many classes with a total membership of nearly 5,000. Up to the time of the Detroit Convention nearly 700 volunteers had sailed; since then the number has nearly trebled. At that time there was in many places an unfortunate chasm existing between volunteers and non-volunteers; now these two classes are united in spirit and in effort, and the students who are not volunteers recognize increasingly that a burden of responsibility, equal to that borne by the volunteers, rest also upon them for the world's evangelization. Then there was no organized missionary effort carried on by students among the young people of the churches; now there are well organized student campaigns in connection with a dozen or more denominations and participated in by hundreds of students. In 1894 the Volunteer Movement was established only in North America and the British Isles, with beginnings also in Scandinavia and South Africa; now it is firmly planted in every Protestant country of the world, and the volunteer idea has been successfully transplanted to the student centers of non-Christian lands. Then there were Christian Student Movements in only three or four countries, and these were not related to each other; now there are eleven national or international Student Movements bound together in sympathy and effort by the World's Student Christian Federation.

V. SECRET OF THE FRUITFULNESS AND POWER OF THE MOVEMENT

What is the secret of the fruitfulness and power of the Volunteer Movement? The composition of the Movement suggests in part the explanation. It is made up of those who are young, active, and vigorous, whose minds are educated and disciplined, and whose lives have been consecrated to the service of God and man. The *esprit de corps* resulting from a world-wide union of students of like ambitions and purposes is also an element of strength. Moreover, the Movement has focussed all its energies on a distinctive work. Time after time efforts have been made to deflect it from its course, but all such pressure has been steadfastly resisted. No feature of work has been added which had not a vital bearing on the realization of the main objects of its existence. Use has been made of the agencies of supervision which have been employed by the most successful organizations, both secular and religious. From the beginning the Movement has had the benefit of the counsel of board secretaries, missionaries, and other mission experts. It presents to the student world no narrow program, for it seeks to unite the students of all branches of the Church of Christ, of all nations and races, in the sublime effort to evangelize the whole world and to establish completely the Kingdom of Christ. The watchword is a tower of strength. It appeals to the heroic, the strenuous, the self-sacrificing, and strong young men respond to such an appeal. In the appeal for nothing less than the lives of men lies one of the deep secrets of the strength of the Volunteer Movement. The fact that its highest ambition is to serve and not to govern, indicates another source of power to which Christ called emphatic attention. By giving prayer a large place in its life, and by honoring the work of the Spirit of God, the Movement has related itself to the source of all power. In a word, the Movement has always sought to place itself in line with the great purposes of God, and in so far as it has done so, there have been manifested in its life and work His presence and blessing. What might not the Movement have accomplished had it recognized and heeded more fully these secrets of fruitfulness and power.

VI. The Program of the Movement

Only a beginning has been made in the work of the Volunteer Movement. We must not count ourselves as having attained. The next four years should witness marked advance in every department of the work. We would call attention to several of the points to be chiefly emphasized in the policy of the Movement between now and the next convention.

The number of students engaged in the study of missions should be greatly increased. While the progress in this department has been great, as we have already seen, yet when we compare the less than 5,000 members of mission study classes with the more than 40,000 active members of the Student Young Men's and Young Women's Christian Associations, or even with the 6,000 and more theological students of North America, we realize how much remains to be done. Every reason which has influenced those who have already entered these classes applies with like force to those who have not. It is of fundamental importance that at this stage of the missionary enterprise those who are going out from the colleges to guide the opinion and activity of the Church at home and abroad, whether as clergymen or laymen, should be intelligent concerning the progress, present position, and outlook of the Kingdom of Christ throughout the world. Progress in this department should embrace not only the enlistment of larger numbers in study classes, but also a higher grade of work by the members of classes, the cooperation of more professors and advanced students as teachers, and the preparation of more textbooks of high grade. And have we not a right to expect that, under the influence of the Volunteer Movement, an increasing number of students and professors will be led to become foreign mission specialists—thinkers, writers, and authorities on foreign missionary problems?

Far more students of real promise and ability should be enrolled as volunteers. The present number of volunteers is too small, even if all possessed the proper qualifications to warrant their being accepted by the boards. Many of the boards are asking for more men than are now available, and the probability is that this demand will continue to increase. The non-Christian world imperatively needs more men. They are needed to fill up gaps in the missionary ranks. They are needed to press into unevangelized regions. Let us not forget that we stand for a forward evangelistic movement. More volunteers are needed to keep up the missionary interest in the colleges. The vitality of the home Church depends on giving up more of her sons and daughters for the work of extending Christ's Kingdom in less favored lands. The Volunteer Movement will cease to be a movement if the day comes when students fail to offer themselves willingly for this great work. Let it not be forgotten that the supreme purpose of the Movement is to enlist soldiers. All other phases of its work are of secondary importance. God called it into being for this specific purpose. Unless it keeps the supply equal to the demand, it will in so far fail of its mission.

Notwithstanding the need, the Movement has found it very difficult during the past few years to secure a sufficient number of well-qualified volunteers. What are the reasons? During the years of financial depression the boards were unable to send out all the qualified volunteers who applied. For example, one board issued the statement that so far as their denomination was concerned, the fires of the Volunteer Movement would have to be banked. This resulted in a noticeable decrease in the number of men volunteering. The impression that there are more volunteers than the boards can send, has persisted so strongly that our secretaries have found it difficult, and in some instances impossible, to counteract it. The fact that the boards have become more rigid in their requirements has, in not a few cases, discouraged students from volunteering, through fear that they would not be accepted. The stay-at-home volunteers, especially those who have not been providentially detained, are a real stumbling block in the way of securing recruits. Another hindrance is the fact that so many relatives, friends, and even professors in theological seminaries and colleges not only do not encourage students to decide to become missionaries, but positively discourage such decisions. The lack of missionary interest and zeal in some churches is prejudicial to consecration to missionary service.

Thus far we have been dealing with reasons external to the Movement. There are two reasons within the Movement: With the growing complexity of missionary organization and work in the colleges, our traveling secretaries have had so many things to attend to that they have not been able to give so much time to pressing on students the claims of missions as a lifework as was given in the early days of the Movement. We have sought to help the situation somewhat by increasing the length of their visits. We appeal to the Young Men's and Young Women's Christian Association secretaries to relieve the volunteer secretaries as much as possible, and set them free to do the work for which they are specially qualified and primarily responsible. At the same time we would urge national, state, and provincial association secretaries themselves to help us in this recruiting work. One of the principal reasons why more students have not volunteered is that the volunteers themselves in too many cases have not been urging upon their fellow students the truths which govern their own life purposes. Nothing which the members and secretaries of the Executive Committee do can relieve the volunteers of their personal responsibility. It will be a serious day for the Volunteer Movement if it itself loses the missionary spirit and ceases to be a self-propagating force.

Fully recognizing all the difficulties in the way of enlisting students for missionary service, and observing more clearly than ever the need of reinforcements, let the delegates of this Convention see to it that these difficulties are overcome and that this need is met. What higher ambition could we have for our colleges than that of making them mighty centers for the propagation of the gospel? What a rich heritage to an institution is such a missionary record as that of Cambridge University or of Mount Holyoke College? And let the emphasis of this point of policy be not without its appeal to individual student delegations. The fact that certain volunteers have failed to carry out their purpose should not keep us from missing the plan of God for our lives. "One man's responsibility cannot be measured by another man's delinquency." The fear that he may not be sent should not keep any student from volunteering who possesses the right qualifications. There never was, so far as we know, a well-qualified volunteer who had exhausted all the means at his command who could not get out to the field. The need of men who are willing to sail soon is urgent. Fifteen mission boards have reported to us that they need nearly 200 volunteers to send out this year, and that a majority of these have not yet been forthcoming.

The Movement should promote the best possible preparation of volunteers for their lifework. Our responsibility is not discharged by simply recruiting volunteers. Until they pass under the immediate direction of the Boards we should seek in every way to help them in their preparation. There is need that the Movement take steps to increase the literature bearing on the preparation of missionary candidates. A complete or all-round equipment should be emphasized. As a student movement, limiting our membership to students, we stand for volunteers availing themselves of the best educational advantages which the colleges, theological seminaries, and Bible schools afford. Moreover, the Movement is in a position to supplement the work in connection with the regular curricula of the educational institutions. Through its four years' cycle of mission study, it enables volunteers to make a careful study of missions. Even more important than this is the practical preparation afforded through organic connection with the Student Young Men's and Young Women's Christian Associations. These enable volunteers to acquire the habits of systematic, progressive, devotional Bible study, of the observance of the morning watch, and of intercessory prayer. Nothing is more important or essential. If these habits are not formed before the volunteer leaves home, he will enter upon his lifework fearfully handicapped. He will find it far more difficult to form them in the mission field than at home, and without such habits he cannot accomplish a large and enduring work. He goes out to do a spiritual work. If he is to do a spiritual work, he himself must be spiritual. He should, therefore, come to know in personal experience at home what it is to be filled with the Holy Spirit. He goes out to make Christ known. To do this he must become more and more Christlike. To this end he should not think of sailing until he has come to know Christ as his own personal Saviour—until he has learned through Christ to get victory over his temptations. If he learns to live a victorious life here, he will be able on the mission field to stand against the strong and subtle temptations of spiritual indolence, failure to put first things first, professionalism, pessimism, discouragement, unbelief or little faith, and lowering of spiritual ideals. The volunteer should also be trained to become a missionary before he goes abroad; that is, he should learn here and now to win men to become disciples of Jesus Christ. This is the essential work of the missionary. If a student cannot use the truth of God successfully here to lead people to yield themselves to the claims of Christ, he cannot in Asia or Africa.

Every effort should be put forth to hold volunteers true to their life-purpose and to get them to press out to the mission field. This is one of the most serious problems of the Movement. While the proportion of sailed volunteers has increased in recent years, the fact remains that many volunteers are apparently not resolutely carrying forward their work of preparation and pressing to the front. What deflects these volunteers from carrying out their purpose? Some have applied to the boards and have not been accepted because they lacked the proper qualifications. If it is clear that in the judgment of the mission board they are disqualified from going out, such volunteers, while regarding themselves as providentially hindered, should all the more resolve to make their lives at home tell for world-wide missions. It is an interesting fact that so many volunteers hindered providentially from going to the foreign field have thrown themselves into home mission work in destitute fields, while still others have taken hold of city churches and made them a power for foreign missions. It is noticeable that only those who have been hindered by God have made their churches a great missionary force. Others have been hindered because of the lack of funds of the boards of their denominations. Without doubt the Movement is still suffering from the results of the widespread reports of recent years to the effect that certain boards were financially unable to send out new missionaries. It is not strange that volunteers, when discouraged by their own boards and given clearly to understand that they could not be sent out, entered other forms of work at home. And yet a volunteer before abandoning the hope of getting out to the field soon would do well to make earnest efforts to carry out his original purpose. It may be that he will be able to secure for his board his own support. This has been done by a large number of volunteers. If he fails in this for any reason he may find it possible to go out to the field under some other society.

Some volunteers in theological seminaries, because receiving no appointment from their boards by the time they were well along in their senior year, have naturally been induced to accept, temporarily, definite and pressing calls to service at home. These men are not to blame for wanting to get to work, but it is just in this way that scores of capable volunteers have been unconsciously drawn away from their missionary purposes. They soon pass the age limit, or from other causes become unavailable for foreign service. The machinery of the Movement and of most of the boards is not sufficiently effective to enable them to keep in close touch with such isolated volunteers.

A larger number of volunteers than is generally realized have been lost because of their inability to complete their education. They have been obliged to leave college through lack of funds, ill-health, or sickness or death in their own families, and in a majority of instances have not returned. Removed from the sources of missionary interest, and cut off entirely from touch with the Movement, it is not a matter to occasion surprise that they have practically abandoned their missionary plans.

Doubtless the chief cause accounting for the loss of volunteers is the failure on the part of many of them to put their missionary life-purpose first. If they do not make it the great controlling factor in all their plans, to which everything else must bend, they are in peril of being turned aside. We do not wonder that the purpose of some volunteers has been weakened. They seem to think that they have done all when they have signed the volunteer declaration. They have not kept the missionary fires burning by regular Bible study and mission study, by prayer for missions, and by earnest effort on behalf of the world's evangelization. They have not been trying to enroll other volunteers. They have not applied to their missionary society.

It certainly is not easy for a volunteer to hold himself true to his life-purpose. On the whole it is just as well that the pathway to the mission field is beset with so many difficulties. These difficulties help to purify the motives of volunteers. They tend to keep unworthy men out of the mission field. They discipline and strengthen faith. They lead men to look more beyond themselves to God. In overcoming difficulties men are made strong. In this way volunteers are prepared for meeting the greater obstacles and problems which await them in non-Christian lands. The missionary enterprise does not want men who can be deflected from their purpose. It calls for men of undiscourageable resolution. Our volunteers should be as ready and eager to sail after their preparation is finished as is the British soldier to hasten to the seat of war. "In the beginning of the Movement the Church needed men who were willing to go; now she needs men unwilling to stay."

The whole problem needs to be grappled with more thoroughly than ever. The boards and the Movement must come into a closer relation to each other. There is need of developing the clearing house machinery of the Movement, so that it can keep in more intelligent, constant, and vital touch with the volunteers on the one hand, and sustain on the other hand a more helpful relation to the boards.

The Christian students whom God calls to spend their lives in Christian lands should be led to feel their missionary responsibility, and to resolve to make their lives tell on the world's evangelization. It is an idle dream to think of giving all mankind an opportunity to know Christ in our generation unless all Christian students stand together and work to this end. Therefore, the fact that a large majority of the members of mission study classes, and also that a large majority of the delegates at this Convention, are not volunteers, is most encouraging. Let the Volunteer Movement and the Christian Associations carry on an unceasing missionary propaganda in all the colleges and theological seminaries, and let Christian professors in these institutions co-operate in this great campaign. If this plan be patiently and earnestly followed, it will not be a matter of many years before the missionary life in the educational centers will tremendously influence the missionary activity of the entire Church.

It is impossible to have missionary churches without missionary pastors. The key to the problem of the world's evangelization lies in kindling the hearts of divinity students with the missionary passion. Special attention must, therefore, be directed to keeping the missionary fires burning brightly in all the theological seminaries.

Both directly and indirectly the Volunteer Movement should seek to develop the spiritual life of the colleges and theological seminaries. This is essential to the best life of the Movement. Missionary consecration and missionary progress depend on spiritual life. The missionary revival in the English universities was made possible by the spiritual awakening in connection with Mr. Moody's visit. The Forward Movement of the Church Missionary Society, as Mr. Stock has pointed out, was closely connected with a deep revival in the Church.

The Volunteer Movement had its rise at the Mount Hermon Bible Conference, which was one of the most powerful spiritual conferences ever held in America. A careful study of the reports of our traveling secretaries makes plain that in the colleges where there is a low state of spirituality the missionary interest is feeble. Unless students are bringing to bear upon their lives day by day the Word of God, unless they are giving themselves to secret and united prayer, unless they are experiencing the saving power of Jesus Christ, and unless their hearts burn with the desire to please and to serve Him, the conditions are wanting for the development and manifestation of real missionary life. Where men are conscious of the presence of God they are most likely to hear and to heed His voice. A spiritual atmosphere is indeed essential to safe volunteering and to all self-denying effort on behalf of the extension of Christ's Kingdom. Therefore let the Movement, including all its members, place greater emphasis than ever before on the cultivation of a strong spiritual life at all our student centers.

The solidarity of the Student Volunteer Movement as a world-wide student missionary uprising should be accentuated. The advantages of a close union of all the volunteers of North America are admitted. The same may be said of each of the other countries having similar movements. But the desirability of cultivating closer relations between the various national organizations of volunteers has not been generally recognized or discussed. Through the World's Student

Christian Federation it is possible for these bodies of volunteers, who are animated by a common purpose and spirit to come to know each other better and to be mutually helpful. The cultivation of a more intimate fellowship on the part of the volunteers of all Protestant lands will not be without its influence on the large questions of comity and of occupying the unevangelized regions beyond.

The time has come when we should also endeavor to establish a closer union between the volunteers at home and those who have gone to the field. The 2,000 sailed volunteers are in a position to exert an immense influence on the missionary life of the home colleges by correspondence, by prayer, and, when at home on furlough, by conversation and public appeal. A Student Volunteer League has recently been formed in Japan by about 100 former American, Canadian, and Britist volunteers for the purpose of fostering the purposes and practices which made the Volunteer Movement powerful in their lives at home, and of communicating the volunteer idea more largely to Christian Japanese students. This is an interesting and hopeful development. If the plan were adopted in China, India, and other mission fields it would do much to preserve the unity of the Volunteer Movement and to increase its influence in the world.

A special responsibility rests upon the sailed volunteers from Christian lands for developing among the Christian students of mission lands Volunteer Movements which shall work hand in hand with the Movements in the West. The difficulties in the way of getting native students to volunteer in non-Christian lands are many and great. Among them are the secular openings for educated men, the low salaries paid to Christian workers, the opposition of relatives, the unfavorable light in which religious callings are regarded, and the relation in which the native workers stand to the missionaries. But the existence of these difficulties only emphasizes the need and value of the Volunteer Movement. If it be needed in Christian lands, how much more in the more difficult fields of the non-Christian world? Foreign missionaries alone cannot evangelize the world. They must have the help of a mighty host of native Christian workers. In fact the sons and daughters of the soil must do the larger part of the work. If thousands of new missionaries are required, tens of thousands of native workers are needed to join them in accomplishing the task of the evangelization of the world in our day. That the Volunteer Movement has a large mission to perform among the Christian students of the non-Christian nations is therefore most evident.

VII. WHAT THE MOVEMENT NEEDS

The continued counsel and prayerful co-operation of members and secretaries of mission boards and of missionaries is needed if the Movement is to render the largest possible service to the mission field.

Nothing less than an army of thoroughly capable, Spirit-filled volunteers must be forthcoming if the Church is to be in a position to do the fair thing by the present generation of the unevangelized world. The truth should not be disguised that a vast number of men and women are needed. And it should be reiterated that even more important than the matter of numbers is that of qualifications. The volunteers needed are those who have large capacity and who are thoroughly furnished.

The field of the Movement stands in need of more thorough cultivation and supervision. To this end the staff of secretaries should be enlarged. To ask the present force of workers to cultivate adequately for missions the continental student field of North America is to call upon them to do an impossible thing.

The budget of the Movement should be increased from $16,000 a year to $20,000 in order that we may carry out the enlarged program which has been placed by God before us.

The leaders and members of the Movement need vision, enthusiasm, resolution and faith, that we may be true to the marvelous opportunity presented to our generation.

There is need of having more volunteers and other Christian students make the watchword—"The evangelization of the world in this generation"—the commanding or determining purpose of their lives. When it takes strong hold on their convictions and becomes a practical, regulative force in their lives day by day, the Church of God will be mightily stirred and witness the greatest triumphs in all her history.

Without question there is need that the Church of Christ rise up in her might and enter into the heritage which God has prepared for her as a result of the Student Volunteer Movement. This student missionary uprising presents to her an irresistible challenge and appeal to devise and to undertake great things for this generation. God grant that she may not fail to recognize the day of her visitation.

Deeper than all other needs, is that of prayer for the outpouring of the Holy Spirit upon the members of the Movement. This need is indescribably great. Christ, in commanding His disciples to pray the Lord of the harvest that He thrust forth laborers into His harvest, went to the center of the missionary problem. In a pre-eminent sense His command strikes at the heart of the problems of the Volunteer Movement, because the distinguishing work of the Movement is that of raising up laborers for the world-wide harvest field. If the Volunteer Movement is to continue to be a movement—that is, if the volunteers are to keep pressing out to distant fields—there must be on the part of Christians everywhere a larger obedience to the prayer command of our Lord

> *O Lord of the Harvest,*
> *Send forth laborers made sufficient by Thee*
> *Into Thy harvest.*

JOHN R. MOTT, *Chairman*
J. ROSS STEVENSON, *Vice-Chairman*
W. HARLEY SMITH
H. P. ANDERSEN
PAULINE ROOT
BERTHA CONDÉ

The Executive Committee

REPORT PRESENTED AT
THE FIFTH INTERNATIONAL CONVENTION
NASHVILLE, TENNESSEE, FEBRUARY 28 - MARCH 4, 1906

A REVIEW OF THE FIRST TWO DECADES

The year 1906 is a year of two anniversaries of unusual interest and significance to the student world. It is the twentieth anniversary of the inauguration of the Student Volunteer Movement for Foreign Missions at Mount Hermon, and also the centennial anniversary of the American foreign missionary enterprise which began with the memorable Haystack Prayer-meeting at Williams College in 1806. It is a suggestive coincidence that the earnest band of Christian students at Williams and the hundred student delegates who volunteered at Mount Hermon had before them the common ambition of creating and extending a student missionary movement. The conditions, however, for the development of an intercollegiate society were not favorable in the days of the Haystack Band. In those days the colleges were few and isolated. The means of communication were poor. The intercollegiate idea had not been worked out in any other department of college life. There were no strong religious societies of undergraduates to furnish the field and atmosphere for a comprehensive missionary movement.

The situation had entirely changed eighty years later when 251 delegates from eighty-nine colleges of all parts of the United States and Canada assembled at Mount Hermon on the banks of the Connecticut for the first international Christian student conference ever held. They came together as representatives of an intercollegiate

Christian society with branches in over 200 colleges. There was a corresponding movement among the college women of the country. There were two others among the theological students of the United States and Canada respectively. These societies, closely bound together by the intercollegiate tie, furnished the most favorable conditions for a successful missionary propaganda. Although at the beginning of this conference less than a score of the delegates were thinking of becoming missionaries, by its close, 100 had indicated their willingness and desire, God permitting, to become foreign missionaries. The story of the spread of this missionary uprising to all parts of the student field of North America is familiar and need not be repeated. It has seemed appropriate, in view of the anniversary character of our Convention this year, to depart from the custom of confining our report to the progress of the preceding quadrennium and instead to survey the achievements of the Volunteer Movement during the two decades of its history and make a forecast of the tasks confronting us in the new decade upon which we now enter.

It will be well to reiterate the fourfold purpose of the Volunteer Movement, namely, (1) to lead students to a thorough consideration of the claims upon them of foreign missions as a lifework; (2) to foster the purpose of all students who decide to become foreign missionaries by helping to guide and to stimulate them in mission study and in work for missions until they pass under the immediate direction of the mission boards; (3) to unite all volunteers in an organized, aggressive movement; (4) to create and maintain an intelligent, sympathetic, active interest in foreign missions among the students who are to remain on the home field in order that they may back up this great enterprise by their prayers, their gifts, and their efforts. Thus it will be seen that this Movement is not a missionary society or board in the sense of being an organization to send out to the foreign field its own missionaries. It is rather a recruiting society for the various missionary boards. Its highest ambition is to serve the Church.

The field for the cultivation of which the Movement holds itself responsible is the student field of the United States and Canada. This embraces all classes of institutions of higher learning, both denominational and undenominational. The Movement is under the direction of an executive committee composed of six representatives of the Student Young Men's and Young Women's Christian Associations, which, as is well-known, are the two comprehensive Christian organizations among students of North America. There is an advisory committee made up of secretaries and members of several of the principal mission boards of North America, and also a board of trustees.

I. Achievements

Before this Movement was a year old, President McCosh of Princeton said of it in writing to *The Philadelphian,* "The deepest feeling which I have is that of wonder as to what this work may grow to." The Church certainly had a right to expect that a movement with such a personnel, operating in such a field as that of the colleges and theological seminaries of North America, engaged in an undertaking so sublime and inspiring as the evangelization of the world, would accomplish large and beneficent results. That this has been the case will be apparent as we consider in outline a number of the outstanding facts of progress which have been achieved by this Movement during its short life of twenty years.

The Volunteer Movement has touched by its propaganda nearly if not quite 1,000 institutions of higher learning in North America. Upon 800 of these institutions it has brought to bear one or more of its agencies with such constancy and thoroughness as to make an effective missionary impression. These include nearly all of the American and Canadian colleges and theological seminaries of importance. In the case of a large majority of these institutions the work of the Movement has been the first real missionary cultivation which they have ever received. It is the testimony of professors and other observers that even in the rest of the institutions which had already been influenced in different ways by the missionary idea, the Volunteer Movement has very greatly developed missionary interest and activity.

There are few student communities in which the spirit of missions is not stronger and more fruitful because of the work of the Student Volunteer Movement. As a result of the visits of its secretaries, the training of leaders for student missionary activities at the various student conferences, the promotion of its mission study scheme, and the pressing upon educated young men and women of the claims of the world-wide extension of Christ's Kingdom at its great international conventions and on other occasions, the subject of missions has taken a stronger hold on the student class of North America than has any other theme or undertaking. The vital importance and moral grandeur of the missionary enterprise have been presented in such a way as to command the respect and allegiance of the educated classes. It may be said with truth that no class of people believe so strongly in missions as do the students. This is a fact of the largest possible significance because from their ranks come the leaders in the realm of thought and also of action.

As a result of disseminating missionary intelligence, of personal effort on the part of student volunteers and traveling secretaries, and of the promotion of the ministry of intercession, not to mention other causes, the Movement has increased greatly the number of missionary candidates. Thousands of students have become volunteers by signing the volunteer declaration, thus indicating their desire and purpose, God permitting, to become foreign missionaries. This campaign for missionary recruits has been waged with earnestness for five student generations. Profiting by mistakes made in the early years of its history, the Movement has become more and more conservative in this work of raising up missionary candidates. No one familiar with the methods now employed finds ground for unfavorable criticism.

Some mission board secretaries have recently raised the question whether the Movement has not swung in its policy to an extreme of caution and conservatism. Notwithstanding the ultra-conservative policy in recent years, the number of students intending to become missionaries is over five times as great in the colleges and fully twice as great in the theological seminaries as was the case when the Volunteer Movement was inaugurated. This is no small achievement, because it is not easy to influence young men and young women to become missionaries. The many misconceptions and prejudices concerning the missionary call, the opposition of relatives and friends, the prevailing spirit of mercantilism and materialism, and the tendency to inconclusive thinking among so many students, combine to render the work of securing missionary recruits one of extreme difficulty.

A larger number of new volunteers have been enlisted during the past four years than during any one of the three preceding quadrenniums.

The growing number of missionary candidates stands out in striking contrast with the decline in the number of candidates for the Christian ministry. Some people have thought that the increase in the number of student volunteers accounts for the decrease in the number of ministerial candidates. This is a superficial view for actual investigations show that in those colleges where the claims of foreign missions have been most successfully emphasized there has been the largest increase in the number of men deciding to enter the ministry. If the Volunteer Movement has been more successful in its effort to obtain recruits than has the propaganda for ministerial candidates, this result is due to the methods it has employed, the earnestness with which these methods have been promoted, and the motives to which appeal has been made.

Because the Volunteer Movement is a movement and because

it is a movement for foreign missions, the principal proof of its efficiency is to be found in the going forth of its members to the foreign
mission field. No matter what its other achievements may be, nothing
can take the place of this result. This is its distinctive mission. It is
gratifying therefore to note that the Movement has on its records
the names of 2,953 volunteers who, before January 1, 1906, had
sailed to the mission field. At the Toronto Convention the hope was
expressed that during the next quadrennium 1,000 volunteers might
go forth. It is a striking coincidence that the number who have sailed
during the past four years so far as we have information is an even
1,000. About one-third of the sailed volunteers are women. Not
fewer than fifty denominations are represented in the sailed list.

Including the regular denominational boards under which nearly
all the volunteers have gone out, and also certain undenominational
and special societies, the number of different agencies under which
volunteers are serving is very nearly 100. While the greatest proportion are engaged in evangelistic work, a large number have entered
medical and educational missions, and every other phase of missionary activity is represented in the forms of service in which the volunteers are occupied. The sailed volunteers are distributed as follows:

Among Indians and Eskimos of Alaska and British North America	39
Mexico	86
Central America	17
South America	167
West Indies	69
Latin and Greek Church Countries of Europe	18
Africa	313
Turkish Empire	121
Arabia	10
Persia	30
India, Burma, and Ceylon	624
Siam, Laos, and Straits Settlements	61
China	826
Korea	117
Japan	275
Philippine Islands	64
Oceania	43
Miscellaneous	73
Total	2,953

The question is sometimes raised: Would not many of these volunteers have gone abroad even had there been no Volunteer Movement? A question like this can never be completely answered. A

somewhat extensive investigation involving interviews with a large number of volunteers in different foreign fields by a member of the Executive Committee of the Movement, has furnished data for the conclusion that about 75 per cent of the sailed volunteers assign the work of the Movement as the determining cause in influencing them to go abroad in missionary service. Reasons could be given for increasing this proportion. It should be pointed out also that a considerable number who never signed the volunteer declaration have reached the foreign field as a direct result of the Movement. Volunteers whose missionary decision is traceable to other causes testify that the Movement did much to strengthen their purpose, to help them in preparation for their lifework, and to hasten their going abroad.

Further proof that this organization is well characterized as a movement is its increasing momentum. Two and one-half times as many volunteers have sailed during the last ten years as during the preceding ten years. Nothing illustrates the spirit of this Movement better than the way in which its leaders have pressed to the front. Of the sixty-nine members of the Executive Committee and secretaries of the Movement who have been volunteers, forty-eight have sailed, six have applied to the boards but have been detained by them for missionary purposes, five are under appointment to sail in the near future, two are securing final preparation, and eight have thus far been unable to go on account of poor health, none have renounced their purpose.

Secretaries of the mission boards testify that the Movement has been helpful in making possible the raising of the standards of qualifications of intending missionaries. During the past twelve years in particular it has emphasized that those who are to become missionaries should possess the highest qualifications. It invariably encourages students to take a regular and thorough college or university course and to press on to such graduate courses as may be required by the agencies under which they expect to go abroad. It urges upon students that whenever practicable they should supplement the regular courses by special studies in departments of learning which will better equip them for the difficult and responsible task of laying secure foundations in non-Christian fields.

The promotion of the progressive study of missions through its educational department has in itself been a most helpful influence in preparation for the missionary career. Leading board secretaries have repeatedly emphasized the indispensable value of the educational department of the Movement in affording facilities for securing such knowledge of missionary subjects. The volunteers as a rule have been encouraged to throw themselves into the active work of the Young Men's and Young Women's Christian Associations during their student days. This has helped to develop their executive, administrative, and inventive abilities. It has accustomed them to working with others. It has given them experience in personal evangelism, which is one of the principal methods they will employ all their lives on the foreign field. It would be impossible to overstate the importance of the service which the Movement has rendered in guiding and stimulating volunteers to form right devotional habits such as that of personal Bible study, secret prayer, the observance of the Morning Watch, and the practice of religious meditation, because those who are familiar with the conditions which obtain on the mission field know that when these habits are not formed during undergraduate days it is a most difficult and discouraging experience to try to form them after one enters upon missionary service. Above all the Movement insists that each volunteer should come to know in actual personal experience day by day Jesus Christ as the only sufficient Saviour, and the Spirit of God as the only adequate power in Christian service. It is evident, therefore, that the Movement in ways like these has accomplished much in promoting a higher quality of missionary effort as truly as it has increased the volume of missionary service.

From the beginning the Volunteer Movement has observed in its policy the principle of the cantilever bridge, that is, that the one way to make possible the thrusting forth and sustaining of the volunteers who constitute the foreign arm of the service is by enlisting the intelligent, sympathetic, and active support of the students who are to spend their lives in work on the home field and who in turn constitute the home arm of the service. The old antithesis between the claims of the home and foreign fields has, therefore, as a result of this policy been rapidly disappearing. Each volunteer who sails means more than one additional helper in this world-wide missionary campaign. He stands for a constituency of his fellow students who largely as a result of his going have acquired a special interest in the enterprise and have come to feel a sense of responsibility for its successful accomplishment.

Thousands of young men and young women in the colleges are year by year entering other callings with the missionary spirit. Great as has been the service rendered by the Movement in helping to make the coming ministry of the Church a missionary ministry, a service equally great and in some respects more needed has been that of influencing the men who are to become the statesmen, lawyers, doctors, editors, teachers, engineers, and educated commercial and industrial leaders to recognize and to accept their personal responsibility for the extension of Christ's Kingdom throughout the world. Moreover, in interesting in the missionary cause the educated young men who are later to represent us in the diplomatic, consular, civil, military, and naval service in distant parts of the world, the Movement has greatly strengthened the hands of foreign missions. It is a fact of unusual interest and significance that nineteen of the present secretaries of twelve foreign mission boards have come from the ranks of the Movement. Several of these men were called to this work after they had rendered service on the foreign mission field.

Before the Volunteer Movement was organized, comparatively little was being done to inform, still less to educate students on the subject of foreign missions. In a few institutions missionary meetings were held from time to time. Now and then a missionary on furlough would visit a college or seminary. But as soon as the Movement entered the field, it inaugurated an educational missionary campaign which has become increasingly extensive and efficient. Formerly, the subject of missions was not brought to the attention of one student in twenty. Now few if any Christian students pass through college without being brought face to face with the most important facts about the non-Christian world and the missionary responsibility of the Church. It is now the general rule for each student Christian association to hold regular missionary meetings. A large staff of traveling secretaries of the Volunteer Movement make effective appeals in hundreds of colleges and seminaries each year. Scores of returned missionaries are invited to visit the different institutions. Missionary libraries have been established in most important student centers. Missionary lectureships have been inaugurated in several of the theological seminaries and in a few colleges. Most of these advances are traceable directly to the Volunteer Movement.

By far the greatest service, however, in promoting missionary education has been through the education department, which was organized twelve years ago. At that time an investigation revealed that in all the student field of North America there were less than a score of classes carrying on a progressive study of missions. Since then the Movement has organized mission study classes in 668 different institutions. During the past year there were 1,049 mission classes with an enrollment of 12,629 different students. As an indication that this work is growing rapidly it need only be pointed out that at Toronto four years ago it was reported that there were but 325 classes with an enrollment of less than 5,000. Fully three-fourths of the members of these classes are not volunteers. This in itself is a further indication of the great change which has come over the college world for, a generation ago, the special study of mission subjects was confined almost exclusively to those students who themselves expected to become foreign missionaries.

The object of the education department of the Movement is to stimulate systematic, thorough, and progressive lines of study by volunteer bands, mission study classes, and individual students. Much of the success of this department of the work is due to the fact that for several years there has been a secretary of education to devote himself exclusively to its interests. Mr. D. Willard Lyon occupied this responsible post for one year before going to China, and during the eleven subsequent years Mr. Harlan P. Beach has held the position. During this period the Movement has authorized the use of thirty-six different courses of mission study either written or adapted for use among students. Prior to this there were no mission textbooks available. Seventeen of these courses have been prepared entirely under the auspices of the Movement. Among the principal contributions to missionary learning have been such books as *The Geography and Atlas of Protestant Missions, Dawn on the Hills of T'ang,* and *India and Christian Opportunity,* by Beach; *Japan and Its Regeneration* by Cary; and *The Religions of Mission Fields as Viewed by Protestant Missionaries* by different authors. Several of the textbooks of the Movement have had a sale of 10,000 or more copies and three of them a sale of 20,000 or more. The promotion of mission study has greatly stimulated reading on missions. This in turn has led to the building up of large collections of missionary books in many of the colleges and seminaries. Without doubt, students as a class, in proportion to their numbers, constitute the largest purchasers and readers of missionary literature.

There are marked advantages in connection with this mission study work. It is developing an intelligent and strong missionary interest. It is doing much to make such interest permanent. It is an invaluable help in preparing missionary candidates for their lifework. It is making the conditions favorable for the multiplying of the number of capable volunteers. It is developing right habits of praying and giving for missions. It is promoting reality in Christian experience. It is equipping those who are to become leaders at home to be real citizens of a world-wide kingdom. When such writers as Benjamin Kidd, Captain Mahan, John W. Foster, and Professor Reinsch have emphasized so strongly, on the commercial and political sides alone, that the leaders of our own time must know the life of the peoples of the non-Christian world and prepare to enter into relations with them, it is most fortunate that the Volunteer Movement affords such favorable facilities for accomplishing this desired end.

Not a little has been done by the Movement to improve the provision in theological seminaries for missionary instruction. Two conferences of theological professors for the discussion of this most vital question were called by the Volunteer Movement. To these special conferences as well as to the discussions in the meetings of professors at the international conventions are traceable some of the most important advance steps yet taken in this direction. In considering the great progress which is now being made by the Young People's Missionary Movement and by denominational young people's societies, it should be noted that Mr. Beach has sustained an advisory relation to this part of their work, and their leaders bear testimony that he has rendered indispensable service. Similar testimony has also been given by workers in the women's boards in connection with which there has also been marked advance in the promotion of mission study. No better evidence could be given of the real worth of the splendid work accomplished by Mr. Beach as educational secretary than the fact that Yale University has appointed him to the new professorship of the Theory and Practice of Missions.

The Movement has sought to enlist the financial cooperation of students. When it began its work less than $10,000 a year was being contributed toward missionary objects by all the institutions of the United States and Canada. Last year 25,000 students and professors gave over $80,000, of which $60,000 was given to foreign missions. This is an increase of 50 per cent over what was reported at the Toronto Convention four years ago. If the members of the various churches gave on a corresponding scale the various mission boards would not be troubled by the financial problem, for that would mean to them an income of over $50,000,000 a year. Seventy institutions gave $300 or more each. Many colleges and theological seminaries are now supporting entirely or in large part their own representative on the foreign field. The growing missionary interest has culminated in the organization of large mission enterprises in some of the leading universities, such as Yale Mission, the Harvard missionary undertaking, the Princeton movement on behalf of the literati of China, and the plan of the University of Pennsylvania to build up a medical college in Canton. As a rule students give toward some regular missionary object and in all cases are giving toward enterprises which have the approval of the mission boards.

An increasing number of the largest givers to foreign missions in our various churches trace their missionary interest to the influence exerted upon them by the Volunteer Movement during undergraduate days. There are a great many recent graduates who as a result of this influence are now supporting missionaries as their own substitutes. The Movement in promoting the support of a missionary by a college or seminary has familiarized the churches with the idea of the support of an individual missionary by an individual congregation. Hundreds of theological seminary graduates, with this object lesson fresh in mind, have gone out into the churches to lead them to adopt a similar plan. The existence of the Volunteer Movement with its large and increasing number of intending missionaries constitutes possibly the strongest basis of appeal to the churches to increase their gifts to missions. The experience of the field workers of the different boards clearly establishes this point. It is also being used by the Young People's Missionary Movement as an unanswerable argument in its work among the multitude of young people in the churches.

Important as has been the work of the Volunteer Movement as an agency to promote the evangelization of foreign mission lands, many consider that it has exerted an equally indispensable influence on the development of the best Christian life at home. Its direct and indirect influence on the religious life of the student communities has been very great indeed. Who can measure its effect on the faith of the students of this generation? It has greatly strengthened their belief in the fundamentals of Christianity. It has enlarged the content of their faith by its contribution in the sphere of apologetics. By bringing before them the difficulties involved in the evangelization of the world, it has exercised and developed their faith. By bringing to their attention the triumphs of Christianity in the most difficult fields it has strengthened faith. By exhibiting to them the present day power of Christ among the nations it has tended to steady faith at a period when in the case of so many students the foundations of belief are shaken. The marvelous spiritual power of the Movement itself and the intimate association it affords our students with the students of other lands have greatly enlarged the reach of their faith.

The influence of the Movement on the religious life of students is observable also in the realm of character as well as of faith. Culture or education for culture's sake is not sufficient. Education for the development of character and the increase of power to use in the service of others is the true conception which is promoted by the work of the Movement. The missionary spirit is the spirit of Christ Himself. Wherever the Volunteer Movement works, therefore, it exerts a humanizing and broadening influence. It promotes the spirit of brotherhood and unselfishness. It develops the spirit of love and compassion for men as a result of inculcating the spirit of obedience to Christ. The Movement leads men to be honest in dealing with evidence. It promotes decision of character. It requires a life of reality. It develops the heroic and self-sacrificing spirit so much needed in our time. Phillips Brooks was right in insisting that missions are necessary for the enrichment and fulfillment of the Christian life. It would be difficult to overstate the value of the service rendered by the Volunteer Movement in helping to counteract certain perils of student life such as selfishness, intellectual pride, tendency to growing luxury and ease, materialism, and skepticism. In summoning men to a life of unselfish, Christlike service it is promoting the highest possible ideal.

It has tremendously stimulated Christian activity in all institutions. Not least among the causes of the increasing movement of evangelism in the colleges has been the Volunteer Movement. A point often overlooked is the place this foreign movement has had in developing the home missionary spirit.

During all these years the secretaries of the Movement, as they have gone in and out among the colleges and seminaries and conferences and conventions, have emphasized among the students the formation of right devotional habits. Who can calculate what they have accomplished in enlisting thousands of young men and women in the habit of unselfishness and definiteness in prayer, in introducing them to the best devotional literature, in inducting them into the habit of daily, devotional Bible study, in leading them to observe the Morning Watch? Secretaries of the Young Men's and Young Women's Christian Associations testify that the volunteers in many places have created an atmosphere in which men have been enabled better to discern the will of God and in which they have been energized to be obedient to their heavenly vision. The dominant note in all the work of the Movement has been the recognition of the Lordship of Jesus Christ. This one idea of regarding one's life, not as one's own, but as belonging to Christ, has without doubt done more to revolutionize and transform the religious life of the colleges and theological seminaries than any other idea which has been emphasized during the past twenty years.

The Volunteer Movement early recognized that the young people of the churches furnish an ideal field for a successful propaganda in the interest of enlisting workers and supporters. Within a year after the Volunteer Movement was inaugurated the volunteers began to work among the young people in the churches. As far back as 1890, the secretaries of one of the leading mission boards sent a letter to the Executive Committee expressing appreciation of the work done by the volunteers to kindle missionary spirit in the young people's societies and churches. At the first Convention of the Movement held in Cleveland in 1891, one of the seven points of policy announced by the Executive Committee was the following: "Recognizing the wonderful possibilities of the various young people's societies of the day, the Volunteer Movement shall seek to spread the missionary spirit among them. It is believed that these two movements are destined to sustain a very important relation to each other." From that year onward an increasing number of Volunteer Bands and of other earnest companies of Christian students have devoted themselves to developing missionary interest among various classes of young people.

The first organized effort on a denominational scale was that carried on under the leadership of Dr. F. C. Stephenson, a Canadian Methodist volunteer, among and through the students of his own denomination. The effort which he inaugurated in 1895 has continued to go from strength to strength and has been one of the most effective object-lessons for other denominations. About the same time Mr. F. S. Brockman, one of the leaders of the Movement, without knowledge of the good work being done on these lines in Canada, was so impressed with the possibilities of awakening missionary interest among young people that he decided to give special attention to developing these possibilities. He devoted much of his time and attention for two years as the representative of the Movement in inaugurating a similar campaign in the Methodist Episcopal Church and in facilitating like efforts in several other denominations. After Mr. Brockman went to China, Mr. S. Earl Taylor represented the Movement in carrying forward the work to a higher stage of development. This kind of work for a time was characterized as the Student Missionary Campaign, by which was meant an organized effort by students, both volunteers and non-volunteers, to communicate to the churches through the young people their missionary knowledge, enthusiasm, and consecration, as well as to introduce among them their practical methods and agencies. Many denominational enterprises of this kind were thus promoted directly and indirectly by the Volunteer Movement. Some of the most successful were carried on by individual bands, such as the Yale band, and the bands of Denison University, Northwestern University, and Wooster College. In the first stages, the work of developing this kind of activity in the different denominations and among the various bands was financed largely by the Volunteer Movement. Two conferences of leaders of such activities in the different denominations were called and conducted by the Movement in 1899 and 1900.

All along, however, it has been the policy of the Executive Committee not to take on such work as a permanent feature of the Volunteer Movement, but to encourage its organization as an independent movement working on lines parallel to the Volunteer Movement, either in the different denominations, or as an interdenominational arrangement. The organization in July, 1902, of the Young People's Missionary Movement was regarded, therefore, as clearly providential. This comprehensive, interdenominational agency has the responsibility for the cultivation of the missionary spirit among all classes of young people apart from those in the student field. It is under the direction of a committee composed of representatives of the missionary societies. It holds summer conferences, conducts missionary institutes at metropolitan centers, promotes mission study, prepares suitable programs and literature for Sunday Schools and young people's organizations, issues and promotes the circulation of missionary textbooks and effective leaflets, and organizes and conducts missionary exhibits. Its leaders and those of the Volunteer Movement are in close consultation with each other and are seeking in all ways within their power to strengthen each other's hands. The fact that the leaders of the Young People's Missionary Movement and of the different denominational missionary activities among the young have come so largely from the ranks of the student movement ensures the highest degree of unity and co-operation. The possibilities of the Young People's Missionary Movement are simply boundless. If its campaign can be adequately waged, within fifteen years the entire Church of North America will be flooded with the missionary spirit. This in turn will make possible the going forth of the large number of recruits to be raised up by the Volunteer Movement to meet the great need of our generation in the non-Christian world.

Apart from furnishing recruits for the foreign field and intelligent leaders of the missionary forces of the Church at home, apart likewise from stimulating the missionary spirit among the hosts of young people, the Volunteer Movement has exerted a great influence upon the Church as a whole. The very fact of the existence of such a Movement, uniting the coming leaders of the aggressive forces of Christianity, has appealed to the imagination of the Church. The cosmopolitan sweep and growing momentum and spiritual power of the enterprise have given an impression of its providential character. Christians have been encouraged by the sight of such a comprehensive and aggressive league to believe in the possibility of making the knowledge of Christ accessible to all mankind in our generation. The Movement has presented an irresistible challenge to the churches. Dr. Charles Cuthbert Hall, in writing to the *Bombay Guardian* regarding the Church at home, said: "There is an advance toward the world-view in certain sections of the Church. I attribute the advance, very largely, to the indirect influence of the Student Volunteer Movement. Our universities and colleges are getting the world-view. They are becoming impregnated with the spirit of missions. A reflex influence, radiating from university life, is smiting with new earnestness the occupants of many a pulpit and many a pew."

Although this Movement has spanned but two decades, it has exerted a large influence in promoting Christian unity and co-operation among various bodies of Christians. Uniting as it does so many of the future leaders of the Church who have spent from four to seven years or more in the most intimate spiritual fellowship and united Christian service in student life, it is not strange that this should be true. These workers going forth to the foreign field after being so closely united during the years of preparation do not lose touch with one another. The bonds of mutual esteem and affection still unite them. Animated in their most plastic years by a common life purpose and spirit, familiar with each other's points of view, and accustomed to grapple together with difficult tasks, they would find it hard, if not impossible, not to stand together in the great conflict at the front. Face to face with the powerfully entrenched forces of the non-Christian religions, they recognize even more clearly than they could have done in the homelands that nothing short of unity of spirit and effort can hope to prevail. Therefore, we observe in several of the principal mission fields of the world the attractive and inspiring spectacle of concerted effort on the part of the volunteers who have gone out to represent the different Churches of the United States, Canada, Great Britain, the Continent of Europe, and Australasia.

Already in Japan and China these volunteers from the countries of Christendom have organized national Unions to promote Christian fellowship, united prayer, associated study of problems, and practical comity and co-operation. Although the volunteers are still in the minority in the different mission fields, they are wielding an influence out of all proportion to their numbers. What they have accomplished to deepen the spiritual life of workers, both native and foreign, through interdenominational conferences has in itself been a service of such importance as to call forth most hearty expressions of appreciation from many of the oldest missionaries. Under the influence of these united volunteers, in common with other causes at work, the idea of Christian unity has been much more fully realized on the mission field than at home. Even greater progress would have been made abroad had it not been for the denominational ambitions and lack of vision of some of the home Churches. As was clearly brought out in the recent Interchurch Conference on Federation, the mission fields have much to teach the home Churches in the practice of Christian unity and co-operation.

The good that has been accomplished is a ground for great gratitude and confirms the prophetic words of Dr. Temple, the late Arch-bishop of Canterbury, who said, "The recognition of the common task imposed upon every variety of Christian belief will be likely indeed to do more to bring us all into one than any other endeavor that we may make."

In some ways, the largest multiplication of the influence of the Volunteer Movement has been its extension to the students of other lands. It first spread as an organized enterprise to the universities and colleges of the British Isles under the leadership of Mr. Robert P. Wilder, one of the founders of the Movement. It was next trans-planted to South Africa by one of the American women volunteers, although it did not assume large proportions in that part of the world until the memorable visit of Mr. Donald Fraser and Mr. Luther D. Wishard in 1896. The leaders of the British movement, particularly Mr. Fraser, transplanted the volunteer idea to the universities of France, Switzerland, Germany, Holland, and Scandinavia. The inter-national volunteer conventions held in Great Britain have exerted an immense influence upon the further development of missionary life and activity on the Continent.

While none of the Volunteer Unions on the Continent are very large, they represent a great advance, especially when the baffling dif-ficulties of that part of the student field are borne in mind. The chair-man of the Executive Committee of the American Movement organ-ized the Volunteer Movement among the universities of Australia and New Zealand in 1896. Thus there are now Volunteer Movements organized among the students in all parts of Christendom. Of all the Volunteer Unions in other lands, without doubt not only the largest, but also the strongest, is that of the British Isles. The results accom-plished by this Union are, in proportion to the number of its members, as large as those achieved by our own Movement, if not larger. One of the most significant steps in the enterprise of world evangelism was the transplanting of the volunteer idea to the schools and colleges of the Levant, India, Ceylon, China, and Japan, during the years 1895 to 1897. This also was accomplished by one of the workers of the Volunteer Movement. As a result of this action the Christian students of the Orient join hands with the Christian students of the Occident in the effort to establish the Kingdom of Christ in all the world. The student Christian movements in non-Christian lands in helping to raise up an army of native workers are striking at the heart of the problem of missions, because, if Christianity is to be rapidly and firmly estab-lished in these lands, there must be not only an adequate staff of for-eign missionaries but also strong, resourceful, self-propagating native churches.

It is a well-known fact that in all countries where the Volunteer Movement is established there is a larger and more comprehensive student movement corresponding to the Student Young Men's and Young Women's Christian Associations of North America. It embraces in each country not only volunteers, but also a much larger number of students who are not volunteers. It cultivates the whole range of Christian life and work among students. It is significant that the Student Volunteer Movement in several of these countries, especially in Great Britain, on the Continent, in South Africa, and, in a measure, in Asia, pioneered the way for the larger and more comprehensive enterprise. This John the Baptist service should not be overlooked in any estimate of the achievements of the Volunteer Movement.

In 1895 was formed the World's Student Christian Federation, which now embraces all Christian Student Movements and societies of the different nations and races. Under the influence of the Volunteer Movement one of its three principal purposes is the missionary purpose. The study of the formation and development of this world-wide Federation of students makes plain that the missionary idea has had a larger federative and unifying power than any other influence save the uplifted Christ. It is no mere coincidence that in the very generation which has seen the whole world made open and accessible and the nations and races drawn so closely together by the influence of commerce, there has been created this world-wide student brotherhood. God has been aligning the forces for a movement of such magnitude as the world has never known in all the centuries.

One of the mightiest factors in the influence exerted by the Volunteer Movement has been the proclamation of its watchword, "The Evangelization of the World in This Generation." This has been sounded out with convincing force by the workers of the Movement for twenty years in conferences and conventions, in institutes and summer schools, in books and pamphlets, in public addresses and private interviews. The exposition, defence, and advocacy of this great ideal have had a great effect in shaping the convictions and purposes of the students of our time and have begun to influence powerfully the missionary life and policy of the Church. When it was first proclaimed, nearly twenty years ago, it met with distrust, unsympathetic questionings, and much opposition. Year by year it has been received with increasing favor. Among its strongest advocates from the beginning have been the missionaries, board secretaries, and travelers who are among those best acquainted with the real difficulties involved in the world's evangelization.

Some of the greatest missionary conferences held on the foreign field during the past ten years have emphasized the central idea of the watchword. The appeal issued by the great ecumenical missionary conference in New York in 1900 said, "We who live now and have this message must carry it to those who live now and are without it. It is the duty of each generation of Christians to make Jesus Christ known to their fellow creatures." The most influential bodies of Christians in the British Isles such as the Lambeth Conference of Bishops of the Anglican Communion have endorsed this watchword. The deliverances of these influential conferences and conventions held in America, England, and Asia are traceable directly to the agitation carried on by the volunteers. One of the most conservative and effective denominations in America, the United Presbyterian Church, has virtually made the carrying out of the idea of this watchword a part of its missionary policy, so far as the parts of the non-Christian world to which it as a denomination is providentially related, are concerned. This step was taken by its General Assembly after prolonged discussion preceded by a thorough consideration on the part of its missions on the foreign field of the problems involved. It is believed that other denominations in this and other Christian lands are more and more coming to shape their policies in accordance with this great objective.

Among the principal benefits of such a watchword is the power that it exerts in the life of the individual student who adopts it as a personal watchword, thus letting it govern his life plans and determine the use he makes of his time, money, nervous energy, and opportunities. It widens and enriches his sympathy. It exercises and strengthens his faith. It throws him back on his supernatural resources. It lends intensity to life. It necessitates a life of reality. It promotes the spirit of self-denial and heroism. It imparts vision. Comparatively weak indeed would have been the spirit and faith of the Volunteer Movement without this ideal. Eliminate from the Volunteer Movement this element of urgency, which so markedly characterized the life of our Lord and the practice of the early Christians, and its achievements would have been insignificant in comparison with what has been accomplished. If tens of thousands of Christian students and hundreds of thousands of the other members of the churches could have given this watchword right of way in their lives as many of the members of this Movement have done, what marvels might not have been accomplished during the past twenty years in hastening the extension of the Kingdom of Christ in the world.

II. CONTRAST

In no way can we realize more fully the great change wrought in the missionary life of the student field of North America through the influence of the Volunteer Movement than by contrasting the situation as it was twenty years ago, before the Movement was inaugurated, with that of the present time. Then in hundreds of colleges and other institutions of higher learning including many of the leading universities of this continent, the claims of world-wide missions were never brought before the students; now there is scarcely an institution of prominence in either the United States or Canada in which the facts of missions in their relation to educated young men and women are not brought to the attention of the undergraduates of each student generation. Then interest in the world-wide program of Christ was confined almost exclusively to the theological seminaries and a few scores of denominational colleges and with the exception of a few medical student centers was a matter of concern chiefly to those expecting to enter the ministry; now the missionary spirit is as strong in state and undenominational institutions as in most of the Christian colleges, and students of all faculties or departments of learning alike are recognizing their common opportunity and responsibility for spreading the knowledge of Christ throughout the world. Then the attitude of students toward missions was as a rule apologetic or indifferent; now wherever the Volunteer Movement is well established it is one of growing interest and practical co-operation.

Then there were not more than a dozen collections of up-to-date missionary books accessible to students; now there are several hundreds of missionary libraries in the colleges and seminaries. Then there was no such thing as the scientific and progressive study of missions carried on in connection with the Christian societies of students; now, as we have seen, more than 12,000 students in over 1,000 groups with capable leaders are carrying forward such studies under the guidance of a highly developed education department at the New York office and have access to well-nigh two scores of systematic courses of printed studies prepared primarily for use among students. Then there was no literature devoted to the methods and means of developing missionary life and activity; now there are many booklets and pamphlets on such subjects written for use in student communities. Then, with the exception of a series of effective conferences confined strictly to theological students, there were no student missionary gatherings; now, year by year, at thirteen sectional student conferences the college men and women of different parts of North America gather for ten days to consider among other things the world-wide interests of Christ's Kingdom, and once each student generation assemble in a great international convention over 3,000 strong to view together the great battlefields of the Church and to take counsel as to the most suc-cessful prosecution of the world-wide war.

Then there was not one person devoting his entire time to planting and developing the missionary idea among students; now the Volunteer Movement has never fewer than ten secretaries in the field and at the headquarters, devoting themselves exclusively to serving the missionary interests of the colleges and seminaries. Then in only a handful of colleges were students helping missions financially; now in over 300 different institutions there are growing financial enterprises on behalf of the world's evangelization and many institutions are supporting their own missionaries. Thousands of young men and women are going out from the colleges each year on graduation to throw themselves into the great work of developing, under the leadership of the Young People's Missionary Movement, among the millions of members in the young people's societies and in the Sunday schools, an adequate financial constituency to sustain the growing army of student volunteers.

Then only the most pronouncedly Christian institutions were furnishing missionary candidates; now volunteers are forthcoming from nearly all institutions of higher learning and, as has been stated, in the student field as a whole, the proportion of missionary candidates is five times as great in the colleges and twice as great in the seminaries as it was twenty years ago. Then there was no missionary organization binding together missionary candidates; now we have the Student Volunteer Movement for Foreign Missions organically related to similar volunteer unions in other countries of Protestant Christendom and in the principal non-Christian nations, all bound together through the more comprehensive Christian student societies of the different lands by the World's Student Christian Federation, which embraces nearly 2,000 student religious organizations with a membership of 105,000 students and professors in forty countries. Then there was no great unifying objective; now the student world has as an inspiring ideal to call out its heroic devotion and self-sacrificing zeal, the noble and apostolic purpose, the evangelization of the world in this generation.

III. NEED FOR A GREAT ADVANCE

Great as have been the encouragements in the pathway of the work of the Volunteer Movement during the first two decades of its history, far greater things will be required of it in the new decade upon which we now enter. We are summoned to tasks of the greatest difficulty and of the most vital importance to the Kingdom. First of all we are called upon to raise up a much greater number of capable missionary recruits. Let us never forget that the continued strength of the Movement lies in its appeal for life.

The need of more volunteers is convincing. Several mission boards are calling for a larger number of candidates than are now available.

Interviews with the secretaries of the boards reveal the fact that their requirements are sure to increase rather than diminish. There must be a growing supply to meet this growing demand. Hundreds of mission stations are seriously undermanned. If this situation continues it means overwork, imperfect work, lost opportunities. Nearly every mission has large plans for extension. As a rule their demands are supported by the most telling evidence. There are still vast regions including hundreds of millions of people which require pioneer work. The need of men in these regions as well as in fields partially occupied is not only extensive but intensive and this intensive need is indescribably great. To those who have hearts of compassion and who actually know the facts from first-hand knowledge, this need constitutes the great pathetic fact of the world. The calls from large bodies of missionaries should in themselves command a large response on our part. Let us never forget the strong appeal issued by the Decennial Missionary Conference held at Madras in December 1902, in some ways the most weighty body of missionaries ever assembled, calling upon the Churches of Christendom to send out to India as soon as practicable 9,000 additional missionaries. Remember also the call from the responsible missionary leaders of China two years ago asking the Christians of the home lands to double the staff of missionaries in China by the time of the Morrison Centennial in 1907. We as students should be peculiarly responsive to the appeal for large reinforcements which reached us a little over a year ago signed by the names of 343 of the volunteers of North America, Europe, and Australasia now working in the Chinese Empire. The fact that the spiritual tide is rising in every great mission field and the enterprise of missions has begun to yield on such a large scale suggests a special reason why we should press our present unprecedented advantage. To a degree not heretofore experienced this is a time of great crisis in some of the principal fields. For example, when in all the history of Christianity has there been a more momentous crisis than the one now confronting the Church in the Far East in the light of the Russo-Japanese war? And let us bear in mind that a great offering of the best lives of our colleges and seminaries from year to year is absolutely indispensable to the best welfare of the United States and Canada. Without such real sacrifice we cannot hope to preserve spiritual life, a pure faith, and a conquering spirit. "The army that remains in its entrenchments is beaten."

Reasons like these for a great and growing army of volunteers impose a tremendous responsibility on the Volunteer Movement. In view of our providential mission, in view of God's dealings with us in the years that are gone, we cannot escape this responsibility if we would. And the task should not stagger the faith of any of us. This is apparent when we remember that it would take only one of every twenty Christian students who are to graduate from the institutions of higher learning of the United States and Canada during the next twenty years to furnish a sufficient number of new missionaries to make possible a large enough staff to accomplish the evangelization of the world in this generation, so far as this undertaking depends upon foreign missionaries.

We can readily obtain the numbers of workers required to meet all providential calls upon us if we will but multiply and faithfully employ the agencies which have already proved so effective. An expansion and deepening of our educational work, a wiser use of our large opportunities at the many student conferences, a considerable enlargement of our traveling secretarial staff, a general acceptance on the part of all volunteers of the solemn responsibility resting upon them for securing new recruits, the continued conservative yet confident aggressive use of the volunteer declaration, the deepening of the spiritual life of the colleges and seminaries by a great expansion of the Bible study activities, the calling forth of more intercession for laborers on the part of the Christian students in general and of the pastors of the churches, the encouragement in every way in our power of the Young People's Missionary Movement in its essential work of preparing the minds and hearts of the youth before they enter colleges for the days of missionary decision—the unwearied use of these and other means will, as surely as the operation of any other well-known laws, result in giving us all the missionary candidates needed.

In all this work of enlisting new recruits we should continue to stand for quality. The ultimate success of the missionary enterprise does not depend primarily on vast numbers of missionaries so much as upon thoroughly furnished missionaries. For the very reason that our watchword requires haste we, above all others, should insist on the most thorough preparation and training of workers, knowing full well that this will save time in the long run and enormously increase the fruitage. Let it be reiterated in this convention as it has been in all preceding conventions that our great need is not that of volunteers who will go when they are drafted, but of those who will press through the hindrances not of God to the work and place which He has appointed.

Next to the demand for more volunteers of capacity is the need of young men and young women who, being providentially detained, stay at home for the express purpose of developing on this continent the strongest possible base for the adequate maintenance of this gigantic world-wide campaign of evangelism. To stay for any lower reason will defeat the object of the Movement and prevent the largest expansion of the lives of those who thus hold aloof from carrying out the comprehensive and sublime purposes of Christ for His Kingdom in the hearts of men. All students should be ambitious to exercise the rights and responsibilities of world citizenship. There should be no exception among those who are to work in North America as to taking the watchword of this Movement as the governing principle of their lives.

We should all associate our efforts to increase from among those whom God does not call to be missionaries the number of young men of large ability and genuine consecration who will devote themselves to the Christian ministry. No class of people should be more concerned with multiplying the number of efficient ministers than the leaders and members of the Volunteer Movement; for without an adequate leadership of the 130,000 or more parishes of the various Protestant churches of the United States and Canada it is an idle dream to talk about evangelizing the world in this generation.

Those who are not providentially led into missionary service or into the ministry should devote themselves with as much earnestness and self-sacrifice and lifelong persistence to the promotion of the missionary campaign as do those who are separated by the Holy Spirit unto these two callings. We must have thousands of earnest young men and young women passing out of the colleges each year into positions of lay leadership in the forces of the Church. If in some way during the next two years 10,000 of the choicest Christian spirits of our colleges could be led to specialize on the promotion of missionary life and activity among young people, it would take far less than one generation to bring up the forces of the home Church to the point of maintaining as large a campaign as that required for the realization of the watchword. There is no unworked lead which will for a moment compare in financial and spiritual possibilities for world-wide missions with that of the 20,000,000 children and youth in the Sunday Schools and various Christian societies of young people in the United States and Canada. May God give the delegates of this Convention, and the tens of thousands of Christian students whom they can influence, vision to recognize and undiscourageable purpose and enthusiasm to exploit this marvelous lead.

There is need of laying hold with a far more masterly hand on the student field of North America and cultivating it with such thoroughness as to realize more fully its missionary possibilities. What has been said about the achievements of the Volunteer Movement and the Young Men's and Young Women's Christian Associations may seem to some like boasting, but these achievements when placed in contrast with what ought to have been done, what might have been done, what ought to be done, and what can be done, are meager and unsatisfactory indeed. No one recognizes the shortcomings and sins of omission and commission of these organizations more keenly than do their leaders. Well may they and their members humble themselves before God as they reflect on how poorly they have discharged their great trust. May such humiliation be so genuine as to make it possible for God to trust them with continued opportunity, that there may be more efficient and fruitful service rendered in the decade before us than in the two which have passed.

The students of a nation offer an unparalleled field for any noble propaganda. Their minds are impressionable, generous, and open. The special training which they are receiving prepares them for holding a vastly disproportionate share of the positions of leadership in the affairs of men. The student field of North America is ripe for far larger missionary harvests. What has been actually accomplished in certain denominational colleges, state institutions, and theological seminaries shows what might be done if the causes which account for the large fruitage in these institutions are but made operative in all the other institutions. There is no reason why institutions like Ohio Wesleyan, Northwestern, Oberlin, Mt. Holyoke, Cambridge University, Alexandria Seminary, Wycliffe College, should be exceptions in this matter of yielding large missionary results.

The difficulty reduces itself largely to one of close supervision and thorough and constant cultivation. To this end the staff of secretaries of the Volunteer Movement should be largely increased so that every institution may receive at least one unhurried visit each year from an expert on student missionary matters. The traveling secretaries of the Young Men's and Young Women's Christian Associations should give much larger attention to the missionary policy of the student Associations than at present. The splendid results of such close attention on their part to the Bible study department during the past two years illustrate what might be done for missions with the benefit of such co-operation. Hundreds of sympathetic professors should be led to assume as one of their outside specialties the developing of the missionary spirit through the promotion of the scientific and progressive study of missions. The mission boards should release for the service of the Volunteer Movement propaganda such of their returned missionaries as may be desired to ensure the adequate cultivation of the entire field. Every volunteer should become a propagating center for multiplying the number of missionaries and the number of missionary leaders for the home Church.

The persistent use of such means as these would result in vastly greater missionary achievements throughout the North American student field. It would make possible the doubling of the number in mission study classes before the next convention, the large multiplication of the number of institutions supporting their own missionaries, the steady increase in the number of missionary volunteers and of candidates for the Christian ministry, and the sending out into the ranks of the millions of young people thousands of new leaders to kindle their missionary zeal and devotion. Not many years would pass before there would be in every student community at least one band of earnest students whose hearts God had purified and touched with His hand of power, that would constitute a veritable spiritual dynamo from which would course forth missionary light, heat, and energy.

The time has come for our Movement and for the entire missionary enterprise to undertake things on a vastly larger scale. The conditions on the mission field favor as never before a great onward movement. The world is open and accessible as to no preceding generation. Its needs are more articulate and intelligible than ever. The forces of Christianity, both native and foreign, are widely distributed and occupy commanding positions. The forces which oppose the missionary movement have been markedly weakened. Momentous changes are in progress. On all the great battlefields the conflict has reached the climax and if the present attack be adequately sustained, triumph is assured.

The conditions on the home field are likewise favorable for taking advantage of this unparalleled situation abroad. Our missionary organizations have acquired a large fund of experience and have perfected their methods to such an extent that they are prepared for the prosecution of the campaign of evangelism on a scale and with a promise, a parallel to which the Church has never known. The material resources of the home Church are so stupendous as to constitute her principal peril. The various bodies of Christians have recently in the Interchurch Federation movement been drawn more closely together than ever for purposes of practical co-operation.

In the student field also the outlook is most encouraging. The Christian Student Movement has a secure foothold in nearly every student community of North America. In the ranks of the various Christian societies of students are to be found large numbers of the young men and young women of large capacity, high attainment, and choicest spirit. The Student Movement has wrought out plans and methods in years of experience which prepare it for cultivating its field more effectively than in any preceding time. It has a realizing sense of its perils and is availing itself of the best counsel as to how to avoid them. It commands the sympathy and co-operation of every missionary agency and of the leaders of the Church. It is animated by the spirit of enterprise, faith, and victory. In view of considerations like these our Movement must press forward to greater tasks or decline, suffer atrophy, and give way to some new movement.

What are some of the greater things to which we as a Movement should give ourselves? The leaders of the volunteers in different lands together with the leaders of the missionary forces should make a fresh study of the entire world field and arrive at some plan by which it will be thoroughly mapped out and adequately occupied. It is possible to accomplish this now as at no preceding time. It is absurd to assume that the Christian Church does not possess the requisite ability and consecration to accomplish an undertaking which is so obviously in accordance with the desires and purposes of Jesus Christ. We should not permit ourselves to entertain further doubt on this subject, until the best constructive statesmanship has been exercised upon it, and until we have given ourselves far more to prayer than we have hitherto done that this great end may be realized.

We should lay siege to the Port Arthurs of the non-Christian world with the undiscourageable purpose to capture them. We should not shrink or falter before such apparently impregnable fortresses as the Mohammedan world, the literati class of China, the principal citadels of Hinduism, the great strategic capital cities of Latin America. Moreover, we should not be staggered by the comparative indifference, inertia, and unreality of vast bodies of Christians on the home field or by the general materialism and worldliness of our time. This should rather lend added intensity to our attack.

Let it be reiterated, also, that another great undertaking to which we should set our hands is that of raising up by the use of all good human devices, and above all by the superhuman assistance of the Spirit of the living God, nothing less than a great army of volunteers of such furnishing that they will meet the requirements of the situation and of such purpose of heart that they will reach the fields. Of like magnitude and importance is the work of greatly enlarging the financial plans and achievements of the missionary movement. There are literally thousands of individuals and families, not to mention churches, which should each be supporting one or more missionaries and in many instances whole mission stations. The rising generation of young people must be made a generously giving generation. The missionary enterprise must be so presented as to command some benefactions as princely as those made in recent years in the interest of the higher educational institutions of America and Britain.

The watchword of the Movement, "The Evangelization of the World in This Generation," must be taken up in dead earnest by different bodies of Christians as the cardinal point in their policy. Especially must it lay hold of individual Christian students, both volunteers and non-volunteers, with such conviction that it will become in very deed a governing principle in their lives and relationships. This work of making Christ known to all men is urgent beyond all power of expression. It is the unmistakable duty of Christians to evangelize the world in this generation. It is high time that the attempt be made in serious earnest. We appeal to the Church by all the compulsions of Calvary and Olivet to accept the challenge which the Volunteer Movement presents in the proclamation of this watchword.

IV. THE PRICE THAT MUST BE PAID

If these great things are to be achieved we must pay what it costs. What will be the price? Undoubtedly it involves giving ourselves to the study of missionary problems and strategy with all the thoroughness and tirelessness which have characterized the intellectual work of those men who have brought most benefit to mankind. It will cost genuine self-denial. In no sphere so much as that of extending the knowledge and sway of Christ is the truth of His own word illustrated, "Except a grain of wheat fall into the earth and die, it abideth by itself alone; but if it die, it beareth much fruit." In the pathway of giving up not only of our lives and possessions, but likewise and more especially of our selfish ambitions and preferences and plans shall we most surely reach the great goal that we have set before us. In all the hard persevering labor to which we must give ourselves not least must be the work of intercession. It is only when we come to look upon prayer as the most important method of work, as an absolutely triumphant method of work, that we shall discover the real secret of largest achievement.

That undertakings like those which we have set before us require that we give ourselves to them with undying enthusiasm must not be overlooked. Important as is the most comprehensive and exhaustive preparation for any great work, there comes the time when the work of preparation ceases to be a virtue and when those who have done their best to prepare must give themselves with daring abandon to putting their plans into execution. God grant that this Movement may never lose its first flush of optimism and aggressive enthusiasm. Let the Crusader spirit which characterized the early Christians when they flung themselves against the Roman world, more and more possess it.

Of transcendent importance is it that we exalt Jesus Christ increasingly in the life of this Movement. He must continue to be at once its attractive and impelling force. It is His program which we are to carry out. He is our divine triumphant Leader. By His Spirit we shall conquer. The one word which sums up our great need and ambition is that the individual members of this convention yield themselves absolutely to the will of God and the domination of Christ. "A body of free men, who love God with all their might, and yet know how to cling together could conquer this modern world of ours."

> John R. Mott, *Chairman*
> J. Ross Stevenson, *Vice-Chairman*
> Hans P. Andersen
> W. Harley Smith
> Bertha Condé
> Susie Tittle
> *The Executive Committee*

REPORT PRESENTED AT
THE SIXTH INTERNATIONAL CONVENTION
ROCHESTER, NEW YORK, DECEMBER 29, 1909 - JANUARY 2, 1910

The Student Volunteer Movement is primarily a movement, not an organization. True it unites by a common declaration of life purpose a growing company of American and Canadian students who have dedicated their lives to foreign missionary service, but this by no means represents all that the Movement is and does. As a vital force, as a new spirit, as a pervasive influence, its life and activities are far more widely manifested and felt. Regarded in this light and not as a formal and visible organization, it is the most comprehensive student movement of the United States and Canada, because its mission embraces both men and women students, and its field comprises institutions of higher learning throughout these two nations. Its following includes the students of all Christian communions.

The primary and paramount function of the Movement is that of recruiting. It seeks to enroll a sufficient number of well-qualified volunteers to meet the requirements of the mission boards of North America. Its well-understood purpose also involves the cultivation of the whole range of missionary interest and activity among all classes of students and the leading of the students who are not to become missionaries to recognize, accept, and prepare themselves to discharge their responsibility to maintain the missionary enterprise by their advocacy, by their gifts, and by their prayers. That it may better realize these two great purposes, the Movement seeks to carry forward its work on the one hand in close relationship to the mission boards and on the other hand in intimate touch and co-operation with the Student Young Men's and Young Women's Christian Association Movements and with other student religious societies.

I. ACHIEVEMENTS OF THE QUADRENNIUM

The quadrennium which has elapsed since the Nashville Convention has been characterized by closer unification of the interests of the Volunteers and non-volunteers, by marked expansion of the activities of the Movement, by greater intensification of its life, and by a notable increase of momentum in the going forth of its members to their life-work in all parts of the non-Christian world. Among the many developments and achievements, attention is called to a few of the most outstanding and significant.

The best evidence of the efficiency and power of the Student Volunteer Movement is the number of sailed volunteers. In fact, this is the great test by which the Movement should be judged. The enlisting of volunteers who will actually go to the front and serve there is its distinctive mission. This in itself is a sufficient reason for the existence of such a movement. Measured by this standard, the Movement has steadily gone from strength to strength. At the Toronto Convention in 1902 it was reported that 780 volunteers had sailed during the preceding four years. In the quadrennium following the Toronto Convention and ending with the Nashville Convention in 1906, 1,000 volunteers sailed. During the four years which have since elapsed, ending with the Rochester Convention, 1,275 volunteers have sailed, or 275 more than we were able to report for the quadrennium ending with the Nashville Convention. Thus this Movement is markedly increasing in volume.

It is interesting to note that volunteers constitute a steadily increasing proportion of the number of men and women sent out by the mission boards. This is particularly true of the men and of the unmarried women sent out.

The total number of volunteers who have sailed under the various mission boards since the beginning of the Movement in 1886 is 4,346. Some fifty different communions are represented in the list of sailed volunteers. They are distributed by countries as follows:

Japan	374
Korea	200
China	1,253
Siam, Laos, and Straits Settlements	79
India, Burma, and Ceylon	840
Persia	39
Turkish Empire	157
Arabia	21
Philippine Islands	127
Oceania	57
Africa	466

Mexico	133
Central America	28
West Indies	128
South America	266
Latin and Greek Church countries of Europe	21
Miscellaneous	157
Total	4,346

The question from time to time presents itself: Do the leaders of this Movement press to the front? In answer it is gratifying to state that of the volunteers who have been traveling secretaries sixty-four have sailed, four have been rejected by the boards because they lacked necessary qualifications, three are still in course of preparation, two are detained by the boards for special service, and five are at work on the present staff. All the members of the Executive Committee who have been volunteers have either become missionaries or have applied to the boards and been detained for missionary service in connection with the home base. No facts could better illustrate the aggressive spirit of the Movement.

Since the Nashville Convention, one of the principal developments which, more than anything else, explains the great increase in the number of sailed volunteers has been the creation of what is known as the Candidates Department. This department was established to serve as a clearing house between the volunteers on the one hand and the agencies and fields calling for men on the other hand. S. M. Zwemer consented to defer his return to the mission field for two or three years in order to help establish this department. He has been ably seconded by W. B. Smith. They have become experts on the subject of missionary demand and supply. With the co-operation of a strong Candidates Council, composed of secretaries of different mission boards, they have been enabled to obtain accurate information as to the present and prospective demand for various kinds of missionary workers in the different mission fields. With the help of the large staff of state, national, and international traveling secretaries of the Young Men's and Young Women's Christian Associations and of the traveling staff of the Volunteer Movement they have kept in touch with the sources of supply. All of these traveling workers have furnished, as it were, eyes and ears for the Candidates Department in their constant search for workers required by the boards. Many local secretaries, and also professors in theological, medical, and other institutions, have rendered valuable assistance in this important search.

Each year special posters or bulletins have been published and placed by the Department in hundreds of colleges and professional schools in the United States and Canada, thus bringing to the attention of thousands of students the urgent needs of the regular boards and of other agencies. An enormous correspondence has been conducted with volunteers and non-volunteers whose names have been suggested as possible candidates. Many articles have been written for religious periodicals, medical journals, and college papers, setting forth definite opportunities for service on the foreign field. Through these and various other means the Candidates Department has enabled the Movement in the past few years to render larger service to the mission fields than in any preceding period of its history. The great increase in the number of sailed volunteers during the past four years is all the more significant in view of the fact that these years included a period of serious financial depression, and of the further fact that the requirements as to qualifications of many of the mission boards have become more exacting. Moreover, the Movement has been steadily increasing the number of volunteers. In view of the very conservative methods which it employs in its recruiting work the fact that the number of missionary candidates has increased year by year is remarkable. This has afforded the mission boards a wider basis for selection, and this in turn has had an important bearing on the quality of approved candidates.

The past four years have been characterized by a growing sense of responsibility on the part of American and Canadian students who are to spend their lives in work on the home field, to sustain those of their fellow-students who are to devote their lives to work in the non-Christian world. The recognition of the fact that the work of Christ at home and abroad is one work was evident at Toronto and even more apparent at Nashville. This has become more and more pronounced, so that in most parts of the student field we find the satisfactory and hopeful spectacle of the students who are to go and the students who are to stay at home standing together unitedly in the common enterprise of world evangelization. The students who do not volunteer are coming more and more to see that the determining consideration in choosing and fulfilling their lifework should be its helpful bearing on the world plans of Christ. Many of the students who are becoming clergymen regard their parishes not alone or chiefly as a field to be cultivated, but primarily as a force to be wielded on behalf of the whole world. Students who are to become teachers, editors, lawyers, statesmen, jurists, commercial and industrial leaders, in short, who are to become leaders in all important realms of thought and action, are inspired with the ambition to bring all the resources and influence which they have or may command, to bear upon the problem of making the Church in the United States and Canada an adequate base for the proper maintenance of a world-wide war. This change in feeling, attitude, and purpose of such large numbers of educated men and women is without doubt one of the most hopeful signs of the time.

Another test of the rising tide of practical missionary interest among students is the increase in their missionary giving. At Nashville it was reported that the students of North America were contributing $80,000 a year to missionary objects. They are now giving $131,000 toward such objects, or an increase in four years of over sixty per cent. There are scores of colleges and schools each supporting entirely or in large part its own representative on the foreign field.

Some of the larger universities have launched special missionary enterprises of their own, for example, the new Yale at Changsha, China, supported by the Yale constituency; the Princeton Association enterprise in Peking, China; the medical missionary establishment in Canton, maintained by the University of Pennsylvania; and undertakings like that of Oberlin in the Province of Shansi in China. But by far the larger part of the missionary contributions goes to the mission boards of the Church. The students of Yale head the list with their contribution last year of fully $10,000 to missionary objects. Among institutions for women the Misses Masters' School made the largest contribution, having given last year $3,385. Possibly the most notable gift proportionately was that of $1,070 by forty students of the Episcopal Theological Seminary of Virginia at Alexandria. If we limit ourselves strictly to the students who contributed to missionary objects last year, we find that the average contribution was $2.51 per student. This does not take account of amounts which these students raised for missions from members of the faculty and friends, or of what they may have given through their home churches, but simply what they themselves gave through college channels.

The value of this important result of the work of the Movement lies not so much in the amount of money given as in the influence upon the thought and habits of the students. Tens of thousands of them are thus helped to acquire the habit of systematic and proportionate giving. Large numbers of them who are to become ministers and lay leaders will later influence the churches to which they belong to adopt a plan of supporting one or more missionaries as a result of observing the successful working of the plan of an Association or institution supporting its own representative on the foreign field. Many sons of the wealthy by this experience in their college days catch the idea and form the purpose of supporting missionaries, mission stations, colleges, and hospitals. Another great advantage of the plan is that young men and women during their student days become related to the Church agencies which carry on the missionary enterprise. As a result they will be more interested in these agencies and better prepared to co-operate with them. The Movement is thus helping to raise up and train efficient collectors, organizers, and administrators of the auxiliary missionary agencies of the Church. The further fact should not be lost sight of that through financial co-operation with missions many a student has been led to dedicate his life to missionary service.

The past four years have been a record-breaking period in the promotion of mission study among students. In the year preceding the Nashville Convention there were 1,049 mission study classes in institutions of higher learning in the United States and Canada. Last year there were 2,084. In the year before the Nashville Convention the total number engaged in mission study was 12,629. During the past year it was 25,208. It will be seen that the number has doubled in four years. The increase has been greater during the past four years than during the twelve years preceding the Nashville Convention. Moreover, as a result of the wise direction of the mission study work by J. Lovell Murray, the attitude of the leaders in Christian work in the different colleges and seminaries toward the subject of mission study has changed to such an extent that this work is now regarded by most of them to rank with Bible study as one of the two foremost and fundamental Christian activities among students. In a number of institutions the entire student body has been enrolled in voluntary mission study classes. Even where curriculum instruction on the subject of missions is provided, voluntary groups are often formed. For example, at one theological seminary where every student receives curriculum instruction in missions and where there is a missionary lecture foundation as well, thirteen voluntary mission study groups have been formed enrolling nearly all the students of the seminary.

The quality of mission study class leadership has also markedly improved. This is due partly to the fact that more of the ablest students and professors have been enlisted as teachers, but even more is it traceable to the better training of leaders. The leaders are now usually appointed for a longer period in advance than formerly and therefore have more time to prepare. A larger number of them now receive training at the summer conferences. The normal training class method is more widely employed. Much special literature for leaders has been published. The influence of Dr. T. H. P. Sailer has been most helpful in improving the leadership of the mission study class work. Nothing better illustrates the growing recognition of the vital importance of mission study than the remarkable increase in the number of delegates at student summer conferences who enter the mission study classes in connection with these gatherings. At the men's conferences last year it is reported that of 1,930 delegates nearly 1,900 were in such classes, and it is estimated that including both men's and women's conferences, nearly if not quite 90 per cent of the total number of delegates registered were enrolled in mission study classes. Reference should also be made to the increasing number of professors who have been related to this work. Last year over 300 college and seminary professors sustained a responsible relation to mission study work either as leaders of classes, teachers of normal groups, or advisors of committees.

Some of the best textbooks prepared by the Movement were issued during the past four years. Among those which should be particularly noticed are Zwemer's *Islam: a Challenge to Faith*, Barton's *The Unfinished Task*, Miss Fiske's *The Word and the World*, outline studies on *The Work of the Medical Missionary* by Edwards, and outline studies on *The Apologetic of Modern Missions* by Murray. One of the most useful publications has been the special edition of Brown's *The Foreign Missionary* which has been widely used as a textbook especially by volunteer bands. In addition to the books specially prepared for the Movement, we have used the textbooks prepared by other agencies including the British Student Volunteer Missionary Union, the Young People's Missionary Movement, and the United Study Committee. Besides the new textbooks and the revisions of old textbooks, the Movement has issued a number of new and effective pamphlets which have been largely used in promoting the mission study propaganda and in helping mission study class leaders.

The Mission Study Department of the Movement has been the principal factor in building up splendid missionary libraries in all parts of the student field of North America. It has also had much influence in the enlargement and improvement of curriculum instruction in missions. The indirect influence of this department in stimulating students to pray for missions, to give to missions, and to work for missions, has been great indeed. Even more vital has been its influence on the offering of many lives for foreign service. Testimonies to this effect are constantly coming to our attention. A recent letter from a southern college, where there were 200 students among whom were no volunteers, stated that as a result of a mission study class on *The Unfinished Task*, seven students, including the leader of the class, volunteered for foreign missions. It is generally recognized that the mission study work now conducted in the colleges and professional schools has had very much to do with preparing intending missionaries for their life service on the foreign field. True it is that it has served to steady and strengthen the missionary purpose of almost every volunteer. Moreover, the influence and importance of mission study in widening the horizon, enriching the lives, purifying the ambitions, and enlarging and shaping the life purposes of students cannot be easily overstated.

In some respects the indirect results of the work of the Student Volunteer Movement have been quite as remarkable as what it has accomplished directly in the way of carrying out its distinctive purposes. These indirect results have been accomplished without definite aim or plan. First among them should be mentioned the influence of the Movement on the religious life of the institutions of higher learning throughout the United States and Canada. The propaganda of this Movement has given to the Christian students of our day the world vision and made real to them the brotherhood of man. In appealing to students to meet the needs of the non-Christian world, it has sounded out the call to serve in such a compelling manner as to fire a multitude of college men and college women with the passion for helpfulness. In emphasizing Christ's desire to extend His Kingdom over the entire world, it has at the same time helped students to acknowledge His sway and to give Him His rightful place as Lord over their own lives. In summoning students to world conquest, it has appealed to the heroic and self-sacrificing in men, and has enlisted the students of our day as of no previous generation to lives of unselfish devotion and self-discipline. As a result of its activities, more students today have forgotten or lost themselves in the great cause of Christ than at any time in the history of colleges. Thus this Movement has dealt a powerful blow to some of the gravest perils of modern student life in North America—the perils of selfishness, of narrowness, of materialism and worldly ideals, of extravagance and luxury, of softness and love of ease.

By bringing vividly and thoroughly before students the marvelous individual and social transformations wrought by the Living Christ in the midst of the most discouraging and difficult conditions of the non-Christian world, the Movement has furnished to inquiring and thoughtful students present-day, satisfying evidences of the vitality and conquering power of the Christian faith. As an apologetic factor and force its influence has become enormous. The literature and conferences of the Movement, as well as the practices and appeals of its members and secretaries, have done much to lead students into the formation of the most helpful devotional habits. One comes to realize best what a vast contribution this Movement is making to the ethical and spiritual life of our institutions by contrasting them with those student communities either on this continent or in other parts of the world which have not yet been exposed to the full stream of its life and power.

The work and influence of detained volunteers should be mentioned among the indirect results of the Movement. It is well known that quite a large number of the volunteers have been prevented from pressing to the front, because of the fact that they could not meet some of the requirements of the mission boards, or because of personal or family problems and difficulties. Some of these volunteers, by persistent and prayerful effort, might have overcome their obstacles and have gone out to the foreign field, but a careful study has convinced us that a large majority of those who have been detained in recent years have been hindered through providential causes. Those volunteers who know beyond question that in deferring temporarily or permanently entrance upon foreign missionary service they are following the clearly indicated will of God, constitute one of the most fruitful classes spiritually to be found on the home field. Many of them are actively engaged in the work of the Christian ministry, especially in frontier churches and in the needier metropolitan and suburban parishes. Others are engaged in educational work in connection with home mission institutions, especially in the most needy fields of the United States and Canada. A few are medical missionaries among the Indians. Some are secretaries of foreign mission boards and auxiliary agencies. Some are secretaries of Young Men's and Young Women's Christian Associations, and yet others are engaged in settlement work or other Christian social betterment activities. Detained volunteers are also found here and there among the laymen who are accomplishing large things for the Kingdom. Such providentially hindered volunteers, who devote themselves with enthusiasm to the work of developing a strong Christian base in North America for the world-wide operations of the Church, are as truly helping to realize the high aims of the Movement as are those whom God permits to carry out their purpose on the foreign field.

Time will doubtless show that the most significant missionary development on the home field during the last four years was the inauguration of the Laymen's Missionary Movement. Its founder has borne testimony that he received his vision of the necessity and practicability of such a Movement while attending the Nashville Convention. This led later to the calling of the notable interdenominational prayer-meeting of November 1906, held in the Fifth Avenue Presbyterian Church of New York City (in commemoration of the Centennial of the Williams College Haystack Prayer-meeting), at which the Laymen's Missionary Movement was formally organized. The progress of this Movement during the three years which have elapsed has been truly wonderful. In Canada it has become both a national and a world force, and is rapidly coming into like prominence in the United States. It has been transplanted to Great Britain and bids fair to develop in the near future into an effective agency there and in other parts of the world. It has adopted as its watchword that of the Student Volunteer Movement: "The Evangelization of the World in This Generation." This Movement, in relating the aggressive laymen to the missionary plans of the Church, is destined to affect profoundly the realization of the aims of the Volunteer Movement. In fact, the Laymen's Movement is the complement of the Student Volunteer Movement. While it will inevitably accomplish other large ends, its greatest service will be that of making possible the sending out of a sufficient number of volunteers to accomplish the world's evangelization in our day.

The Student Volunteer Movement of the United States and Canada, as well as the corresponding movements in Great Britain, on the Continent, in Australasia and in South Africa, has through the medium of the World's Student Christian Federation, indirectly extended its influence among universities and colleges in all parts of the world. In these days, as a result of the work of the Federation, all parts of the vast student world have been brought into intimate relation to each other and it is now possible as at no time in the past for the students of one country to influence those of other lands. That this influence is as a rule exercised unconsciously does not change the fact. If the Student Movement of any country, or even a band of students in any college, does a thoroughly creditable work, the example is sure to become widely contagious, even in parts of the world where least expected. It is not strange, therefore, to find many examples, both near and far, of the effect on the students of other nations of the missionary consecration and activity of faithful groups of students of different Canadian and American colleges. In this connection we would call appreciative attention to the fact that the past quadrennium has witnessed the most remarkable series of student missionary conferences ever held—those of Nashville, Liverpool, Halle, and Cape Town. Even more notable, from the point of view of unifying the Christian students of the world for the purposes of world-wide conquest, were the conferences of the World's Student Christian Federation held in Tokyo in 1907 and in Oxford in 1909. Recent years, therefore, as no preceding period, have seen a coming together of the students of the world and a recognition of their common responsibility for the world's evangelization.

Largely under the influence of sailed volunteers engaged in educa tional missionary work and in the work of the Young Men's and Young Women's Christian Associations on the foreign field, the student volunteer idea has been planted and developed among the Christian students in different parts of the Orient. A genuine missionary spirit has manifested itself among them in certain centers, and the day is not far distant when in each principal mission field there will be a Student Volunteer Movement. While there have been encouraging illustrations of missionary consecration among Indian and Japanese Christian students, the most remarkable examples in recent years have been afforded by students of China. Particularly notable are the volunteer bands in Peking University and in Shantung University. In the latter over 100 students and in the former over 200 have dedicated their lives to Christian work, notwithstanding the fact that in so-called secular pursuits they would receive far larger salaries. When all the difficulties are considered, these are the two most remarkable offerings of student lives to the cause of the world's evangelization which have been made in recent years by any universities in the world. They suggest the boundless possibilities of the native Christian student communities of the Orient when the volunteer idea lays hold of them powerfully under the influence of the Spirit of missions.

Some consider that the greatest by-product of the Student Movement is its far-reaching influence in the direction of Christian co-operation, federation, and union. The Student Volunteers of North America and Great Britain, who have been bound together so closely in this Movement during their college days, have, since reaching the mission fields, regarded it as both a duty and a privilege to continue to plan and work together. Now that the number of sailed volunteers from these countries is over 5,500, or about one-third of the total missionary body, it is but natural to find them exerting a large unifying influence. That that influence will soon become irresistible, as their number continues to increase, is perfectly evident, and when they succeed in realizing their present visions of co-operation and union, the result will be more than the equivalent of adding thousands of new missionaries.

II. POINTS FOR CHIEF EMPHASIS

As we, the members and friends of the Volunteer Movement, enter upon another period of achievement, on what points of policy should we place chief emphasis? The watchword—"The Evangelization of the World in This Generation"—must be given a larger place in the life of the Movement and of the Church. The watchword was adopted by the North American Movement, as well as by the movements in some of the other nations, after prolonged consideration and under the highest spiritual influences. It has come to mean more and more in the life of the Movement from year to year. It has grown steadily in favor both among the volunteers and other Christian students, and has been accepted increasingly by leaders of the Church and recently by large numbers of the best informed and most deeply interested laymen. It has appealed profoundly to thoughtful Christians of different nationalities and different communions. Christians everywhere are coming to recognize that there is a responsibility resting upon each generation of Christians to make the gospel fully known to the non-Christians of their own generation. They know of no reason which commends itself to their judgment and conscience why they should not make a resolute and sustained effort to make Christ known to every section of the human race now living; and the conviction ever deepens upon them that this great claim of the non-Christian world upon them can be fulfilled if the Church of today will but give itself to the task.

The history of the Movement shows that there are great advantages in having such a watchword as a commanding ideal. The fact that it is a startling word, calling for explanation, compels attention and stimulates inquiry and thought regarding Christ's great program for the world. To get Christians to reflect upon such matters as the vastness of the task and the urgency of the situation is most desirable. If earnest Christians will think this matter through, it is certain that the subject will lay powerful hold upon their convictions and profoundly influence their practices. Among the best propagators of the watchword have been its critics. The faithful criticisms of men like Professor Warneck have had great influence in leading people to investigate the meaning of the watchword and as a result many have been led to adopt it. It brings home to each Christian his responsibility in a way which causes him to recognize it and to accept it.

The watchword emphasizes the pressing and overwhelming urgency of the missionary situation and appeal. It reminds us constantly that our problem is a living one—one which living men have to face on behalf of men now living. It does not present an academic problem but one which is personal and pressing. It keeps us asking ourselves the question: Are we doing all that we can to reach our living brothers? It is a stirring reminder that our plan must embrace the whole world and that we must act without delay. None recognize so keenly the necessity and value of this aspect of the watchword as do many of the volunteers who are now at the front face to face with the crisis which confronts the Church on every hand. The watchword is a vast and bold challenge which appeals, therefore, with special force to strong natures. It lays hold of and calls out the strongest elements in men. It has discovered to the Church the attraction which hard things have for young men. The watchword is helping to raise up and develop missionary strategists and statesmen. Those who have thought deeply upon the requirements of such a watchword have come to see that the wisest strategy and the largest statesmanship are indispensable to its realization.

Contrary to the impression of some the watchword is promoting thoroughness. Its advocates clearly see that the task to be accomplished is so vast and so difficult that nothing short of the most thorough methods and processes will avail. They recognize that the principal human factor in the undertaking is the native Church and therefore they are emphasizing the development of the native arm of the service. None have made stronger deliverances against superficiality and in support of thorough work than old volunteers who have accepted the watchword. The official statements of the Volunteer Movement on this very subject, the mission study propaganda, the insistence by leaders of the Movement on the most thorough preparation of volunteers, the fact that such a large proportion of volunteers devote themselves to educational and training work, the constant emphasis at volunteer conventions on the formation of right intellectual and devotional habits, and the insistent appeal of leaders to the strongest students to devote themselves to missionary service—these are among the many evidences that the Volunteer Movement under the influence of its watchword is a great exponent of thoroughness.

Many are inspired by the thought that the realization of the watchword will give us a larger Christ and a larger gospel. They believe that each race of mankind has some fresh contribution of thought, character, and experience to make, and that only as they have had opportunity to learn of Christ and to receive Him can they make these contributions. How desirable it is that the Church should avail itself as soon as possible of all that nations as yet spiritually unborn are able to interpret of Christ's excellencies and to communicate of His power.

Increasing experience shows that the watchword exerts a profound spiritual influence. If it is to be realized there must be not so much a change in missionary methods and policy as a change in the lives of the Christians of our day. The emphasis, therefore, which the Movement places must not be so much on the number of workers, or on the increase in gifts, or on the power of human strategy, as on the sufficiency and availability of the Divine resources. To give chief prominence to the matter of numbers and quantity is to neglect the most important thing of all, the hiding of our power. Such a watchword inevitably drives its adherents to the Divine sources. It makes convincingly plain to them and to all who come under its influence, that we must have a great accession of superhuman power if the gospel is to be carried in purity to all men in our day.

If arguments like these influenced students and others years ago to adopt the watchword, with what cumulative force should they appeal to us today, in view of the special urgency of the situation throughout the non-Christian world and God's unmistakable summons to us to make a great and adequate advance. The time has come for us to urge upon Christians everywhere the acceptance of this watchword as a personal watchword.

The practical question with us as delegates and leaders is how to make the watchword a real power in our own lives, because if it dominates us it is sure to lay powerful hold upon others through us. We should continue to read and to reflect upon the various discussions of the watchword and of all that is involved in its realization. We should welcome criticism and promote discussion. We should constantly be expounding the watchword to others and urging them to accept it. We should plan and act as though we had, which as a matter of fact we do have, but one generation in which to accomplish all that we do in the way of making Christ known to the world. Far too many students and professors are planning and acting as though they had two or more generations in which to accomplish their lifework. Rather let each one so plan and so work that, if a sufficient number of students and professors would do likewise, Christ might readily be made known to all people in our day. This means that we must regulate our manner of life in such a way as the realization of such a watchword requires. This will affect profoundly our habits as to the use of time, energy, money, opportunity, and influence. It will determine all our important decisions. It will be an effective call to constant consecration, discipline, and sacrifice. Intercession will become a great reality with us, especially prayer for members of the Movement now at the front, prayer for the thrusting forth of those now ready to sail, prayer for those in preparation, prayer for the quickening and energizing of the workers on the home field. If the watchword is to continue to be a living power with us, we must renew from time to time the sense of the reality, urgency, and personal responsibility involved in it. There have been times in the life of each one who has taken this watchword when it deeply moved and influenced him. Our concern must be that of making this a more nearly constant experience. What idea can possess us which will be more potent, more purifying, and more inspiring? May God keep the Christian students of our day from drifting into lives of mediocrity or lives lacking the enthusiasm of this world-conquering idea.

By far the most important concern of the Volunteer Movement and of its friends is to augment greatly the number of well-equipped volunteers who can in the immediate or near future press out to the mission fields. The present demand for such workers is greater than at any time in the past and is sure to increase in the years just before us. Without doubt the student field of the United States and Canada at the beginning of the present decade is to be subjected to a heavier pressure to furnish missionaries and other helpers for the establishment of Christ's Kingdom abroad than it has thus far felt. This pressure is being brought to bear from two sides. In the first place, from the side of the non-Christian world itself. The present student generation is facing an absolutely unique world situation. There have been other times when in one or a few portions of the world the Church was confronted with a grave crisis, but never before has there been such a world-wide synchronizing of crises. Today throughout the entire Far East, in all the principal parts of the Near East, such as Turkey and Persia, in Southern Asia, in the East Indies, throughout the larger part of the African continent, and even in parts of Latin America, the Christian Church faces nothing less than an acute and momentous crisis. This crisis can be met only by the sending out of a far larger number than are now forthcoming of thoroughly capable and well-furnished missionaries.

On the home side we are subject to the growing pressure of the expanding ability of the Church to send forth an army of workers, primarily as a result of the uprising of Christian men in the Laymen's Missionary Movement, not to speak of the activities of the Forward Movements in some of the Christian communions and of the very effective work of the Young People's Missionary Movement in the Sunday Schools and among the large numbers of other young people. The burden of responsibility thus imposed upon our Movement and upon all the Christian forces at work in the North American student field is such as to justify in itself the holding of the Rochester Convention, and as to require a great enlargement in the plans of the Volunteer Movement, and also to call for the united and hearty co-operation of all who are in any way concerned with the full Christlike outreach of our universities, colleges, and seminaries. The Christian Church has the right to look to us with confidence at such a time. Though the Volunteer Movement and the related Association Movements will be tested as never before, we cannot but believe that they will not be found wanting in this hour of supreme and inspiring opportunity and solemn responsibility.

The urgency of the situation must not tempt us or in any way deflect us from the well established policy of the Movement to secure missionary candidates who are thoroughly well qualified. On the contrary the demand of the present time is for missionaries of the highest order of ability. In most countries the problems confronting the missionary are so difficult and so important as to demand missionaries of exceptional ability and preparation. Never was the need of constructive missionary statesmanship and of missionary strategy so imperative. The growing movements of co-operation, federation, and union on the foreign field will be carried to a successful issue only by men possessing the gifts of true leadership. The Volunteer Movement in its propaganda for recruits, while earnestly seeking to increase greatly the number of volunteers, must therefore concern itself even more with the questions pertaining to their qualifications and thorough preparation. As in the past, chief stress will be placed on securing men of well-established faith and of genuine Christian character.

To meet the great demands of the present unparalleled situation calls for enlargement in every direction. It is evident that the staff of traveling secretaries should be doubled. This is necessary if all the important educational institutions are to receive a visit each year. It is essential also if the Movement is to do a more intensive work in each institution, and without doubt this is needed. Only in this way can we hope to secure a sufficient number of volunteers to ensure the number required for sailing after the thorough sifting processes of the boards have been employed. The highly productive work of the Candidates Department must be further developed. It is the function of this department to help the boards find young men and young women who can sail in the near and not in the distant future. This is a most difficult work and requires the expenditure of far more time than is usually realized. The work of this department must be brought through frequent conferences and in other ways into even closer relation to that of the Candidates Departments of the different mission boards.

Splendid as has been the increase in the number of mission study classes, there must be a very great enlargement of the enrollment in mission study. This is entirely feasible. The reasons which have influenced 25,000 students now in mission study classes to devote themselves to such studies apply with equal force to fivefold this number of their fellow students. In no other way can we better help to supply the conditions which will enable students of our day to discover their life relation to the extension of Christ's Kingdom. Mission study does much to make possible safe and sound missionary decisions. The volunteer band organization and life need to be strengthened. A careful study has made plain that the institutions which have been furnishing continuously the largest number of satisfactory volunteers are those in which there have been progressive, vital, and active volunteer bands. The history of the Student Volunteer Union of Great Britain enforces the same lesson. Unfortunately we have allowed the mission study classes in some institutions to take the place of the old time volunteer bands. This they can never do. Both agencies are indispensable.

Possibly the best recruiting ground for missionaries is the sixteen or more student summer and winter conferences of the Young Men's and Young Women's Christian Associations and also the still more numerous district, metropolitan, and state missionary conferences. These conferences furnish an atmosphere favorable for the discovery of the will of God and also release influences in the lives of students which prompt them to Christlike obedience to the will of God. It may be questioned, however, whether we have begun to utilize the possibilities of these gatherings as places for the dedication of lives to the world-embracing plans of Christ. At the same time conservatism should be exercised that students may volunteer only after the most thorough and prayerful consideration and not as a result of the enthusiasm of the hour. The leaders of these conferences and of the different college delegations may well give more thought and prayer to this most highly-multiplying work, that of raising up leaders for the missionary forces.

Christian college and seminary presidents and professors and schoolmasters should also recognize and accept a larger measure of responsibility for recruiting laborers for the fully ripe harvest fields of the non-Christian world. They are in a position to do more to influence life decisions than any other class of workers. They have the largest influence with the students. Their counsel is regarded as impartial and unselfish. When we see what individual professors here and there are doing as a result of setting apart systematically each week a few hours for the definite purpose of receiving students to talk over with them their life purposes and plans, we cannot but wish that more of them would adjust their professional and administrative duties so as to admit of their devoting themselves more largely to this most productive and enduring work. We believe the day is near at hand when more of our leading educators will come to regard the missionary contribution of the colleges as their crowning glory.

The deepest lesson of all to be learned is the Christ-appointed lesson that the real secret underlying the adequate supply of truly qualified workers is the work of intercession. Anything which the delegates of the Rochester Convention and the other friends of this Movement can do to make prayer for laborers a vital practice in their own lives and to communicate the prayer passion to others will more directly and more potently than anything else result in the actual distribution throughout the fields of the non-Christian world of the workers of God's own appointment. Wherever else we may fail, therefore, let us not permit ourselves to fail at this point.

The time has come when the Volunteer Movement must widen its program so as to do more to improve the opportunities for advancing the interests of Christ's Kingdom which present themselves in the non-Christian world to those who are not missionaries. Such opportunities are multiplying on every hand. Some of them are quite as important as the opportunities presented by the regular missionary career. How important it is, for example, that the men who are to fill the positions in the diplomatic and consular service and in various departments of the civil service of our own and other Christian countries, shall be men of genuine Christian character and men who by word and work will not only safeguard the missionary interests committed to their charge, but will also throw the full weight of their influence on the side of Jesus Christ and His program. When we think of the great service recently rendered by such Christian civilians as Sir Andrew Fraser in India, Sir Mortimer Durand in Persia, Judge Wilfley in China, and Mr. R. S. Miller, Jr., in Japan, we recognize the possibilities before the young men who devote their lives with Christian purpose to the service of the Government in other lands.

The educated men who relate themselves to the Army and Navy are from time to time placed in positions where their influence on non-Christian peoples of other races will do much either to strengthen or weaken the influence of Christianity. The attitude and actions of Admiral Watson while in the Far East is a good example. In this day of commercial and industrial expansion, an increasing number of our most ambitious and enterprising young men will be scattered over different sections of the foreign mission field to help exploit the material resources or to extend the movements of commerce. In some instances such men, if they have the missionary purpose and spirit, can do as much as missionaries themselves to advance the interests of Christianity, especially among classes of men not reached by the ordinary missionary methods. A great many of our best engineering students and students connected with other departments of applied science will go forth to lands like China, Africa, and Turkey in the near future to aid industrial development. If all these should go with the determination to make their influence tell for Christ they would greatly advance the interests of Christian missions. An increasing number of college men and women, especially the sons of the wealthy and well-to-do classes, are making the tour around the world at the close of their college course. The visits of some of these students have been a benediction to the missionaries and native Christian workers and their living witness an evidence of Christianity to the non-Christians with whom they have mingled, while others have concealed their Christian profession and abandoned their Christian practices, thus weakening the hands of the missionary movement.

Unquestionably the greatest opportunity before the students of North America who do not contemplate becoming regular missionaries is that which presents itself in the realm of education. There is a large and growing demand for American and Canadian students, both men and women, to go out to different parts of the non-Christian world to teach in government schools and colleges and in other non-missionary institutions. Scores of our fellow-students are now holding such positions in the Philippines, in Japan, in China, and in Latin America. The demand for such workers will increase; hundreds will probably be required within the next few years. Such teachers outside of the classroom, in the several hours each day at their disposal, have a wonderful opportunity to expound and illustrate the teaching of Christianity among those over whom they have won such large influence in their regular work, and to help the missionaries in many other directions. The teacher in all of these countries wields an enormous influence over the youth.

One opportunity, which comes to most of us but which many have overlooked, is that presented by the large and increasing number of students among us from Oriental and other non-Christian lands. These students are to furnish a vastly disproportionate share of the future leaders of their respective nations. They come among us as strangers and are peculiarly susceptible to the offices of kindness. They are at the most plastic period in life. Who can estimate the great good which could be accomplished by our carrying on among them a campaign of real friendship, remembering that the highest office of friendship is to help our friends in the deepest things of life? These foreign students are in a position to do more than some missionaries to extend the domain of Christ among their countrymen.

If the great number of new volunteers, so imperatively demanded, are to be forthcoming; if the large and growing stream of Christian students going forth to the non-Christian world in the so-called secular enterprises are to improve the opportunities which await them; and if the type of Christianity which both these classes bear from us is to be really worth propagating, then the delegates of this convention and all those who have at heart the spiritual welfare of the universities, colleges, and schools of North America must give more thought and attention to making the conditions in them favorable for this great expansion of pure Christianity. In a word, if there are to be such great results witnessed abroad, there must be supplied a commensurate cause at home. The centers of learning of the United States and Canada must become more than at present abounding centers of Christianity in its purest and therefore most highly propagating form. This means that campaigns of evangelism must be waged with wisdom and power in all our principal student communities. We note with appreciation the extensive plans which have been made for presenting the Living Christ to college men at many universities during the coming term. The number of men adapted to lead in this life-giving work must be multiplied.

Special efforts must be put forth through apologetic lectures and apologetic writings by men of learning and devotion, who can gain and hold the confidence of students, to establish firmly in the essentials of the Christian faith those who are to propagate that faith abroad as well as those who are to maintain it at home. The present comparatively superficial knowledge which many Christian college students have of the foundation facts of the Christian faith does not qualify them for spreading triumphantly the Christian faith in the lands of the other religions. The Christian students must also acquire an experimental knowledge of the power of Jesus Christ to give them victory day by day over their temptations. It is such first-hand knowledge of the Living Christ which will give them a gospel to proclaim with unshakable conviction. They must be helped to develop a character of Christlike sympathy and love so that, as they go forth to non-Christian lands, they will be able to win the hearts of the people by kindness as well as to persuade their minds by truth, for this has always been the key with which to open the doors for the wide spread of the Christian faith. Every college should send forth men of saintliness and might. The present day calls for men of power, pre-eminently for men of spirituality. To propagate a superhuman gospel necessitates workers who are under the control of a Superhuman Power.

There is need also of sounding out in every college the stern call to self-denial. Men influenced by the growing tendency to ways of extravagance, pleasure-seeking indulgence, and slackness among the students of North America will not conquer the Hinduism, Mohammedanism, and materialism of Asia. Nothing short of entering into fellowship with Christ Himself in the life of daily self-denial will generate truly world-conquering power. Great also is the demand today on every mission field for men of heroic mould. We must look to our schools and colleges to supply them. If we can help the students there to face courageously the subtle perils and evils of modern college life and to win the victory over their own spirits, we may confidently expect to see these same men meet victoriously every foe which awaits them at the front. Our Christian student movements must also abound more fully with the spirit of unselfish service. Those who are to devote their lives as ministers or laymen to the service of their fellows must not only catch the spirit of such devotion during student days but must also preserve it by actually engaging in helpful effort among those within the range of their influence. There is something strangely inconsistent in studying and planning to make Christ known and obeyed in distant lands and not to be concerned about extending His sway among those within our college walls and among those before our college gates.

Above all, the college men and college women throughout our whole field must be led to surrender themselves wholly to Jesus Christ as Lord and to let Him determine their life decisions and dominate them in every relationship. The great question which must be pressed insistently upon them is not the question of whether or not they will become missionaries, not the relative claims of the home and foreign fields, but the one crucial, all-important question whether or not they will yield to Christ His rightful place as the Lord and Master of their lives. In proportion as the students of our day are influenced to answer affirmatively and whole-heartedly this question of questions will be the realization of the sublime purpose of the Volunteer Movement —to give to all men in our day an adequate opportunity to know and to receive the Living Christ.

> John R. Mott, *Chairman*
> J. Ross Stevenson, *Vice-Chairman*
> Hans P. Andersen
> Bertha Condé
> W. Harley Smith
>   *The Executive Committee*

REPORT PRESENTED AT
THE SEVENTH INTERNATIONAL CONVENTION
KANSAS CITY, MISSOURI, DECEMBER 31, 1913 - JANUARY 4, 1914

"It is a holy sight," said Disraeli, "to see a nation saved by its youth." Is it not a more inspiring sight to see the students of the North American continent dedicating themselves to the sublime undertaking of making Jesus Christ known, loved, and obeyed throughout the entire non-Christian world? The Student Volunteer Movement for Foreign Missions, called into being nearly a generation ago under the influence of the mighty working of the Spirit of God, has already profoundly impressed the religious life of the colleges of the United States and Canada, widely influenced the missionary life of the churches, and furnished to the mission boards the greatest offering of lives ever made in one generation by two Christian nations. The simple but highly significant purpose of this Movement is, in the first place, to furnish the mission boards of the United States and Canada with a supply of capable student volunteers sufficient to meet the demands made upon them in the effort to give all living men the opportunity to know the living Christ; and, secondly, to lead the students whom God does not call to become missionaries to make their lives count most as clergymen and laymen in developing in North America a strong home base for world-wide missions and in backing up that enterprise in all ways within their power.

While related organically to the Student Young Men's and Young Women's Christian Associations, the Volunteer Movement exists primarily to serve the foreign missionary societies of the North American churches. In carrying out its twofold object it has developed methods and agencies which have enabled it to render increasingly valuable service. Among these means one of the most potent is the Quadrennial Volunteer Convention. These conventions, which are the largest and most representative gatherings of Christian students held anywhere in the world, have literally marked epochs in the missionary life of the American and Canadian colleges. They afford the one opportunity we have to realize and to accentuate the spiritual solidarity of the complex and varied Christian forces of the wide student field of this continent. They make it possible also to review together the progress made during the preceding student generation of four years and to set before ourselves tasks to engage us in the years to come. As we now let pass before us the outstanding facts of progress during the last quadrennium, we shall recognize clearly that it has surpassed in fruitfulness any corresponding period in the life of the Movement.

The distinctive purpose of the Volunteer Movement is to secure student volunteers who will actually go forth from the United States and Canada and spend their lives in non-Christian lands in the work of establishing Christ's Kingdom. The supreme and only sufficient test by which it should be tried and judged is its efficiency in this vital respect. It is a ground for sincere gratitude, therefore, that within the lifetime of the Movement 5,882 of its members have sailed. They have gone out to the foreign field under the auspices of over seventy missionary agencies, practically all being connected with the recognized missionary societies of the various Christian communions of the

United States and Canada. They are distributed throughout the non-Christian world as follows:

Africa	638
Arabia	26
Central America	40
China	1,739
India, Burma, and Ceylon	1,133
Japan and Korea	743
Latin and Greek Countries of Europe	28
Mexico	168
Oceania	67
Persia	51
Philippine Islands	163
Siam, Laos, and Straits Settlements	104
South America	359
Turkish Empire	221
West Indies	177
Other Countries	225
	5,882

I. ACHIEVEMENTS OF THE QUADRENNIUM

Most gratifying is the fact that during the four years which have elapsed since the Rochester Convention 1,466 volunteers have sailed. This is a far larger number than have gone out during any preceding quadrennium. It exceeds the number who sailed during the first twelve years of the life of the Movement. It is interesting to note that nearly twice as many student volunteers have gone out from the United States and Canada during the last four years as from the universities and colleges of all the other Christian nations combined. A study of the record blanks of these sailed volunteers, as well as conversations and correspondence with many of them, reveals that in nearly every instance the Volunteer Movement was an important if not the principal factor in influencing them to become missionaries.

Not a few volunteers are hindered from pressing to the front: some because of personal responsibilities with reference to their families; some because of their inability to comply with the physical, intellectual, and other requirements of the boards; some because of personal debts or other financial problems; and some through lack of consecration and force of character. On the whole, however, the strongest appreciation should be expressed with reference to the determination and persistence of so many volunteers, who in the face of serious opposition and discouragement have persevered until they have realized their volunteer purpose. It is this spirit of steadfastness and heroism which constitutes the real glory of the Movement. It would be difficult to overstate the value of the many obstacles which confront volunteers, viewing these as means of purifying their motives, solidifying their purpose, developing their character, strengthening their faith, calling out their latent energies, and thus preparing them to grapple more successfully with the most serious difficulties and problems which await them on the mission field.

Without doubt, one of the secrets of the going forth of this continuous and expanding stream of volunteers is the fact that the leaders of the Movement, its recruiting officers, continue to press to the front. At Rochester we were able to state that of the volunteers who had been traveling secretaries sixty-four had sailed, four only had been rejected by the boards because they lacked necessary qualifications, three were still in course of preparation, and two were detained by the boards for special service. Of the twenty-nine different traveling secretaries who have served the Movement since the convention at Rochester twelve have sailed; one is under appointment; four are detained temporarily on account of health; two are still carrying on preparatory studies, and ten are members of the present staff of the Movement, and on completing their preparation will proceed to the field.

The Candidates Department of the Movement, established under the inspiring leadership of Dr. Zwemer, has been carried forward by Mr. W. B. Smith during the last four years to a stage of very high efficiency. Now that he lays down this work to press out to India in fulfillment of his life purpose, we wish to express appreciation of the masterly way in which he has conducted this part of the work. The purpose of this department is to bring the qualified candidate, whether he be a volunteer or non-volunteer, in touch with the position to be filled on the mission field. It seeks to present concrete or definite calls to students who are now actually qualified to go to the front. It serves, therefore, as an indispensable clearinghouse between the source of supply, that is, the prepared students, and the demand, that is, the needs on the various fields as known and emphasized by the mission boards. It has enabled the Movement to become more and more of practical service to the boards. Of this fact they have borne recent emphatic testimony. Its helpful relationship to the boards has been greatly facilitated by the cooperation of the candidate secretaries of the various general and women's boards, who come together from time to time to discuss with the Movement this side of its work.

General bulletins or lists of calls, setting forth in a clear and orderly way the requirements of the different societies, are issued at least twice a year, and circulated widely among the institutions of North America. Besides these, certain special denominational lists are published, and also circulars calling attention to certain specific openings on the foreign field. Wide use is made of periodicals which will help to bring the needs of the boards to the attention of students and graduates. The hundreds of secretaries of the Student Young Men's and Young Women's Christian Associations, as well as over 600 other trusted correspondents, are used to help discover men and women required to meet the specific needs of the different boards. The many student conferences are also utilized as opportunities for the discovery of suitable candidates. An extensive correspondence is conducted from the central office. Last year the candidate secretary communicated with 8,000 different persons and as a result was able to submit to the missionary societies the names of over 500 suitable candidates. This work is of the greatest possible value to the mission boards. It has greatly increased the number of persons from whom they can choose candidates. It influences many to decide to become missionaries, because some of the strongest young men and women are most influenced by a call to some definite post. Moreover, it helps to hold many volunteers to their life purpose who might otherwise become lost to the missionary movement. Above all and through all it makes possible the much more prompt manning of critically important positions.

During the last four years a larger number of new volunteers has been enrolled than during any corresponding period in the history of the colleges of North America. This is all the more remarkable because the recruiting methods of the Movement have become more conservative from year to year; and because experience has shown that it has become more difficult in recent years to secure candidates because of the multiplying demands and attractions for workers on the home field. It should be a source of encouragement and thanksgiving for all to know that the present student generation is not lacking in willingness to respond to the heroic appeal and to the stern requirements of missionary service.

Next to the persistent personal work of the volunteers themselves, the principal agency for securing new recruits has been that of the traveling secretaries of the Movement. As a result of the larger vision and larger initiative of the Nashville and Rochester Conventions, we have been enabled during the last eight years to double the number of traveling secretaries. This in turn has made possible the reaching of many more colleges and universities and of laying more effective siege to the principal student centers. With our present staff we are able to make each year over 500 visits to some 400 different institutions. We cannot speak too highly of the wonderful influence which has been exerted by these devoted and able workers who have come with their deeply moving message, pressing upon successive generations of students the surpassing claims of Christ and His world-wide plans. Where the conditions have been favorable for the manifestation of the Divine Presence and working, these occasions have frequently marked the beginning of new epochs in the spiritual life as well as the missionary fruitfulness of the colleges.

In this immediate connection emphatic reference should be made to the invaluable service rendered to the missionary work of the Church by the traveling and local student secretaries of the Young Men's Christian Associations and Young Women's Christian Associations. Under their leadership these agencies have become increasingly fruitful missionary auxiliaries. In view of their unique opportunity it is not surprising that some of these workers who are dominated by the missionary purpose have been able to accomplish results second only to those of the recruiting officers of the Volunteer Movement.

The many conferences held in the student field of North America have also been tributary to the expanding missionary interest and consecration of the present student generation. The Rochester Convention, which ushered in the last quadrennium, exerted an even more profound influence on the student field of North America than any of its predecessors, and this is saying much, for we have not yet begun to see the end of the influence exerted by the conventions at Nashville, Toronto, Cleveland, and Detroit. Besides these great international official gatherings of the Movement, there have been inaugurated in different parts of the field, under the initiative of the volunteers themselves, many state, provincial, or district volunteer conferences. Last year, for example, there were held as many as thirty-two such gatherings attended by an aggregate of 4,415 student delegates from 468 institutions. When wisely planned, ably led, and properly correlated with the other Christian activities in the student field, these more informal meetings have often furnished the occasion for demonstrations of spiritual power and have kindled missionary fires in many places.

Without doubt, however, far more productive in permanent missionary results have been the various summer and winter conferences of the Christian Association Movements of North America. At least sixteen gatherings of this kind are held each year, attended by over 6,000 carefully selected student delegates. As a rule these conferences continue for ten days. This makes possible intensive work. Over 75 per cent of the delegates from year to year receive systematic training for the leadership of the mission study classes and for the other missionary activities of the colleges. Moreover, experience shows that these conferences yield a surprisingly large number of the strongest volunteers.

A most fundamental activity of the Volunteer Movement is the promotion of mission study. This underlies and makes possible the largest and most satisfactory achievements in other directions, such as enlisting new recruits, training missionary candidates, the preparation of intelligent leaders for the home base, the promotion of missionary giving, and the multiplying of missionary intercessors. It means much, therefore, to be able to state that within the last four years there has been an increase in the number of young men and young women in mission study classes in the colleges from 29,300 to 40,400. This addition of 11,000 or of nearly 40 per cent represents one of the greatest advances ever made. It equals the expansion made during the first twelve years of the history of the Mission Study Department of the Movement. When we remember that at the time this feature of the work was introduced in the year 1894 there were not more than 200 students enlisted in the thirty mission study groups then in existence, the fact that we now have about 2,700 mission study circles in over 700 different institutions is indeed highly significant. The increase of the recent years has been shared by all classes of institutions; but the most encouraging advance has been made in the theological seminaries, where there has been an increase of some 60 per cent and in the medical schools, which report an increase of 100 per cent. It should be pointed out that of the 40,000 students thus engaged in the investigation and discussion of missionary subjects fully seven-eighths are non-volunteers. This fact in itself is indicative of a great change which has taken place in recent years, and gives promise of a leadership of the Christian forces which will be intelligently sympathetic with the missionary program of Christianity.

Satisfactory progress has been made in the production of new courses of mission study. Among the most helpful and most widely used courses recently issued by the Movement are *The Unoccupied Mission Fields* by Zwemer, *South American Problems* by Speer, *The Chinese Revolution* by Brown, *Educational Missions* by Barton (the first of a series of works to deal with the main branches of missionary service), and *The Decisive Hour of Christian Missions* by Mott. In this connection attention should be called to the most notable book published by the Movement, the one issued in connection with Commission I of the Edinburgh Missionary Conference, *The World Atlas of Christian Missions.*

Even more important than the marked increase in the number engaged in mission study and the advance recorded in the production of new courses has been the steady improvement in the quality of the mission study work. This is due primarily to the strong emphasis placed upon the qualitative aspect of the work by the leaders of the Mission Study Department. More attention has been given to the selection and training of teachers for study groups, especially at the summer conferences. The literature on the subject has been enriched. The co-operation of college and seminary professors has become more general and helpful. The attention paid to such subjects in the curriculum of our institutions has also had an indirect but strong influence. Moreover, the closer correlation of mission study and the Bible study and social problems study has contributed in a marked degree to the improvement of all these activities.

On an occasion like this it is fitting that attention should be called to the remarkable development of mission study throughout the Churches as a result of the wise and aggressive propaganda of the Missionary Education Movement, of the Central Committee of United Study of Missions of Women's Boards, and also of the Laymen's Missionary Movement. It will be recalled that the Volunteer Movement was the principal contributory cause leading to the inauguration of these three beneficent enterprises. In any true estimate, therefore, of the influence of the Volunteer Movement one should not lose sight of its great indirect services to the missionary enterprise.

From its earliest days the Volunteer Movement has emphasized the financial responsibility of undergraduates. It has believed that it is literally true that where one's treasure is there one's heart is also. During the last year the colleges and seminaries secured $220,804 for missionary objects, of which about one-half was contributed by the students themselves and the rest was secured by them from the professors and immediate friends. This is of course in addition to what the students and professors give in connection with the Churches they attend. It represents an increase of over 60 per cent in the gifts reported for the year preceding the Rochester Convention. Over 100 institutions are each subscribing $300 or more. Among the institutions which are giving most largely are Yale, Princeton, the University of Toronto, the University of Pennsylvania, Oberlin, the University of Michigan, and the Southern Baptist Theological Seminary. The institutions whose members are giving most per capita are the Misses Masters School, where the gifts last year averaged $15; the Groton School, where the average was $17, and Auburn Theological Seminary, where the average was $8. The institutions which have had a mission station, a college, a missionary, or some other special object to support have kept up their giving steadily, and, as a rule, have increased their annual gifts; but those which have not had such special objects have been more spasmodic in their giving, and in several instances have even ceased to make missionary gifts. It is gratifying to know that by far the larger part of the student contributions is given through the regular mission boards.

The chief value of missionary giving in the colleges and seminaries is seen not so much in the amount of money which is thus obtained for the missionary cause, although this now represents the equivalent of the support of possibly 150 missionaries, as in the influence which this practice exerts upon the future attitude and activities of the students. Among their number are not a few of the sons and daughters of the wealthy. These will some day inherit and administer vast sums of money which, if related to the plans of the expanding Kingdom of Christ, may accomplish untold good. Others will some day through their own efforts be in a position to wield large financial power, and, as a result of the habit formed in student days, will use this power in furthering the missionary work of the Church. Thousands of those now giving will some day be pastors in charge of churches and will then apply the same principles with reference to the support of missionaries and missionary institutions as those which they have become accustomed to use in their student days. Tens of thousands of the present student givers to missions will later become leaders of the lay forces of the Church, and, with their practical missionary interest, will be in a position to augment greatly the financial support of the missionary enterprise.

While concentrating all its attention and energy upon its direct propaganda, the Student Volunteer Movement has had a profound reflex influence on the religious life of the students of the universities and colleges of North America. In summoning successive generations of Christian students to consider the world claims of Christianity, it has indirectly promoted among them conclusive thinking with reference to their lifework problems. In influencing thousands to dedicate themselves to foreign missionary service, it has at the same time indirectly influenced even greater numbers to devote their lives to some other form of Christian service as a lifework. Countless young men and young women, who have felt that they could not go abroad, have resolved that they would devote themselves to Christian service at home. It is the very genius of the Movement to bring students into right relation to Jesus Christ as Lord. Nearly all Christian students had come to know Christ as Saviour, but many had not been led to recognize Him as the Lord or Master of their lives. The Volunteer Movement has been even more concerned in influencing them to acknowledge His sovereign sway than in urging them to decide to serve Him in any particular part of His world-wide Kingdom. It has thus afforded a challenge for every Christian student for testing his devotion to Christ. Nothing could be more valuable to a man than to be obliged to answer the question whether his loyalty to Christ is limited and fractional or thoroughgoing, complete, and absolute. Whether he becomes a student volunteer or not, the experience of facing this question fearlessly and honestly is of the greatest possible help. The Movement in sounding out the missionary call has promoted reality in Christian experience in every college which it has touched. Its appeal tries men's motives as by fire and exposes relentlessly all sham and hypocrisy.

Through all the years, and never more than in the recent past, the Movement has emphasized the vital processes. Some think that it has done more than any other one factor to develop the prayer life of the colleges. All over the field it has raised up and trained intelligent and faithful intercessors. It has widened and intensified the prayer life of every student who has come under its direct influence. The wide observance of the Morning Watch is traceable in large part to the constant emphasis placed upon this life-expanding habit by the secretaries and members of the Movement. The study of inspiring Christian biographies and of the most dynamic devotional literature has also been widely promoted in the same way.

Who can estimate the influence of the Movement in maintaining and extending the influence of the Christian faith in our universities? Without doubt it has exerted a profound apologetic influence. This it has done through acquainting men with Christianity as a present-day, vital, world-wide, triumphant force. It has done so also by showing through its missionary studies not only the total inadequacy of the non-Christian religions, but also the absolute sufficiency of pure Christianity. It is well to remember that only a Christianity powerful enough to conquer the minds and hearts of the followers of the non-Christian religions in Asia and Africa can show itself able to meet the deepest needs in the lives of the students of North America. Moreover, the influence of the example of the volunteers thinking enough of their own religion to go forth with conviction to propagate it in the very homes of the non-Christian religions, is in itself an apologetic of the very highest order and has been used by God to lead many an open-minded and honest unbelieving student to investigate afresh the claims of Christianity and to yield to these claims.

The student missionary uprising has been a mighty help in the direction of counteracting the perils of our modern college life. At a time when growing luxury, self-indulgence, and the tendency to softness are manifesting themselves in our colleges, it is well that we have a Movement which makes such an appeal to the heroic, which summons men to such a stern and rugged self-discipline, and which assigns to them such stupendous tasks.

The influence of the Movement on the home Church has also been both wide and deep. It has inspired thousands of young men who are to lead the home churches, with the world vision and the world passion, and influenced them to make their lives tell for the realization of Christ's world program. In giving to the mission boards year after year such a priceless offering of lives dedicated to the missionary career, the Movement has presented to the Christian Church a most compelling appeal or challenge for its generosity, sacrifice and fellowship in prayer. In doing so much also to bind together in true friendship the future leaders of all of our Christian communions the Movement has become one of the greatest factors, if not the greatest, in realizing the prayer of our Lord that we all may be one.

It should be emphasized that once a student volunteer, always a student volunteer. It is a striking fact that the students, who under the spell of this Movement are led to offer themselves for missionary service and go out to the foreign field, never lose the original impulse. The ideals, principles, and spirit which did so much to determine their life purpose continue in a remarkable degree to dominate their attitude and practice. The discerning traveler in mission lands today is impressed by the fact that the old volunteers have become a tremendous force in nearly all these fields. There are now on the foreign field approximately 7,500 volunteers who have gone out from North America, the British Isles, the Continent of Europe, and the Christian lands of the Southern Hemisphere. On only one mission field, that is, Japan, are they organized; but in many other fields they assemble each year in greater or less numbers at hill stations and in conferences. Nearly all of them during their furloughs renew their touch with the Movement at home, and by means of periodicals, correspondence, and intercession preserve a more or less intimate relation to it.

One is conscious in meeting these volunteers, even in the most isolated places, that there is a spiritual solidarity among them. They seem to understand each other, and from widely differing angles are working together toward certain great common goals. A careful study of the missionary conferences held on the different fields as well as at home shows clearly that the volunteers have become a recognized factor in the development of missionary policy. Their influence is thrown strongly on the side of increasing the efficiency of the missionary enterprise in all its parts. From their ranks have risen some of the outstanding missionary statesmen of our day. They have had a leading part in nearly every notable movement on the foreign field for more than a decade. By life practices as well as by word they have stood for the spiritual emphasis in mission work. On every field can be seen the influence which the watchword has had upon them and through them upon others. It is observable in the way in which they have sought to communicate this ideal and motive to the native Christian students. It is recognized in the way in which they have emphasized the importance of the adequate occupation of the field, a good illustration being the initiative given to the recent remarkable study made in Japan on the distribution of the forces. It is seen again in the countless appeals which they have individually and collectively sent back to the students and Churches at the home base emphasizing the urgency of the situation.

The volunteers now at the front have also become the greatest single human force in the promotion of co-operation and unity. It would be strange were this not the case. Here are over 7,000 able men and women who during their student days, though belonging to different Christian communions and nationalities, worked together as members of a common Movement, animated with a common objective. In that plastic, vision-forming period they learned to respect, trust, and love each other. Now they stand face to face with a task so stupendous, so difficult, and so urgent, that they are convinced that they are necessary to each other, that nothing less than a policy and practice of co-operation and a spirit of Christlike oneness will prevail. On every field, therefore, they may be found in the forefront in all wise, constructive efforts to draw together the Christian forces. Moreover, their indirect influence on the cause of unity at the home base is destined to be both extensive and profound.

II. SPREAD OF THE MOVEMENT TO OTHER LANDS

For a number of years the Student Volunteer Movement of the United States and Canada was the only organization of its kind in all the student world. Under the influence of one of its founders a similar Movement was later developed as an organized force in the British universities. Still later the volunteer idea was transplanted, either from North America or from the British Isles, to many other lands, such as the Scandinavian countries, Germany, Holland, Switzerland, Australasia, and South Africa. The North American Movement has never lost its deep interest in these sister Movements, but continues to follow their development with keen and prayerful interest. It is appropriate, therefore, on this occasion that attention be called to some of the more recent facts bearing upon their activities and influence.

The Student Volunteer Missionary Union of Great Britain and Ireland has from the beginning been a mighty factor in the missionary life of the British universities and of the British Empire. Over 1,800 of its members have sailed, this being a larger proportion of the total number than in the case of our own Movement. Each year between 200 and 300 new volunteers are enrolled, although it is reported that there has recently been a slight falling off. Each year about 100 complete their preparation and sail. The number in mission study circles ranges between 1,600 and 2,000. Among the most effective textbooks recently produced and most widely used are *The Renaissance in India* by Andrews, *The Outcaste's Hope* by Phillips, and *The Missionary Motive*. The Fifth Quadrennial Conference of the Union was held just two years ago at Liverpool. It differed from the preceding gatherings in that it dealt with the social problems of the home field as well as with the needs and opportunities of the foreign field, thus emphasizing the solidarity and interdependence of the work of Christ at home and abroad. In the recent reorganization of their work steps have been taken to make the general Christian Student Movement of the British Isles responsible for promoting missionary interest and intelligence among all classes of students, and to have the Volunteer Union concentrate on recruiting volunteers and facilitating their preparation. This Union has rendered a unique service in promoting unity among the Christian forces of the British Isles. It has also through its quadrennial conferences greatly stimulated the missionary and general religious life and activity of the universities of the Continent.

The Student Missionary Movement in Germany, in the face of very great difficulties, has continued to carry forward its helpful activities. It has thus far enrolled about 110 volunteers, of whom over sixty have already sailed, nine going out during the last year. It has about 400 students in mission study circles. Last April it held its Fifth Triennial Conference at Halle. There were present over 900 delegates, or twice as many as ever before. This conference made a profound impression upon all who were present and has greatly quickened the missionary interest in a number of the leading universities. The recent visit by Dr. Zwemer and many addresses given by other missionary authorities have helped to develop the interest. In view of the fact that such a very small fraction of the candidates sent out by the German missionary societies have been students, the development of this Student Missionary Movement is of the greatest possible importance to the future of German missions and the German Churches.

Within the last four years the Volunteer Movement has been organized in the Swiss universities. It has enrolled over thirty volunteers, a few of whom have already sailed. It is confined largely to French-speaking Switzerland, but it is hoped that it will soon spread more widely among the German-speaking universities of the country. A few scores have been enlisted in mission study. A most important missionary conference, which will deal also with the social problems, is now being organized and will be the first of its kind ever held in this field.

In Holland a Student Missionary Movement has been established which includes not only those who plan to go to the mission field, but others who are especially interested in missionary questions. It has fewer than 100 members in all. It is reported that fourteen of the Dutch students have sailed since the beginning of their Student Movement. Encouraging results in mission study are being secured.

The universities of Norway, Sweden, Denmark, and Finland have for years been centers of missionary interest. In recent years much more attention has been given to the study and discussion of missionary questions. Although the Volunteer Movement in an organized form exists in only part of the universities, especially those of Denmark and Finland, the number of students who have sailed from Scandinavian universities has been greater during the last decade or two than during earlier periods. The most notable event of the past year was the Student Missionary Conference at Gothenburg, Sweden, attended by nearly 200 students from different Scandinavian countries.

In the French universities there has recently been developed a promising force known as the Volunteers of Christ. Those who belong to this Movement seek to develop and express the missionary spirit in whatever career they may undertake, or in whatever field they may be called to work. While it is not an extensive Movement, it has already exerted a deep influence. In Hungary and also in Austria there are the beginnings of missionary movements. The students are interesting themselves chiefly in the Mohammedan problem in the Near East.

The Student Volunteer Movement of Australasia is one of the most promising in the world. Although its student field is not extensive, it has up to the present time enrolled between 300 and 400 volunteers of whom 106 have already sailed. Last year more new volunteers were enrolled than in any preceding year. There is growing interest in mission study, there being a total enrollment last year of 734. Largely under the influence of this Movement, the Laymen's Missionary Movement was introduced into Australasia. The two organizations work in the closest possible co-operation and actually join in deputation work in the churches. The Volunteer Movement of Australasia is doing more than any other in the world to promote the missionary spirit in the churches of the country. Its activity is a splendid illustration of how a comparatively small company of earnest students can impress the spirit and policy of the Church throughout an entire nation.

The Volunteer Movement in South Africa has also accomplished a work in some respects quite as remarkable as the one in Australia and New Zealand. It was established in the same year (1896). It has enrolled over 300 volunteers, of whom nearly 100 have already gone to the mission field. It has recently appointed a candidates secretary with reference to meeting more fully the demands of the missionary societies. The missionary conference held recently at Worcester was a gathering of great power. The students of the native colleges and schools of South Africa are also being summoned to devote themselves more largely to the work of Christ among their own people. A burden of responsibility is being placed upon the Movement of South Africa to have a larger part in meeting and resisting the Moslem advance.

One of the most remarkable developments among the students of foreign lands during the last four years has been the organization in China of the Chinese Student Volunteer Movement for the Ministry. This Movement has been raised up in answer to prayer to help solve the greatest problem of the Church in China, that of securing a sufficient number of well-qualified native students for the Christian ministry. Without such able leaders the Church cannot minister successfully to the educated classes of China. In view of the special difficulty involved in securing this kind of men for the leadership of the churches, it was decided to limit this Movement to those who would volunteer to become Christian ministers. The declaration therefore reads, "It is my purpose, if God permit, to become a minister." The watchword of the Movement is "The Evangelization of Our Mother Country and the World in This Generation." From the beginning, the principal traveling secretary has been Pastor Ding Li-mei, in whose wonderful work in some of the colleges of North China the Movement may be said to have originated. He has gone as a flame of fire among the students of ten or more of the provinces. As a rule he has remained in a college long enough for an unhurried visit—long enough for the fires to kindle and burn. Each year, during the past three years, from 150 to 250 volunteers have been secured. Never before in a non-Christian land has there been such an offering of strong students for the Christian ministry. In some of the colleges the volunteers include a majority of the ablest students of the upper classes.

Among the score of volunteer bands already established in China are some which in size, character of personnel, and spiritual power are the equal of any of the student volunteer bands which have ever existed in our North American colleges. Although these Chinese volunteers are subjected to the strongest possible pressure to enter lucrative callings in government or commercial pursuits, practically none of them have turned their backs upon their missionary purpose. The indirect influence of their example has been such as to lead many of the Chinese students who are to enter other callings to do so with a genuinely unselfish spirit and with a determination to make their lives also count in the evangelization of China. The Chinese Volunteer Movement, as an organic department of the Student Young Men's Christian Association, exists primarily to serve the Christian Church. It emphasizes the absolute necessity of securing the most thorough preparation in order that the leaders of the Church may be qualified to meet the unprecedented opportunities now presented in all parts of China. The Christian students in North America should remember with special intercession this uprising of Chinese Christian students. We should also pray that in the not distant future there may be developed similar Movements among the students of India, Japan, and other parts of the non-Christian world. The remarkable conference of Indian Christian students held last winter at Serampore, a gathering which did so much to Indianize the Christian Student Movement in that vast field, the activities of the Indian National Missionary Association, and the recent consecration of Mr. Azariah as the first Indian bishop, have done much to inspire the Christian students of India with the spirit of service and to facilitate the development of a Volunteer Movement in that part of the world.

The World's Student Christian Federation, which embraces not only the Volunteer Movements, but the more comprehensive Christian Student Movements of all lands, has continued to go from strength to strength. Through its name and world-wide field, through its missionary objective and activities it serves as a constant reminder to the students of all lands of the world relations of Christianity. More than any other influence, unless it be possibly the advocacy of the watchword, the Federation has helped to hold in prominence in the thought of the students of our generation their responsibility to make the reign of Christ co-extensive with the inhabited earth. During the last quadrennium there have been added to the constituent Movements of the Federation 300 student Associations with over 20,000 members, until now the Federation embraces over 2,300 Christian Associations with a total membership of 156,000 students and professors.

During this period the Federation has held two of its most notable conferences—the one in 1911 at Constantinople, within the gates of the Moslem world, which opened the way to a wonderful expansion of the Student Movement in the Near East, both within and outside the Oriental Churches; the other last June at Lake Mohonk, which through its personnel, representing over forty nations, did so much to make the Federation and its world mission vivid and real to the students of North America. In binding together the Christian students of all lands and races, and in concentrating their attention and activities on bringing the power of the universities and colleges to bear upon the problem of the evangelization and Christianization of the whole world, the Federation is rendering a service to Christian missions which is of so great importance that discerning leaders of the Church speak of it as one of the most remarkable facts of modern times.

III. THE DEMAND OF THE COMING DAY

The greatest demand made upon the Volunteer Movement today is that of furnishing a much larger number of well-qualified volunteers. In fact, this demand is more insistent than ever before. The appeal comes from every mission field and is supported by virtually every missionary society. Why are many more volunteers required? They are needed in order to fill the vacant places in the missionary staff occasioned by death, or by permanent withdrawal from the field owing to ill-health or other providential reasons. They are needed in order to relieve from impossible strain the present missionary force which in all quarters of the world is so fearfully undermanned. The strain is due not so much to impending failure as to recent remarkable triumphs. This suggests that more volunteers are demanded in order that the Church may safeguard the great expansion of its missionary work which has taken place recently in so many countries. More missionaries should be sent out at once in order to make more productive the colleges, hospitals, and other departments of the missionary enterprise. A careful study of the missionary movement today gives one the impression that a relatively small addition to the existing staff would result in greatly augmenting the spiritual results.

It is inspiring to add that many more volunteers should be forthcoming to press the present unparalleled advantage which the Christian Church now has in the Far East and in the Near East, in Southern Asia and in Africa, and in other regions. Without doubt it is true that Christianity has never before had such a combination of opportunities among both primitive and cultured races. It must be remembered also that the era of higher specialization on which the missionary movement has entered demands in itself a great increase in the number of missionaries. There is so much to do in the non-Christian world today that the task cannot be accomplished save by a vast enlargement of the native Christian forces. This in turn calls for an increase in the number of missionaries in order that there may be raised up and trained in the immediate future the necessary staff of capable native Christian workers. The very enlargement of the native Christian community requires an enlargement of the missionary staff, that these rising, plastic, native Churches may be wisely developed at this most critical stage in their life.

No convention like this, moreover, should overlook the fact that there are still many totally unoccupied fields. We would sound out the call for students of heroic spirit to become pioneers in these lands where Christ has not been named. Our watchword demands a vast consecration of the lives of the students of our day to the work of world evangelization; because it is our fixed and unalterable purpose to give all men now living an adequate opportunity to know the Living Christ. To accomplish this calls for nothing less than an uprising far surpassing that wonderful offering in the first two years of the life of the Movement. What event could take place which would do so much to quicken the life and faith of our colleges and universities, in fact, of all the churches of the United States and Canada, as the dedication of an unprecedented number of the choicest men and women to the carrying out of the sublime purposes of our Lord and Saviour for all mankind? At a time like this when the facts and forces of our material world are presenting such a colossal and dazzling appeal to the student class, it is necessary for the spiritual welfare of the colleges that the world-claims of Christ be pressed as never before.

Our student centers are well able to supply this great increase in the number of volunteers so imperatively needed. We have not yet begun to realize the missionary possibilities of the institutions of higher learning in North America. The complete and convincing proof of this is the example of what certain universities and theological seminaries have done and are doing. If other institutions similarly situated would do as well we should have far more than enough volunteers forthcoming to meet every requirement. In one sense, therefore, this matter of securing a sufficient number of suitable volunteers reduces itself on the human side to a matter of mathematics. It involves, possibly, a doubling of the present force of traveling secretaries of our Movement. If the present staff by visiting 400 institutions are able to set in motion influences resulting in a certain number of volunteers, then if arrangements can be made to double the number of visits, and, if possible, to do more siege work at certain institutions, there should be a corresponding increase in the number of missionary candidates. Moreover, experience shows that certain summer conferences and other student conferences and institutes yield a disproportionately large number of volunteers. The causes for this result should be carefully studied, and similar principles, methods, and influences should be applied to the other gatherings.

The missionary fruitage secured by some of the local and traveling secretaries of the Association movements suggests what large results in the aggregate would follow if the other workers possessing similar or greater opportunities were to recognize and accept their responsibility for becoming enlargers of the Kingdom. Everything which has been stated regarding the need of expanding several-fold the number of earnest students of missions takes on added meaning in this immediate connection, for it is more evident than ever that widening missionary intelligence is a necessary precursor to large and satisfactory results in recruiting work. Behind all that has been said lies the need that the leaders of this Movement and all others who are to have a large part in recruiting work make a more careful study of the problems of vocational guidance, and of the psychological aspects of the work of recruiting. They should make a fresh examination of the soundest motives of appeal, of the wisest ways of appeal, of the dangers and human limitations of appeal, and of the lessons of history and present-day experience in securing Christian workers.

Lest a misleading impression may be left by what has been said concerning the mathematical and human aspects of this vital problem, it should be emphasized with full conviction that the securing of the workers needed for the expansion of Christianity is primarily and essentially a superhuman matter. It is the sovereign work of the Spirit of the Living God to separate men unto the work whereunto He has called them. Unless, therefore, the recruiting secretaries, the Association secretaries, the Christian professors and teachers, and the student volunteers devote themselves to this infinitely important work with a sense of conscious and humble dependence upon Him, and wield with conscientiousness and earnestness the irresistible forces of intercession, we shall absolutely fail to discover and enlist the army of student volunteers demanded in this generation of unique opportunity.

The state universities and other higher educational institutions under government control should be made far more largely than at present missionary strongholds and propagating centers. This class of institutions includes a majority of the largest universities. The number of students in them is increasing much more rapidly than in the denominational colleges. A greater proportion of the students than is generally realized are Christians. They are open-minded, aggressive, honest of purpose, and possess much decision of character. Contrary to the popular impression, these students as a class are idealistic in the best sense. Experience shows that they are responsive to reality and do not shrink from large and difficult undertakings. Most of the state institutions are still in a plastic condition, owing to their comparative youth and rapid growth. It is not difficult, therefore, to influence them profoundly with the missionary ideal. There is not one of these institutions which could not with proper cultivation be made a center of genuine and expanding missionary spirit. Each one of them should furnish an increasing number of missionaries. Possibly they will not yield so large a proportion of volunteers who will become regular ordained missionaries. On the other hand, more than other colleges, they should furnish the men and women who will be needed in increasing numbers for the specialized forms of missionary work such as the educational, the medical, the industrial, the literary, the administrative, also for the work among special classes such as young men and young women.

As these are government universities and not under the supervision and control of the Churches, the Student Volunteer Movement and the related Association movements are under special obligation to give them the missionary outlook, to cultivate in them the missionary spirit and to call forth from them missionary recruits. It is especially gratifying to note that some of the leading Christian denominations have come to recognize their responsibility for safeguarding at these centers the religious interests of the young men and young women belonging to their respective communions, and are putting forth effective efforts to accomplish this end. It is to be hoped that everything possible will be done to develop in these large student communities well equipped Christian churches, and that in charge of them may be placed ministers of such experience and gifts of personality and leadership that they will command the intellectual and spiritual confidence of the students and professors, and thus be in a position to influence pronouncedly their religious life. All this will tend to prepare the ground for bringing forth the large missionary fruitage which we have a right to expect from these important educational institutions.

Quite as important as augmenting the number of volunteers is the work of increasing their efficiency. The success of Christian missions on the foreign field depends, under God, on the qualifications and preparation of the missionaries. This point received great emphasis at the Edinburgh Conference and in the series of Continuation Committee Conferences recently held throughout Asia. Student volunteers should be given to understand that in the judgment of the wisest missionaries a much more thorough training of missionary candidates while on the home field is called for today than in the past. This is due to the great advance in the education of the peoples in the non-Christian world, including the native Christian communities. It is occasioned also by the marked growth of the spirit of independence in the native Churches. It is demanded by the abler leadership of the forces of the non-Christian religions. It is made necessary by certain dangerous tendencies, including that of syncretism or eclecticism. Moreover, if the Church is to take and hold a position of leadership among the educated and influential classes, its native workers must receive more advanced training; and this, in turn, calls for even better qualified missionaries than in the earlier and simpler stages of the missionary enterprise.

In view of these more exacting educational requirements, it is a ground for sincere gratitude that as a result of the Edinburgh Conference there has been established in North America, as well as in Great Britain, a Board of Missionary Preparation, and also that, owing to the same initiative, there are being organized in different mission fields union language schools. These agencies have been called into being to facilitate the better preparation of missionary candidates. Steps are being taken to bring about a closer co-ordination between what is done on the home field to further missionary preparation and what is done on the foreign field.

The recent Continuation Committee Conferences in Asia strongly urged that the volunteer, in addition to securing a general education as complete in all respects as that required for corresponding work at home, should have opportunity, if possible, before going out to the mission field to study such subjects as the following: the history and philosophy of the religions of the country to which he goes, as well as the subject of comparative religion; the history, social conditions, and characteristics of the people to whom he is to minister; the history and methods of Christian missions, especially of the land where he is to work; exceptionally full and thorough Bible study; actual experience and training in personal work and other forms of evangelistic effort; bookkeeping and business methods; philology and the principles of phonetics; and, in many cases, the theory and practice of teaching.

To secure all or even a large part of this special preparation will not be easy. Few, if any, of the mission boards themselves make provision for affording such preparation. Unfortunately, moreover, few of the colleges and theological seminaries provide the necessary facilities. It is the belief of many that the curricula of the theological seminaries and of some of the denominational colleges should be radically revised with reference to furnishing more specific preparation for the foreign missionary career. In far too many institutions of this kind the instruction and other facilities afforded are not calculated to give students a true and large comprehension of the races to which they are to minister, of the religions or systems of belief which they must meet, of the present-day statement of the Christian message which will win its way most largely, of the growing sense of the expansion of the Kingdom, and of the time of all times in which we live and work. It is believed that it will be better for our existing denominational institutions to adapt themselves to meet these needs than to have established special missionary training institutions as has been done so largely in European countries. Possibly much could be done in a temporary way by the Board of Missionary Preparation in furnishing summer courses such as those provided during the past two summers in Great Britain by the Board of Mission Studies.

It seems to be the impression also among the volunteers now on the mission field that it would be well for the boards to allocate intending missionaries to the fields to which they are to be sent much earlier than is now usually done, in order that they may sooner begin to specialize in their preparation. While the Volunteer Movement is primarily a recruiting agency as contrasted with a training agency, it should preserve the most intimate relation with the Board of Missionary Preparation, and should seek to do all in its power to fulfill the expressed wishes of the mission boards in furthering the best possible preparation of its members for the exacting requirements of the missionary career. We should continue to stand in season and out of season for the most thorough preparation and should enroll as volunteers only students who possess strong character, power of initiative, gifts of true leadership, consciousness of divine call, and willingness to pay what it costs to secure an unusually complete preparation.

For every reason this convention should mark the greatest advance in mission study ever made in the institutions of North America. We should augment the number in study classes literally by the tens of thousands. What reasons were there which influenced the 40,000 who engaged in such study last year, that do not apply with equal force to the over 100,000 other Christian students who are not now identified with these classes? The plans recently introduced for the closer correlation of the mission study with Bible and social problems study should contribute largely to this end. The statistics show that of the total number enlisted in mission study in the colleges, three-fifths are women students. As the number of men students in both the United States and Canada exceeds the number of women students, it suggests that far greater emphasis than heretofore must be placed on pressing this propaganda among the men students. While there has been an encouraging increase in the number of study classes in medical colleges, there is an imperative demand that this number be greatly enlarged, especially in view of the fact that so many of the missionary societies are finding it impossible to secure a sufficient number of candidates for the influential medical missionary service. It is vitally important also that hundreds of mission study groups be formed in the normal schools, because of the special influence which the teachers have in all our communities and Churches.

As the preparatory and high schools are the keys to the colleges and universities, the time has come when we must put forth wise but aggressive efforts to enlist a multitude of the schoolboys and schoolgirls in the study of missionary biography as well as of certain aspects of the missionary movement. This is desirable not only for the sake of preparing those who are later to enter the colleges, there to be brought under the influence of the volunteer appeal, but also for the sake of that vastly larger number who do not proceed to college.

It is a great mistake also that in many theological seminaries the study of missions is so seriously neglected. An investigation has revealed the fact that only about one-third of the 172 theological seminaries and theological colleges in the United States and Canada make a serious attempt in connection with their curricula to provide adequate instruction on the subject of Christian missions; that one-third furnish partial provision, and that the remaining one-third entirely ignore the subject. There is thus added reason why the voluntary study of Christian missions should be greatly promoted among theological students. The fact that not a few of these students have been in mission study classes in their undergraduate days should not be allowed to weaken the force of this emphasis, because it is expected that the leaders of the Churches shall have a more comprehensive and advanced knowledge of the subject than other members of the educated classes. How otherwise the Christian Church is to be led to perform her full duty in this great missionary age is more than can be seen.

The matter of augmenting the numbers engaged in mission study should be grappled with by every delegation in this convention, for in accomplishing this purpose we facilitate the realization of all our other missionary desires and obligations. The plans recently introduced for the closer correlation of the mission study with the Bible study and social problems study should be of very great help. The example of what has been accomplished in some institutions should stimulate the rest of us. If it has been possible at the University of Toronto, to have, as was the case during one year since the Rochester Convention, over 600 students in mission study circles, it is possible to have from 500 to 1,000 engaged in such study in each of thirty or more other large universities represented in this convention. If it has been possible to have twenty classes with an aggregate of over 200 members in William Jewell College, one of our typical denominational colleges, there are at least 300 other denominational colleges represented in the Convention, nearly all of which might have as many, were the delegates present to devote themselves energetically and persistently to accomplishing this result. If it has been possible for one women's college in Virginia to have nearly 400 of its students enlisted in mission study, and, in addition, one mission study class composed of twenty of the teachers and professors, then the delegates from other women's colleges may well ask themselves whether much larger things are not possible in each of their fields.

It is of first importance that this work of mission study be conducted in a genuinely spiritual manner. Otherwise, mission study is dangerous, because through this means we bring vividly before young men and young women at the most impressionable time in life some of the gravest problems and deepest needs of the human race, some of the most inspiring opportunities ever known, and some of the greatest trusts which God has ever committed to a generation of Christians. A further and determining reason why this whole work should be carried on in the spirit of prayerful dependence on God, is that it involves the possible revelation of His will for the lives of all who engage in such study, and through them for other lives and even nations. This fact suggests that above all things, in season and out of season, the leaders of mission study in each institution should bear in mind the objective of all such study—that is, the leading of the students to adjust their lives honestly and courageously to the new knowledge which they receive. Mission study should be regarded as a failure and a danger unless it results in a large and more intelligent consecration of those who engage in such study to the great task of the world-wide establishment of Christ's Kingdom.

Among the many things which the Volunteer Movement is called upon to do, it is well to keep clearly in mind that our central responsibility is that of projecting our members into the mission fields. Nothing else can take the place of lives thus transplanted and lived out in the non-Christian lands. Unless there be a constant human stream flowing out from our American and Canadian universities to the ends of the earth this Movement cannot preserve its reality, its contagious enthusiasm, and its world-conquering power. We should give most thoroughgoing study and intense attention, therefore, to the development of our Candidates Department. The Church has a right to expect that a Department like this, which is in constant and intimate touch with all the sending agencies and with the principal sources of supply, should become increasingly expert on the subject of the discovery and releasing of men qualified to meet immediate needs. To this end we welcome the frank, constructive criticism and suggestions of board secretaries, missionaries, students, and others who are in a position to throw any light on this question, which is the very crux of one of the most vital problems of Christian missions.

While the Candidates Department of the Volunteer Movement

should do all that it can, there is a part which can best if not only be done by the mission boards themselves. Each missionary society should have its own candidates department, and each of the principal societies should have a secretary devoting all or a large part of his time to the work of dealing with candidates. He should be a man of experience, wide knowledge, much sympathy and tact, as well as of marked sincerity and courage. The lack of such candidates departments and secretaries among the societies goes far to explain why the results of the volunteer propaganda have not been more largely conserved. The mission boards only are in a position to deal authoritatively with young men and young women who have decided to become missionaries, for the simple reason that they are the sending societies, whereas the Volunteer Movement is solely a recruiting agency. Why should each board build up an efficient candidates department? It should do so in order to weed out early any volunteers who, it believes, in the light of its expert knowledge, cannot qualify to go out as missionaries. It should do so in order to help hold suitable volunteers true to their life purpose. It should do so in order to enable all volunteers to secure a more nearly adequate preparation for their life career. The existence of the Board of Missionary Preparation accentuates the need of such a candidates department in each mission board, because the ideals of this new agency as to more thorough preparation cannot be realized until there are those representing the missionary societies who can deal authoritatively with candidates as to the kind of preparation which they should have. Without doubt the following of this plan will result in greatly increasing the likelihood of each board having a sufficient number of good men available to meet the requirements of its work.

In our report this year we would call attention to the presence in our North American institutions of higher learning of the large and increasing number of students from Oriental and other non-Christian countries. These student migrations bid fair to increase in volume. The students who have thus come among us will on their return to their native lands wield an unusually large influence. This is particularly true of those coming from lands like China, which are in such a plastic condition and which are now adopting the Western civilization. The members of the Volunteer Movement, as well as of the all-embracing Student Christian Association movements, should interest themselves in the most genuine and wholehearted manner in these students who are to become the leaders of tomorrow in their important nations. We should befriend them in every way in our power, seeking to facilitate their plans and to render them practical service. We should see that they are exposed fully to the best side of our civilization, and are led to understand clearly that what they most admire and we most value in our national and social life is traceable to the principles and spirit of pure Christianity, and that the things about our civilization which most displease them as well as ourselves are due not to Jesus Christ, but to the lack of Jesus Christ. We should lead them to investigate thoroughly the teachings of our religion, and especially the life and work of Christ Himself. We should seek to guide them into a reasonable and vital faith in the living Christ, and should pray that an increasing number of them may devote their lives to the service of Christ in their native lands, some as Christian ministers and others as lay leaders. These men and women, who in so many cases represent the flower of the lands from which they come, were they to consecrate their lives to Christ's cause, could do far more to advance His Kingdom among their people than an equal number of foreign missionaries.

We note with keenest appreciation the development in our student field of the Chinese Students' Christian Association, which is doing such a remarkable work among the Chinese students and also that most encouraging beginnings are being made by the Christian students of other nationalities to render a similar service among their countrymen in our colleges. We rejoice in the presence of so many of the Oriental students in this Convention. We should gladly co-operate with them in any ways which they may indicate for the accomplishment of their high aims. It is well that we American and Canadian students remind ourselves of the great reflex benefits which will come from the development of the work of Christ among the students from non-Christian lands now in North America and from intimate association with them. What will it not do in the widening of our sympathies, in the strengthening and enriching of our own faith, in the enlarging of our hope in the ultimate victory. Moreover, it will make more vivid and real to us the meaning of the missionary enterprise. It will do much to promote international good will. It will make possible that larger unity in which the leaders and workers of the different nations and races come to recognize how indispensable they are to each other. Above all, it will give each of us a larger Christ, for the more deeply we enter into fellowship with the Christians of other lands and other races, the more clearly we see that He has required all the different members of his world-wide family through whom to express adequately His excellencies and to communicate His power.

The most critical battlefield from the point of view of the Volunteer Movement is not the Moslem world, not the educated classes of Japan, not the literati of China, not the citadels of Hinduism, not the areas of neglect in Latin America, but our own American and

Canadian universities and colleges. If the Churches of North America are to wage triumphant warfare in these distant, difficult fields which call today so loudly for our help, the missionary facts and spirit must first dominate our own seats of learning. If we are to go forth to attempt world conquest we must have no untaken forts in our rear. This attaches the greatest possible importance to all well-considered efforts to promote the moral and religious welfare of the North American student field. The moral evils, the prevailing student temptations, the unfavorable college traditions and customs, and everything else in modern college life which is contrary to the teachings and spirit of Christ, must be overthrown if there is to be most largely developed among us truly world-conquering power. If we are to go forth with unshakable confidence to preach Christ as a world Saviour we must know beyond peradventure His saving power in our own lives and in the lives of our fellow students.

We must be able to present Christ and His work in terms that will command the intellectual and spiritual assent of the most thoughtful men in our own universities, if we are to have a message which will challenge the attention and win the intellectual confidence of the educated classes of the Orient and of Latin America. If the colleges and seminaries are to furnish the missionary consecration requisite to meet the demands of the mission boards and of the mission fields, they must be brought under the wonderful sway of the Living Christ Himself. To this end we should give ourselves even more than heretofore to the promotion of thorough, constructive, reverent study of the Scriptures. We should seek to kindle the evangelistic fires far and wide among the students of North America. We should try to discover and utilize for apologetic lectures and writing and for evangelistic work a larger number of our best Christian ministers and professors. The social study and social service program of our student movements should be pressed with the greatest vigor and intelligence. The leaders of the Christian forces should seek in every way to promote united prayer on behalf of students. Thus will be supplied the conditions essential to the raising up of a sufficient number of student volunteers to meet the present world situation.

Moreover, it is of equal importance that the students to whom the way does not open providentially to go out as missionaries, will be led to recognize with conviction and to accept cheerfully their equal responsibility to sustain the student volunteers by their prayers, by their sacrifices, by their intelligent advocacy, and by their aggressive work for world-wide missions. For the proper maintenance of this world-wide enterprise there must be a very strong home base in North America. It must be so strong, and therefore its Christianity must be so vital, that the impact of the United States and Canada on the non-Christian world through commerce, through industry, through political relations, through social contacts, through the mingling of students, investigators, and travelers, shall be a Christian impact. Those who represent us abroad in these other relations must speak the same voice to non-Christian peoples which these peoples hear from our missionaries. Moreover, as the representatives of these lands come within our gates they must find that the Christianity being lived and applied among us here agrees essentially with the claims made for it by the missionaries whom we send to them. Only a gospel and a Christian spirit which show themselves able to deal successfully with the sad and tragic social facts of our North American communities can break the power of caste in India and lift the other indescribably great social burdens which so heavily oppress the inhabitants of Asia and Africa.

IV. EMPHASIS ON THE WATCHWORD

There is need of placing stronger emphasis than ever upon the watchword of the Movement—"The Evangelization of the World in this Generation." Nearly a generation has elapsed since this watchword was adopted. The question has been raised in one quarter whether it might not be wise to abandon the watchword in view of the fact that a generation has gone and the world still remains unevangelized. This reveals evident misunderstanding. From the beginning the Movement has insisted that although the watchword was to be taken as an ideal for the Movement as a whole, the secret of realizing it lay in having a sufficient number, not only of individual student volunteers, but also of other individual Christians, adopt it as their personal watchword and as a governing principle in their lives. Therefore, the Movement has constantly sought to multiply the number of those who would bring their lives under the sway of this ideal and purpose. Who will say that the Movement did not do its duty in taking this inspiring idea as one of its great objectives? Who will say that had a sufficient number of Christians accepted the watchword as their own, the necessary facts about Christ might not have been brought to the attention of all men? Judged by the influence which the watchword has had upon the lives of those who have accepted it, it seems entirely reasonable to infer that had Christians far more widely been brought under its influence, this great ideal might have been translated from theory into fact.

What have been some of the results of the watchword where it has been proclaimed and most widely accepted? It has arrested the attention of earnest men and compelled them to consider the claims of world-wide missions; it has emphasized as no other one thing the urgency of the task of world evangelization; it has served as a constant reminder of the fact that making Christ known is a living question and not a matter for mere reflection and discussion; it has developed decision of character in dealing with the great and pressing missionary facts; it has attracted heroic men everywhere—men who shrink not from vast and most difficult undertakings; it has called out the latent energies of the students of our day as no other challenge which has been presented to them, and has developed some of the most attractive and solid traits of Christian character; it has widely promoted unity and co-operation because the very magnitude and difficulty of the task have helped to fuse together the coming leaders of the Christian forces; it has led to a larger discovery of God and a deepening acquaintance with Him, and has for an increasing number lifted the whole missionary enterprise to the superhuman plane. The more earnestly the watchword has been discussed and criticized, the more strongly have men come to believe in it as expressing the solemn obligation resting upon the Christians of our day. It is a most striking fact that as the volunteers have gone to the front, and have become more familiar with the difficulties and conditions obtaining on the mission field, their belief in the providential character and need of such a watchword has in most instances been intensified rather than weakened.

If such a watchword has been appropriate in the past, what shall we not say of its aptness and timeliness for the present day. The present is a time of unprecedented opportunity. Never has there been a time when simultaneously in so many parts of the world the doors were so wide open as now. It is a time of unprecedented danger. Above all, it is a time of unprecedented urgency, owing to the fact that so many nations are in a plastic and changing condition; owing to the growing spirit of nationalism and racial patriotism; owing to the rapid spread of the corrupt influences of our so-called Western civilization; owing to the dangerous tendencies in connection with the non-Christian religions; owing to the recent unparalleled triumphs of Christianity and the rising tide of spiritual success on every hand; and owing to the possibility of entering into the marvelous heritage prepared by the recent period of thorough preparation. Why has God made the world known and accessible today as never before? Why has He provided such extensive and well-equipped missionary agencies at the home base and on the foreign field in our day? Why has He at this particular time placed such boundless resources at the disposal of the Church? Surely such vast preparations must have been made for some great and commensurate purpose. Can we question, in view of the character of God and the present-day facts of the world, that it is His will that the whole field be occupied and evangelized in our day, and that, however great and difficult the undertaking, there are resources in our Lord Jesus Christ and latent in His followers available and sufficient to enable us to carry out that will.

If the years right at hand are to witness what is easily possible, the entering more largely than we have dreamed into the realization of the watchword, the plans of the Church must be widened accordingly. In honesty it must be said that these plans today do not make the impression upon one that it is the deliberate and dominating purpose of Christian missions to make the living Christ known to all living men in our day. The time has come when there can no longer be any reasonable excuse for not taking literally the whole world into our plan. A half-generation hence it should not be possible to point to an unoccupied field or to any considerable area in which it is impossible for men to know the essential facts concerning the mission of Christ. To this end let the members and friends of our Movement reassert with fresh conviction the obligation embodied in our inspiring watchword. Two things in particular should be emphasized. In the first place let each volunteer and each Christian student make the watchword his personal watchword. This means that we will let it influence our ideals, our motives, our attitude, our spirit, and our habits. It means that we will let it determine the use of all our talents, whether they are talents of time, money, opportunity, strength, or influence. It means that we will study its bearings on our preparation, on the time of our pressing out to the field, and on the manner and method of our work. In short, it involves our making it a governing or guiding principle in all our life and relationships.

In the second place, we who take the watchword as our own should persistently plan to get other Christians to accept it as their ideal and governing principle. A serious mistake has been made by us in neglecting to do this. We have assumed too much that others would learn about the watchword and be interested in it and adopt it on their own initiative. Experience shows that this is not the case. In our propaganda we cannot wisely omit for even one year giving great prominence to this dynamic and quickening idea. We must wage a constant educational campaign on the subject. Each year there should be in every institution of higher learning in North America at least one study circle having as the basis for its study the book on the watchword, or the one entitled *Decisive Hour of Christian Missions,* or the one entitled *Unoccupied Mission Fields,* or some other theme which lends itself to creating clear and strong convictions upon the urgency of the task. Far wider use should be made of the pamphlet literature bearing on this subject. Speakers and writers should be called upon as in earlier years to treat the theme in an up-to-date, practical, and convincing manner. We should welcome the most penetrating criticism and discussion of all the subjects involved in the understanding of the watchword and in its application to the missionary problem. We should give ourselves to personal siege work with men and women who are in a position to have large influence for or against the realization of this God-given ideal, that they in turn may become most helpful propagandists. We do a great injustice to our fellow students and other Christians if we do not give them the benefit which will come to their lives as a result of accepting with full knowledge and conviction this new and powerful motive which has done so much to enlarge the views, the lives, the plans, and the practical co-operation of all who have come fully under its power.

V. Our Immediate Responsibility

A unique responsibility rests on the delegates of this Convention. Never in the history of the student world has there been a Convention in which so many Christian students have come together to face the wholeness of the task and the oneness of the task which confronts the forces of Christianity in the non-Christian world. Never has a body of Christian students been exposed to such a flood of light on the needs and opportunities of the less favored lands and races of their generation. Never has there assembled a company of educated men and women with so great latent energies to place at the disposal of Christ for the accomplishment of His world-wide purpose. "Unto whomsoever much has been given of him shall much be required." In view of the great things which we have received in the universities and colleges of these two great lands of privilege, and in view of the wonderful vision and opportunity which come to us in this remarkable convention, what does our Lord Jesus Christ require of us?

Christ requires that each of us individually place himself absolutely and irrevocably at His disposal, henceforth to do His will and not our own. Let us be thoroughgoing and decisive on this point, cost what it may. Right here lies our most strategic battleground. If we win on this field, that is, if we let Him dominate here, all else can be accomplished.

Are we not called to make the ideal set forth in the watchword our personal ideal and to resolve to let it govern the shaping of our plans, the use of our powers, and the outreach of our influence?

Is it not the wish of Christ that the members of each delegation shall seek corporately to study how we can do most to realize in our separate colleges the advanced policy of the Convention as set forth in this report? Let us not be satisfied with things as they are, even at the best. Let us remember how God has mightily used the delegates of preceding Conventions as they have returned to their universities, colleges, and seminaries. May the Kansas City Convention be no exception in this vital respect. Rather, as a result of each delegation becoming closely united and catching the vision of the new and vastly larger spiritual possibilities, let its members give themselves to prayer, and be inspired to usher in a new era in all that pertains to giving Christ and the plans of His Kingdom their proper central place in the life of the institution. Let us not be satisfied with small things when God so obviously desires and designs that we attempt large things for Him. Our plans have been regulated too much by precedent and by our visible resources. Let them henceforth be determined rather in the light of the character and plans of God and of our invisible but aboundingly sufficient superhuman resources.

Does not Christ desire that we as a Convention associate our efforts, our gifts, and our sacrifices, that the beneficent work of the Volunteer Movement be very greatly enlarged? Why should its valuable service be limited to 400 or 500 institutions each year when 1000 colleges and universities stand in so great need of its practical and spiritual helpfulness?

Christ summons us to more faithful intercession, and also to enlist others as intercessors. Beyond question this is the primary need of the Church today. In view of the vastness of our missionary task, its baffling difficulties, the impending critical dangers, and the pressing urgency of the undertaking to make Christ known to all men in our day, nothing less than a marvelous manifestation of superhuman wisdom, superhuman love, and superhuman power will avail. History clearly teaches that such a manifestation is conditioned on the faithfulness of the Christians in prayer. The most highly multiplying thing, therefore, which we can do in this convention, and as we go forth from it, is to seek as never before to enter into the life of intercession and to lead others to join us in the discovery of its boundless possibilities.

JOHN R. MOTT, *Chairman*
J. ROSS STEVENSON, *Vice-Chairman*
CLARA C. BENSON
BERTHA CONDÉ
W. HARLEY SMITH, M.D.
CHARLES D. HURREY
The Executive Committee

REPORT PRESENTED AT
THE EIGHTH INTERNATIONAL CONVENTION
DES MOINES, IOWA, DECEMBER 31, 1919 - JANUARY 4, 1920

THE ACHIEVEMENTS OF THE STUDENT VOLUNTEER MOVEMENT
FOR FOREIGN MISSIONS DURING THE FIRST GENERATION
OF ITS HISTORY — 1886 - 1919

The Student Volunteer Movement for Foreign Missions, which had its rise at Mount Hermon, Massachusetts, in the summer of 1886, has rounded out in the year just closed the first full generation of its life. It is not our purpose to recount at this time the story of its beginning at that first International Student Christian Conference nor to call attention to the more remote springs of this modern student missionary uprising, which has already become world-wide in its scope and influence as in its objective and program. We do wish, however, to record, with reverent gratitude to God, the record of what He has wrought both in and through this Movement. We would that we might "abundantly utter the memory of His great goodness."

At the outset it is well to remind ourselves of the well-established purposes of the Student Volunteer Movement—purposes which have been held in prominence and steadfastly adhered to through all the years: (1) to awaken and maintain among all Christian students of the United States and Canada intelligent and active interest in foreign missions; (2) to enroll a sufficient number of properly qualified volunteers to meet the successive demands of the various mission boards of North America in their effort to give all living men the opportunity to know the Living Christ; (3) to help all such intending missionaries in preparing for their lifework and to enlist their co-operation in developing the missionary life of the colleges and of the home churches; (4) to lay an equal burden of responsibility on all students who are to remain at home as ministers and lay workers, that they may actively promote the missionary enterprise by their intelligent advocacy, by their gifts, and by their prayers.

This Movement is a recruiting agency and summons students to a world-wide crusade. It is not, however, an organization to send missionaries nor does it assume the functions of a missionary-sending agency. It is unswervingly loyal to the Churches. While related organically to the Student Young Men's Christian Association and the Student Young Women's Christian Association movements of the United States and Canada, the Volunteer Movement exists primarily to serve the foreign missionary societies of the North American churches. It is a student movement. The field for which it has ever held itself responsible has been and is the universities, colleges, theological seminaries, medical schools, normal schools, advanced training schools; in short, all institutions of higher learning in the United States and Canada. The field embraces fully 1,000 institutions, which have in them today approximately 300,000 students. The Movement has brought within the range of its helpful influence more colleges than has any other national or international student movement, save the all-embracing World's Student Christian Federation. In the development of the Movement its leaders have endeavored to keep in close touch with the student forces so far as the organization and administration of the work is concerned. The Executive Committee has recently been enlarged to admit of larger representation of students themselves.

From the colleges come the leaders in all influential walks of life. No work could be more important than that of making the student communities strongholds and propagating centers of missionary intelligence, enthusiasm, and activity. The fact that under the influence of this Movement the student class has been enlisted on behalf of the world-wide program of Jesus Christ is, therefore, a fact of the largest possible significance. No other subject has taken such deep hold on the convictions of college men and college women or called forth from them such unselfish devotion. What class of people have believed more strongly in missions than have the students of the generation now under review, as judged by every test? That this is true is due mainly to the comprehensive campaign waged by this Movement through all the recent years. Before college men and college women has been opened the world-wide horizon of Jesus Christ. The chief concern has been to get students to acknowledge the sovereign sway of Christ rather than to urge them to decide to serve Him in any particular part of His Kingdom. This has afforded every student a challenge by which to test his devotion to Christ. Nothing could be more valuable to any student than to be obliged to answer the question whether his loyalty to Christ is limited and fractional or thorough-going, complete, and absolute.

I. The Distinctive Achievement of the Movement

The distinctive achievement of the Student Volunteer Movement has been the enlistment of volunteers for foreign missionary service. It has pressed upon eight successive student generations the claims of foreign missionary service. Formerly the missionaries of North America came almost entirely from a few scores of Christian colleges and seminaries; under the influence of the widespread propaganda of this Movement, they are now drawn from nearly all our institutions of higher learning. Even the colleges which before the Movement began its work yielded the largest number of missionary candidates now with few exceptions furnish much larger numbers. Few Christian students in any part of Canada and the United States have passed through their college life without having been confronted with a presentation of the claims of the missionary career.

Because the Student Volunteer Movement is a movement and because it is a movement for foreign missions, the principal test of its efficiency is found in the going forth of its members to the foreign mission fields. Since the Movement was organized, the records show that 8,140 of the students whom it has enrolled as volunteers have gone out to the mission fields. Of this large number, 2,202 have gone out since the Kansas City Convention six years ago. When it is remembered that this period embraced the World War, the effect of which was to interrupt and contract so much of the missionary work of the world, this showing is indeed remarkable. The going forth of the North American volunteers has been increasing in volume and momentum throughout the thirty-three years of the life of the Movement. In the last eleven years as many sailed as during the preceding twenty-two years; that is, as many went forth in the last one-third of the generation as during the preceding two-thirds.

The 8,140 volunteers who have sailed have gone to virtually all of the battlefields of Christianity throughout the entire non-Christian world. They have been distributed over the world as follows:

Africa	867
Arabia	31
Central America	60
China	2,524
India, Burma, and Ceylon	1,570
Japan and Korea	987
Latin and Greek Countries of Europe	42
Mexico	202
Oceania	68
Persia	76
Philippines	216
Siam and Straits Settlements	155
South America	571
Turkey	270
West Indies	226
Other Countries	275
Total	**8,140**

The Volunteer Movement for some time has furnished approximately 75 per cent of the men missionaries of North America and 70 per cent of the unmarried women missionaries. The proportion would be even larger were it not for the practice of certain missionary societies of sending out non-students as missionaries, whereas the Volunteer Movement enrolls volunteers from the student class only. The sailed volunteers have gone out under the auspices of sixty-six foreign missionary agencies and include members of not less than sixty Christian communions or denominations.

The question has sometimes been raised as to whether most of these volunteers would not have sailed anyhow, regardless of the Volunteer Movement. Repeated investigations have shown that nearly, if not quite, 75 per cent of the volunteers assign the activities of the Movement as the principal or determining factor in their decision to become missionaries, and the others have borne testimony to the influence of the Movement in strengthening their purpose, furthering their preparation, and hastening their going forth to the field. Next to the Christian home the Movement has been the principal factor in influencing life decisions for missions.

The real test of the power of a Movement like this is seen not so much in the remarkably large number of its members who have sailed, as in the greatness of the difficulties which have been overcome by these members in achieving their purpose. The most impressive and highly reassuring chapter in the life of this Movement is the one which tells of the resolute, heroic, and self-sacrificing efforts put forth by countless volunteers in surmounting the difficulties which beset their path—difficulties pertaining to ill health, difficulties related to securing thorough preparation, difficulties involving family ties, difficulties incident to the financial position of the mission boards or due to their ultra-conservative policy as to expansion, difficulties of the most personal character, involving conflicts with temptation, doubt, and selfish ambition. Such hindrances have not been without their great advantages. They have constituted an invaluable drillground for faith and character. Every volunteer worthy of a place on the foreign field has had obstacles in his path. In surmounting them, motives have been purified, faith has been disciplined and strengthened, men have been led to look beyond themselves to God, unworthy candidates have been kept out of the field, the fitttest have survived and pressed to the front. The missionary enterprise does not want and does not need men who can be deflected from their purpose.

One secret of the propulsive power of the Movement has been the fact that from the beginning its leaders have themselves pressed on to the foreign field. Of the members of the Executive Committee and

the secretaries of the Movement who have been volunteers, numbering in all 196, thirty-seven were missionaries on furlough, all the rest
have sailed except fifty-four, and of this number three are under appointment, seven have been declined by their boards for good reasons,
eleven are in preparation, twenty were prevented from going by ill
health, four have died, and the remaining nine are serving on this
year's staff of the Movement.

II. INFLUENCE OF VOLUNTEERS ON THE FIELD

It would be difficult to overstate the far-reaching influence on the
world's evangelization and Christianization exerted by the Movement
through the going forth of these more than 8,000 volunteers. What
have they not accomplished in the way of pioneering new fields and
widening the limits of Christ's Kingdom; in the planting and developing of Christian schools, colleges, and universities; in the opening up
and conducting of missionary hospitals and dispensaries and the in-
stituting of other measures for the relief of the physical sufferings of
countless millions of mankind; in the bringing to bear of the principles
and spirit of Christ upon the economic, social, political, and racial
problems of nations and peoples; in the waging of a ceaseless and well-
nigh world-wide campaign of personal and social evangelism; in the
planting of Christian Churches and the enlisting and training of leaders of the Christian forces; in the shaping of missionary policy and
the exercise of Christian statesmanship! Through their direct and
indirect influence, hundreds of thousands have been converted to the
Christian faith and indigenous Christian forces of propagating and
world-conquering power have been developed. The unwearied labors,
the constructive achievements, the Christlike lives and, in not a few
cases, the martyr deaths of this first generation of North American
volunteers have added an heroic and inspiring chapter to the annals
of the Christian Church.

III. MISSIONARY EDUCATION

One of the outstanding features of the Volunteer Movement,
which has in turn been one of the principal contributory causes of its
growing fruitfulness, has been the evolution of its plan to further the
scientific and progressive study of missions. As a result of much ex-
perimentation in the pathway of its promotion of missionary reading
and discussion during the early years of its history, it was led in the
year 1894 to establish a Mission Study Department and to set apart
a specialist to develop a comprehensive missionary study program.
At that time there were less than a score of groups of young men and
young women in the colleges engaged in what might properly be called

mission study, and these were working apart from each other, without a concerted plan, and without expert guidance. In contrast, last year, in the student field of North America, 47,666 students in nearly 3,000 classes were engaged in the study of missionary subjects under trained leadership. The number in such classes today is nearly twice what it was ten years ago. The Young Men's and Young Women's Christian Associations and the Church boards have had a large and valuable part in making possible this marked advance. The character of the leadership of this work has steadily improved, as a result of normal classes in the various colleges and at the summer training conferences, of the co-operation of hundreds of college and seminary professors, and, above all, of the wise guidance given by the educational secretaries of the Movement.

In connection with the work of the Educational Department, scores of courses, with textbooks, have been prepared. Most of these were written especially for the Movement and among them are a number of notable works. Among those which have had the largest circulation of any publications in the realm of missionary literature are the following: *Dawn on the Hills of T'ang, South American Problems, The Unoccupied Mission Fields, Africa Waiting, Islam, a Challenge to Faith, The Evangelization of the World in This Generation, Social Evils of the Non-Christian World, The Healing of the Nations, Educational Missions, The Foreign Missionary, The Decisive Hour of Christian Missions, Geography and Atlas of Protestant Missions, World Atlas of Christian Missions, The Call of a World Task.*

As a precursor and accompaniment of the development of the mission study activities of the Movement there has been the establishment, under its influence, of hundreds of valuable missionary libraries in the colleges and universities of the United States and Canada. This work of the Movement was one of the influences leading to the establishment of the Missionary Research Library, at 25 Madison Avenue, New York City, which has become the largest and richest collection of missionary literature in the world. Another result of the propaganda conducted by the leaders of the Movement has been the establishment of missionary chairs and lectureships in many colleges and theological seminaries and the introduction of the study of missions into the curricula of many other institutions. Some examples are Yale, the Kennedy School of Missions at Hartford, Princeton Theological Seminary, the Southern Baptist Theological Seminary at Louisville, Drew Theological Seminary, Ohio Wesleyan University, Northwestern University, Union Theological Seminary, the College of Missions in Indianapolis, Vanderbilt University.

As a result of the wise direction given to the mission study feature of its work and the rapid increase in the number of students enrolled in mission study classes and other means of missionary education, there has come over the student body of North America a marked change of attitude toward the subject of missions and toward world problems. Students today have a broader intelligence regarding the social conditions and religious problems, as well as the possibilities of the various non-Christian nations. They feel and manifest a wider sympathy for men of other races. They have been helped to form the true conception, that backward and depressed races and peoples are not to be exploited by stronger nations but are to be served and helped along the pathway of progress and self-determination. They have a larger understanding of the worth as well as the inadequacy of the non-Christian religions and, above all, of the indispensable character and mission of pure Christianity. They entertain a deeper appreciation of the missionary enterprise and of the missionary career. They have come to feel a new sense of responsibility for the evangelization of the world and for the Christianizing of national life and of international and interracial relations. In the pathway of the study of the social and religious problems of foreign lands has come the great development of the study of North American social problems. Thus students are being prepared today as never before for the responsibilities of Church membership and of world citizenship. At a time when such writers as Benjamin Kidd, Viscount Bryce, Ambassador Reinsch, Lord Robert Cecil, General Smuts, Viscount Grey, and President Wilson are emphasizing so strongly the importance of bringing to bear Christian ideals and principles on the pressing world problems, it is highly fortunate and clearly providential that the Student Volunteer Movement has, through its Educational Department, reaching out to every center of learning in North America, introduced means and methods for raising up and educating young men and women for their new world responsibilities.

In holding to its distinctive mission in the realm of missionary education, that of preparing students for determining intelligently and conclusively their relation to the world-wide program of Christ, the Movement has indirectly exerted a wide and profound influence on the promotion of mission study beyond the confines of the colleges and universities. It is within the facts to state that the modern mission study movement was originated by the Student Volunteer Movement. This part of its work led to the corresponding activities of the Central Committee of United Study of Missions of Women's Boards, of the Young People's Missionary Movement, later known as the Missionary Education Movement, and likewise of the Laymen's Missionary Movement. These agencies and others, both at home and abroad, have in turn carried the plans, methods, facilities, and inspiration of mission study far and wide among millions of members of the Christian Church.

IV. Fostering Financial Stewardship

From the beginning, the Movement has been a financial force for missions. A generation ago the combined missionary gifts of the colleges and seminaries were less than $5,000 a year. As a result of constant emphasis on the importance of missionary giving, the gifts of university, college, and seminary constituencies of the two countries have increased year by year until last year they amounted to a little over $300,000. It is a striking fact that during the war period, when the number of students was greatly diminished, the scale of missionary giving was augmented. This is all the more remarkable when it is recalled that during the last three years of the war period the American students gave such large sums in connection with what is known as the Student Friendship Fund, the gifts for this purpose, not to mention other war gifts, being over $200,000 in the year 1916-1917, $1,295,000 in the year 1917-18, and over $2,300,000 in the year 1918-19. Scores of universities and colleges have been encouraged by the Movement to adopt the plan of supporting entirely or in large part their own representative on the foreign field. Never were so many other colleges planning to undertake similar obligations. Some of them, such as Yale, Princeton, and Oberlin, maintain entire mission stations or establishments, each having on its staff several missionaries. The giving in some colleges and schools has been so generous and even sacrificial that it has put to shame the missionary giving in the churches. In some institutions the undergraduates have given on the average $10 to $20 each per annum. Were the giving of the churches on the same scale the financial problem of missions would be solved.

As a result of this feature of the work of the Movement, tens of thousands of students are being trained year by year in habits of systematic and proportionate giving. Large numbers of students have been led to assume the support of one or more representatives on the foreign field, and some of them, as a result of the impulse and education received in their student days, have subsequently given hundreds of thousands of dollars toward missionary objects. Many hundreds of ministers, keeping in mind what was done in their student days in colleges or seminary, have led their churches to become responsible for the support of a missionary or a mission station or institution. Thus, under the influence of the Movement, the centers of learning have become experiment stations and propagating centers for far greater financial achievements for missions than had ever before been contemplated.

REPORTS OF THE EXECUTIVE COMMITTEE

V. CONTRIBUTION TO THE MORAL AND SPIRITUAL LIFE
OF THE COLLEGES

The influence of the Movement on the religious life of the colleges
and universities of North America has been both wide and profound.
It is not too much to say that within the generation the outlook of a
vast majority of Christian students has been changed from the provincial to the cosmopolitan. The words "missionary" and "missions"
mean something entirely different to the student mind today even in
denominational colleges and seminaries from what they connoted to
the preceding generation. Under the influence of the addresses of the
traveling secretaries, of the many mission study and discussion groups
and forums, and of the various student conferences and conventions,
contracted ideas have fast given way to enlarged conceptions of the
grandeur and transcendent possibilities of this greatest work which
confronts the Church of God.

A strong, well-rounded type of character is developed under the
influence of the missionary idea because the missionary spirit is in
reality the spirit of Christ Himself. Where it dominates the thinking
and action of students, they are not only broadened but humanized.
The spirit of brotherhood and unselfishness is manifested. Compassion and love are developed. The missionary challenge appeals to the
spirit of adventure, the heroic, and the sacrificial in students and thus
calls out the strongest strains of their nature. It promotes honesty in
dealing with evidence and, therefore, makes for decision of character
and for a life of reality. It prevents the hardening of sympathy and
conscience by demanding that generous impulses be expressed in action,
instead of being allowed to evaporate. The dominant note of the
Movement, as has already been emphasized, is the recognition of the
Lordship of Jesus Christ. The emphasis on this idea of regarding
one's life not as one's own but as belonging to Christ has done more
to give reality and depth to the religious life of the colleges and seminaries than any idea which has been pressed upon students in the last
three decades.

The work of the Movement has been most wholesome in counteracting the subtle dangers which tend to weaken character and contract
the influence of students. The Volunteer program and spirit are a living protest against the forces of materialism and selfishness as well
as against all that is narrow and intolerant. The summons of the
Movement calling men to stupendous tasks and to lives of stern and
rugged discipline cuts across habits of luxury and the subtle perils of
love of ease. By developing in students the power of vision to realize
and the impulse to respond to the needs and claims of distant nations
and peoples, the Movement renders the greatest possible service to

the home land, for as the late Jacob Riis has pointed out, "every dollar given to foreign countries develops ten dollars' worth of energy for dealing effectively with the tasks at our own doors."

The Student Volunteer Movement has likewise made an enormous contribution to the faith of the students of our day. The vast and overwhelmingly difficult program to which it has summoned them has served to exercise, strengthen, and quicken their faith. Its emphasis upon the fundamental points of the Christian religion has given men a vivid appreciation of the incomparable worth of the Christian Gospel. Through its promotion of fairminded study of the non-Christian religions, it has not only made students aware of the inadequacy of these religions but at the same time has caused to stand out the absolute sufficiency of pure Christianity to meet the needs of the human heart and of the human race. It has shown impressively that only a Christianity powerful enough to conquer the minds and hearts of the followers of the non-Christian religions in Asia and Africa, can show itself able to meet the deepest needs in the life of the United States and Canada. The influence of the example of thousands of volunteers thinking enough of their own religion to go forth to propagate it with conviction in the homes of the non-Christian religions is in itself an apologetic which has led many unbelieving students to investigate afresh the claims of Christ and to yield themselves to Him. We are just beginning to recognize also the rich apologetic value of the work of the Volunteer Movement through its presentation to students of the world-wide, vital, and triumphant power of the Living Christ.

The great war revealed as never before the limitless capacities of the students of our generation. There were disclosed within them latent powers of courageous and unselfish effort, of capacity for extreme sacrifice, of ability to lose themselves in great causes, of power of initiative, leadership, and co-operation, which, if released and related to the great plans of Christ for all mankind, would make possible an absolutely unprecedented and hitherto unbelievable expansion of His Kingdom. The missionary program alone furnishes an adequate outlet for these newly disclosed and well-nigh boundless energies. It is not surprising that the strongest students, under the spell of the attraction of hard things, have been dedicating themselves in increasing numbers to the missionary career.

VI. INFLUENCE OF DETAINED VOLUNTEERS
AND OF NON-VOLUNTEERS

It speaks much for the spirit of genuineness in the Volunteer Movement that its detained volunteers have likewise been a mighty power in the world. The thoroughgoing volunteer who has been providentially hindered does not become discouraged or self-indulgent. Instead of losing his interest in the Movement and renouncing its ideals, he rather redoubles his efforts and seeks to devote his life on the home field to backing up the missionary enterprise as earnestly as he would have done had he been privileged to hasten to the front. Thus hundreds of hindered volunteers have thrown themselves with added intensity into home missionary work in frontier fields of the United States and Canada or in needy metropolitan or suburban parishes. Not a few of them who have been detained have exerted as teachers or as pastors a wonderful influence in raising up volunteers and in furthering the missionary plans of the Churches. It is an impressive fact that a large proportion of the most influential secretaries of both the foreign and home mission boards of these two countries are either hindered volunteers or students whose point of view and spirit were profoundly influenced by the Volunteer Movement. A number of them have been permitted to spend a part of their lives on the foreign field and it is characteristic of most of them that they never wholly abandon the hope that the way may yet open for them to go forth again to proclaim Christ where He has not been named.

A study of the causes which have influenced students to enter the Christian ministry and other distinctively religious callings on the home field reveals the strong reflex influence exerted by the Movement. A multitude of young men and young women to whom the way did not providentially open to go abroad have under the power of the volunteer appeal dedicated themselves to Christ's service at home. Moreover, each volunteer stands for more than one volunteer. He represents a number of student friends and classmates who, because of his example, or better, because of the reasons which influenced his life decision, will with conviction back him and the missionary enterprise itself. Indeed, one of the most encouraging developments in the last decade of the period under review has been this recognition on the part of students, who have not considered themselves called of God to be either foreign missionaries or pastors, that it is equally their duty as laymen to spend their lives for the sake of world evangelization and Christianization. If the message of Jesus Christ is to be taken to every part of the world in our lifetime, it is absolutely imperative that the entire body of Christian students of this generation see eye to eye and work as one mind to this end. In the early part of the generation there was a tendency among students to look upon the active promotion of the missionary movement as something quite outside the ordinary Christian life. They assumed that to extend Christ's Kingdom was purely optional and the peculiar duty of clergymen and missionaries. The Volunteer Movement pressed upon them the truth that an

active missionary spirit is inseparable from a genuine Christian life
and that a man might well question whether he is a Christian at all if
he finds himself indifferent to making Christ accessible to all mankind
Therefore, the fact that the old antithesis between the claims of the
home and the foreign fields has so largely disappeared is highly re
assuring. Next to the need of students dedicated to the work of foreign
missions is the need of young men and young women who stay at home
for the express purpose of developing on this continent the strongest
possible base for the maintenance of the world-wide Christian cam
paign. To stay at home for any lower reason would defeat the object
of the Movement and at the same time impoverish the lives of those
who hold aloof from carrying out the inspiring plans of Christ for His
Kingdom in the hearts of all men.

VII. Far-reaching Influence of Volunteer Conventions

It has been the custom of the Student Volunteer Movement to
hold a great international convention once in each student generation
of approximately four years. The chain of these gatherings is as
follows:

City	Year	Attendance
Cleveland	1891	680
Detroit	1894	1,325
Cleveland	1898	2,221
Toronto	1902	2,957
Nashville	1906	4,235
Rochester	1910	3,747
Kansas City	1914	5,031

Owing to the war a wider interval has elapsed since the last convention. Those who are most familiar with these gatherings and with
the outreach of their influence regard them as having been among the
most creative and potent of all the influences set in motion by the
Movement. They go further and insist that had the Movement done
nothing else than make possible these large, representative, and vital
assemblies of the coming leaders of the nations, it would have justified
its existence. It is true that the Volunteer conventions hold a unique
place in the life of the students of North America. They have literally
marked epochs in the missionary and religious life of the colleges of
Canada and the United States. They are the touchstone to all that
pertains to widest vision, to highest ideals, and to most highly multiplying influence. They have done more than any other one thing to
make vivid and commanding the world-wide program of Christianity.
They have also been the principal factor in enabling the students of
North America to recognize not only the wholeness but likewise the

oneness of the task confronting North American Christian forces as they face the non-Christian world as well as the unchristian aspects of our own civilization. Moreover, these gatherings have enabled the American and Canadian students to realize their spiritual solidarity. In a gathering like this, where we have represented almost every university and college of all the American states and Canadian provinces, we come to appreciate afresh that we of these two young Anglo-Saxon lands have behind us a common tradition in the deepest things of life—those that pertain to religion, language, and laws that we are inspired by common ideals and destinies, that we are summoned to share common responsibilities in extending throughout the world the limits of Christ's Kingdom. This solidarity has come to mean something richer and more profound as a result of the common, sacred experience which has tinged with blood and tears the recent fateful years.

In addition to these great international conventions, it should be pointed out that each year there assemble in various regional summer conferences of the Student Young Men's Christian Association and the Student Young Women's Christian Association of the United States and Canada and in different state and district conferences of the Student Volunteer Movement not less than 10,000 students and professors to prepare themselves for efficient leadership of the Christian activities in the colleges and universities. These gatherings constitute an invaluable recruiting ground for the Volunteer Movement as well as opportunities for furthering its other high aims. Grateful recognition should also be given to the series of Student Volunteer conferences which have been conducted in the British Isles and to similar gatherings which have been held on the continent of Europe, in Australia, and in South Africa under the auspices of the Student Missionary Movements of these lands. These gatherings have meant to the students of those parts of the world what our volunteer conventions have meant to the student life of North America.

VIII. Influence of the Movement Upon Students of Other Lands

The Student Volunteer Movement of North America has sent out powerful waves of influence to the student life of other lands. The religious life of the North American and British universities interacted for many years especially through the visits of certain religious leaders; for example, the visits of Mr. Moody to the British universities in the 70's and early 80's, the visit of Henry Drummond and of J. E. K. Studd to American colleges somewhat later, and through visits made by British students to Northfield. The story of the Cambridge band early served to kindle missionary interest and faith among American students. After the inauguration of the Volunteer Movement on this side of the Atlantic, Mr. Wilder and Mr. Forman, its founders, were possibly the chief human instruments in bringing about the organization along similar lines of what first became known as the Student Volunteer Missionary Union of the British Isles. This organization has accomplished a wonderful work in the colleges of Great Britain and Ireland and has exerted a great influence on the missionary life of the Churches. Under its influence over 2,000 student volunteers have sailed in connection with various missionary societies of the British Isles. Its series of missionary conferences as well as the visits of its members have constituted one of the chief factors in transplanting the volunteer idea to the universities of the Continent, especially to those of Holland, France, Switzerland, and Germany.

The visits of Mr. Wilder had much to do with quickening the missionary interest, activity, and consecration of the students of Norway, Sweden, Denmark, and Finland, and later of other student fields of the Continent. Representatives of the North American Movement were instrumental in transplanting the Volunteer Movement to the universities of Australia and New Zealand and a joint deputation of American and British student leaders rendered a similar service in South Africa.

A most significant development was that which came through the visits of American student workers to Asia, resulting in the raising up from among students a large number of volunteers for the ministry. This impulse has been strengthened through the years in India, Ceylon, China, Japan, Korea, the Levant, and native South Africa by the increasing number of volunteers who have gone out to these fields from the United States, Canada, Great Britain, the Continent, and Australasia. The most fruitful of these indigenous movements is that in China where, under the Christlike leadership of Ding Li-mei, within the past few years hundreds of Chinese students have been led to dedicate their lives to the Christian ministry. While these movements on the mission field are primarily concerned with recruiting for home missions, they all share with the Movement of so-called Christian countries its world-wide vision and purpose.

Next in point of missionary importance to the student missionary uprising itself, was the organization of the World's Student Christian Federation in Sweden in 1895 which today federates all the Christian Student Movements of the world. This has greatly facilitated the interchange of ideas and experience among students of the nations and has thus made it possible for each national Student Movement to make its missionary influence most powerfully felt in other parts of the world. The Federation, in binding together the coming leaders of all lands and races, and focussing their attention and influence on the evangelization and Christianization of the whole world, is rendering an inestimable service to Christian missions.

Thus we have seen realized within our day the word of prophecy uttered by the Executive Committee of the Volunteer Movement in their report at the first Volunteer convention, held in Cleveland in 1891, in which they said: "If the students of the Protestant world were linked together by the power of the Spirit in this Movement, it would greatly hasten the establishment of Christ's Kingdom through-out the world." The late Dr. George Smith, of Edinburgh, in an address some time ago, acknowledged this great contribution of the Student Volunteer Movement in these apt words, "The Movement has created a Christian nucleus which in East and West has made every college in its degree a missionary institute or a missionary station."

IX. Reflex Influence Upon Home Churches

The Student Volunteer Movement has sown much seed beyond its self-appointed student fields and this seed has already brought forth fruit. Special attention should be called to the influence which it has exerted upon the Churches of North America. From the beginning of its life it appealed powerfully to the imagination of the North American churches. At a time when vast multitudes of church members were indifferent to the missionary obligation, the sudden uprising of the student missionary host presented a living, irresistible challenge. The first volunteer bands sent their members out to speak in the churches and this plan has continued to be followed as the Movement has grown in numbers. Many thousands of student volunteers and of other earnest Christian students under their guidance have brought into the churches their commanding world vision, their kindling enthusiasm and their life dedication to the world plans of their Divine Master. In season and out of season they have proclaimed their watchword, "The Evangelization of the World in This Generation." This new missionary challenge and program have come with quickening power to the churches and have done much to enlarge their faith and call forth their sacrificial devotion.

Soon after the beginning of the Volunteer Movement, America experienced a rather prolonged period of financial stringency. This had its effect in contracting the missionary plans of the churches. It bade fair to exert a chilling influence on the new and burning missionary zeal kindled by the Movement. In fact, the secretary of one of the leading mission boards urged on an important occasion, although doubtless with great reluctance, "We must bank the fires of the Student Volunteer Movement." At a time like that the Volunteer Movement furnished the churches an appeal which never failed to call forth self-sacrificing liberality. Hundreds of volunteers went among the churches, saying, "We have given our lives to the missionary career; we want to go to the field; the mission boards cannot send us. Will you send us as your representatives or substitutes under the boards?" Hundreds of congregations, families, and individuals found it impossible to resist such an appeal, and assumed, often through deep and rewarding sacrifice, the financial support of such workers. In fact, it was the volunteers who introduced the living link idea; that is, the plan of an individual or a family or a parish supporting a missionary, or a mission station, or institution. The leaders and members of the Movement elaborated this plan in pamphlets which were circulated in countless communities. The leaders of the mission boards recognized this unique service and repeatedly expressed their deep appreciation. The practice of many an American and Canadian volunteer might well be expressed in the following description of Samuel J. Mills, that first student volunteer of the North American continent: "When not ready to go to the foreign field, he could not wait in idleness. No dreams of a field more to his liking kept him from tilling the field at his feet. He waited not for an opportunity to turn up; he made the opportunity. He made himself master of facts and used them as shot and shell to beat down the walls of carelessness and indifference."

Through all the thirty-three years of the life of the Movement the volunteers have interested themselves especially in the young people of the churches. Volunteer bands were in the habit of sending deputations to work in the young people's societies, seeking to spread missionary information, to promote the study of missionary books, and to lead young people into right habits of giving and of prayer for missions. At every Volunteer convention it was likewise customary to have present official representatives of the young people's movements. Thus the Volunteer Movement and these young people's movements have always regarded themselves as complementary to each other. The thought was that the millions who made up the membership of the young people's organizations should send the thousands who constituted the membership of the Volunteer Movement. At a later stage leading members of the Volunteer Movement initiated what came to be known as the Student Missionary Campaign, beginning in 1898 with the activities of Dr. F. C. Stephenson in the Methodist Church in Canada, and of Mr. F. S. Brockman and Mr. S. Earl Taylor among the Methodist bodies in the United States. It was not long until similar projects were launched in a score of denominations. This led ultimately to the formation of the Young People's Missionary Movement in 1902, later known as the Missionary Education Movement, an agency which has accomplished untold good in influencing the missionary ideals and activities of the new generation. The leaders of these various denominational and interdenominational missionary activities among young people were student volunteers or men and women who bore testimony that they had received much of their vision and training from the Volunteer Movement.

A layman, Mr. John B. Sleman of Washington, who attended the Volunteer Convention in Nashville in 1906, conceived while there the idea of rallying the lay forces of the American and Canadian Churches to make possible the sending forth in larger numbers of student volunteers. As a result of his obedience to that vision, there was organized in the month of November of that year the Laymen's Missionary Movement of the United States and Canada. Subsequently it led to the formation of similar movements in Great Britain, in Australasia, and on the Continent of Europe. It came at a providential moment to help prepare the North American churches for the immeasurably greater opportunities and responsibilities which crowded the subsequent years. In the Laymen's Movement in North America and elsewhere, it is significant that many of the moving spirits were those who, like its founder, received their impulse from the Volunteer Movement.

It is not too much to state that the splendid missionary leadership now being given the Churches of North America is traceable chiefly, under God, to the thirty-three years of unresting missionary propaganda waged by the Volunteer Movement. During this entire period it has been the exception when there has not been at least one visit made each year in each theological seminary as well as in each college by some accredited, capable representative of the Movement. This means that the vast majority of the educated young men who are now in the home ministry have been exposed to the vision, program, challenge, and passion of the Volunteer Movement. Most of them have also come under the influence of its conferences and conventions and have done intensive study in its classes and discussion groups. It would be surprising, therefore, had the Movement not exerted a profound and truly formative influence on the preaching, the planning, and the spirit of the leaders of the churches.

X. INFLUENCE ON MISSIONARY STATESMANSHIP AND ACTION

The Volunteer Movement has exerted an enormous influence on missionary thinking, missionary policy, and missionary action in the various fields. The hundreds of volunteer bands, the thousands of mission study classes, the countless training institutes and conferences and the international conventions have throughout the generation resulted in raising up in all the churches scientific students of the wide range of questions involved in the extension of the Christian religion. At the most plastic or formative time in the character and thought-life of young men and young women, a multitude have been trained to think deeply and courageously on these questions. Their thinking has been stimulated and guided by the foremost missionary scholars of modern times, who, by the initiative of the Movement, have been brought to the colleges, seminaries, and conferences in order that the young student life might have the benefit of their knowledge and experience and come under the influence of their personalities. The hundreds of traveling secretaries who have been chosen from the ranks of the leading students of the day or from the returned missionaries of most progressive spirit have also been a great factor in the widening and deepening of the mental processes of the student volunteers and of those who were destined to become leaders of the Christian forces on the home field. All this has resulted in introducing into the mission fields an element of statesmanship already well-advanced. The student volunteers scattered over the mission fields have taken a position of leadership in the most comprehensive surveys which have been made and in the furthering of the scientific study of the missionary problems. The same might be said of the home field, particularly in Anglo-Saxon countries.

The volunteers have been most active in the past generation in pushing into unoccupied regions. The Volunteer Movement leaders have on home platforms and through the printed page been the principal advocates on behalf of the unoccupied fields of the world. It is not strange that their appeals have influenced adventurous and heroic spirits to become missionary pioneers in neglected parts of Asia and Africa. The now generally accepted idea of the duty and possibility of the complete and prompt occupation of each field and of the world as a whole was derived in large measure from the Volunteer watchword and from the persistent emphasis placed upon it in all the gatherings and activities of the Movement. The ideal of the world's evangelization has done much to kindle the membership of the Movement with the passion of evangelism and on nearly every field student volunteers are among the most fruitful reapers. The largest ingatherings among the educated classes have been secured through their leadership.

The leaders of the Movement have ever placed the emphasis on developing indigenous leadership in the lands where its members are serving. The volunteers have helped to plant and develop native student movements which in great fields like China have become most hopeful factors in the life of rising churches. In India, the National Missionary Society is an indirect result of the work of the Indian

Student Movement. The volunteers have done much toward elevating able native workers to places of real leadership in the churches. They have also promoted a feeling and attitude of democracy and fellowship in the relations between the native and the foreign workers. In the keenness of their desire to help each people to make its own contribution to the life and spiritual wealth of the Church, they have greatly promoted larger understanding and sympathy.

Volunteers have during the past two or three decades been among the foremost leaders and at times initiators of forward missionary movements, both on the foreign field and at the home base. We need only recall the forward-looking and aggressive plans projected during this period in the national and international conferences of missionaries in the Orient and in the Occident. They have been particularly active and helpful in promoting co-operation and unity among the Christian forces. The Volunteer Movement came into being a number of years before the mission boards of North America or Europe had established any stated forum for interdenominational discussion of missionary problems or any plan for interdenominational study and investigation of missionary questions. Indeed, the Volunteer Movement had its first international convention before the Annual Conference of Foreign Mission Boards of North America held its first meeting. For over a quarter of a century, during which there has been developing an increasing co-operative procedure on the part of the mission boards, such development has been paralleled by the growing activities of the Volunteer Movement, which have been preparing the student volunteers to make effective on the mission field the co-operative purposes and processes of their own mission boards. It would be impossible for the student volunteers to spend from four to ten years in the intimate spiritual fellowship and united service of student days at home and then, after reaching the field of their lifework, to lose touch and fall apart. The enduring bonds of friendship and esteem of college days still unite them. They never wholly lose the spell of the missionary vision which came to them together and commanded their united devotion in their early years. Animated in the most plastic days of their lives by common purposes, familiar with each other's points of view, and accustomed to grapple with common tasks, they inevitably have stood together in the great conflict at the front. Face to face with the powerfully entrenched systems of the non-Christian religions, of unbelief and of sin, they have come to believe with deep conviction that the cause of Christ must present an unbroken front.

The Student Volunteer Movement has ever stood, not for undenominationalism, but for interdenominationalism. Its leaders believe in the providential character and mission of the various Christian communions or denominations; and, in their administration of the Movement as well as in their personal life and influence, they have sought not in vain to strengthen the hands of the various churches. But with similar conviction and devotion they have recognized the desirability and necessity of concerted thinking and effort to further those processes which tend to draw together in common understanding and triumphant unity of action all true disciples of Jesus Christ. It may be questioned whether there is any other one unifying influence among Christians which is today more potent than that of the life and work of the 8,000 American and Canadian student volunteers and the nearly 3,000 British, Australasian, South African, and Continental European volunteers, who constitute over one-third of the foreign missionaries of the world. From widely different angles, they are working toward certain common goals, and in their spirit and work present to an unbelieving world one of the most dynamic of the apologetics of Christianity. Dr. Temple, late Archbishop of Canterbury, father of William Temple, in commenting on this Movement, said, "The recognition of the common task imposed upon every variety of Christian belief will be likely indeed to do more to bring us all into one than any other endeavor that we may make." Many of the leaders of interdenominational movements in fields like China, Japan, India, and Latin America, as well as at the home bases in North America, in Europe, and in the Southern Hemisphere are volunteers of former days.

XI. Most Notable Contributions of the Movement

One of the foremost thinkers of Europe has recently raised the question: What has been the most distinctive contribution of the Student Volunteer Movement? Some would insist that the idea of the Volunteer Declaration, "It is my purpose, if God permit, to become a foreign missionary," has been the contribution of largest power. It is true that there would have been no continuous and ever-expanding Volunteer Movement with all of its abounding fruitage had it not been for the clear-cut, unequivocal statement of personal purpose which has done so much to burn the bridges behind and to carry resolute men and women across seas and over mountains of difficulties. Those words, so simple and yet so full of meaning, epitomizing as they do the soul struggles, the life resolution, and the commanding vision of so many thousands of students, have resulted in pushing out within our day on every continent the wide limits of Christ's Kingdom. Without doubt, the strength of the Movement is and ever will be in its appeal for life.

Others would maintain that the principal contribution of the

Movement has been the solidarity which it has developed among its members and the members of kindred movements throughout the world. Boundless indeed are the possibilities for Christ's Kingdom of having in the leadership of the aggressive forces of Christianity throughout the foreign battlefields thousands of men and women who share the same vision, who are commanded by the same purpose, who have developed in such large measure the ability to co-operate and who have so largely communicated their spirit of unity and spiritual conquest to the tens of thousands of their non-volunteer fellow students of all lands and races.

XII. The Watchword

Still others, and their number seems to be by far the greatest, believe that the most distinctive, the most original, most daring, and most truly notable contribution of the Volunteer Movement has been its watchword, "The Evangelization of the World in This Generation." While the history of this idea shows that it has recurred and been emphasized from time to time since the early days of Christianity, it was not until the Volunteer Movement, almost on the threshold of its career, adopted it formally as its great motive ideal and thenceforth waged a persistent propaganda in its advocacy, that it could be said to have become a power in the missionary life of the churches. When it was first proclaimed by the Movement, it met with distrust and opposition. It has grown steadily in favor among both the volunteers and other Christian students and has been accepted increasingly by leaders of the churches. Christians everywhere have come to recognize that there is a responsibility resting upon each generation of Christians to make the gospel fully known to the non-Christians of their own generation. They know of no reason which commends itself to their judgment and conscience why they should not put forth a resolute and sustained effort to make Christ known to every living man, and the conviction ever deepens that this great claim of the non-Christian world upon them can be fulfilled, if the Church will but give itself to the task.

The question has been raised in one quarter whether it might not be wise to abandon the watchword, in view of the fact that a full generation has gone and the world still remains unevangelized. This reveals evident misunderstanding. From the beginning the Movement has insisted that, although the watchword was to be taken as an ideal for the Movement as a whole, the secret of realizing it lay in having a sufficient number not only of individual student volunteers, but also of other individual Christians, adopt it as their personal watchword and as a governing principle in their lives. Who will deny that, had a sufficient number of Christians accepted the watchword as their own, the necessary vital facts about Christ might have been brought during the generation within the comprehension of all men? Judged by the influence the watchword has had upon the lives of those who have accepted it, it seems entirely reasonable to infer that, had Christians far more widely been brought under its influence, this great ideal might have been translated from theory into fact.

The history of the Movement shows that there are great advantages in having such a watchword as a commanding ideal. The fact that it is a startling phrase, calling for explanation, has arrested the attention of earnest men and stimulated their thought regarding Christ's great program for the world. It has emphasized as has no other one thing the urgency of the world's evangelization. It constantly reminds men that the missionary problem is a living one—one which living men have to face on behalf of men now living. It does not present an academic problem but one which is personal and pressing. It keeps men asking themselves the question: Are we doing all that we can to reach our living brothers? It is a stirring reminder that our plan must embrace the whole world and that we must act without delay. None recognize so keenly the necessity and value of this aspect of the watchword as do volunteers at the front, face to face with the crisis which there confronts the Church. The watchword is a vast and bold challenge, which appeals, therefore, with special force to heroic men—men who shrink not from most difficult undertakings. It has called out the latent energies of the students of the generation as has no other challenge ever presented to them.

Contrary to the impression of some, the watchword has promoted thoroughness. Its advocates have clearly seen that the task to be accomplished is so vast and so difficult that nothing short of the most thorough processes will avail. They also early recognized that the principal human factor in the undertaking is the native Church and therefore they have emphasized the slow but sure process of building it up at whatever cost of labor and money. None have made stronger deliverances against superficiality than volunteers who have been governed by the watchword.

The watchword has widely promoted unity and co-operation, because the very magnitude and difficulty of the task have helped to draw together the coming leaders of the Christian forces. It has led to a larger discovery of God and to deepening acquaintance with Him, and has for an increasing number lifted the whole missionary enterprise to the superhuman plane. Its emphasis upon the whole world, including all races and peoples, has disclosed to many a larger Christ and a larger Gospel. They have come to see that each race of mankind has some fresh contribution of thought, character, and experience to make, and that only as each race has had opportunity to learn of Christ can it make these contributions. How desirable it is that the Church should avail itself as soon as possible of all that nations as yet spiritually unborn are able to interpret of Christ's excellences and to communicate of His power!

If such a watchword has been appropriate in the past, what shall we not say of its aptness and timeliness for the present day! With the ending of the great world convulsion, the Church has come into a time of unprecedented opportunity. Never has there been a day when simultaneously in so many parts of the world the doors were so wide open as now. It is a time of unprecedented danger, because of the new forces, which have recently been released. Above all, it is a time of unprecedented urgency, owing to the fact that so many nations are in a plastic and changing condition, owing to the revived spirit of nationalism and racial patriotism, owing to the rapid spread of the corrupt influences of western civilization, owing to the dangerous tendencies in connection with the non-Christian religions and, on the other hand, owing to the recent unparalleled triumphs of Christianity and the rising tide of spiritual success on every hand and the possibility of entering into the marvelous heritage prepared by the recent period of thorough preparation. Why has God made the world known and accessible today as never before? Why has He provided such extensive and well-equipped missionary agencies at the home base and on the foreign field in our day? Why has He placed such boundless resources at the disposal of the Church? Surely such vast preparations have been made for some great and commensurate purpose. Can we question, in view of the character of God and the present state of the world, that it is His will that the whole field be occupied and evangelized in our day, and that, however difficult and vast the undertaking, there are resources in our Lord Jesus Christ, and latent in His followers, available and sufficient to enable them to carry out that will?

XIII. CHRISTIANIZING INTERNATIONAL RELATIONSHIPS

There are multiplying evidences that the Volunteer Movement has been exerting a much-needed influence toward Christianizing the impact of North America on the non-Christian world. The widely pervasive work of the Movement has not been without its powerful effect on the ideals and character of students entering the so-called secular pursuits. They, in common with the students entering the missionary career, have caught visions of Christ's Kingdom and have begun to recognize their responsibility to further its world-wide extension. From among these educated men, thousands have gone forth to all quarters of the world. Many of them are responsible leaders in industrial and commercial undertakings who within the sphere of their daily calling have sought to commend Christianity. Not a few others in the diplomatic and consular service of the United States and the British Empire have rendered great services not only in safeguarding missionary interests but also in bearing faithful witness to Christ among officials of non-Christian nations. We may also well be proud of the courageous Christian influence which has been exerted by officers and enlisted men of the Army and Navy who received their original Christian impulse through the Volunteer Movement and the closely related Student Association movement. It has become the practice of sons and daughters of well-to-do families to make journeys to various parts of Asia, Africa, and Latin America and it has been gratifying to observe that many of these, who at home had felt the influence of the student movement, have, while abroad, done much to further the missionary work. One of the most highly multiplying influences has been that exerted by the students who have gone out to these foreign lands to serve as teachers in government and other secular schools. Possibly the greatest factor in the Christianizing of the relations of the United States and Canada with non-Christian people has been the friendliness shown to foreign students studying in the American and Canadian universities and colleges. There are now fully 10,000 such students, representing all nations, enrolled in our institutions. Many of them are here as a result of the efforts of missionaries recruited by the Volunteer Movement. Their character and achievements are mightily affecting the attitude and spirit of American students; social prejudice is being overcome and a new respect is being engendered for those of different national and religious viewpoints. Moreover, the Christian students among us from other lands are greatly strengthening the appeal for volunteers. Irresistible is their call to participate in a genuine co-operative effort on behalf of their people. The Volunteer Movement, working hand in hand with the Student Young Men's and Young Women's Christian Associations and especially under the wise leadership of the Committee to Promote Friendly Relations among Foreign Students, has influenced profoundly these future leaders of the non-Christian world. These strangers and friends within our gates have been most open and responsive to such fraternal influences. Many of them have thus been exposed to the best side of our civilization. They have been led to look beneath the surface and to see that what they most value in North American life and institutions is traceable to Christ and His teachings and that what they, in common with ourselves, most deplore is due not to Christ but to the lack of Christ. As a result, hundreds of them have been influenced to investigate His teachings and to identify themselves with His program and service. Much has been done to promote international and interracial understanding and goodwill. In fact, it may be questioned whether among all the influences at work today to Christianize international relations and to put vital, unselfish content into the new international arrangements which are taking shape in the world, there is one comparable in importance to that exerted by this and the other phases of the all-embracing Christian Student Movement in its splendid, constructive, and fraternal efforts to lead the future leaders of all lands and all races to realize in Christ their essential unity.

XIV. The Springs of Power

The Volunteer Movement at the end of thirty-three years is strong and vital and never more so. Why has it gone from strength to strength all these years and what has been the secret of its productive power? The true answer to this penetrating question will point the way to the larger achievements which lie before the student missionary uprising. In the first place, its personnel has been made up of those who are young and vigorous, whose minds are educated and whose lives are consecrated to the service of God and man. Its members have been fired with undying enthusiasm and have ever been responsive to new and larger visions and plans. Their eyes have been fixed on the coming day and they have never lost the first flush of optimistic hope.

Vigilant and constant supervision has been one of the prices paid for the growing fruitfulness of the Movement. Only one year was it left without administrative direction and in that short time it broke into parts and its impact on the college life of the continent was greatly weakened. The lesson, however, was learned and ever since the Movement has had the benefit of wise guidance. In this connection attention should be called to the mutual benefits which have obtained from the close organic relation which has ever existed between the Volunteer Movement on the one hand and the Young Men's Christian Association and the Young Women's Christian Association of the United States and Canada on the other. Throughout the whole generation they have acted and reacted most helpfully upon each other. Moreover, the Movement has had the invaluable counsel of trusted leaders of the foreign mission boards of the churches. It has regarded itself as their servant and has never lost touch with them. Now that so many of the boards have candidate secretaries or departments closely articulated with the Movement, and now that so many of their administrative officers are men or women who were once volunteers or whose early lives were profoundly influenced by the Movement, this relationship has become closer than ever.

Through all the years the Movement has focussed its energies on its distinctive work, that of recruiting men and women for the missionary career. It has furnished a splendid example of undeflected energy. Time after time efforts have been made to induce it to interest itself in other objects or to broaden or weaken its purpose but it has held without wavering to its objective and has continued to find its strength in the appeal for life.

The Student Volunteer Movement has been preserved from stagnation because it has kept a continuous human stream flowing out from the American and Canadian universities to the nations of the earth. This has made possible the preservation of its reality, its contagious enthusiasm, and its world-conquering power. Had it not thus preserved its crusading character, it would, like so many other organizations, have stagnated and died.

The path of boldness is the path of growth. The Student Volunteer Movement addressed itself to a colossal task which made an heroic appeal. In undertaking to give all people now living an adequate opportunity to know the Living Christ, and in adopting the audacious program of making the reign of Christ co-extensive with the inhabited earth, it confronted the students of the world with a challenge great and bold enough to call out their latent capacities and to command their extreme devotion.

The realization of the watchword of the Movement has necessitated its traveling by the way of the Cross. In those colleges and seminaries and in those countries where its leaders have recognized this most clearly, the spirit of the Movement has been preserved in greatest purity and in truly world-conquering power. The program of the Movement might well be characterized as a campaign of unselfishness. It has never sought to develop into a permanent organization or to become an end in itself. In a sense it has violated all canons of building up a strong organization in that every year of its life it has pushed out to foreign lands nearly all of its leaders. Its ambition has been not to perfect an organization but to lose itself in the world's greatest cause. Thus it has expressed itself through many Christian communions and through countless Christian organizations and agencies. It has decreased; they have increased. It is this deep, sacrificial strain running through all its activities which goes so far to explain its multiplying power. "Except a grain of wheat fall into the ground and die it abideth by itself alone; but if it die it bringeth forth much fruit."

The true source of the vital energy of the Movement has been its relation, through the exercise of prayer, to the Source of all life and power. The streams that turn the machinery of the world rise in solitary places. The origins of this incomparable offering of life lie in secret places—in the lives of individual students in communion with the Living God. The Movement assumed visible, corporate expression in the never-to-be-forgotten gatherings for united prayer of the undergraduates at Mount Hermon. Every onward impulse in its career was generated in prayer. Everything vital or essential to its triumphant progress among the nations—the separating of workers, the thrusting them forth as God-sent men, the overcoming of apparently insuperable obstacles, the coming upon them of accessions of superhuman power, the manifesting through them of the Spirit of Christ, the fountain of all the real beauty that is in the world, the laying of the foundations and raising of the walls of the Kingdom of Christ among the nations—these and everything else bearing the Divine marks are traceable to prayer. Jesus Christ is at once the attractive and the impelling force of the Movement. It is occupied with His program. It acknowledges Him as its Divine Leader. In so far as it humbles itself and yields itself to His sway, He will continue to be its productive power. "A body of free men who love God with all their might, and yet know how to cling together, could conquer this modern world of ours."

On behalf of the Executive Committee
JOHN R. MOTT, *Chairman*

PART THREE

ADDRESSES AND PAPERS OF THE CHAIRMAN

✤✤

ADDRESSES AND PAPERS OF THE CHAIRMAN

✠✠

THE PURPOSE OF THE CONVENTION

ADDRESS DELIVERED AT
THE STUDENT VOLUNTEER CONVENTION
KANSAS CITY, MISSOURI, DECEMBER 31, 1913

IT IS WELL, as we enter upon this wonderful convention, that we pause to remind ourselves of the purposes which have brought us together. Why have we traveled from virtually every state and every province of North America to come here? Why have there come among us fraternal delegates from the nations of Europe? Why have we among us those who have been warriors on nearly all of the battle-fields of the Christian Church? Why have the responsible leaders of the aggressive forces of the Christian religion laid aside their work to come and sit with us and to counsel with us? Why have the editors of the religious press and the representatives of the secular press identified themselves with this great convention?

We have come here in order to face the wholeness of the task which confronts the forces of Christianity as they look into the non-Christian world. Necessarily, each one of us has been largely occupied with a fraction of the work before our religion. It is well that we should have an opportunity like this which, as no other opportunity that comes in North America, enables us to come into one another's presence and to view the great task in its complexity, in its entirety, as Jesus Christ, the founder of our religion, views it. This will necessarily enlarge us, widen our vision, expand our hearts, enrich our characters, send us away with fuller purposes and with higher ideals.

We have come here, also, in order to accentuate the oneness of the task in which we are all interested; not only to view the wholeness of the undertaking, but to remind ourselves that we who acknowledge Jesus Christ as our Lord, and who honestly desire to become more and more like Him, and who have as our ambition to make His reign co-extensive with the inhabited earth, are all one, no matter how we may feel, and no matter what we may think; that being one in those essentials, we are one actually. It is well to accentuate this fact.

We are here also to realize—notice the language—to realize the spiritual solidarity of the Christian students of North America, and to remind ourselves also of a larger unity, one that binds us to the Christian students of other lands and other races. Happily, you and I live in a generation in which there is a world-wide Christian Student Movement. Ours is one of the first generations of which this could be said. We are to be envied by the students of other generations, in that our lines have been cast in a time when this spiritual solidarity takes on a larger meaning and a greater momentum than at any time in the past. Not at Northfield, not at Silver Bay, not at Lake Geneva, not at Black Mountain, not at Asheville, or on the Pacific coast, either in California or in the Northwest; not in any of these other gatherings of the United States and Canada can we realize this vast spiritual solidarity as at this gathering which comes only once in each student generation; which draws into one great assemblage the representatives of all of the divisions and movements of the Christian student organizations of the United States and Canada, with delegates of the student movements of other nations, enabling us to catch and feel the pulse, too, of those wonderful uprisings of the Christian students and professors of the nations of the world, to make Christ king. Let us realize all this in its fullness these days.

We are here, also, to emphasize—I would go further and say we are here to demonstrate—the reality, the vitality, and the conquering power of our religion. Nothing so emphasizes this as coming together and discussing with the leaders of the aggressive forces of Christianity of all the continents of the world the program of Christ. Here we shall find during this never-to-be-forgotten time that our cause is not a losing one but one of victory. The genuineness, the abounding vitality of the conquering power of our Lord and Master will be borne in upon us, and through us upon others throughout this continent.

Fellow delegates, more important than this, we are here in this convention to send out the call to the present generation of students of North America to face the absolutely unprecedented world situation. In other words, this convention takes on intensity as it reminds us that we must serve our generation by following the will of God. We shall consider during these days another definition of the word "generation" than the one that I am using this afternoon, in which we shall have in mind the whole life that you and I are to live, but this convention is concerned primarily with the generation to which you as students belong. It would concentrate its rays, its energies, its light and its power, upon the few years—how few they are!—that you are to spend in that college, in that university, in that theological seminary, in that medical school, that you may have stamped upon your own life and upon the life of your student generation this wonderful vision that will be borne in upon us during these days.

My friends, the possibilities of this particular convention are boundless. Where shall we find a limitation that we can place on these possibilities? Surely not in the purposes that have brought us together; as we have already seen these purposes are sufficiently vast, sufficiently deep, sufficiently far-reaching, to take in not only every delegate of this convention, but the colleges and societies that we represent, the nations to which we belong; yes, and those other nations to which some day a multitude of us will belong. There is no limitation that will compress this convention so far as our objects are concerned. Nor do I find a limitation when I think of the part of the world in which we are meeting this year. For the first time, our International Convention meets in the Upper Mississippi Valley. To my mind that is a significant and fortunate fact. It may be because I spent so much of my life in this part of North America, but I think it is for other reasons, that I recognize in the atmosphere, in the environment, in the tides of life and power of this Upper Mississippi Valley, conditions that will help us to realize the sublime purposes of this convention, not to speak of other things that I always associate with this region, a spaciousness which has ever given men power of vision to see things in the large. That is greatly needed just now and as we go back to our homes in all parts of this continent. I find also associated with this Upper Mississippi Valley, not only spaciousness, its great open plains, its vast reaches, but I find here the pioneer spirit, the spirit of adventure, the spirit that not only sees visions but is not afraid of them, that rises up to put into effect what it sees. To my mind this is one of the reasons why a larger proportion of volunteers have come from Upper Mississippi Valley than from any other part of the United States, a proportion that is almost the same as that which we find in that other spacious realm, the Dominion of Canada, which is an integral part of this vision-forming and vision-sharing convention.

I see no limit, therefore, in the part of the world where we are meeting. Nor do I see a limitation in the outreach of this convention, as I think of the particular time at which we have assembled, not only on the threshold of a new year, but on what some of us believe in our souls to be the threshold of a new era of the world expansion of Christianity. Since the Rochester Convention I have visited the principal battlefields of Christianity and I wish to state my conviction now, and possibly again later, of the fact that this generation of students is facing the most wonderful world situation which has ever confronted a generation of students; and if we live to be very old, I cannot imagine a generation coming when students will have a larger situation to face. The limit is not there, then.

We do not find, do we, today, a limitation to the possibilities of this convention, in God? Am I not right when I say that there are undiscovered, unexplored, and unassimilated resources in God, the like of which we have never dreamed? We are summoned in this convention to enter into these marvelous possessions.

Where, then, shall we find a limitation to this convention? There is only one place, and that is a place where we do not need to find it, thank God. What is that place? That place is in the life of each delegate. My friends, I remind you now, and you will be reminded in every hour of this convention, that in your life are latent capacities that transcend, if realized, anything that has been crowded into your past experience, capacities for adventure, capacities for sacrifice, capacities for heroism, capacities for unselfishness, capacities for faith that will make your future transcend your past so far that this will be a wonderful convention.

God forbid that any delegate should let a limitation be placed upon this convention in his own life; rather let us in this first hour reverently gather around the supreme, the only figure around which we may gather, our Lord Jesus Christ, and let Him revise our plans and if need be our lives. Let us fall down before Him, let Him dominate us individually and corporately. Then what a convention it will be!

THE WORLD OPPORTUNITY

ADDRESS GIVEN AT
THE STUDENT VOLUNTEER CONVENTION
DES MOINES, IOWA, JANUARY, 1920

We stand on the threshold of the greatest opportunity which North American students have ever confronted. It is characteristic of opportunity that it is passing. As the Arab proverb would express it, "The dawn comes not twice to awaken man." It is supremely important, therefore, that each of the 6000 delegates here be in such attitude of mind and heart that he may both see and seize opportunity. The nature and wonder of our opportunity will appear as we remind ourselves of the purposes of this great international convention of the Student Volunteer Movement.

We have come here to get a commanding vision of the new world. What a different world it is from that upon which the delegates gazed at the last convention, held in Kansas City just six years ago. What an old world that was. How absolutely different is the world which we view today. It need not be pointed out that it is a shaken world. The old foundations were heaved and broken up and were found to be but shifting sand.

Parts of the world which but yesterday we regarded as most stable are still trembling. It is an impoverished and overburdened world. The backs of innocent generations will bend low in toil and sacrifice as a result of impossible burdens imposed by the recent war. It is an exhausted and overwrought world. The nerves of the peoples have been worn threadbare.

The world is still torn and embittered. Not only is there hatred between the groups of nations which have been at war, but there has been a falling out among certain of the countries which were united in the struggle.

More ominous still is the fact that in virtually every nation which was at war, and in neutral countries as well, there has come a great fissure or rift between different classes. The bolshevist movement has not been concerned with dividing the nations and peoples vertically into separate compartments, as it were, but rather has aimed to cast a horizontal cleavage across the entire human race, arraying class against class.

The world is also still sorrowing and suffering. We need only remind ourselves of the 11,000,000 graves filled by the war. The physical sufferings continue over vast areas of mankind. Some who are in touch with the facts maintain that more people will die from starvation and exposure during the present winter than during any one year of the war.

The world is confused and bewildered. How few, even among the leaders of the nations, give one the impression that they know the way. Reversing the terrible picture, we may, on the other hand, thank God that the world is plastic to a degree hitherto unknown. It may now be cast in new molds. It is a humbled world. What nation today gives one the impression of pride and self-sufficiency, as was true of not a few nations but six years ago? This suggests the hopeful fact that the new world is a teachable world. Wherever one goes one hears the three questions: How did we miss the way? What is the way out? How long, O God, how long? Compared with the days preceding the war, the world is still unselfish, although, unfortunately, by no means as unselfish as a year ago or still less two years ago. Nevertheless, it is still responsive to a wonderful degree to the appeal for help and co-operation.

Moreover, wherever one looks, one receives the impression that we are living in an expectant world. The most backward, depressed, oppressed, and discouraged peoples seem to have their faces lifted with a new hope as they look toward the coming day. As trusted leaders who have come to us from recent observation of nearly every land bring us during the next five days their reports, and as we confer here with students of every race and people, the impression will become overwhelming that old things are literally passing away and that all things may become new.

We have assembled here not only to take the wide view, the view or vision of a new world, but also to receive a new challenge—a fresh commission. God speaks to each generation of students. Never has he spoken with greater clearness and power than to this generation. This convention has assembled in God's own hour for us. Suppose we had met at the end of the usual interval of four years, that is, two years ago, or suppose we had convened even a year ago, right after the signing of the armistice; what an inadequate view we should have had of the colossal and overpowering tasks awaiting our particular generation. Or suppose we had decided not to assemble until a year hence; so far as one can now see, we should have missed the day of our visitation. God speaks to our generation, to the students gathered in this Coliseum, and through them to those whom we represent.

What a generation this is. I sometimes think that God has accomplished a hundred years' work in the past five years. We must quicken our pace. Let me reiterate what I have said more than once, that I would rather be alive the next five or ten years than at any other time of which I can dream.

What is God's call to the colleges and universities of this particular day? It may be summed up in the one word, the call for leadership— leadership in the sense which Christ had in mind when He taught that he who would be greatest must be the servant of all. There comes to the students of our day a demand for a great and unparalleled offering of lives dedicated to the service of God and man. To use the language of Samuel J. Mills of over two generations ago, "Would that we might break out upon the non-Christian world like the Irish rebellion, 40,000 strong."

To what are the students of today summoned? Many of them are needed in industry, commerce, and finance, to apply the principles of Jesus Christ to these great energies and to wield them in the interests of His Kingdom. Others are needed in national and international politics, to Christianize the impact of our western civilization upon the non-Christian world. Men and women of the colleges are needed as investigators, thinkers, writers, and editors, to master and interpret the facts of our day in terms which will command the attention and following of the masses of mankind.

Others are called to become professors and teachers, for, as the old maxim expresses it, "What you would put into the life of a nation, put into its schools." The universities must furnish mediators, true statesmen, in this day of clashing and strife among classes and races and nationalities. Above all, there must be a great uprising of young men and women who will become ministers of religion, missionaries, prophets, and apostles with great social, ethical, and spiritual concern and passion. In a word, the challenge will sound out through this Convention to the student world of today for leaders of the forces of righteousness and unselfishness.

Or, in another and possibly a better word for these days, the call comes for builders of the new order. The period of building has arrived. Every American and Canadian student of wide outlook, unselfish spirit, and constructive ability is needed. An added responsibility comes upon us, as we shall see tomorrow, because of the startling depletion of the universities of Europe. Why did hundreds of thousands of the students and schoolboys of the nations with which we made common cause in recent years lay down their lives? They did so that their lives might become foundation stones of the new order. They laid down their lives with smiling faces. Why? In the first place, because they believed in their great, unselfish cause, and in the second place, because they trusted us. Their lives became foundation stones. Shall we not rear the superstructure?

Again, why have we come together here on the Iowa plains? Immanuel Kant has spoken of the starry heavens and the moral law within as influences which fill the mind with awe. I always feel like adding the mountains, the high seas, and the great plains. It seems to me, for example, that here, in this great Middle West, in this land of large dimensions and of wide horizons, it becomes easier to take in the vastness of the world field, the boundlessness of our opportunity. We students of a continent have come together here to realize our unity and spiritual solidarity. Here, in the heart of North America, almost equidistant between the colleges of New England and those of the mountain states and Pacific slope, also equidistant between the colleges of Manitoba and those of the gulf states, the radius of the Convention gathers within its sweep well nigh 1,000 institutions of higher learning which have sent delegates representing every American state and virtually every Canadian province.

Especially significant and full of promise is the union between the American and Canadian students, who are bound together by a common tradition in the deepest things of life—those pertaining to religion, language, and laws; by the recent sacrificial experiences, through the blending of hopes and fears, of blood and tears; and, above all, by common responsibilities and destinies in the realm of the unselfish outreach of these two nations.

In a convention like this, moreover, our horizon widens as we look into the faces of the hundreds of our foreign guests. Looking southward, we remind ourselves that here are delegates from Mexico, Cuba, Puerto Rico, Honduras, Venezuela, Colombia, Brazil, Argentina, Chile, and Peru. Looking eastward, we find in our midst delegates from England, Scotland, France, Holland, Switzerland, Portugal, Italy, Scandinavia, Poland, Czecho-Slovakia, Greece, Rumania, and Russia. Looking westward across Asia, we recognize representatives of Japan, Korea, Siberia, China, Siam, the Philippines, India, Ceylon, Armenia, Syria, and other parts of the old Turkish areas. Looking even farther afield, we remind ourselves that here are gathered representatives from different parts of the African continent and from far away Australia. The Des Moines Convention unquestionably constitutes the most cosmopolitan student convention ever held.

This lends the largest possible significance to the third purpose which has brought us together, that of realizing our unity. How essential this is, because the undertaking of rebuilding the world along Christian lines is so vast, so difficult, so urgent, that it is hopeless to expect to accomplish it unless the coming leaders of all lands and races are brought into common understanding and sympathy and devote themselves to a common program. Tremendous unifying forces are operating in a convention like this. The greatest ideas known to man and around which the program of this convention is built have wonderful federating power. Coming together to accentuate the vital teachings and principles of the Christian religion, on which we are all agreed, inevitably tends to fuse us together. Rising up together into the mountain peak of a deep and inspiring Christian experience—a mount on which we see no man save Jesus only, and an elevation from which we behold the kingdom of our Lord and his Christ—facilitates very greatly our coming into most intimate spiritual relationship to one another.

A convention, likewise, conducted on the platform, not of undenominationalism, but of interdenominationalism, by which is meant that the students of each denomination or communion are free to preserve and develop and give largest expression to that which is most distinctive to them, makes possible a larger, richer, and more potent unity than a process which would seek to reduce us all to the least common denominator. Associating, as we shall here be from time to time, in united intercession, which is our most potent and truly Christlike service, (for He ever liveth to make intercession) insures triumphant unity.

We face here also stupendous tasks, tasks which are admittedly far too great for any of us working singly or along separate denominational, national, or racial lines. All this tends to push us in upon each other, that we may present a united front to a united opposition, a united ignorance, a united sinfulness, a united unbelief. Above all, coming, as we shall be here, into a deeper personal experience of loyalty or allegiance to our common Lord necessarily implies a truer loyalty to one another. And this splendid unity or solidarity resulting from the free working of these mighty forces is intended to be not an end in itself. God has some vast designs to accomplish through us unitedly—designs which far transcend in sweep and importance those which have ever assembled a North American student convention.

We have come apart, from every quarter of the continent, yes, and through the persons of our foreign guests, from every corner of the wide world, to receive a fresh accession of superhuman power. The past five fateful and tragic years have constituted a great process of exclusion. One by one the pillars of our so-called civilization, to which we have pointed with such confidence and pride, have crumbled and fallen at our feet, until at last but one has been left standing— Jesus Christ, the same yesterday, today, and forever—never so unique, never so necessary, never so sufficient. With unshakable conviction and with larger content than ever may we say,

> Sufficient is thine arm alone
> And our defense is sure.

How great is the need on the part of the delegates to this convention for a power infinitely greater than their own. Such power is indispensable in order that the Christian religion may be made a triumphant reality in our lives and, through us, in the life of our colleges. It is essential in order that we may bring the principles and spirit of Christ to bear upon the obstinate and pressing problems of our social, industrial, racial, and international life. Such power is needed that the program of this convention—to make the reign of Christ coextensive with the inhabited world—may be made effective. Only a gospel adequate to meet all the needs of all the peoples of all the world is adequate to meet the needs of any one man here or in any community to which we may return. It is highly important to afford just now to these two sister Anglo-Saxon nations, in the midst of their social, industrial and racial unrest, antagonism and strife, and at a time of so much religious uncertainty and dissatisfaction, a fresh and mighty apologetic of the vitality, adequacy and conquering power of the Christian Gospel.

If these four great objectives which have brought us together are to be realized; if this convention is to become a mighty force for the rebuilding of the world, then our lives must undergo reconstruction— reconstruction as to their outlook, as to their moving ambitions, as to their guiding principles, as to their animating spirit. What should, therefore, be the attitude and spirit with which we enter upon the boundless opportunity presented to us singly and corporatively as members of this convention? After all, there are few really great days, great sights, great experiences in any life, whether it be long or short. What calamity could be greater than to miss the day of God's own visitation or to fall short of entering into a life-transforming experience or of catching what is literally a heavenly vision? What, then, should be our attitude or spirit that we may enter the door which now opens before us? It should be a spirit of downright earnestness. If ever men or women should be at their best and be true to their best selves it should be the students of the Des Moines Convention, because we meet in the shadow of an incomparable world sacrifice. We meet at a time when the world is still on fire. I remind you that twenty-three wars are now actually being fought, as an aftermath of the great war. Whole nations, as Hoover and others have reminded us, are still stretched on a cross of suffering. "When thy judgments are in the earth, the inhabitants of the world learn righteousness." The living God is moving among the nations. "Behold, I am re-creating all things." Madam Guyon speaks of creative hours with God. It is a notable fact that the hours of greatest suffering have ever been hours of creation. How vitally important it is, therefore, that our souls be attuned to the voices and movements of our time.

Our spirit should also be one of responsive open-mindedness. Lord Bacon has insisted that "he who would enter the kingdom of the natural sciences must do so as a little child," and did not Christ press home the same principle when he said that "except ye become as little children ye shall in no wise see (still less enter) the kingdom of heaven"? Here at the Des Moines Convention the boundless kingdom is to open —a kingdom of attainment and a kingdom of achievement. Who shall place a limit on what the living Christ may do in and through those delegates who yield themselves to His leading with open minds, responsive hearts, and active wills?

A spirit of courageous faith should dominate us all—faith in God, that He is, that He works, that the things which are impossible with men are possible with Him, faith in the incomparable worth of the

Christian gospel. Its wondrous scope embraces the whole human race in the entire range of its being, in all its varied relationships. It comprehends the full program of Christianity; it releases the boundless resources of Jesus Christ. It is because we believe that this gospel is going to work such great transformation in and through us here in the United States and Canada that we have unshakable courage to go forth with it into all the world. Above all, faith that God will use us. As we enter upon the high and holy activities of the Convention, let us prepare ourselves by a great corporate act of faith that God may make us, one and all, strongest where now we are weakest, and that as a result He may send us back to overcome the evils of modern college life and out into our respective nations to conquer their social and racial injustices, cruelties, and neglects and far on into the great open spaces of the non-Christian world to reveal His excellences and to communicate His power.

WHAT CONSTRUCTIVE FORCES ARE AVAILABLE?

ADDRESS GIVEN AT
THE STUDENT VOLUNTEER CONVENTION
DETROIT, MICHIGAN, 1928

It has been my privilege to attend the entire series of conventions of the Student Volunteer Movement, beginning with the one held at Cleveland in 1891. Throughout the period spanned by these notable gatherings, one associates an ever enlarging conception of the requirements of the world mission and expansion of the Christian religion. It assists my own memory to recall the shifting of emphasis as I returned from various world journeys to these gatherings. For example, after my first round-the-world trip, which consumed the larger part of two years, my message in public addresses, pamphlet literature, and study circles was chiefly the need of a great enlargement in the number of well-qualified foreign missionaries in order to accomplish our watchword, "The Evangelization of the World in This Generation." The Volunteer Movement, however, did not at that time overlook other fundamental factors involved in the world-wide extension and establishment of the Kingdom of Christ. I came back from my second world tour just in time to be present at the memorable convention in Toronto. I joined with others in pressing the point that, while we still needed and should continue to need large numbers of volunteers of the highest qualifications for the foreign missionary career, even greater was the need of an army of the choicest spirits from among the sons and daughters of the soil, that is, the young men and women of the rising indigenous churches who, under the command of our Lord, would dedicate their whole lives to Christian service. After my next extensive journeys, which included Africa and Latin America as well as large parts of Asia, and, in the light of deeper study of the relative importance of the different factors, I was led to share in another and more needed emphasis, namely, the supremacy of the super-human factor in every part of the world-wide Christian enterprise. How prone we had been, and still are, to take this too much for granted, with the result that all other essential factors in the accomplishment of Christ's will are robbed of their highest efficacy and power.

Beginning with the World Missionary Conference at Edinburgh in 1910, and continuing through the successive chains of regional and national conferences which, as Chairman of its Continuation Committee, I was called upon to conduct in different parts of the world, we were led to lay very special and timely stress on the absolute necessity of bringing about closer unity and co-operation on the part of the Christian forces. It was maintained in a memorable discussion at Edinburgh that a well-thought-out plan of practical co-operation, entered into heartily and adhered to loyally by the various missionary agencies and churches, would result in more than doubling the missionary force of the world. This statement has never been disproved. The contacts of my latest journeys throughout the Near East, around the Pacific Basin, and, more recently, in the World Conferences of Christian Workers among Jews have led me to recognize the peculiar need and timeliness of the note which is being sounded in this convention and elsewhere among discerning Christian thinkers, writers, and speakers, and that is the need of a vastly greater synthesis, if Christ's Kingdom is to come in power. It must be a synthesis between the old and never-to-be-neglected individual gospel and the equally true and indispensable social Gospel of Christ; a synthesis that embraces the older and younger churches as never before in mutual respect, confidence, practical support, and constant sharing; and, what has been far too much overlooked, a synthesis in the plans and activities of the so-called Christian and the so-called secular organizations and movements which are multiplying and expanding on every hand. Again let it be observed that these separate emphases which have characterized different periods spanned by the life of the Volunteer Movement, and have been stated with conviction by its leaders from generation to generation, are not to be regarded as having been mutually exclusive. With greater or less faithfulness, all the factors included in these different points of emphasis have been recognized and stressed by the leaders through the years. Rather than thinking of them as exclusive in any sense, we have come to a time when with clearness we must recognize that they are cumulative and mutually supporting.

The present Detroit Convention meets at a wonderful moment. This new and comprehensive emphasis is of peculiar timeliness because of the startling development and manifestation of divisive influences among men. In addition to the cleavages and misunderstandings of sectional, social, national, and international character, there may be recognized now, as never before, divisions and antagonisms that are intercontinental and world-wide in their reach. Among such divisive influences we recognize the economic, as seen in ruthless competition, in exploitation, in economic imperialism, in the unfair practices involved in the control of raw material, and, in general, in the wide disregard of the social and ethical consequences of such practices. Moreover, in the international political realm the fact of the existence and working of divisive influences is most ominous. How true it is that on every hand there are still grave international misunderstandings, as, for example, between the United States and Japan. What an alarming weakening of prestige and influence of western nations over non-European peoples is now observable in the Far East, in the Near East, in Africa, in Latin America! Is it not true also that there has never been quite so much discontent with reference to existing treaties, not only in the Orient, from which so much has recently been heard, but also in the West? How conscious the observant traveler through parts of Europe and the Near East must be today of maladjustments as a result of international treaties. The international atmosphere is sadly but truly surcharged with suspicion. Nation after nation, to use the expression of an American ambassador, is oscillating between fear and cupidity. There has been nothing short of a recrudescence of militarism in very recent years. Within a week we have read in our papers that thirteen European nations now have military dictatorships. The military and naval expenditures of the world are in excess even of those in the years that immediately preceded the War.

Above all, we observe in the sphere of race relations alarming manifestations of divisive tendencies. This fact is due in part to the shrinkage of the world caused by greatly improved means of communication. This, in turn, has resulted in augmenting the tides of emigration and immigration, likewise in a vast expansion of the volume of travel. Thus there has come about, as at no other time in the history of mankind, a constant mingling of the peoples on both the higher and the lower levels of life. The races have been set to acting and reacting upon one another with startling directness, power, and, at times, virulence. Wherever two or more races are thrown against each other without some superhuman guidance and restraint, something seems to take place which tends to draw the worst out of each race; but it is also true, thank God, that the interracial contacts call forth the best from each race concerned when there is exerted the influence of a more than human direction and control. There is in a race, just as in an individual, not only the height which lays hold of heaven, but also the depth which reaches down to hell; and the deepest of these depths may be seen in the zones of most bitter race conflict. The War greatly accentuated the gravity of this peril because races, as well as nations, were awakened under the impulse of ideals of freedom and self-determination. As a result, the friction points between races are doubtless more numerous than they were a few years ago. Of this friction we have solemn examples between Whites and Blacks in the United States of America, and possibly even more in South Africa; also between Orientals and Occidentals in the lands around the fringes of the Pacific Basin. The words of Dr. S. K. Datta, of India, may be somewhat exaggerated, but on the other hand they have their solemn warning, "There seems to be hardly any interracial trust and good will." The race problem is of world-wide interest and imminent concern. Now that the world has found itself as one body, it cannot be a matter of indifference to any one nation if in any other part of the international body there be friction, bitterness, and strife. Let us, as a student gathering, not overlook the fact that the racial problem is not without its inspiring aspect. Are not many of its manifestations an evidence of the movement of the higher spirit in man inspired with the desire and hope, even among the most abject and backward races, of a freer, fairer, and nobler life? Do we not recognize in it the purpose of the Heavenly Father brooding over His whole family with the desire that it be brought into accord and unity? The very difficulties associated with the problem, which cannot be minimized, are an added attraction to heroic and unselfish natures.

Great and alarming as are the factors, forces, and influences which today tend to divide men and peoples, to array them against one another, and to generate misunderstanding, bitterness, and strife, it is my profound conviction that far greater, and far more expansive, potent, and hopeful are the agencies, movements, and forces which are tending to draw them together. In the light of many years of travel and world contacts, I would record my belief that the world is immensely nearer than ever before to the unity which we of this convention long to see. Let us now look at the two great streams of international and interracial co-operative activities which we and those of other lands and races should dedicate ourselves to blending or combining in what I have characterized as the larger synthesis now needed. I refer to the stream of so-called secular agencies and the stream of those which are avowedly Christian. We shall see that they are now happily and increasingly blending, and that they are in reality indispensable to each other. First, then, let us note some of the so-called secular factors.

The improved means of communication are on the whole, I am persuaded, making for better understanding, closer co-operation, and the maintenance of more friendly relations between nations and races. In recent years there has been an enormous expansion of the steamship lines on all the great seas, as well as an outreach of railway systems in most difficult and out-of-the-way areas of different continents. The whole world has been linked up almost beyond belief by the perfection of the cable and telegraphic systems and the development of the radio. The automobile has led to the opening up of almost inaccessible haunts of men the world over. The brilliant triumphs of the airplane have accelerated enormously these processes of unification. Thus the world has been contracted within late days literally into a whispering gallery. Hundreds of millions of people have been made readily accessible to one another. Thus there has been made possible a sense of solidarity and interdependence among peoples. For the first time in history it has become possible for all the races of mankind to have a realization that they are members one of another. This has advanced in a marvelous way the possibilities of co-operation in the constructive work of the world. It now becomes actually possible for different nations and races to enter into a life of sharing—above all, in the deepest things of life. This breaking down of barriers of time and space has thus achieved a cohesiveness of human interest of which a very few years ago we had no conception. The social consequences are simply incalculable. No preceding generation of students has ever faced a world with such possibilities.

The expansion of commerce, industry, and finance constitutes another great force which should tell more and more for the stabilization, unification, and upbuilding of the world. A study of the more recent commercial maps of Bartholomew and other map makers, and of the official statistics of the bureaus of economics in different countries, reveals that the achievements in these realms in recent years have been overwhelming in their volume and power. Here again I am persuaded that their operations are being conducted on an increasingly higher level, both from the point of view of ethical standards and from that of social responsibility. The reason doubtless lies in the fact that under present conditions there is turned upon these areas of the life of nations the fuller blaze of the light of truth and of the requirements of social and international obligation. To be persuaded of this fact, one needed only to scan the proceedings and activities of the World's Bankers' Association, of the World's Chamber of Commerce, of the World's Advertisers' Clubs, and other such agencies of an international character. A distinguished educator in New England has pointed out that the great task of the years immediately before us is that of giving spiritual significance to the vast material accumulations and almost unbelievable activities of applied science which have marked the years of the recent past.

The past decade has witnessed the most significant development of international political machinery. The great central fact in this connection has been the creation of the League of Nations. This has become literally an annual world parliament of over fifty nations— nations which have in them approximately four-fifths of the population of the world. Its machinery—the Assembly, the Council, and the Secretariat—has shown increasing efficiency. It has the great advantage of being always ready for action. Its permanent aspect constitutes the foundation of deepening confidence. Its prestige has grown steadily. While it has not been without its limitations and shortcomings, it constitutes without doubt the greatest political experiment of modern times. In spite of all discouragements and difficulties, its volume of achievement has increased year by year. It has conducted successfully the return of nearly half a million war prisoners. It has helped to succor over 2,000,000 refugees, chiefly Greeks and Russians. It has greatly facilitated the reconstructive processes, and has actually saved whole nations from bankruptcy and disintegration. To a wonderful degree it has checked and controlled diseases; through its intelligence work, through its co-ordination of scientific research, and through securing joint action in combating deadly perils. It has put forth effective efforts against dangerous and criminal commerce. It has come to close grapple with gigantic evils, such as the opium curse, the traffic in women and girls, and forced labor. Minorities have been befriended. Backward peoples have been protected, notably through the Mandates Commission. It has taken significant steps in the direction of furthering intellectual co-operation among peoples. Apart from all these practical ministries and constructive services, we think of the League of Nations as having composed many political disputes. It is believed that it has averted certain wars. It has dealt constructively with the problems of security and armaments, and it has made public not fewer than 700 treaties. Faith in the League as a method of conciliation, conference, and co-operation has, therefore, grown stronger year by year. All these varied activities have constituted a training school in the realm of international co-operation.

Another remarkable piece of international machinery is the Per-

manent Court of International Justice. Of all international agencies
set up in modern times to insure peace, none has evoked wider interest.
It crowns a generation of determined effort. It has already won the
adhesion of over fifty nations, among which none has had a more important or honored part at the stage of initiation or at the later stage
of final formulation, than America. In reality it fulfills an ideal which
for many years has commanded some of the most creative thinking and
enthusiastic devotion of American statesmen. Here again, as in the
case of the League of Nations, the permanent aspect of the organization is the highly significant thing. It is not surprising that this Permanent Court of International Justice is being appealed to increasingly.

The International Labor Office, likewise closely integrated with
the League of Nations, has become a great factor in drawing together
the nations and races. Not fewer than fifty-six nations are constituent
members, and several others participate to a greater or less degree in
its constructive activities. Through its annual international labor conferences; through its governing body representing governments, employers, and workers; and through its highly efficient office, with its
intelligence, research, and diplomatic sections, it has without doubt
become the leading factor in the world today in promoting social justice, without which there can be no permanent international peace, in
ensuring improved human conditions in labor, and in waging warfare
against hardship, privation, forced labor, and unfair international
competition.

In addition to such permanent international political and judicial
agencies, the last few years have witnessed not a few special conferences of great international significance. Chief among them in many
respects was the Washington Conference of 1922, which exerted such
a far-reaching influence that we are only beginning to see and estimate
its results.

Attention should be called to activities for the physical betterment
of mankind which are international in scope or outreach. It is not
necessary to reiterate the great contribution made through the health
work of the League of Nations. Another agency is that of the League
of National Red Cross Societies, not to speak of the fine work of the
International Committee of the Red Cross. This League, which has
developed so rapidly since its organization in Paris in 1919, now includes fifty-two national Red Cross societies, with 16,000,000 members. It seeks to promote the physical welfare of mankind through
pooling the experience of all nations, and to furnish a medium for co-
ordinating relief work in great national and international calamities.
It preserves close contacts with the many other international health

agencies. Important and influential as have been its multiform activities through its Relief Division and Nursing Division, of even farther-reaching significance have been the modern developments in the pathway of the work of its Health Division. Nor should we overlook the Junior Division which was initiated in Canada only a little more than a decade ago, and which has expanded so rapidly that it now includes among the youth 8,000,000 members in some thirty or more national unions.

The International Health Board of the Rockefeller Foundation, which has developed on such scientifically thorough lines, has become a great factor in achieving genuine international co-operation. Last year alone it conducted activities on all continents, extending its beneficent work to the remotest corners of the earth. It patricipated in public health work in eighty-eight separate states and nations. It is concerned not only with the conquest, but more specially with the prevention of disease. In addition to its thorough work of field research, it aids public health organizations of different nations in the development of effective administrative measures. Its successful concentration on diseases of world-wide distribution such as malaria, yellow fever, and hookworm, constitutes an inspiring record of helpfulness to mankind.

The China Medical Board, working especially through the Peking University Medical College and its related activities, is in itself a splendid illustration of what can be achieved by associating the best-furnished minds of the medical profession of America, Europe, and Asia in a great constructive enterprise. It has already done much to raise the standards of the medical profession in a great area of the world.

International athletic competitions, such as the Olympic Games and other international meets have revealed what a factor well-conducted sports may be in furthering understanding, good feeling, and co-operation among the youth of the nations.

The activities of the Near East Relief afford a bright chapter in the fostering of good international relations. This great unselfish enterprise in the course of a decade has not only saved thousands of lives, furnished practical relief in the form of food and clothing to millions, combated successfully deadly diseases and prevented their becoming an international menace, rehabilitated millions of refugees, restored hope to whole peoples, reorganized industry in many a community, reunited broken families, trained and placed many orphans, but also accomplished untold good in abating racial antagonisms and laying secure foundations for peace and brotherhood in the Near East. Through incarnating the Golden Rule, it has lifted this great principle proclaimed by Christ into its proper central prominence and made it a great unifying as well as a rallying cry in all lands for people animated with a passion for helpfulness. This, however, is only one illustration of many which might be given of widespread philanthropy and great constructive relief enterprises which have given the post-war period distinction.

In the educational realm, moreover, as well as in the spheres of physical betterment and political action, we find a bewildering number and variety of enterprises and projects, launched within the recent past, which are making for closer and more helpful relations internationally and interracially. The Pan-Pacific Science Congress, which has recently held its third session in Japan (the two earlier triennial meetings have been held in the Hawaiian Islands and Australia, respectively), has associated the representatives of the science faculties of the universities and the leaders in scientific research councils or other learned groups of the lands around the Pacific Basin. In addition to its most distinctive purpose, that of initiating and promoting co-operation in the study of scientific problems in the Pacific region, it is most interesting to note that a second and co-ordinate object is that of strengthening the bonds of peace among Pacific peoples by means of promoting a feeling of brotherhood among the scientists, and through them among citizens in general in all Pacific countries. This suggests the long list of regular international meetings of societies in virtually every department of learning and of intellectual progress. The number is legion, as given in the list prepared by the League of Nations, and earlier by the organization in Belgium which was formed a few years ago to catalogue and in a measure federate international societies of every description throughout the world—lists including hundreds and hundreds of such agencies. They have served to throw down countless strands of friendliness and co-operation based on understanding and human interest.

The Scholarship Foundations of an international character, and international fellowships of universities, which have multiplied so greatly since the War, are destined to exert a great influence among the many unifying processes. Most of them specifically state in their annoucements that one of their main objectives is to foster international understanding as a basis for continuing peace.

The Carnegie Endowment for International Peace, with its divisions of Intercourse and Education, Economics and History, and International Law, concentrates on hastening the abolition of war. It wisely utilizes many other existing agencies wherever they will best serve the central purpose. Some of these subordinate agencies, although little heralded, are accomplishing untold good toward the realization of the inspiring ideal of international friendship and universal peace.

The Williamstown Institute of Politics, although it has been at work less than a decade, has already exerted a far-reaching influence. This is true not only through the drawing together of leading minds on national and international subjects, but also through stimulating and guiding them each in turn to become a center of helpful propaganda in the furtherance of sound policies and plans of international agreement. Its work has been so well done that it has become contagious in the sense that it has led to the formation of similar institutes in America and other parts of the world.

Particular attention should be called to the Institute of Pacific Relations, organized in Honolulu under the impulse of a business man of wide outlook and genuine sense of mission, to bring about right relations among the peoples of the Pacific. This organization has brought together at its two biennial meetings outstanding groups of influential men of all the nations which surround the Pacific Basin. It seeks to ensure international understanding and good will through facing frankly and thoroughly the outstanding problems of the Pacific, and through establishing friendships among leading men of widely different points of view and of all walks of life. It has been well characterized as an adventure in friendship. Its moving spirits are determined to profit by the unfortunate international experiences on the European side of the world in the dominant hope that these may not be repeated in days to come in the Pacific.

The foregoing list of so-called secular co-operative agencies of an international or interracial character is simply suggestive and in no sense exhaustive. Before proceeding to call attention to so-called Christian agencies of co-operation for a better world, let me make a few comments on the list which has just been outlined. With the exception of certain aspects of such factors as improved means of communication and the activities of commerce, industry, and finance, it is a remarkable fact that nearly all of this vast, varied, and beneficent organized activity has been inaugurated and carried forward during the last decade. None of these agencies bears the Christian name, but we must recognize that one and all of them are of profound concern to all who are working for the coming of Christ's Kingdom. They are constructive in their action. Now and then one of them may have been prostituted to selfish or unworthy ends, but generally speaking, they have been building and not tearing down. They are concerned, in fact most of them are chiefly concerned, with getting at and removing causes which make for misunderstanding, distrust, and strife, and not simply with dealing with ill results. They are facilitating the larger

discovery and application of truth, and this lies at the base of an enduring structure. They are avowedly working to bring about better understanding and sympathy among nations and races. Beyond question
they are one and all throwing down strands of friendliness and brotherhood, not only among individuals but, as a result of that process,
among whole peoples. It should be observed that their contribution
to the physical betterment, the social emancipation, the intellectual
enrichment of mankind may be regarded as an integral part of the
Christian gospel—as a natural expression of Christ's own spirit of
love and helpfulness, for was not this the very genius of His emphasis
on the world, the development of human personality and of right
relationships among men? Thus, all these so-called secular agencies
may and should be accepted and utilized to further His world-wide
cause. All of them in the facing of their impossible problems and in
the frank acknowledgment of their limitations, will be led increasingly
to Christ in the vital sense of finding in Him not only the adequate
ideal and purpose, but also the only sufficient power.

Therefore, none of these means, agencies, and movements is to be
regarded by us, the members of this convention, as against Christ, or
as having objectives out of accord with Christ, or as apart from Christ.
Rather may we not, as a generation of Christian students, regard them
as priceless assets and allies, and seek to make them increasingly tributary in all our plans for the extension of His Kingdom. Remember
His own teaching that he who is not against us is for us, and, therefore,
should be with us. May we not with new meaning heed the words of
the great apostle, "All are yours; and ye are Christ's; and Christ is
God's." It is highly impressive to observe what a disproportionately
large number of the founders, leaders, and moving spirits of these
so-called secular enterprises which are making for international and
interracial co-operation are sincere followers of Christ. As we recall
their names, of how many of them could we not say, Christ gave them
their vision; Christ motivated their lives and imparted to them their
sense of mission; Christ was their inspiration; at His feet they would
lay in humility their tribute. Even some of them who do not bear His
name admit, nevertheless, that to Him they owe their governing ideas,
ideals, and inspiration. In my college days I read a book of great sug-
gestiveness entitled *Gesta Christi,* by Loring Brace, which was devoted
largely to showing to what a great extent the philanthropic and social
betterment activities in Europe through the centuries might be traced
to the influence of Jesus Christ. During the first half of the life of the
Student Volunteer Movement there appeared a very notable work of
several volumes on *Missions and Social Progress* by Dr. James S.
Dennis. A fresh work might well be prepared at the present time

translating into terms of Asia, Africa, and the rest of the non-Christian world a record of the wonderful achievements of the present generation traceable to the influence of Jesus Christ, not only in the realm of social uplift but also in the spheres of improved international and interracial relations.

Great as has been the unifying influence of the organizations and movements which do not bear the Christian name and which are not avowedly Christian, by far the most potent, fruitful, and hopeful instrumentalities making for international and interracial accord and co-operation in the life of the world today are those which humbly avow their allegiance to Christ, openly bear His Name, courageously seek to find and travel His Way, and, if need be, bear His Cross, and consciously look to Him and draw from Him their life and power. With all its faults, shortcomings, and sins, the Church of Christ, in its multiform Communions, is the great Divine Society or Fellowship transcending all differences of class, nationality, and race, and dedicated to the supreme purpose of the world-wide establishment of His Kingdom. Here we would pay a special tribute to those, chiefly students of North America and other lands, who heeded the call of Christ Himself and devoted themselves to the world mission of His religion and to making it dominant not only in the lives of individuals but also in the whole range of the life of society and the relationships of men. I love to think of the 29,000 and more Protestant missionaries (and why not also those of the other great Communions) including the more than 11,000 Student Volunteers, who have gone forth from the universities and colleges of North America. In truth they are pioneers of international and interracial friendship and co-operation. They are ambassadors from the highest levels of their own native lands to the peoples of countries to which they had been accredited. They are interpreters of the best side of the life and thought of each land to the other. They are illustrators or demonstrators of the reality of the Christ in whose name they have gone forth, and of His way of life. Many of them have proved by their lives that racial barriers can be overcome. They have counteracted also the unfavorable impressions produced by certain sinister social contacts. They have been mediators —mediating between peoples or races which have misunderstood each other and where there have been bitterness, friction, and strife.

With equal satisfaction, also, we think today of individuals, of little bands, and, in certain fields, of great companies of the Christians of the vital, rising indigenous Churches of Asia, the Pacific islands, Latin America, and Africa. These men and women are convincing witnesses and demonstrations of the power of Christ to transform lives and human conditions, and are also veritable bridge builders in co-operation with the missionaries and other Christians of the West, spanning great chasms which have separated East from West.

Our minds dwell not alone on the Churches, both older and younger, both parents and daughters, and likewise upon the many auxiliary agencies which have sprung from them and which are so intimately related to them. Among these we would call attention to but a few which are international or interracial in character and which today are exerting a remarkable unifying influence. At once we think of certain phases of the work of the Federal Council of Churches of Christ in America, such as its Commission on International Justice, and its Commission on Interracial Co-operation. Again there comes to mind the World's Alliance for Promoting Friendship Through the Churches, supported so fully by the Church Peace Union. This Alliance has as constituent members national bodies in over thirty countries. It has a practical, constructive program which not a few think has done more during the past decade to insure thinking, planning, speaking, and action by the Churches on all that pertains to international good will and unity than has been achieved by them during the preceding centuries. The recent Stockholm Conference on Christian Life and Work with its Continuation Committee and permanent office, is another splendid illustration of the unifying power of the Churches, both Protestant and Eastern Orthodox.

The International Fellowship of Reconciliation, composed of groups in between twenty and thirty countries east and west, though a relatively small organization and not widely advertised, has proved to be one of the most vital and truly creative forces at work for true peace. With heroic and sacrificial devotion, many of its members have gone the way of the Cross in their sincere efforts to apply the central principle of the organization that the love of Jesus of Nazareth is the only power which can overcome evil and call forth the undiscovered good in men. The Fellowship for a Christian Social Order, which during these days is being brought into an intimate relation with the Fellowship of Reconciliation, was conceived in the same spirit and in its useful work has been governed by the same principles.

The Young Men's and Young Women's Christian Associations have become in reality a world power for unity, with their 12,000 and more branches in over fifty nations, having a membership of over two and a half million young men and young women, not to speak of many other millions who were members in their youth and have gone out into the world to apply the principles inculcated by the Associations. These Movements in their fellowship and activities are blending increasingly the strongest races of mankind. They recognize and accept the solemn obligation to make Christ known and trusted and obeyed in all human relationships. They believe that each nation and race has an essential contribution to make in the working out of the Christian program. Most fortunately their work is established in some of the zones of greatest racial conflict. Particular attention should be called to the work of the Interracial Commission of the Young Men's Christian Association, which during the years since the War has worked with such efficiency and splendid effect. Through its national, as well as its various state, county, and community commissions, composed of the very best elements among the white and black races, it has been demonstrated that good will and co-operation rather than antagonism and violence are the most effective methods of interracial adjustment.

The World's Student Christian Federation, which unites all the national and international Christian Student Movements of the world, is admittedly one of the most important factors at work in the world for ensuring the realization of the great Christian objective of international and interracial accord and co-operation. Its branches now exist in over 3,000 universities and colleges in some forty or more different nations, with a membership of at least 300,000 students and professors, not to mention the large numbers of graduates now engaged in various influential callings who were active members in their undergraduate days. This Movement constitutes in its present fellowship a body which in some respects is the most intelligent, the most idealistic, and the most unfettered among all the youth movements. Including as it does so many who tomorrow will be the recognized leaders of the nations, it is in a unique position to establish enduring bonds of friendship between nations.

Great as has been the direct and indirect influence of the Student Volunteer Movement for Foreign Missions, in binding together in sympathetic understanding and active co-operation the races of mankind, it now stands on the threshold of opportunities for even more significant service in this sphere. For reasons which have already been emphasized in virtually every session of this convention, this mission of the Volunteer Movement, while more difficult and exacting than in the past, is more necessary and hopeful. In the early days of the life of this Movement, President McCosh of Princeton voiced the conviction that the Volunteer Movement constituted the greatest offering of young life for the world's evangelization which had been thus far made in all the history of the Christian religion. With how much more aptness and force might such a statement be made today; but more significant still would be the claim which could be made and well supported that this Movement has likewise made an absolutely unique and wonderful contribution toward the unification of the races of mankind. By its policy during these later years of weaving together the

Student Volunteers and the students who have become clergymen and lay workers in all walks of life in united planning and effort on behalf of the world-wide establishment of Christ's Kingdom, it is dealing more comprehensively and successfully with the world situation and its requirements than in the earlier days when its objectives were more restricted. A high tribute should also be paid to the Missionary Education Movement of North America and other lands, and likewise the Laymen's Missionary Movement, as mighty forces for the liberation, combination and stimulation of great constituencies for the realization of the international mission of Christianity.

The International Missionary Council, as the successor of the Continuation Committee of the World Missionary Conference of Edinburgh in 1910, has succeeded in uniting the Protestant missionary forces of the world, and thus, from the very nature of the case, is a demonstration of the possibility, the reality, and the necessity of international and interracial co-operation. Its enlarged meeting, soon to be held on the Mount of Olives in Jerusalem, will be, in some respects, one of the most notable gatherings of modern times. It is to bring together a limited number of the recognized leaders of the various mission boards of all the sending countries and of the rising indigenous Churches of Asia, Africa, Latin America, and the Island World. For the first time in anything like equal numbers, there will meet in intimate fellowship the trusted representatives of the older Churches and the younger Churches. The very genius of this meeting will be that of sharing—that is, the Churches of the East and those of the West coming together to share with each other their vision, insight, experience, and hopes. They come together, moreover, corporately to rethink, to restate, and, where necessary, to revise programs and policies for the world-wide mission of the Christian religion. A most happy arrangement has been made by which each Christian Student Movement is invited to be represented at Jerusalem by one of its leaders who on his return will devote a year or more to communicating to the students of the universities and colleges of his country the message of this great creative gathering.

It has been my opportunity in recent years to be thrown into the very middle of the life stream of the Christian Churches and of virtually all of these auxiliary interdenominational and international Christian movements. This has come about through world journeys, through attendance upon world conferences, and through the countless contacts which have come in the intimacies of one's official relation to four or five of these world-wide agencies. With this as background, I wish to state that this world-wide movement flowing forth from Jesus Christ, the Fountain Head of vitality and unity, is in reality the great internationalism. The topic assigned to me is "Jesus Christ and International and Interracial Co-operation for a Better World." The leaders and members of all the Churches, of all these auxiliary Christian agencies, and of all the so-called secular organizations and movements which we have today reviewed in outline, together with not a few others of great importance which have not been named, must increasingly go to Jesus Christ Himself, if they are to enter into the full realization of international and interracial co-operation for a better world. Unless we wish to miss the way, we shall go to Him for the guiding principles which are unerring, principles which, if applied in international and interracial contacts, ensure good will and accord—such principles, for example, as the infinite worth of each nation and race; the true brotherhood of man based on recognition of the fatherhood of God; recognition that inequalities among nations and races are not intended to signify an opportunity for domination and exploitation, but rather for justice and service, especially on the part of the strong on behalf of the weak; the fact that the nations and races are members one of another, and therefore absolutely essential to each other; the applicability of the Golden Rule between nations and races just as truly as between individuals; repentance and forgiveness among nations and races as among individuals; the commandment of love, with its implications of vicarious and aggressive manifestation of love; and the all-embracing principle of the Kingdom of God. Shortly after Viscount Grey came over to serve as British Ambassador I called upon him in Washington to invite him to make an address at the Volunteer Convention in Des Moines. He accepted the invitation though he was unable to fill the appointment on account of his early recall to Great Britain. (Later, in substitution, he gave an address at the Volunteer Convention in Great Britain.) In this memorable conversation he made the significant remark that the great need of the world internationally was the moralization of international affairs. As he enlarged on the statement, it became quite clear that he had in mind nothing short of the application of the principles of Christ to the relationships between nations. To whom else shall the nations go? Christ only has the word for international and interracial life as well as for individual life.

We go to Christ for the only adequate and comprehensive program. One might summarize it in a single sentence. On His own word His program concerns every human being of every nation, of ever race, of every condition, in the whole range of his being, in all his relationships—social, international, interracial—in all time and eternity. Surely here is a program the realization of which requires us all, and likewise demands the collaboration of the leaders and members of all the constructive and unselfish forces which have been passing in review before us.

We go to Him, moreover, for the only power sufficient to meet and to satisfy every need and every aspiration of the human heart and of the human race. He has power to quicken conscience and to make it tremble, and thus to make men truly penitent because of their share in the guilt of their own nation or race. He has power to enable men to take the step between knowing their duty with reference to other lands and races and doing their duty, even though this involves traveling by way of the Cross. He has power to transform whole peoples, making them strongest where once perchance they were weakest. As Principal Fairbairn was wont to insist, "Christ is the most powerful spiritual force that ever operated for good on and in humanity." He has power to lift men up on wings as eagles, and to impart to them the unfading vision of the kingdoms of this world becoming the Kingdoms of our Lord and of His Christ, that He may reign over them in true accord. Beyond question, He has power to unite the nations and the races. By His incarnation, by the inclusiveness and comprehensiveness of His wondrous gospel and Kingdom, by His breaking down the middle wall of partition between God and man, and, therefore, between man and man, on the Cross, by the world-wide sweep of the program which He has committed to His followers, by His high-priestly prayer "that they all may be one," by His ever-living intercession, and by the witness and sacrificial service of His Body, the Church—Christ reveals Himself as the One through whom the unity of the human race is discovered and realized. "He showed me the river of the water of life, bright as crystal, flowing from the throne of God and of the Lamb, through the streets of the city; on both sides of the river grew the tree of life . . . and the leaves served to heal the nations." To heal the nations—both in their inner life and in their outer relationships.

It should bring Christ very close to us in the convention this morning, as we remind ourselves that He has power to brood over our universities and colleges, yes, over this great convention, and to raise up from among us and among our fellow students to whom we soon return, a new generation of leaders. In using the word "leaders," we have in mind leaders in Christ's own sense, when He said that he who would be greatest among you should be the servant of all. Great and imperative is the need of leaders who in all realms of thought and action will consecrate themselves to that high and holy mission of being apostles of reconciliation. Jesus Christ, before Whom we stand, is the Living Christ, Christ the real Leader of us all, the World Conqueror. He only can kindle the enduring enthusiasm, command the loyalty, and call forth the undying devotion of the students of our day in this sublime cause. He summons us here today to a dedication of our lives to His appointed task of the world-wide extension of His Kingdom—some to go forth as medical missionaries, some as educationalists, some as Christian writers, some as evangelists. Others under His guidance will, in relation to the so-called secular agencies near and far, make the governing purpose of their lives that of bringing to bear the principles and spirit of Christ in the entire range of the life and relationships of men and nations. All of us, in these and in other capacities, will hold in true central prominence the great unifying objective of the Christian faith. To this end the Christ present among us is ushering us into a wondrous fellowship. Each one of the preceding Volunteer conventions has constituted in itself a fellowship which has ever continued to widen and deepen. The notes of reality which have been struck with such insistence and faithfulness throughout this convention also constitute a call of Christ to each one of us singly and collectively, for the groups of us who return together to the different universities, colleges, and seminaries, to afford to our fellow students and to the outer world a demonstration of fresh evidence of the working of the Living Christ within us. It is an inspiration to remind ourselves that Christ Himself is here seeking to clothe Himself with us, that is, to communicate Himself inwardly to us and through us. With a definite act of will and with unselfish and heroic abandon let us yield ourselves afresh to His sway.

Let me appeal to the students here today to dedicate their lives to that noblest task—that truly Christlike and Christ-appointed endeavor—the drawing together in closer co-operation and unity of the Christian forces and the other constructive and vital forces of the nations and races. Such international and interracial union in thought, planning, intercession, and action is absolutely essential to the establishment of the Kingdom of God. It is the most highly-multiplying activity in which men can engage. It has been suggested that to this end I indicate in outline a practical working program.

1. Success in any co-operative effort depends on a right attitude. We should resolutely set ourselves to cultivate and maintain an attitude characterized by willingness to recognize the place and value of other nations and races, by appreciation of their heritage and customs, by open-mindedness to learn from them, and by determination to understand them and to work with them however much we may differ.

2. Seek to discover the mind of Christ and then make that mind our own. The attitude and spirit of Christ are revealed in His teachings and in His contacts with those of other races and faiths. The

extent of our reaching the soul of any people is determined by our sense of the Living Christ.

3. Engage in and promote in all our institutions more serious and scientific study of race relations and international problems from the point of view of Christ. The present generation has no excuse for not making great progress in this quest, because it has manifold more incitements and facilities in these realms than had any of our predecessors.

4. Master a few of the most notable books. It is a most interesting fact that the five or six books on race relations from the Christian point of view, which are admittedly in the front line, have come out within the past five years, and were prepared by former leaders or workers in the Student Christian Movements of North America and Europe, namely:

> *Christianity and the Race Problem,* J. H. Oldham
> *Race and Race Relations,* Robert E. Speer
> *The Negro from Africa to America,* W. D. Weatherford
> *The Clash of Color,* Basil Matthews
> *The Race Problem and the Teaching of Jesus Christ,* J. S. Hoyland
> *Who Is My Neighbor?* by leaders of The Inquiry.

5. Foster the establishment and best working of open forums, institutes, conferences, and retreats on interracial and international issues. It would be difficult to overstate the value of such international group meetings as those conducted in recent years by the World's Student Christian Federation, and by other Christian organizations, both in the Occident and in the Orient. In this connection we look forward with eagerness and hopefulness to the meeting of the Federation to be held in India a year hence.

6. Emphasize the enlarged meeting of the International Missionary Council, to be held so soon in Jerusalem. The representatives of the Christian Movements here in the United States and Canada should bring to this creative gathering the needs, aspirations, and purposes of the Christian students of these two countries. On their return, they should communicate to all of their centers of learning the vision, insight, outlook, challenges, constructive program, and sense of the unity of the Christian forces and of the Jerusalem meeting itself.

7. Cultivate the habit of making personal friends of individuals of the different races. Our trouble with reference to the race problem

is that we generalize it too much. So long as it is an abstraction, we shall never understand or appreciate it. Each intimate friendship established with some one of another race will prove to serve as an effective key, enabling us to unlock with understanding and sympathy difficult race situations.

8. It is well also to multiply contacts with the home life of the people of other races. This serves to break down the superiority complex. There is a Japanese proverb which says: "To be together for ten minutes under the same tree unites our destinies even beyond the tomb." With even more aptness might this be said of intimate and unhurried contacts with home life.

9. There should be a great improvement in our program and practice of promoting friendly relations among foreign students. Splendid work has been accomplished during the last twenty-five years, largely through the initiative and leadership of the Committee on Friendly Relations among Foreign Students. The time has come to expand enormously, in all countries which receive student migrations, helpful ministries of this sort. It should not be regarded as an impossible ideal and undertaking for the World's Student Christian Federation, together with all related national Student Movements and the Churches, to spread so thoroughly the network of friendly interest and co-operation that no foreign student would fail to be served by them. In all such friendly ministries we should keep vividly in mind that the highest office of friendship is to help those whom we would befriend in the deepest things of life.

10. The West should invite, welcome, and give open-minded and sympathetic heed to individual messengers and groups from the Orient. The sending forth of our own deputations to Europe, Asia, and Latin America which has characterized recent years is also to be heartily commended.

11. The only really safe and profitable way for us to study the interracial and the international problem is in the pathway of attempting to do something. We have learned the wisdom of this course in the pursuit of other studies in connection with which we have made the most satisfying progress. In this sphere, which has to deal with some of the most tragic realities, we shall find no exception.

12. Recognition of this truth at once summons us Christians and all who would go Christ's way to a more fearless following of Him, whatever the cost. This means the clear-cut determination to bring His principles to bear in all our own interracial and international contacts. It means banishing cowardly cautions and foolish fears. The leaders among the early Christians were always venturing something,

always risking something. So today there is no making terms with things as they are. The call is always to what is beyond.

13. To this end we are challenged to wage uncompromising warfare against national and racial prejudice, against unjust or unequal social and political arrangements and practices, and against those attitudes and habits which hinder fellowship, such as luxury, arrogance, and, above all, war itself as the final denial of brotherhood.

14. The clear call to mind, conscience, and will comes to us here in North America to help right wrongs which we personally or, as members of our nations, collectively, have done to other peoples; for example, the spread of corrupt films or movies throughout the Far East, the Near East, and the islands of the Southern Seas; the toleration of lynching; the leaving unrighted of the harm done by the Japanese Exclusion Act.

15. Let us seek to propagate the idea and practice around which this convention has been built and which it has so well illustrated—the conception of mutual sharing on the part of all nations and races on the higher levels of their life. We have been in the habit of speaking of sending-countries and receiving-countries but let us henceforth look upon every nation represented here as a country which is under obligation to share its best and under like obligation to welcome and receive the best of other lands. Every nation, every race, every little band of Christians, every individual Christian, has a unique and absolutely indispensable contribution to make to the all-embracing Christian fellowship and program. Let every people be given adequate opportunity to bring their glory and honor into the Kingdom of God. Let us henceforth as never before seek to work out together fresh interpretations of the Person, teaching, work, and spirit of Jesus Christ. Let us afford to an unbelieving world the demonstration of the reality that we are "workers together with God," and thus let us present the triumphant apologetic.

STUDENTS AND THE FUTURE OF CHRISTIAN MISSIONS

ADDRESS GIVEN AT
THE STUDENT VOLUNTEER CONVENTION
BUFFALO, NEW YORK, 1932

The future of Christian missions rests with the delegates to this convention and with your colleagues and comrades among the Christian students, not only in the colleges and universities which you represent, but also in the educational institutions across the breadth of the world, as upon no other group. This is not theory; it is supported by the unfolding centuries of the history of the Christian Church. Never was it more true of a student generation than of yours which is now taking the torch, and which is one so fittingly represented in this creative gathering.

I have unlimited confidence in this particular group and those who are your comrades, for I know them from recent contacts with the student communities over the wide world.

I have attended all the conventions of the Student Volunteer Movement. In a sense there have been thirteen, though nominally we might say there have been only twelve. We often overlook the first of the series, the one that met by the banks of the Connecticut at Mount Hermon, in the summer of 1886, the first international Christian student conference ever held. There we had representatives of eighty-nine Canadian and American universities and colleges; likewise foreign students from some eight or ten other nations. We were there to the number of 251. It was not a hasty weekend. It did not last, as some of our modern conferences do, a week or possibly ten days, but four full weeks. There was only one general meeting each day, so that ample time was left for the most intimate fellowship one with the other, and a deepening and expanding acquaintance with the living God.

It is not altogether surprising that under those conditions God's voice became very audible, very distinct, and very personal, and that an even 100 of the 251, by the last morning before we separated, had decided that, God willing, they would become foreign missionaries. I make bold to say that in the history of the Christian conferences of students the world over, there has been no other quite so highly productive. I refer not so much to the numerical aspect as to the fact that the Mount Hermon conference made possible the creation of the Student Volunteer Movement. The other twelve conventions that we hear more about would not have taken place had it not been for that great creative act of God, working through a generation of undergraduates on both sides of the line here in North America, and on both sides of the Atlantic and of the Pacific.

Then came Cleveland in '91; Detroit in '94; Cleveland again in '98; the memorable meeting in Massey Hall, Toronto, in 1902; the likewise dynamic meeting in Nashville in 1906; the one in the neighboring city, Rochester, in 1910. Contrary to my early impressions, I find in my travels that this latter was one of the most productive of all the series. We cannot judge, again I say, by numbers. God breaks out in little companies, I am inclined to think, more than in the great masses. But after all what counts is what follows the assembly. I have come in these long years to judge gatherings not so much by what takes place in the days of never-to-be-forgotten fellowship as by the measure in which we follow through and fill with living content the visions and high and holy and unselfish purposes we form during these creative days.

Some in this hall will remember the next meeting in 1914 out in Kansas City, possibly the most largely attended of the whole series and certainly one of the most powerful. Then came those tragic war years; but we did not let them pass without a calling together of the shattered ranks, more especially in Canada, but also in the United States. At this meeting, very fittingly held in Northfield, in the midst of those solemn days God did speak to us some very deep and challenging as well as humbling words.

The interval changed as the war came to a close, and the meeting held at Northfield in 1918 was followed by one at Des Moines in 1920. There we met under the pressure of changed world conditions and confronting almost impossible situations, but God conquered the difficulties, over-mastered the gathering, and creative results followed. In 1924 the Indianapolis meeting was held, followed in 1928 by the convention at Detroit. Some people speak lightly of these, contrasting them with some of the earlier gatherings. I do not share this opinion. I should find it difficult to overstate my sense of the importance of the Indianapolis and Detroit conferences, meeting in the most difficult moment in the life of the Student Volunteer Movement. How necessary those gatherings were to make possible united thinking, united vision, united planning, and united action!

Now we assemble in this thirteenth gathering. My good friends Robert Speer and Dr. Sailer, and I are the only persons here who have been present at the twelve gatherings. I am the only one who has attended the entire thirteen, and you will agree with me that this has not proved to be an unlucky number.

Those of us who belong to an older generation will do our best in any years that remain to us and will gladly lay down our lives fighting shoulder to shoulder with you and seeking to strengthen your hands in any way in our power; but our generation will not live long enough to effect the extensive and profound changes involved in meeting the demands of the world mission of Christianity. You will. Your unspent years, your unexhausted energies, your abounding idealism and hope, your undimmed vision, and your spirit of courage and adventure place the future in your hands.

You ask, what is the task of the world mission of Christianity in the years which lie ahead? Let me attempt to state it quite simply. The governing purpose of the Church in the world is to make Jesus

Christ known, trusted, loved, obeyed, and exemplified in the whole range of individual life and in all human relationships. This requires on the part of your generation a fresh apprehension of the great Central Figure of the Ages, the Lord Jesus Christ, and a commanding realization of the purpose of God in the life of the world. It involves such an expansion of the Christian program as will bring into view and under fresh, intelligent, sympathetic, and conscientious consideration the vast range of human need. Moreover, it calls for so rethinking, restating, and revising the working program of all the Christian Churches—the older Churches of Europe, North America, and Australasia, and the younger Churches of Asia, Africa, and Latin America —as will lead to such distribution or redistribution of Christ's representatives and agencies as will make possible His vitalizing and transforming truth, love, and power being brought to bear upon all areas of life. All this, in turn, calls for such a liberation, mobilization, and utilization of the latent forces of Christianity as the world has never known. How comparatively latent the powers of Christianity still are! What powers are latent? The clerical leadership of our day, both at home and abroad, is startlingly inadequate to meet the modern demands, whether we have in mind filling existing gaps, or providing a worthy succession for men who must soon transfer their burdens to younger shoulders, or superseding relatively incompetent workers, or keeping from breaking down under impossible strain those who are overburdened, or meeting the multiplying demands of higher specialization. The lay forces are, if possible, even more latent. Think, also, of the financial resources not yet brought under the sway of Christ, and, therefore, absolutely unrelated to the plans of His expanding Kingdom. What alarming lack there is of the powers of statecraft in the affairs of the Church. Even more clamant is the demand for courageous prophets, for inspiring apostles, such as Kagawa, and for sacrificial examples, like Schweitzer. Schweitzer's name calls to memory his vital word: "Those who have felt the discipline of suffering must enter the Fellowship of Pain and seek to deliver others from the fetters of sorrow. It is my desire to be a forerunner preparing the way for this renaissance and to fling my faith in a new humanity like a burning firebrand into the gloomy darkness of our times."

Why must we look to the students now thronging our universities, colleges, and seminaries to augment and strengthen the leadership of the world mission of our Christian faith? The stupendous and profound changes in the world in recent years make necessary a leadership of such capacity and resource as will enable the forces of righteousness and unselfishness to orient themselves to the vast situation and its exacting requirements. Bolshevism and nationalism have broken up the old world; a new world is in the making. Expressed simply the task of leaders of the new day is to mold a future far better than the past.

The summons comes afresh to wage a better-planned, more aggressive, and triumphant warfare against the age-long enemies of mankind—ignorance, poverty, disease, strife, superstition, secularism, and sin. The leaders in that warfare must have a more highly specialized training, and, if possible, even greater accessions of power of every kind than did their predecessors.

Such distinctively qualitative leadership is essential in order that the builders of the new civilization may possess the necessary background, outlook, insight, and grasp to grapple successfully with their large and emergent problems. Never did the undertaking of bringing in a right world-order seem to me to be so difficult as it does now. In virtually every country the situation to be dealt with differs greatly from the past in scale, complexity, and pace—because of modern invention, improved communications, multiplied contacts, new and wider human relationships. This is true in economic issues, in social uplift, in political reform, in sex relations, in racial problems, likewise in the realm of apologetics or the thought bases of the Christian faith.

Internationally, the last few years have brought mankind into a new world. The fact is that the present is the first generation which has been called upon to deal in any large way with international relations, and it finds itself inadequately prepared. The peoples simply do not understand their post-war world. They find themselves more or less committed politically to arrangements and institutions for which the intellectual foundations have not been laid. Countless dangerous prejudices have still to be slain. Whole peoples must be changed in disposition and habits and, therefore, in knowledge and motives. Such a period of reconstruction demands truly great national and international leadership in churchmanship, in statecraft, and in all other spheres dealing with human conduct.

In every relationship of mankind leaders are needed who are qualified to deal with the basic economic facts. Economic questions have come tremendously to the front in every part of the world. Economic and political policies and programs are out of gear, or not integrated. The world's economic life has been shifting rapidly from a national to an international base, and a sense of industrial and economic solidarity is spreading across national boundaries the world over. "Our political conceptions," as Dr. Zimmern points out, "have not caught up with our machines. We are trying to serve a twentieth-century world with eighteenth-century political ideas." As a result tens of millions of unemployed working men and women are walking the streets of European and American cities.

To meet successfully, because constructively, the startling manifestations of divisive forces and influences—economic, social, international, interracial—there must be a leadership competent to effect the closer and more effective co-operation and unification of religious and all other constructive forces.

Such strengthened leadership is needed in order that the constructive forces themselves, including the world mission of Christianity, may be ushered into a more advanced stage of development and usefulness. Their programs must be restudied, restated, and revised in the light of fresh thought and human relations. This statement includes programs of churches at home and abroad. Seldom, if ever, has the Christian Church more needed the awakening and guidance of prophetic voices. And there is no compelling prophecy without clear thinking, sincerity, and courage.

One shrinks from attempting to prophesy, but the topic assigned to me, "The Future of Christian Missions," necessitates that I venture to forecast in some measure the undertakings which should and, I pray God, may, absorb the highest powers of your generation in relation to the world program of Christ. This I will seek to do in concise outline.

In the first place, the Christian missions of the coming day must bring about a vivid recognition of the fact that the frontier of Christian missions must be thought of in the future less as geographical than as having to do with the areas of life and of human relationships —social, economic, rural, racial, international—and likewise with the realm of thought. This great shift in emphasis marks the change in missionary program and policy between the time of the world missionary conference in Edinburgh, in 1910, and the one recently held in Jerusalem.

Having emphasized this significant fact, let me quickly add that there are still vast, totally unoccupied geographical areas. These are inhabited by tens of millions among whom there are still no missionaries or missionary agencies. In other words, the day of the pioneer, the adventurer, I might say, in the spiritual sense, the pathfinder and foundation-layer is by no means over. I appeal, therefore, to the strongest and most heroic strains in present-day student life to fling themselves with apostolic abandon into these regions beyond.

The new day calls upon a new generation to lend themselves to the larger evangelism. The evangelistic objective, from the day when Christ said to his little band "Ye shall be witnesses unto me," has been the governing objective of Christian missions. It must ever be kept central. Incomparably the most vital, the most important, the most highly multiplying, and the most enduring work in which mortal man can possibly engage is that of exposing men to the Living Christ. But the day is at hand for the larger evangelism—larger in the sense of larger desire, larger message, larger adaptation of means to our supreme end, larger unity among the Christian forces, larger accessions of superhuman wisdom, love, and power. Never were the fields to which this convention directs our gaze more ripe unto harvest. How true this is the most recent letters from Sherwood Eddy in China and Stanley Jones in India, not to mention like trustworthy witnesses of other fields, abundantly testify.

Christian missions of tomorrow as well as today must be concerned with taking more seriously the carrying out of the policy of devolution agreed upon at the Jerusalem Conference, that is, the handing over increasingly to the rising indigenous Churches responsibility for initiative, decision, and leadership in the carrying forward of the work of these Churches. It is one thing to take this high ground in conferences and conventions; it is quite another thing to go through the sacrificial and trustful process involved in the implications of our convention resolutions or findings. We need to look on the rising Churches as we would upon youth. Early in my life of service among the students throughout the world I learned to trust youth. Never have I regretted any act of trust of youth, even though they have made mistakes or blunders. At times I have regretted that I had not trusted them more. It is the same way with reference to these rising Churches in different parts of the non-Christian world. They rise to the heights when trusted with impossible loads of responsibility.

The missionary movement is only in the early stage of the period of specialization. The generation to which you belong will be called upon to expand it on every hand. In the early days of the Student Volunteer Movement only three or four phases of missionary service were presented to the students, such as the evangelistic, medical, and educational. Recently I had occasion to draw up a list of not fewer than twenty-six quite different forms of missionary service of which I had witnessed examples in different parts of the world. How this widens the range of the missionary appeal to the student life of the present day! How it multiplies the number of outlets for student consecration of lives of service!

One of the most inspiring aspects of the world-wide opportunity of the days before us is that of carrying forward the wonderful process ushered in at the recent Jerusalem Conference—the process of sharing. In some respects that word and the idea which it connotes were what gave unique distinction to that creative meeting on the Mount of Olives. There for the first time in the history of Christian missions there met on an equality the representatives of the older Churches of the West and the younger Churches of the Orient and Africa. They met on a parity, not only as to numbers, but as to what is more significant: participation, leadership, the exercise of formative influence on program and policy. Never can world missions be the same. All students of today and tomorrow who aspire to lives of largest helpfulness, whether they be students among the nationals of the rising indigenous Churches planted by the missionaries or whether they be the new Student Volunteers going forward from the universities of North America and Europe, are called upon to share with each other. "To share what?" one may ask. To share experience, knowledge, insight, vision, personalities, opportunities, burdens, suffering, creative processes. Toward all these the workers of every land can contribute, and, in addition to what we contribute in common, the Christians of each nation will have something quite original or unique to offer to the Christians of other names and other climes. We are learning increasingly what a large Christ we have who requires all of us through whom to express adequately the wonders of His truth and His power.

This leads me to emphasize that within the sphere of co-operation and unity the Christian missions of tomorrow must make great strides forward if they are to be true to the situation which confronts them. We might divide the great movement of drawing together the Christians into three stages, so far as the world mission is concerned. In the first place, there was the period which preceded the world missionary conference at Edinburgh in 1910—a period characterized by countless detached pieces or demonstrations of co-operative or united effort on the part of Christians of different denominations or races. Then, there came the period between Edinburgh and Jerusalem, the distinguishing characteristic of which was the development of interdenominational and international machinery designed to foster united thinking, planning, and action. This was the period in which the number of national Christian councils was increased from two to twenty-eight. These are the bodies which unite all the Christian Churches and missions of a given national or international field for the realization of their important common ends. It was the period, also, which witnessed the evolution of the International Missionary Council, which federates loosely but effectively all these vital national bodies and for the first time in the history of Christianity is making possible dealing with the world program of Christianity in literally world-wide dimensions. The third period on which in these days we are entering is the one in which the Christian workers of all denominations, nations, and races are going to be called upon, as never before, to take seriously the implications of the machinery created and the programs adopted with reference to co-operation and unity. In other words, we must see clearly that the drawing together of the Christian forces for unity in organization and plan was never intended to be an end in itself but to make possible the realization of the most vital and stupendous results. It will be remembered by all of us that Christ in His high priestly prayer prayed that "they all might be one," not as an end in itself, but "that the world might believe." My faith leads me to congratulate those present and those whom you represent on the possibility which is yours to fill in with practical living content the vision which has increasingly commanded the older generation.

If the multiplying exalted and crushing responsibilities which these advance measures require are to be realized, those of your day must go into training and stay in training longer than did your predecessors. You are to enter into co-operation with peoples who are at a more advanced stage intellectually than characterized the peoples of the earlier generations. The problems confronting you are more numer-our and more exacting than those with which your predecessors had to deal. You do well, therefore, to lay a broader and deeper founda-tion. This leads me to suggest the great desirability of a closer integra-tion on the part of the candidate departments of the various mission boards and the Student Volunteer Movement in all that has to do with the subject of missionary preparation. The emphasis must be increas-ingly on the qualitative as contrasted with the quantitative.

To give effect to the implications of the modern shrinkage of the world—that of the need of Christianizing the impact of the so-called Western Christian nations upon the non-Christian world—requires that all Christian students who may not be called by God to devote their entire lives to the missionary career shall, with like sense of re-sponsibility, resolve that within the sphere of their calling they will do all in their power to strengthen the hands of their comrades who do enter upon the missionary career. This means that Christian students who are to devote themselves to the world-wide expansion of industry, commerce, and finance, or who are to engage in the diplomatic and consular service of their governments, or who may be identified with armies and navies, or who have anything to do with the spread of the moving picture industry to other lands, or who as government teach-ers, or lecturers, or scholars sent abroad on errands of investigation or research, or those who are part of the tides of travel shall recognize and seize their opportunity to commend by word and life the gospel which their missionary colleagues are seeking to propagate. The day has dawned when we must all recognize and seek to realize Christian missions as the great internationalism. Only in our day have many in each country come to recognize that the problems which we had re-garded as national are in reality of world-wide interest and concern, and, therefore, can be solved only in a world context and in a world-wide program. This is seen with great vividness in the economic problem. It is likewise true in the conquest of disease, in the throttling of the opium curse, the drink evil, and the white slave traffic, in the meeting of the difficult questions involved in emigration and immigration, in the realm of race conflict, international misunderstandings, and the outlawry of war. One of my eight visits to China was right after the Boxer War, in connection with which scores of missionaries and thousands of Chinese Christians were massacred. It was a time of intense bitterness between Orientals and Occidentals. You will agree with me that in these recent years the world has had an adequate demonstration of what colossal military power can do; and, am I not right in asserting that it has accentuated rather than relieved misunderstandings, friction, and strife among nations and peoples? Has not the time come, therefore, for us to turn with unshakable conviction to the alternative and lend our lives until death to the spread of Christianity in its purest form? I love to think of the 30,000 missionaries, Protestant, Roman Catholic, Eastern Orthodox, as ambassadors, in the finest and richest content of that term; as interpreters, interpreting the best side of the life of the nation which sent them and, likewise, the best side of the one which has received them; as mediators, in some humble sense breaking down the walls or partitions of misunderstanding between peoples; and as exemplars, reminding those among whom they labor and with whom they co-operate, by their actual presence as well as their teaching, that there is a Christian fellowship or brotherhood which transcends all national and racial boundaries.

What is required of the Christian students of today and tomorrow if they are to usher in this new and greater day of Christian missions? We must project from this convention an educational campaign in all our colleges and other institutions of higher learning, a campaign of such scope, up-to-dateness, vitality, and prophetic quality as will make possible a truly comprehending leadership of the missionary forces, both within and outside these institutions. Such an awareness is our basic need and it should emphasize the present completely changed, expansive, urgent, and perilous world situation near and far. There should be knowledge of the antecedents or background of the peoples to be served, and of their most sacred and powerful traditions. There must be recognition of the trends of thought and feeling which are moving among them, and of their greatly changed psychology. There is needed a grasp of the real issues which profoundly affect human progress. The areas of conflict must be discerned and strategic positions located. Leaders must see clearly the forces which oppose them and likewise recognize favoring conditions and factors of which they may take advantage. In days like these they should know the basi-

unanswered questions, especially in the minds of youth. It is of supreme importance that leaders should have a realizing sense of the values, motives, and possibilities of human personality, and a reverent recognition of superhuman resources.

The leadership so much needed in all lands which we are to serve and in all callings related to Christian missions should be creative. Among the many men and women holding positions of major responsibility in the work of Christ there are all too many merely mechanical workers and all too few thinkers. Bishop Gore has expressed concisely the reason why in every field of human endeavor there are so many unsolved problems and so little progress, "We do not think, and we do not pray." Undoubtedly, undue stress is being placed, especially in our Anglo-Saxon countries, on the need of organizers, promoters, men of action. The heroes of a new generation are, to an extent that many do not realize, highly paid engineers and managers of big business. To an alarming degree this tendency is becoming more and more apparent even in the educational field and in the churches. The curricula of our schools and universities are too much dominated by materialistic aims, and religious bodies are feeling as never before the secular pressure of the age. Not without reason is the charge made that we in our colleges and seminaries are producing Christian activity and organization more than Christian experience, faith, and philosophy. As a result there is a poverty of germinating, dynamic ideas, creative planning, and great prophetic leadership.

How essential it is that those of us who tomorrow are to lead the constructive forces shall pay vigilant heed that the discipline of our lives, the culture of our souls, and the thoroughness of our processes of spiritual discovery and appropriation be such as will enable us to meet the challenge of our day. We must bear in mind that we are dealing not with a static world but with a dynamic world. Even more important, we should live and act as those who are in touch with the Ever-living and, therefore, the Ever-creative God.

A statesmanlike leadership is required today even more, if possible, than ever before in Christian missions as in all other spheres where constructive measures and advance programs are needed. A number of elements enter into true statesmanship. The statesman is a man of vision—a man who sees what the crowd do not see because he sees farther and more clearly. He takes in wider horizons, larger dimensions. How absolutely true it is that where there is no vision the people perish. Conversely, it can be said that where open doors remain unentered, great wrongs go unrighted, sinister forces gather momentum, depths of human need continue unmet, it is because so-called leaders lack vision, or, through disobedience to it, have allowed vision to fade.

The statesman accepts and applies guiding principles. In times of confusion and perplexity he turns to these as he would to the North Star. No matter how strong and conflicting the crosscurrents of popular prejudice and passion, no matter how insinuating the voices of selfish ambition or other unworthy motives, no matter how many oppose him or how few go with him—he trusts and follows his principles. Much of the power of Gandhi lies in the fact that he has wrought out and is seeking to bring to bear upon a vast, complex, and most difficult situation four governing principles, namely, the principles of nonviolence or passive resistance, religious unity, removal of untouchability, and economic independence. The enunciation by Sun Yat Sen of his three principles—nationality, democracy, and livelihood—has already had a great revolutionary and transforming effect on the peoples of China.

The recognition and observance of relationships marks the statesman of widest influence and largest helpfulness. The multiplication of organizations or agencies, the marked development of specialization of knowledge and function in the missionary enterprise, and the great improvement of means of communication with resulting increase of human contacts, combine to accentuate the necessity of this qualification.

Was it not Curzon who said, "We rule by the heart"? If this be true, then heart-power, or sympathy, is one of the sources of the power of the statesman and pre-eminently of the missionary. The study of biography enforces this truth in many of its most moving pages. By contagious examples it shows that in the various spheres of missionary service the men and women who have been most true to the heart (and also to the imagination), and identified themselves with their fellows in the midst of suffering, poverty, loneliness, and burden-bearing, have had deepest and most abiding influence.

Another statesmanlike trait is that of foresight and wisdom in planning. This suggests the aphorism of Theodore Roosevelt that "nine-tenths of wisdom is being wise in time." Next to character, possibly the highest gift of the statesman is that prescience which enables him to recognize in time the days of God's visitation. May He enable us to see that we are now living in such days!

The attitude of open-mindedness and the habit of seeking counsel have been characteristic of many of the greatest among missionary statesmen. A truly great teacher never ceases to be a scholar. The man who maintains his leadership in any calling does not part company with or hold himself aloof from those whom he would lead. "A leader is," Bishop Brent has said, "simply a foremost companion." We are living in a time when the benefits of group thinking are being much

every land, is a growing acquaintance and a deepening fellowship with this Central Figure. In seeking to augment the leadership of the forces of righteousness and unselfishness it is well to follow His unerring lead—as the Way, the Truth, and the Life. Indeed, His lead has been demonstrated beyond peradventure to have been an unerring one. When has He been known to lead one into a blind alley? When has following Him, cost what it might, resulted in contracting the range or weakening the power of one's leadership? Let it be reiterated. He affords the most satisfying definition of true greatness, of enduring leadership: "Whosoever would be greatest (that is, first) among you, shall be the servant of all." He imparts a sense of mission which surmounts all difficulties, opposition, discouragement, and loneliness. To Him we go for those guiding principles which, when resolutely and courageously applied, solve problems and effect the revolutionary and transforming changes. In fellowship with Him and in contact with His enormous consciousness of God men catch the spirit which overcomes the world—the spirit of unselfishness and faith. He, by His penetrating word exemplified on the Cross, ushers us into the real secret of the most highly multiplying influence of any leader: "Except a grain of wheat fall into the ground and die it abideth by itself alone, but if it die it bringeth forth much fruit." The depth of one's experience in this creative realm determines the outreach of one's work and influence. Jesus Christ was the Great Visionary. Alone He looked down through the ages and saw the peoples of all conditions, nations, and races streaming up to His Cross, when He cried, "I, if I be lifted up from the earth, will draw all men unto me."

THE TASKS OF TOMORROW

ADDRESS GIVEN AT
THE STUDENT VOLUNTEER CONVENTION
INDIANAPOLIS, INDIANA, 1936

We have been profoundly impressed by Dr. Speer's recital of the achievements and influence of the Student Volunteer Movement during the half-century of its life. But the best days of the Student Volunteer Movement are before us. It must be so. There could be nothing more dishonoring to our past than to assume or plan or act as though this were not to be the case. Think of numbers alone. When this Movement was launched in 1886 there were scattered throughout the entire student field of the United States and Canada only a few score of students who were even thinking of becoming foreign missionaries. Today we have literally hundreds of announced volunteers for foreign missions in the institutions of higher learning of both countries. Moreover, half a century ago in all the colleges and universities of North America, there were not over 200,000 students, both men and women. Today there are over 1,000,000. Of this great number fully one-half are members of Christian churches. It is inconceivable that these larger numbers of followers of Christ and all those who have already formed the missionary purpose cannot under God accomplish greater things than the smaller number of their predecessors of years ago.

Think also of the great expansion of Christian organization. In the days of the beginning of the Movement, there were only about 300 societies of Christian students in colleges, universities, and seminaries in the United States and Canada. At present there are over 1,500. In those days there were fewer than 200 such organizations in all the other lands, whereas today there are more nearly 2,000. We now have the World's Student Christian Federation uniting some 3,000 Christian societies of various names in over thirty nations on all continents and with a combined membership of 300,000. What is organization but the means of distributing force most advantageously? Surely this makes possible something greater and better than was possible before such facilities were to any such extent available.

Moreover, the Student Volunteer Movement and related societies at home and abroad have accumulated a vast body of knowledge and experience in all that pertains to arresting the attention and enlisting the interest, enthusiasm, and co-operation of Christian students in great unselfish causes. How much more we know today than in those earlier days about the needs of Christian students, their opportunities, their preparation for most useful service, the ways and means of fostering their interest and directing their energies! What a wonderful half century of experience it has been! What does it not teach in the way of warnings; also in the way of incitement for courageous initiative, sacrificial devotion, and triumph over the impossible!

Think also of the momentum of success. I refer to the countless constructive achievements in the pathway of the work of the Student Volunteer Movement, and to the great volume of confidence built up —in a word, to the habit of victory which has been formed. What a priceless thing momentum is! One might change the term and instead speak of a rising tide. It is always wise to take advantage of a rising tide. Then vastly more can be achieved for Christ and his Kingdom in a relatively short time than in long, wearying, waiting periods when the tide of interest and unselfish passion is falling.

We should remind ourselves also of the priceless heritage which is ours as a result of the lives and achievements of the thousands of volunteers who have gone forth from us into all parts of the world field, and who have thus fulfilled their volunteer declaration. Who can estimate the contagious and propulsive power of their dedicated lives? Our memories throng tonight with such examples as Sir William Wanless, Dr. Avison, and Bishop Lea of the Toronto colleges, in their wonderful work in India, Korea, and Japan; Charles Paterson of McGill in his service for schoolboys in Calcutta; and Murdoch Mackenzie, also of McGill, in his great foundation work in Honan, China. We think likewise of men like Tewksbury and Houghton of Harvard; of Horace Pitkin, William Borden, and Sherwood Eddy of Yale; of McKee of Cornell; of MacCracken of Pennsylvania; of F. P. Price and his son, both of Virginia; of George Worth and his son, both of North Carolina; of Fletcher Brockman of Vanderbilt and his marvelous career in China; of Dr. Caroline Macdonald, so worthily honored with one of the highest degrees of Toronto University for her Christlike ministry in Japan; also Dr. B. Chroné Oliver of Canada, an outstanding leader in the medical missionary program of India; Charlotte deForest of Smith College, now the able principal of Kobe College, Japan. We think of others outside our own continent who have been a source of inspiration and help to us on this side the Atlantic by their lives and Christlike deeds, such as Ruth Rouse, for years the woman secretary of the World's Student Christian Federation; Constance Padwick and her remarkable service of fostering the creation of Christian literature for Moslems the world over; of Dr. Donald Fraser, one of the founders of the Student Volunteer Missionary Union of the British Isles, and later one of the noblest of the great missionary host of Africa; Alec Fraser of Oxford, one of the most dynamic Christian leaders in India and later in East and West Africa; the great team in the Nile Valley, Gairdner of Oxford and Thornton of Cambridge; likewise Witt of Germany in his wonderful work; de Vargas of Switzerland in his intensive, constructive work in Yenching, North China; L. P. Larsen, one of the greatest of a long line of Danish missionaries, and his four decades in India; de Pertis, the lone student volunteer going forth from Italy to his great medical work in Abyssinia; Dr. Kraemer of the Dutch universities and his unique leadership in the work for Moslems, not only in the Netherlands Indies, but in the interest of the whole Mohammedan world; and McNeur and Mawson of New Zealand. The list would run on indefinitely. I myself, in my world travels, have met thousands of these former student volunteers, absorbed in their great unselfish cause of making Christ known and regnant in the life of the peoples with whom they have identified themselves. What college or other institution represented here tonight has not been inspired and blessed by some such examples of its own? It would be difficult to exaggerate the kindling and propulsive power of such a heritage.

The greatly enlarged and enriched program of the world mission, and the wider appeal which this makes possible today, should serve to usher us into far greater achievements for Christ and his cause. One need only contrast the programs of the early conventions of the Student Volunteer Movement with that of the present convention to be impressed with the greatly widened range of appeal as well as with the more exacting demands of the period upon which we have entered.

May we not say reverently, also, that we today have a larger Christ than in those days. Not a new Christ, for he is the same yesterday, today, and forever, but larger in the sense that there are today so many more millions of people throughout the non-Christian world than there were five decades ago who, through the preaching, teaching, and living of the volunteers and other missionaries of the past, have come to know Christ and to have an authentic experience of Christ. Moreover, there are many more communities and areas of life which have been completely transformed by the living Christ. There have also been such convincing demonstrations in impossible economic, international, and interracial, situations of the conquering power of Christ that these constitute added apologetics of the Christian faith. Thank God, He is the living Christ, therefore the ever-creative Christ, and therefore able, ready, and eager to work in and through us today and tomorrow to do new things and to manifest fresh wonders to the honor of his Name.

We who are entering upon the work of tomorrow, must meet a tremendous combination of difficulties and of major unsolved problems. Never did our great task of establishing the reign of Christ seem so difficult to me as it does now, as we consider the magnitude, complexity, and pace of these problems. Do not such overwhelming situations and demands make necessary, and thus make possible, the larger manifestations of his wisdom, love, and power? In view of all these and other considerations, I maintain with you that we have immeasurably more to build upon than did our fellow students of half a century back. Surely this should make possible a greater superstructure. When has a generation of Christian students been called upon to face so many heroic challenges?

1. First among these confronting the students of this new day is the challenge to face an unprecedented world situation. Surely this is true in the number of open doors. There has been nothing like it in the annals of the Christian religion. I grant you there have been times

when in certain parts of the world the doors were as widely ajar to the friendly and constructive ministry of the Christian faith as they are today. But never has there been a time when simultaneously on all continents the doors were so wide open to the messengers and agencies of Christ as they are today. If this be true, we are living in one of the most inspiring and fateful moments in the life of mankind. The serious thing is that this opening of the wide world comes at the same time when the Christian forces of the United States and Canada are called upon, I repeat, to deal with the greatest combination of unsolved problems which we have ever had to face. What can be the reason? May it not be the one that came to me on the high seas one day: that our loving, heavenly Father brooding over His vast human family recognized that He has coming forward now a body of Christians with whom He can trust a situation that is literally world-wide? And let it be emphasized that a Christ who cannot deal simultaneously with all the deepest needs of North America and the rest of the world, is not the Christ to whom we bow down and whom we worship.

The world situation today is unparalleled in urgency. This is due to the rising tides of nationalism and of racial patriotism, both in a most sinister aspect and likewise in a most challenging and hopeful aspect. It is due also to the significant fact that the world is still in a plastic state, although soon to become fixed or set. This makes it of supreme urgency that we lose no time in helping to determine the molds in which the new world shall set. Another splendid reason the time is so urgent is because we are living at a time of rising spiritual tide. This is manifest in the spirit of inquiry all over the world; in the vast multiplication of open forums and study classes and discussion groups for group thinking and the sharing of insight, experience, and purpose; in the growing flood of books and other literature dealing with religious subjects; in the growing spirit of criticism both superficial and thorough and well directed; and, above all, in the Christward movement in so many of the difficult fields both East and West, both North and South.

Another indication that we are facing an unexampled situation is the recent startling development of divisive influences among men. Some of these are in the economic realm. Here we have in mind not the obvious, that is, the age-long conflict between the rich and the poor and between employer and employee. We are thinking of something much more serious, and suggested by such phrases as economic imperialism, commercial exploitation, the dislocations and inequalities due to the machine age, the unjust or unfair use of natural resources, and of great open spaces.

Other divisive tendencies are in the international realm. I confess that never has my heart been nearer standing still with concern about the international outlook than in these days. The reasons for this are self-evident on almost every hand. Quite as alarming also is the interracial friction and strife. A little over a year ago this was burned in upon me as never before when I was in that hottest spot of the world from an interracial standpoint, South Africa. But South Africa is not alone in this respect. With shame must we concede that the United States of America is still an inflamed area. What we are hearing about the Jews in Germany is not exceptional. It could be multiplied in other parts of central, southeastern, and eastern Europe. As I think of the misunderstanding, bitterness, and tension between peoples—Oriental and Occidental, and in other zones of conflict—I am reminded of a memorable conversation which I had with that distinguished Irish civilian, Sir Robert Hart in the year following the Boxer War. He had been in China many years and knew the psychology of the East. You will recall that in that war scores of missionaries and thousands of Chinese Christians were slain because they would not stamp on the Cross of Christ. I said, "Sir Robert, what is the way out?" He replied, "There must either be a colossal military and naval establishment,"—and then he went on to say that it must be "so colossal that it would break down the so-called powers of the world to maintain it, or"—and now notice the alternative—"the spread of Christianity in its purest form." Surely, fellow students, we have in the intervening years had a demonstration of the colossal military and naval establishment. Has it relieved the strain? Has it reduced the number of friction points? Has it increased the volume of good will? Has not the moment come for us to turn with unshakable conviction and unselfish abandon to the alternative of Sir Robert, the spread of Christianity in its purest form?

2. This convention is challenged to recognize that the major problems of the United States and Canada can best be solved in an international or world context. Problems and perils which we have been accustomed to regard as purely national have suddenly assumed international significance. What are some of these problems and grave difficulties of ours which must be dealt with in international or, at times, world terms if they are to be understood, solved, or overcome? From the nature of the case the problem of ensuring right international relations and overcoming misunderstanding, ill will, and strife can be solved only in an international setting. The same must be true also of war, whether we are dealing with its causes or its results. Manifestly, this is true also of race and of immigration, which demand today thoroughgoing and heroic treatment. At what a price also are we in these days coming to see more and more clearly that certain aspects

of our economic problems can be met successfully only internationally; for example, questions of tariffs, currencies, use of natural resources, and of the great unoccupied spaces of the world. What great progress has been made in the conquest of some of the most deadly diseases since the world learned that disease does not stop at national boundaries. How much more must this be taken to heart internationally. Think also of certain other evils such as opium and other narcotic drugs, the liquor traffic, and the white slave traffic. The use of the cinema is, to a far greater extent than is generally realized, making for the growth of international misunderstanding, prejudice, and ill will. Then there are the anti-religious movements which are making such challenges for the allegiance of youth across the world; likewise problems related to the thought bases of religion in general and of the Christian religion in particular. Now that the world has found itself as one body, it can no longer be a matter of indifference to any one part of the body what is happening in these respects in other parts of the body. We are indeed members one of another.

The Christian students of this convention and our colleagues at home are challenged more than at any time in the past to go forth and join forces with the Christians of other lands, not as strangers and foreigners, but as neighbors, to make common warfare against common enemies. To the objection that we cannot think of Christianizing the world until we are more Christian ourselves here at home, we must reply that the very enterprise of the world mission of Christianity is a part of our work of Christianization at home. Why then should many of us leave the United States and Canada, some as missionaries and some in other pursuits? We should do so, first, because the West cannot solve its problems alone and cannot without foreign missions of the right kind solve them at all. Secondly, we should go because the East and the lands of the South cannot solve their problems alone. Thirdly, we go because East and West and North and South have each an absolutely unique and essential contribution to make to our common constructive work of true civilization and Christianization. Fourthly, because a universal Christ needs a universal interpretation. As I travel about the world, I am impressed both at home and abroad with the fact that so many Christians have such a small Christ. They give you the impression that their Christ has revealed Himself only to their particular nation, race, or communion. You and I of this great assembly of many lands and of many communions believe with conviction that we have a Christ so infinite that He requires all the nations, all the races, and all the communions through which to communicate His excellencies and His power.

3. We are all summoned to put forth effective efforts to Chris-

tianize the impact of our so-called Western civilization upon other lands. Missionaries alone cannot achieve this great Christian objective. It is my hope and belief that some hundreds of our great company of 3,000 delegates to this convention will, under the call of God, go forth in due time as foreign missionaries. But, doubtless, fully 2,000 or more of our number will have to make their contribution by forming other contacts and by exercising their influence along other lines, some of them in the realm of commerce, which I predict in the case of both the United States and Canada is going to expand enormously during the next two decades. Here we need young men with the spirit that dominated Captain Robert Dollar through over fifty years in his contacts with the Orient. He not only conducted his great commercial enterprise on Christian principles, but in his personal life and advocacy and in the exercise of his influence he commended the Christian gospel in season and out of season. The same could be said of Sir Robert Laidlaw during the years that he gave so much of his personal attention to his chain of stores in India and other parts of the East. Others will have the opportunity to influence financial policies and practices. The example of Sir Robert Hart furnishes a true model. For over forty years he administered with faultless integrity the vast Chinese Imperial Customs and also lived the life of a simple Christian layman in a way that exerted daily a genuine Christian influence. The fine examples set by Professor Jenks of Cornell in his day, and by Professor Kemmerer of Princeton in more recent years, in giving their financial advice to whole nations, may well be followed by many in days to come.

In the enormous expansion of industry in which our two countries are destined to participate, we are going to have one of the worthwhile opportunities to represent Christ. I think of one Western business manager of an industrial enterprise in the East, who had to pick seventeen young men to send out to a certain Oriental country as promoters. He insisted that every one of them should be a tested and trusted Christian, and his intimate instructions to them involved their setting a Christian example in all their relationships. Let us hope that many of our number will prepare to enter upon a diplomatic career in connection with our embassies and consulates in Asia, Africa, and Latin America. Would that we had more men like my classmate, Ransford S. Miller, who went out first as a missionary, but who early became so proficient in knowledge of the Japanese language, that his government commanded him and used his services for forty years in various capacities in Japan, Korea, and at Washington. What does the Christian cause not owe to his fidelity, as a Christian, to his trust, and to his improvement of his other Christian opportunities! Let me also refer to Francis B. Sayre, now Assistant Secretary of State. He was once a student in one of our eastern colleges, active in the Student Christian Association, then he went out into the diplomatic service in connection with the American Embassy in Siam. He was so impressed by the handicap and injustice of the extraterritorial arrangements that then obtained in Siam that his Christian conscience would not let him rest and he devoted himself to getting this wrong righted. Within two or three years his significant negotiations brought about the abolition of the extraterritorial arrangements by the various nations involved, and thus set Siam free. Would to God that other young men of like ability and conviction might have addressed themselves ten years ago, or earlier, to clearing up the same wrong with reference to China! In what a different position would she be standing today if this larger Christian service had been rendered her!

The vast civil service of the British Empire affords one of the greatest opportunities in times like these. Nothing interested me more in the last visit I made to Oxford and Cambridge than the way the leaders of the Student Christian Movement, in planning for the use of my time in each university, arranged for me to meet in intimate groups young men who are contemplating entering the civil service of their government in different parts of India and Africa. I found there was no livelier subject and none that commanded so much interest as this very question of what they could do in the civil service to commend the religion of Christ and to foster its spread. In this connection we might well encourage young men contemplating such service to read the work by Dr. George Smith, *Twelve Indian Statesmen*.

What an opportunity is presented to the thousands and tens of thousands of tourists who go forth from our country to visit other lands, especially lands in which missionaries are working; but in how many instances is their example a stumbling block rather than a help! A former leader of our Student Christian Association is so much impressed with this need that he has decided to become an agent of an important tourist bureau. His employers have agreed to give him a free hand to prepare the tourists under his guidance for visiting the lands where missionary work is in progress, and to make their visits a help and in no sense a hindrance.

In our lifetime I predict that hundreds of our ablest young men and women will be called upon to go forth and work as teachers and professors, not only in missionary colleges, but possibly even more in government institutions. This will open up one of the greatest opportunities that man can possibly have to Christianize our impact on these nations. How important it is that we use our influence to have as many of these positions as possible manned by Christians who will not only see the opportunity for commending Christ and his way of life, but also seize the opportunity! Many years ago we learned that the Japanese Government wanted some scores of young men to go out to teach English in their government schools, the government paying their expenses out and back and their salaries for a period, as I recall, of two years' service. The committee organized to select these workers insisted that their first qualification must be ability to teach English in the best possible manner from a professional point of view; but, secondly, they sought to select those who were genuine Christians possessing a spirit of service. First and last, as I recall, we sent 100. They did a splendid work. Some of them, after two years, were held for additional periods by the government. Some of them became missionaries and remained in Japan for a long period of time. Their work required that they teach some five hours each day, but they were free the rest of the day to serve the students in such ways as they might choose. They conducted a veritable network of Bible classes and groups for the discussion of all kinds of useful subjects bearing on the development of character and faith. I consider that it was one of the most highly productive services ever rendered by a group of men from the West in an eastern country.

Think also of the enormous and alarming influence being exerted by the "movies" from North America and Europe. It is said that this industry in America alone now has investments aggregating nearly $3,000,000,000. It is a startling fact that in all too many instances the influence of the "movies" or cinema from the West has been deleterious. Here is an opportunity for some of the ablest men and women to devise ways and means to make this a powerful agency for good and one that will foster right relations between our countries and the lands of Asia, Africa, and Latin America. The International Missionary Council is sending J. Merle Davis to the Far East in the near future, to give attention to this among other problems, as he has so effectively done in the recent past in Bantu Africa.

One of the most important opportunities that we shall ever have, and this is true of colleges represented here, is that of befriending foreign students who come within our gates. Some 11,000 or more are now in the institutions of learning in North America, representing sixty or more nations. I repeat, we will never have a greater opportunity than this of exposing them to the best life of our two countries, of taking them into our homes, of making true friends of them, and of commending our religion to them by life and work.

4. The challenge comes to all interested in the world mission to press the larger evangelism. Dr. Speer has spoken of the influence in the life of the Movement of its watchword, "The Evangelization

of the World in This Generation." I wish to endorse strongly what
he has said. My study of the influence of this watchword has impressed me with its wonderful power in expanding the conceptions of
Christian students, in vitalizing them, in unifying and concentrating
their forces, and in impelling them to heroic and self-sacrificing endeavors. It should be made clear today, as it always was in the early
days of the Movement, that the evangelization of the world in this
generation did not mean the conversion of the world in a generation,
or its Christianization in a generation, nor was it ever regarded as a
prophecy of what was likely to take place; nor did its advocates ever
stand for any hasty or superficial preaching of the Gospel, or neglect
of the resolute application of the Gospel to the obstinate social facts.
It does mean that it is the duty of each generation of Christians to
bring the knowledge of Christ to its own generation. An up-to-date
and well-reasoned statement concerning the basic arguments for such
a watchword is the recent book by Alexander McLeish of Scotland,
Jesus Christ and World Evangelization.

Be our views of the watchword what they may, we must all recognize the imperative obligation resting on Christians everywhere to
foster this objective. This is the greatest work in the world. Can we
question that it is the work most needed? Judged by results it is also
incomparably the most important. It is the most highly multiplying
and most enduring of all undertakings. The summons comes to us
in these days and those that lie ahead, to enter upon what may be well
called the larger evangelism. Larger in what senses? Basically, larger
in desire—a desire generated by thorough meditation on God and on
the depths of human need. It must be a larger evangelism in point
of comprehension. We must profoundly understand the peoples to
whom we proclaim the Evangel—their antecedents and background,
their greatly changed psychology, their unanswered questions regarding matters of life and destiny, and their battlegrounds. We must also
have a clear comprehension of the forces that are opposing the Christian faith and the Christian way of life, of the other appealing challenges for the allegiance of men today, of the forces and factors that
favor the ongoing of the Kingdom, and, above all, of the times in
which we live—virtually days of God's own visitation. The larger
evangelism involves a larger message. Christ, the heart of our message, is timeless, but there is need from time to time to restate the
message in terms that are relevant to the needs, the questionings, the
longings, the aspirations of men.

Great is the need also of larger adaptation of means, methods,
and measures to the accomplishment of our high and holy ends. A
larger unity is all-important, on the authority of Jesus Christ. When
He prayed that we all might be one, it is well to recall that He

did not mean that this unity was to be regarded as an end in itself. He prayed that "we all might be one, that the world may believe." If in different fields, near and far, we are confronted, as we are, with an unbelief which is not only extensive but profound, we may be sure that one of the causes is that we are not presenting adequately the climactic and triumphant apologetic—the vital, recognized unity of His followers. Let us, therefore, beginning with our college days and in our contacts in our communities in village and city, and then in distant lands in the case of those of us who are favored with the opportunity of spending our lives where Christ has not been named, concern ourselves with the great and primary task of evangelization, ever seeking so to present Christ to men that they will be confronted with the necessity of decision that He may work a complete change in their hearts, in their lives, and in their human relations.

5. We are summoned within the sphere of our lifework to strengthen in every way the rising indigenous Churches throughout Asia, Africa, and Latin America. It is an impressive fact that these, which are sometimes called younger Churches, throughout these continents, today number their communicant members by the millions. Within relatively recent years the center of gravity in the conduct of the world mission has shifted from the mission boards and the missions to these younger or rising, indigenous Churches; that is, to the Christian nationals. This process, spoken of as that of devolution, has made greater progress in some fields than in others, but the process is now in evidence in nearly every mission field. It calls for most intimate identification of the missionary and all that he represents with these developing Churches. All new missionaries must become vividly aware of this and go out prepared to adjust themselves to this new situation with full conviction and in the spirit of John the Baptist. The time has come in this vital matter for far greater acts of trust—trust of the nationals by the missionaries and the boards which send them. We must bear in mind and in plan not only the growing importance of the younger Churches but also their perils. There is serious peril in more than one field that these Churches may become separated from historical Christianity, creedal Christianity, ecumenical Christianity, mystical Christianity, applied Christianity, vital Christianity. This necessitates continued intimate relations between the Churches of the lands that send missionaries and those of the lands which receive the missionaries. Such close union is desirable, I sometimes think, quite as much for the older Churches as for the younger.

The Jerusalem Conference of 1928 brought into prominence and, I am glad to add, into practice, the idea of sharing. We should share knowledge, experience, insight, vision, opportunities, burdens, hopes, and faith. This involves sharing with one another some of our finest and most deeply experienced Christian personalities. I am not at all sure that in this mutual process the older Churches may not gain even more than the younger. If I were going into a new field where Christianity and other beneficent agencies had not been established, and were given the choice as to which institution to plant first, a church, a college, a hospital, or a Young Men's Christian Association, I say after my years of observation and reflection I should plant the Church first, well knowing that with this vital fountainhead insured, the other beneficent agencies and activities would inevitably follow. I do not think that the converse would be true. Therefore, in going forth in connection with the world mission, let the centrality of this aspect of the undertaking be clearly recognized.

6. There is a great demand today that we lend ourselves to the development of a higher specialization in the work of the world mission. A tremendous change has taken place in this respect in the last two or three decades. It has involved a shifting of emphasis from concern chiefly with the matter of numbers to a resolute effort to influence for Christ and by Christ all departments of human life and human relationships. The process of specialization is more advanced in some fields than in others. Moreover, there are certain forms of specialization which have been more widely introduced than have others. To illustrate what a multiplication in number and variety of forms of specialization is taking place, let me mention briefly a number of specialties in foreign mission service concerning which I have been questioned within a few months, either by those on the foreign field desiring such specialists or by persons who had been called upon to consider going out to work along certain special lines. Included in the list were the following: experts in religious education, in vocational guidance, in leadership training; experts to hold such chairs in colleges and seminaries as church history, Christian sociology, the Christian message or apologetics; professors or teachers in chemical engineering, electrical engineering, sanitary engineering; architects; men to organize financial guilds and Christian co-operative trade societies; treasurers and accountants; a research worker; secretaries and stenographers; Young Men's and Young Women's Christian Association secretaries, and Sunday School Association secretaries; workers to foster the preparation of Christian literature, and others to foster the wise use of Christian literature; directors of Christian welfare work for industrial groups; directors of Christian welfare work for rural communities or the countryside; directors of work in furtherance of right race relations; workers to devote themselves to promoting friendly relations among foreign students.

One other very important call came up in connection with my recent visit to China. There I observed the tremedous expansion of the government school system in connection with which there are hundreds of thousands of boys and girls, also young men and young women in high schools but who are largely like sheep without a shepherd. Only in almost a negligible number of cases were there workers centering their attention upon this most plastic and potentially important group. I came to the conclusion that not fewer than 100 Christian young men and young women of choicest qualifications and equipment should be sent out by the mission boards to cultivate this field. They should go prepared to give all their waking hours to winning the friendship of the youth and to helping them to build character and faith and to prepare for lives of unselfish service. These are only a few of the opportunities that are open nowadays for the students of the United States and Canada in connection with the world mission. A much more extensive and significant list could be prepared in a group meeting of the executives of the mission boards. My hope is that simply calling off this list will make clear to those present tonight who may have thought of the missionary career as confined solely to the great tasks of the evangelist and pastor, the educational missionary, and the medical missionary, that there are opportunities for workers of all kinds of experience and equipment, but who have in common the burning desire to be used by Christ in meeting the needs of whole peoples.

7. One of the chief opportunities in the world today, and relatively one of the most neglected fields of the world mission, is that presented by the rural populations of the non-Christian world. Whereas fully eight-tenths of the population of Asia and Africa and of certain other parts of the world are living in villages and the countryside, the missionary agencies are devoting less than two-tenths of their personnel and financial expenditure to this eight-tenths of the population. We would not wish to see less attention paid to the masses of people centering in the cities and to the work in great beneficent educational and other institutions largely located in the cities, but the time has come, yes, is long overdue, when we should devote vastly greater attention than we are now doing to the multitudes throughout the rural fields. It is important, also, that among all those who are to serve rural fields there be developed a genuine rural-mindedness. You will recall that Dr. Kagawa reminded us that nearly, if not quite, 50 per cent of the inhabitants of Japan are found in the country; in China some estimate that fully 85 per cent are found there; and in India possibly as many as 90 per cent.

The need is not only extensive but intensive. In the villages more than in the cities there must be waged the conflict with the age-long enemies, ignorance, poverty, disease, superstition, and sin. With the exception of Japan, the rate of illiteracy in the rural areas of these countries most needing our help ranges from 40 to 90 per cent or more. Their economic lot is desperate. In Japan it is said that two-thirds of the farmers are full- or part-time tenants and that they are carrying an aggregate indebtedness of $2,000,000,000. In India the vast body of the peasants are hopelessly in debt, paying the money lenders in whose clutches they have fallen from thirty upward to sometimes as much as seventy percent interest. While I was in India a well informed person ventured the statement that every night there lie down in India over 100,000,000 hungry people, that is, without having had sufficient food to satisfy the natural cravings of the body. I am told that in China the number would be even larger. In Latin America much of the labor in the hinterlands might still be characterized as peonage. As I think of the prevalence of disease, I am reminded of the impression made upon me in Africa where I found vast areas reeking with disease. Moreover, there are extensive tropical areas of India, Malaysia, and the Pacific islands that are relatively unserved by the medical profession. What shall one say of remote parts of China and other realms of inner Asia? After listening to discussions of authorities on the subject, who differed among themselves, I came to the conclusion that it is probably not an exaggeration to say that one-third of the rural population of Asia and Africa are still without the modern medical profession. As we think of this, let us remember that pain and disease mean precisely the same thing with these multitudes as with us only that there is so vastly much more of it, and, that the forces that oppose disease and mitigate pain are relatively so meager and insufficient. How sadly true it is that the haunts and strongholds of the grossest superstitions are the villages. Here also animism in its crudest forms, as a religion of fear and despair, holds right of way.

A vivid picture may be had of the conditions that obtain today in myriads of villages, not only of India but of many other fields, from a statement submitted to me by a graduate of one of our Eastern women's colleges who has been working in the Indian villages. I had occasion to visit the villages to which this statement, drawn up by this worker and her Indian associate, applies:

> Every family has a well bucket. Not kept clean.
> Clothing washed on edge of well. Soiled water runs back into well again.
> No drains for waste water.
> Illiterate women and girls.
> No occupation for boys who don't go to school.
> Dead animals left about.
> Pigs all over village.

Refuse left in middle of alleys.

Housing below sanitary standards, too few windows, too low doors, no ventilation, too many people to each house.

Cattle in houses and badly kept cattle.

Unscreened meat sold in markets.

Flies (food black with them).

Standing water and consequent mosquito pest.

No paving, and roads almost impassable in rains.

Lepers.

Unlimited pariah dogs.

Considerable tuberculosis and no segregation.

Untrained midwives.

Universal giving of opium to babies.

No health instruction for mothers, prenatal or other kinds.

Superstitions interfering with safe childbirth and aftercare.

Most babies put to sleep in tight cloth hammocks.

No place to leave babies when mothers go to work.

Late nights for children and no rest during day.

Excessive nervousness due to overfatigue.

Child labor; carrying of too heavy water jars, etc.

Every year in certain seasons whooping cough, measles, chickenpox, enteric, mumps, malaria, dysentery, pneumonia, influenza.

Many children unwashed, uncombed.

Skin and eye diseases everywhere.

Pyorrhea.

At least one-third of the children undernourished because of poverty or ignorance.

No care of sick.

No control of communicable diseases.

Unsupervised and uncontrolled cases of insanity.

Superstitions interfering with care of fevers of all kinds.

No recreation or occupation for leisure time for either sex, aside from an occasional *bhajan* (devotional song).

Part-time labor due to cotton gins and idleness part of year.

Beggars.

Hopeless indebtedness.

Gambling.

Habit of sitting and sleeping on damp mud floors and consequent rheumatism.

Not enough food for animals.

Mohammedan women in semi-purdah.

No fruit trees.

Hindu vs. Mohammedan and inter-caste feeling.

Certain depressed classes eat dead animals.

Polygamy.

Prostitution.

No laws to enable us to stop cruelty to women and children.

In the light of this realistic and unexaggerated picture do you wonder that an unusually well-informed authority on the rural problem of India, the late Dr. Kenyon L. Butterfield, said that if he had his way he would send out 1,000 Western women to devote their whole lives to work among the villages of India?

8. One of the sternest challenges that come to the Christian students is to act promptly and with all their power to help save the peoples of Asia and Africa from the perils and evils associated with the spread of Western industrialism to those continents. The conditions and practices which have obtained in America and Europe and which, to our shame be it said, still all too much obtain, should not be visited upon the less highly organized lands and races of the world. The process of the industrialization of the vast African continent, as well as of Asia, is gathering momentum at a startling rate and has already effected revolutionary changes. There is no time to lose. The world mission must adjust its program to these fast changing conditions and to specific alarming situations—notably in the gold, copper, and diamond fields of Africa, and in the manufacturing centers as well as the mining areas of Japan, China, and India. Among the most disquieting facts are the wide prevalence of child labor and the extensive use of women in industry under most unfavorable conditions.

The searching question is whether the rest of the world is to travel the economic path of the West, or whether under Christian guidance and power it shall profit from our unfortunate experiences of inequality, injustice, impossible living conditions, class hatred, destructive communism, and strife, and chart a new course for mankind in industrial life and relations. If the Christian Church fails to afford a lead now it will forfeit effective influence in these lands thus concerned. Its message will lose validity and power. Only the program and spirit of Christ are adequate to meet the challenge. What a career this opens for Christian young men and women of heroic mold! The demand is not only for thinkers but for courageous warriors and self-sacrificing servants of mankind. It reminds one of the great service rendered by the late Mr. Harold Grimshaw of the International Labor Office, who made a thorough, sympathetic, and heroic exploration of the evils of forced labor in certain parts of Africa. When he had finished his report to the commission in Geneva a Roman Catholic priest present rose to his feet and said, "We might well fall on our knees at this time and thank God for this report."

9. A fresh challenge comes to the members of this convention and to the Christian students of other lands of the West to enter more of the unoccupied fields of the world. The world mission of Christianity

is not static, but dynamic and vital. Its mandate is still the great missionary command of Jesus Christ, which has not been fulfilled. It has not been repealed. It is still operative. As we have already seen in connection with other challenges that are ringing in our ears, it has taken on vastly greater meaning. Should we not be startled by the fact that so many centuries after Christ gave His great commission to carry His message to all mankind there should still be so many totally unoccupied fields and so many others virtually unoccupied? By this I mean so many great areas of human life in which there are no effective Christian witnesses and interpreters.

In connection with the World Missionary Conference at Edinburgh in 1910, I was chairman of Commission I, which had to do, among other things, with the occupation of the field. In that connection we presented a list of the unoccupied fields. I am pained to state tonight that not a few of these fields, after this lapse of twenty-five years, are still unoccupied. Among those which are totally or virtually unoccupied may be mentioned Outer Mongolia, Asiatic Russia, Russian Turkestan, the Central Asiatic Soviet Republics, Tibet, Nepal, Bhutan, Afghanistan, and Baluchistan; also nearly, if not quite, 500 of the 562 native states of India, and large sections of the Netherlands Indies. Then Africa, notably the two-thirds or thereabouts under Roman Catholic powers, the vast majority of the nearly 700,000 villages of India, over 300 of the 1,600 counties of China, and much of the hinterland of Latin America have great multitudes among whom the gospel agents and agencies are not at work. Taking the world as a whole, I estimate that there are not less than 250,000,000 people who may, without exaggeration, be spoken of as not being within range of the world mission of Christianity. In reaching these vast numbers the Christian nationals of many of the same countries or neighboring countries should have a part. Wherever possible, missionary societies at work in adjacent fields should take on added responsibility for the unoccupied fields adjoining them, rather than encourage the formation of additional missionary societies. The point I want to stress tonight, however, is that we need not a few of the strongest personalities, with the best possible modern equipment, to enter and serve these difficult fields. Wherever possible some of the wisest and most experienced missionaries should accompany them. The point for us all to carry away clearly is that the day of the pioneer and pathfinder is not over. I think it may be said that every preceding Student Volunteer Convention has yielded some of the choicest men and women for this great adventure. Let not this one prove to be an exception.

10. The challenge comes to liberate the money power at home and abroad and relate it to the work of the world mission. The serious reductions of so many of our missionary boards in North America are endangering the missionary enterprise in field after field. It has been serious enough to cut off many branches here and there—branches that were productive and not the kind that Christ spoke of as branches "that bear not fruit"; but it is vastly more serious to do what has been done in not a few cases, namely, cut off tap roots. This is a matter of practical concern to the Student Volunteer Movement and all its friends in the colleges, as well as to all churches, because that explains why the boards are unable in so many instances to send out additional recruits. This comes at the time, as we have already seen, when reinforcements are most needed.

The present economic situation and its effect on our Movement and the world mission remind me of not dissimilar situations at two earlier stages in the life of the Movement—one at the time of the long depression in the nineties, and the other near the close of the first decade of this century. In the former period one of the leading board secretaries in America, in the company of other board secretaries, made this startling statement, "We must bank the fires of the Student Volunteer Movement." Imagine what a depressing influence was exercised not only by those words but by the policy they connoted. Those of us related to the Movement in those days, however, could not rest with matters in such a position. We deployed ourselves among the churches, we spoke on rare occasions at the Sunday morning church services, more frequently we were permitted to speak in the Sunday evening services, and still more frequently in the sparsely attended midweek prayer meeting services. The volunteers and some of their hindered classmates went before these companies, large and small, with the irresistible argument, "The world needs us abroad; we are ready to give our lives until death to this work; the boards cannot send us; will you?" I once had in my possession lists reaching up into the hundreds of churches and groups of Christians who, in response to these appeals in those days of hard times, undertook and kept up the support of worthy missionary candidates under the various boards. In other cases, individual families and, now and then, a man or a woman alone, would take on a budget. At one time as many as seventy of our colleges, universities, and theological seminaries each undertook the support of a missionary. Not a few young men and young women who could not go to the field but who had sufficient means would give the salary of a comrade that he might go out as a missionary under his board. The reflex influence upon their fellow students of this unselfish initiative and sacrificial action on the part of the volunteers and their comrades was very great and most helpful. There was a similar experience in Scotland when one of the leading boards there was retrenching and had decided it could not send out other candidates. A company, as I recall, of over twenty Scottish student volunteers who had finished their education and were ready to go were allowed to appear at the meeting of the General Assembly of the Church concerned and a simple statement was made of the fact that they were eager to go. They stood as a group before the Assembly. The impression made was profound. It led to a liberating of money of both the well-to-do and the poor, resulting in the sending out of the larger part of the number in the group.

Now, I would remind us that the money is in existence here in the United States and Canada. It has not been burned up. The wealth of these two countries today is greater than that of Great Britain, Ireland, Germany, France, Holland, Norway, Sweden, Denmark, Finland, Australia, and New Zealand combined. I repeat, the money is in existence. Not a little of it is in hiding. Much of it is being held back because of grave uncertainties. Taxation is claiming an increasing part of it. But when allowance has been made for all this and vastly more, the sums that lie latent and that people cannot take out of the world with them far exceed the sums that were available or tied up in the period to which I have just referred. Not only is this money in existence, but a disproportionately large part of it is in the hands of Christians. I am proud, generally speaking, of the giving of American Christians. It is up to us to bring before them vividly the wholeness of the facts, the greatness of the facts, the oneness of the facts, the tragedy of the facts, the inspiration of the facts; and, above all, to make vivid the personal appeal. By this I mean the appeal, "I will give my life, will you not give your money?" Why should not at least 100 of the nearly 500 institutions represented in this convention each undertake the support of a missionary, as in other days? Why should not there go out from this great company as many as 500 groups, small or large, of earnest Christians, together with the volunteers, into the churches in our home towns and our college towns and elsewhere to help liberate the funds needed to make possible a worthwhile advance in this day of unparalleled opportunity? Let us realize the hope that Horace Bushnell voiced nearly two generations ago, "What we wait for and look hopefully to see is the consecration of the vast money power of the world to the work and cause and Kingdom of Jesus Christ. For that day, when it comes, is the morning, so to speak, of the new creation."

11. One of the most important undertakings calling for statesmanlike effort on the part of the Christian students of tomorrow, whether as missionaries abroad, or clergymen and laymen at home, is the significant task of drawing together in closer and more effective co-operation and unity the still all too divided Christian forces. While wonderful advances in this direction have been made, notably in connection with the missionary enterprise, there is still much to be accomplished. The world mission has recently entered upon what I speak of as the third stage of co-operation. The first stage was that preceding the World Missionary Conference in Edinburgh in 1910. During that period countless detached co-operative projects were undertaken in all parts of the world field but these were going on, as a rule, without reference to similar projects elsewhere. The second stage was that between the Edinburgh Conference in 1910 and the Jerusalem Conference in 1928. Within those years there were created many national Christian councils. At the beginning of the period there were only two—one, that of the United States and Canada, and the other, that of Germany. At the end of the period there were approximately fourteen of these bodies in the countries which send missionaries. Each of these united with various missionary boards or societies of the country for purposes of fostering united thinking, planning, and action. Then there were approximately the same number, fourteen, in countries to which missionaries are sent. These united the various missions and rising indigenous churches and had similar objectives, namely, that of securing united thought and action. Moreover, in this period was developed what is now called the International Missionary Council, which is composed of official representatives of the various national Christian councils and which seeks to do for the wide world field what each of its members does for its particular field. While these co-operative organizations were being evolved, and largely under their influence, a great many special undertakings in the realm of co-operation and unity were launched and promoted.

A third period on which we have recently entered is the one in which the various Christian bodies pool not only knowledge and experience, but also personalities, funds, plans in the making, and also, increasingly, administration, and even names. This has been characterized as a period in which we actually undertake to do the things which we have talked about doing and have been preparing to do. It is interesting to note that one of the principal factors in making possible the development of all three of these periods has been the student volunteers and their other Christian student colleagues. They have been moving spirits in the creation and conduct of various national

Christian councils, and of the International Missionary Council. They have had most to do with the establishing and developing of the union Christian universities and colleges. They have been responsible for some of the most co-operative developments in the realm of evangelism. Several of the most progressive and influential agencies for the production and circulation of Christian literature are those led by student volunteers. Volunteers have also been responsible for many of the most hopeful activities in the industrial and rural fields. Again, some of the most promising efforts toward the actual union of the Churches, for example in South India, have been those initiated by student volunteers. Much the same could be said of significant developments in the lands from which the missionaries come. We must look to the Christian students of tomorrow to carry this wonderful Movement from strength to strength. Notwithstanding the many encouragements, and in particular notwithstanding the fact that in the foreign missionary movement greater progress has been achieved than in the fields of the Churches of Europe, North America, and Australia, the fact remains that we of the Protestant Communion are still all too divided in the work of the world mission. Never did such division as still exists seem to me to be so unnecessary, unwise, and un-Christian. If Christ has willed our unity—and can there be any question on this vital point?—then one of the governing ambitions of our lives should be to throw our full weight and influence in the direction of facilitating the processes which issue in successful co-operation and vital union.

12. One of the most urgent tasks which we, and those we represent, are in a better position than any other group to perform, is that of winning the new generation—particularly those who now throng our high schools and colleges—for the world mission. They have by no means been won. Happily, there are exceptions to this statement, and these are of such character as to leave no doubt whatever regarding the practicability of winning the great majority if the same means and spirit are employed to achieve the desired end that explain the happy exceptions. Next to the withdrawal of the presence of Christ himself, what calamity could be greater in our day than that of not having the interest and full-hearted collaboration of the oncoming generation? It is a significant fact that certain other movements which are making rival claims to the allegiance of youth are succeeding in arresting the devotion of youth. Christ and his cause with their far greater challenges must win priority in their thought, their feelings, and their ambitions. To this end it takes like to reach like. If we are to reach the youth we must present to them heroic

challenges. We must afford them adequate outlets for all their powers; above all, we must put burdens of responsibility on them and then trust them. I remember that Woodrow Wilson once said to me that the most conservative and stable power in the world is youth, provided they have burdens of responsibility placed upon them. I used to doubt this, but after years of experience I have come to see that it is strictly true. In recent years when I have been in doubt as to whether or not to trust the youth with great and responsible burdens, I have always thrown my decision on their side and I cannot say they have ever failed. One of the most hopeful developments in the British Isles has been the initiative taken by bands of university students to enlist the interest of the schoolboys and schoolgirls during what we in this country would call the high-school period. Might it not be well for us to consider whether a similar mission and method should not be undertaken by us on this side? As I think of these millions of most promising youth in our high schools, with their unspent years, their unexhausted energies, and their unspoiled powers, youth in their vision-forming years, in their habit-forming years, in the period of determining life attitudes and tendencies, in the years of discovery, of invention, of creation, how I long to see them confronted with the inspiring challenge enfolded in the world-wide program of Christ for the times in which they are to live out their lives.

The present world situation—this alarming situation, this emergent situation, this most hopeful situation—and these great and significant tasks and heroic challenges present an irresistible appeal to the Christian students here assembled and our comrades to whom we are to return. None of the preceding twelve international Student Volunteer conventions has presented a greater summons. As one who has attended the entire series, I should say that it is my impression that in no preceding convention have the Christian students of North America been presented with so great a summons. I base this impression on my more recent journeys in contrast with earlier visits to the great fields of opportunity and service across the world. I find my own impression is confirmed by the opinions of discerning and trustworthy Christian leaders of the various lands and races with whom I have been thrown in these travels. Now and then you hear it said that the day of the missionary is drawing to a close. I do not so interpret the situation and the outlook for the generation to which you belong. The facts set forth in this convention from day to day do not sustain such a view, nor do the findings of the long chains of conferences which as chairman of the International Missionary Council I have been called upon to conduct in recent years in Asia, in Africa, and in other parts of the world. Above all, the best informed and most responsible people with whom I have made it a point to take counsel insist that in the years that lie ahead they simply must have the collaboration and co-operation of more of the strongest young men and women who can be selected and sent out from the West.

It should be added that they all emphasize that what is needed is not so much numbers, although in the aggregate large numbers will be required, as the years unfold, as students of the highest quality, of the finest equipment, and of the most thorough preparation. If asked to characterize the kind of workers needed, I would express the matter quite simply by saying that they should be men and women of vision, of personality, of power to grow, and of determination to die growing. They should be men and women ready to go into training and stay in training even longer than have their predecessors, because of the more exacting demands; they should possess great ethical and social passion and concern; they should be men and women of true humility and of sincere appreciation of the good in the cultures of other lands and races; they should have an authentic, indubitable, first-hand experience of Christ; they should have a clear sense of direction, mission, and companionship.

Why do we need so many workers like not a few in this assembly? Some will be needed to fill major positions which are today unmanned. Many will be needed to provide a worthy succession for those who in a relatively short time will be obliged to lay down their burdens and commit their great trusts to younger shoulders. Others will be needed to replace not a few incompetent persons who are now holding positions of importance simply because there are not enough adequately qualified workers to fill them. Many should be sent out to relieve workers now overburdened and overwrought. Reinforcements are needed to recover the ground lost because of the catastrophic cuts of recent years. Additional workers are essential in order to make much more productive the workers already on the field. I came to the conclusion, after much observation and study, that an increase of possibly fifteen to twenty per cent in the existing staffs in mission colleges, schools, and hospitals, and in connection with comprehensive evangelistic undertakings, might well result in one hundred per cent increase in fruitage. As indicated tonight, a large number will be needed if we are to enter on a period of higher specialization in field after field. If we are to deal realistically and heroically with the many virtually unoccupied fields, we must send forth as pioneers a number of those who hear the call of God, and who, like St. Paul, have as their consuming ambition to preach Christ where He has not been named. We might well sum up the cumulative demand that comes to this convention and through it to our comrades near and far, by saying that the desired reinforcements are absolutely essential if we are to press our present absolutely unprecedented advantage as it now obtains in so many fields. God grant that the Indianapolis Convention may not fail to recognize its great day of visitation!

We stand tonight at a parting of the ways. This has been a dangerous convention in the sense that here have been liberated tremendous energies. Wherever such is the case there are always possibilities of evil as well as of good. During these days much new and vital truth has been proclaimed. Much light has been shed on what God would have us become and what He would have us do. Impulses of unselfish action have been communicated. It is well to remind ourselves that truth is given not simply to be contemplated or admired, and not even to be assented to, but to be incorporated and to be obeyed. New light on our pathway is to be followed. Divine impulses are to lead to Christlike action. In a word, when the followers of Christ come to a fork in the road they must follow their Leader and Lord. Therefore, as we approach our watchnight, and as our great convention draws toward a close, the time has come for conclusive thinking; that is, thinking that ends with definite conclusions. We are called upon to make some momentous decisions, decisions which will make all the difference in the world, the difference between lives of mediocrity on the one hand and, on the other, lives of real significance and, therefore, of increasing helpfulness and fruitfulness. What are the decisions?

Without doubt there comes to many of us the choice between a life of contraction and one of expansion; a life of small dimensions and one of widening horizons and larger visions and plans; a life of self-satisfaction or self-seeking and one of unselfish or truly Christlike sharing. During these days we have faced wide open doors of opportunity. We have been reminded of clamant needs. We have learned of crushing burdens. We have beheld wonderful ripening harvests to be reaped, and have heard our Saviour say, "The harvest truly is plenteous but the laborers are few." We have heard some of the sternest and most heroic challenges ever proclaimed to a body of Christian students. Under these circumstances, what shall we do? At once we ask ourselves, "What would Christ do?" What did Christ do? Even in the face of desperate need and at a time when His disciples said, "All are seeking Thee," He said, "Let us go elsewhere into the next towns, that I may preach there also: for to this end came I forth." In days like these and in a world like the one in which we are living, where does the hand of Christ point for His true followers?

Am I not right when I say that His pierced hand has ever directed His followers into fields of wider opportunity and to the meeting of depths of human need?

In this solemn and creative hour we, the followers of Christ, at the parting of the ways, have the choice of guiding on the future (if I may use a military term) or guiding on the past. Surely, after all we have heard tonight, we recognize that among our duties is the duty at times to look backward. This we should do in order to keep vivid in our consciousness the original mandate given by Christ to all His followers. We should take backward glimpses in order to heed the lessons of experience, some of which give invaluable warnings and others afford wonderful incitements. It is well at times to look backward that faith may be fortified. Nor should we forget that there is a reverent use of the memory in order that we may, in the language of the psalmist, "abundantly utter the memory of Thy great goodness."

Having said this, let me emphasize—and it involves no contradiction—that for those of us gathered on this mount of vision it is absolutely essential that we be dominated by the forward look. The reasons are convincing. Our goal, toward whose attainment everything should bend, is in the future. All our unfought battles are there. The determination of our plans and the completion of our preparation are in the days to come. We must look forward with great intentness to avert the grave perils which await us. The older people present would do well to remember, also, that the new generation are to do their work in the coming days and we are committed, while life lasts, to strengthen their hands. Above all, with all of us, young and old, the great fact is that the Prince Leader of the Faith, our Living Lord, is before us and we must follow His lead.

At the parting of the ways we have another choice of greatest potentialities, and that is the choice between regulating our lives and plans by our visible, human, material resources or by our invisible, superhuman, spiritual resources. In this momentous time, well may we with Elisha proclaim, "The chariots of Israel, and the horsemen thereof!" One of the most arresting words in the Old Testament comes to my memory. I refer to the passage which represents the eyes of God "as running to and fro throughout the whole earth to show Himself strong in behalf of them whose heart is perfect toward Him." Think of the limitless possibilities wrapped up in the phrase that God "may show Himself strong" toward any man. May His eye of flame and at the same time of love, as He searches among our great company, find not a few young men and young women whose hearts are so pure, so humble, so responsive and serviceable, that He may be able in and through them to accomplish His wonder work. May

He in truth find it possible tonight and henceforth to clothe Himself with many of our number. What higher aspiration and what more significant resolution could be ours than to wish and resolve that we may henceforth live God-inhabited lives.

More significant and essential, if possible, than anything that I have said is it that with all seriousness we this night make the great decision, to choose between attentiveness unto God and attentiveness to the conflicting and unreliable voices of the world and of this present age. While among my ancestors were Quakers or members of the Society of Friends, it was not until more recent years that I came to sit at their feet and learn this central lesson. With them, prayer is not monologue but dialogue. At the time when most of us have come to the close of what we call prayer, with them the most important part of prayer begins, that is, the affording of opportunity and the right conditions for God to speak to them. Important as it is that we should speak to God, infinitely more important is it that we should hear what He has to say to us. Let us acquire the habit of pausing after we have poured out our hearts to Him in adoration, confession, thanksgiving, and petition, to say, "My soul, be thou silent unto God"; and then, after due silence, offer the simple but most meaningful prayer that should never be permitted to become a form, "Speak, Lord, for Thy servant heareth." Ours is a living Lord. He ever lives, not only to make intercession but to communicate Himself and His mind. It is an easy matter for Him to communicate with His children, for "My sheep hear my voice, and I know them, and they follow me." Whatever else we miss in this convention, let us not fall short of entering into this great reality as a life experience. Granted this, we best insure the largest realization of all else that God has had in store for us in these never-to-be-forgotten days.

THE TWENTY FIFTH ANNIVERSARY OF THE STUDENT VOLUNTEER MOVEMENT

ADDRESS GIVEN AT MOUNT HERMON, MASSACHUSETTS SEPTEMBER 10, 1911, ON THE TWENTY-FIFTH ANNIVERSARY OF THE FOUNDING OF THE MOVEMENT

We meet on historic ground; we meet on sacred ground as we gather here today at Mount Hermon. Here originated one of the most wonderful of all the spiritual movements in the history of the Christian Church. Here was the fountainhead of a stream which has brought more blessings to the universities and colleges of the world than any other which has gushed out in any nation under the life-giving influence of the Spirit of God. A friend of mine, Mr. Luther D. Wishard, the first college secretary of the International Committee of the Young Men's Christian Association, went down south to see Mr. Moody in the year 1885, some twenty-six years ago, to take counsel with him as to giving larger opportunities for workers in the Christian Associations to receive preparation for Christian service. Mr. Moody had had it on his mind that there might be held here in this valley, either at Mount Hermon or Northfield, a Bible study conference for Young Men's Christian Association secretaries. Mr. Wishard felt that we already had a good many conferences of one kind and another, and that something was needed even more than such a gathering of Association workers. He said to Mr. Moody, "One of the things most needed is a gathering which will do for the college students what you have been doing here at Northfield for Christian workers in general." Mr. Moody was interested and pleased by the suggestion, and said that he would gladly have the invitation go out to bring together for Bible study the students from the different colleges and schools. Mr. Wishard pressed him to allow his name to be used, and also to have it stated that he, Mr. Moody, would preside at such a conference. Mr. Moody shrank from that, although he was not a shrinking man. It is interesting that the man who in Great Britain had moved Oxford and Cambridge as no other man in recent times has moved them, that the man who gathered under his leadership fine, intellectual spirits like Henry Drummond, that the man who deeply stirred Yale and Princeton, that the man who had many more invitations from the American colleges than he could accept, seriously doubted whether he could interest, instruct, and inspire college students. But happily he was prevailed upon to accept the presidency of the first intercollegiate Christian conference ever held on a national or international scale.

So the invitation went out to the colleges of North America, and there was a splendid response. There came together here at Mount Hermon in the month of July, 1886, just twenty-five years ago last summer, 251 student delegates. We came from eighty-nine different universities and colleges. I say *we,* because I had that never-to-be-forgotten privilege of being one of the undergraduate student delegates. With nine of my fellow-students I came from one of the eastern universities, Cornell University. The leading universities of Canada were represented, likewise every section of the United States, unless it was the Pacific Coast. There were some quite large delegations, especially from Dartmouth, Amherst, Yale, Cornell, and Randolph-Macon, one of the colleges of Virginia. As I recall, the state which had the largest number of colleges represented was Iowa, there being represented ten of its colleges, located over 1,200 miles away.

Among the delegates were a few professors and teachers, but speaking generally, it was an undergraduate gathering. We met for a period of four weeks. The more recent conferences, some of which you have attended, and like the one held here last June and July, have continued in session for but ten days. The larger period made possible some things that we do not find possible in gatherings in these days. It made possible unhurried opportunities for meditation, for personal intercourse, for fellowship, for cultivating friendships with the leaders, for discussing at great length personal and college problems. We have missed much of that in the more rushing, intense student conferences of later years. That conference was somewhat simple in its scheme in contrast with the modern gatherings. We had one platform meeting each day, which was what we might call a double-header or a triple-header. Mr. Moody would very seldom let a meeting go with one speaker. He would call for an address at short notice. I have often heard him say to the speaker, "Now give us the best thing you have got." Sometimes he would call on a man with no further notice than the time required for the opening exercises. Sometimes he would have us sing several hymns to get the audience thoroughly in tune. When he asked a man for his best, we usually got it. He conducted the meetings without a great deal of conventionality. He sent men to the divine resources. He threw them back on what was uppermost in their minds, on that which was their strongest conviction. Although these ideas may not have come out in as orderly a way as they otherwise would, they represented deep thinking and genuine heart experience.

Another feature of the daily program was the little company— little, I say, although before the conference was over it included nearly every delegate—which met for an hour every morning to discuss methods of carrying on work among our fellow students in the schools and colleges. Mr. Wishard took charge of this hour. He had a little blue-covered pamphlet from which he read extracts which formed the basis of our discussion. At that time, it was one of only two pamphlets in the world bearing upon the work of Christ among students. The other day in Constantinople I witnessed an exhibit in connection with the World's Student Christian Federation Conference in which were over 800 books and pamphlets bearing upon subjects relating to the Christian student movement. Mr. Wishard would read, for example, a few extracts on individual work in the leading of fellow students to Christ, and then he would call upon delegates to give their testimonies as to what they had seen or done in their different colleges; or he would read extracts upon the religious meetings of college Associations, and then we would discuss plans to arouse interest among the students in the college; or he would read a few pages or paragraphs on the neighborhood work that should be carried on by students while doing their studying, in order to bring blessing to the villages and cities in the vicinity of the colleges; or he would take up something with regard to the foreign missionary activities of students; or he would take up our intercollegiate relations—that is, how the Association of any college or school should keep in touch with similar Associations throughout the country. These were practical discussions. In them were kindled fires of interest and enthusiasm that led to great movements in the colleges in the years that followed.

Another feature that was noticed, not in its early days, but before the conference closed, was a Bible class that was prophetic of the many Bible circles, classes, and discussions that we now have on such an elaborate scale in our different conferences. In those days we did not have a single course of Bible study adapted to work in colleges and college Associations. Now we have literally scores of courses prepared by college professors, ministers, and laymen, men who believe in relating students to the great work of Christ in the world and preparing them for it. Some of you who have attended more recent student gatherings remember that we now have a curriculum that is very elaborate, a curriculum that reminds us somewhat of our college courses. We need to have a guide to show men how to make the most of the many opportunities presented in the modern conferences.

There were other things that characterized the practice of the students in that conference which meant as much as anything I have mentioned. One was our custom of gathering around preachers and teachers in the long afternoons and in the early evening, often beneath these beautiful elm trees, in order that we might ply them with questions regarding the presentations or addresses they had made in the morning. As I drove over here this morning, I reminded those in the carriage of this and that old tree under which we had memorable discussions. I remember some of those discussions about the superhuman work of Christ in conversion, about the principles that should guide one in choosing a lifework, about the second coming of our Lord. As a result of these many discussions under the trees, possibly even more than through public addresses, men's doubts were dissipated, their views on religious subjects made clear, and their faith became a reality; so that they rested on rock-ribbed conviction which nothing could shake.

Another part of the daily program was the opportunity for personal fellowship. We roamed up and down this side of the river, and we crossed the river and climbed along the sides of the distant hills. We would devote entire afternoons to this purpose. Sometimes a man would go alone, again there would be two men; at times a little larger company—it might be an entire college delegation. The evenings also were memorable, for then we would go out for the special purpose of meditation upon what had been presented in public addresses and discussed in conferences and interviews.

I have in my library at home a book that I value very highly indeed. It is a leather-bound notebook in which I wrote down very carefully full notes on all the sermons and addresses and discussions of those four wonderful weeks. I first took them down roughly, and then during the afternoons I copied them in ink, underlining with red ink the points that had most laid hold on me. It is a book that I have not shown much to other people, but it represents a great revolution in my own life with reference to religious questions and my personal responsibility to Christ and His Kingdom. Many delegates worked over their notes, not only copying them but applying them, reflecting upon them, saying, "What does this mean to me? What should this mean to others through me?" It is not the number of sermons we hear, it is not the number of books we read, but it is how much time we spend in thinking about the sermons we hear and the books we read that transforms character.

At the beginning of this conference nobody had thought of it as being a missionary conference. Several days had passed before the word missions was mentioned. If I remember correctly, over two weeks had passed before that great theme was suggested on the platform. But there were causes hidden in the background. For example, a certain returned missionary had his home at Princeton while some of his children were receiving their education in the college, and in that home it was customary to have missionary prayer meetings. Under the influence of that home, missionary fires were made to burn brightly among the undergraduates at Princeton. When that band heard of the conference which Mr. Moody was to hold at Mount Hermon, some one had vision enough to see that there might be God's opportunity. Among the very first to see this with a clear eye was a young woman who went to her reward a few months ago, Miss Grace Wilder. She discerned that conditions were going to be furnished at Mount Hermon that might make possible the generation of a great movement, and she laid upon her brother, Robert Wilder, and upon some of the other Princeton men who were to attend the conference, the burden of prayer and expectation, and charged them before God to persevere in prayer and effort that this Mount Hermon gathering might not close without the inauguration of a missionary movement that in some sense would be worthy of the wonderful situation then confronting the Church on the foreign field. So Robert Wilder and his associates came to Mount Hermon. He was a quiet and modest young man, but he had intense spiritual passion. His great desire was for the world's evangelization. From the very first day at Mount Hermon he began to search for and find kindred spirits. He discovered Tewksbury of Harvard, and Clark of Oberlin, and one or two others who came there with a definite missionary purpose. He found others and brought them together daily for united prayer. They had this meeting with the one object that missionary fires might be kindled in the conference. As they found sympathetic spirits, their number grew. They did not confine their meeting to those who had decided to be missionaries, but added others who were thinking seriously about the subject and who honestly wanted to face the facts. In these meetings many men prayed through the great question of their lifework. Finally they ceased to make it a secret meeting in the sense of concealing the fact of its being held. They began to have it announced from the platform that the missionary volunteers and others interested in missions were meeting for prayer, and others began to come in. The men who attended those meetings found it impossible to pray without work. They could not pray for the world's evangelization without dealing with the question of the missionary call. So a network of personal intercourse spread over the conference. You could hardly go anywhere without somebody crossing your path and presenting this great missionary message. Wherever you went you heard them talking about it. I remember that even when in swimming you would hear conversation about this great subject. But it was impossible to pray and spend over two weeks in honest study of the Christian writings without a moving of the missionary spirit within the breasts of those who studied; so quite apart from the personal conversations this influence became one of the efficient causes for generating the missionary spirit.

Finally some of the student volunteers—if we may call them such, although that word was not used in the beginning of the movement—went to Dr. Pierson, who was known to be a great advocate of missions, and urged him to give a missionary address. "Well," he said, "I don't suppose that will be a popular subject here." But they prevailed upon him to do what they wished. One evening this meeting was held. To the surprise of everybody the room was full. Apparently every delegate was there. He gave a very striking address. I can remember it to this day. He took as his thesis, "All should go and go to all." He summed up in that sentence a message that is quite common nowadays but which came as a revelation in those days when most Christians had a fractional view of the Kingdom of God and of the responsibilities of the subjects of the Kingdom for its extension. That address set many a man to thinking. A little later Dr. Ashmore, one of the great missionaries of the Chinese Mission of the American Baptist Missionary Society, on his way across the United States coming home on furlough, read in the papers about this student conference in session. He was burdened with the sense of the need of more missionaries in China. He said, "Possibly that is the best recruiting ground I can find." He changed his plans and came to Mount Hermon, and while there was called upon to give an address. It was a masterly address. He worthily set forth that greatest missionary field in the world, China with its four hundred millions. I can remember as though it were yesterday how he marshaled province after province and made each one seem to us like a great populous nation. I remember how he dilated upon the strength of the Chinese people, and above all pressed upon us what even then he called an urgent situation. Remember that was in the days when the missionaries were largely confined to the fringe of the country, when the total number of Protestant Christians was possibly less than 30,000. It seems incredible that a man in those days should have had a vision of that empire and its possibilities such as he brought before us. He knew how to get hold of college men. I will tell you the way to do it, and that is to place something before them which is tremendously difficult. He presented missions as a war of conquest and not as a mere wrecking expedition. It appealed to the strong college athletes and other fine spirits of the colleges because of its very difficulty. They wanted to hear more about it. The number of interviews greatly multiplied.

Then came a meeting that I suppose did more to influence decisions than anything else which happened in those memorable days. There was held what is now known, although it is a misnomer, as the Meeting of the Ten Nations. Hastily ten men were found to represent ten nations. Here was a son of a missionary in China, a son of a missionary in India, a son of a missionary in Persia. Besides these there were a North American Indian, a German from Germany, a Dane from Denmark, a Norwegian from Norway. We also had a Japanese, an Armenian, and a Siamese, Boon Itt, who afterwards became one of the great powers of the Christian Church in Siam. That was a night which those of us who were there will never forget. The speeches were short, not averaging more than three minutes in length. Each speaker made one point, the need in the country which he represented, the need for Christianity, the need for men to come out to help meet the crisis. Men were moved to the depth of their souls. We went out of that meeting not discussing the speeches. Everybody was quiet.

We scattered among the groves. I have heard of nights of prayer. That was one of them. I know many men who prayed on into the late watches of the night. The grove back there on the ridge was the scene that night of battles in which the unselfish and heroic in men won the victory. Men surrendered themselves to the great plan of Jesus Christ of conquering this whole world and including it in His Kingdom.

The conference was drawing to a close when another meeting was held of which we do not talk much. It was too sacred. I hesitate even now to say much about it. One of our good friends who is with us, Mr. McWilliams, was this morning talking about this meeting to which I refer. It was held in the old Crossley Hall. We were meeting there in the dusk. Man after man arose and told the reason why he had decided to become a volunteer. God spoke through reality. There was a lack of hypocrisy and of speaking for effect which gave God His opportunity to break through and give a message that men would hear. It was not strange, therefore, that during the closing hours of that memorable conference the number of volunteers greatly increased. At the beginning of the Mount Hermon Conference fewer than half a dozen students were expecting to be missionaries. By the last day ninety-nine had decided and had signed a paper that read, "We are willing and desirous"—that is the old language, we now have better language—"God permitting, to become foreign missionaries." The present language is, "It is my purpose, if God permit, to become a foreign missionary." The old form meant complete consecration, but it was not as definite as that used in these days. Ninety-nine had signed that paper. Mr. Wilder has the old record.

The conference closed, but the next morning those ninety-nine met for a farewell meeting of prayer. As I recall, it was in a room in Recitation Hall. There were not seats enough and some had to stand. We knelt, however, all of us, and while we were kneeling in that closing period of heart-burning prayer the hundredth man came in and knelt with us. So of 251 delegates, 100 decided that they were willing and desirous, God permitting, to give themselves to this great work of giving all men an opportunity to know Christ.

Some of us saw that here was a fire that should spread, and one afternoon a number took a walk over the hills and Charles K. Ober suggested the idea that a deputation of possibly four men from those who had volunteered should go through the colleges. It turned out that only one of the four appointed, Mr. Wilder, could go. But in the autumn, John Forman, also a graduate of Princeton, consented to join Wilder. They went through the colleges like flames of fire. It was a wonderful year. Hundreds and hundreds of the best college men and women in the United States and Canada signed the Student

Volunteer declaration in its original form. The Movement spread like a prairie fire. It was attended with all the perils that attend movements proceeding without restraint and without conservative administration. But people stood in awe and saw that God was in the Movement, judged by its effects. It was not until 1888 that the Movement took the present name of the Student Volunteer Movement for Foreign Missions. It was that year organized under that name and adopted as its watchword, "The Evangelization of the World in This Generation." It was not until a few years later that the wording of the declaration was changed to read, "It is my purpose, if God permit, to become a foreign missionary." But from the days of organization in 1888 the Movement has steadily, and in some years rapidly, spread.

Now notice a few, among many, things which have been accomplished. The Movement has carried with greater or less efficiency the missionary message to over 1,000 institutions in North America. It has developed what is known as the Missionary Department of the Young Men's Christian Association and the Young Women's Christian Association until it is the most productive department of those associations. It has waged a great educational campaign, keeping in the field each year for this purpose from one to ten traveling secretaries, holding each year possibly a score of institutes, as well as district and state conferences, convening every four years a great continental convention attended by from 3,000 to 4,000 students and professors from over 700 institutions. It has built up its literature until it now has nearly 100 books and pamphlets designed for its propaganda. It has inaugurated a thorough educational campaign for the study of missions. Whereas in 1893 there were only about 200 students in the United States and Canada in mission study, there were last year over 34,000 in mission study classes of this Movement. It did the pioneering work for the Young People's Missionary Movement, now known as the Missionary Education Movement, and it also led the way for the organization of the Laymen's Missionary Movement, which its founder said was suggested to his mind in the midst of the sessions of the Nashville Convention of the Student Volunteer Movement. It has given rise to all these great tributary agencies for the Church.

Its distinctive mission, however, has been in its appeal for life. Thousands have responded to that appeal, and you will be glad to know that already nearly 5,000 students of North America have gone out as Student Volunteers under the regular missionary societies to the foreign missionary fields. Just think of it! I read this morning, "A handful of corn dropped in the earth on the top of the mountain, the fruit thereof shall shake like Lebanon." These 5,000 are scattered in nearly fifty different nations on every continent of the world. They have already raised up through direct and indirect influence hundreds of thousands of converts. They have communicated their vision to the sons and daughters of the soil. The Spirit of the living God is working with mighty power through them.

This Movement has not been confined to the North American students. Its central idea has been transplanted from our own to other lands until now Student Volunteer Movements are found in one form or another among the students of the British Isles, Holland, Germany, Norway, Sweden, Denmark, Finland, Switzerland, the Protestant part of France, South Africa, and Australasia. What does this mean? It means that the Movement covers all Protestant Christendom. But it does not stop there. It has still later been transplanted to Christian bands of students in the Turkish Empire, down the Nile Valley, among the Japanese Islands, through the great valleys of China, over the plains of India. Let me mention but one example. Last year the Movement had reached such strength in China that they organized what is known as the Student Volunteer Movement for China. Their watchword is "The evangelization of China and of the world in this generation." They already have over 600 Chinese volunteers. In one Presbyterian college 120 out of 300 became volunteers. In another institution 150 out of 450 declared themselves. It is as though 1,000 men were to volunteer in Yale. In one medical college in Peking twenty students out of their small student body volunteered. It is as though 600 had volunteered from the College of Physicians and Surgeons in New York. In another small college eighty out of 150 have volunteered. They have said, "We will spend our lives preaching Christ to our own countrymen."

Think of it, you who are favored in being students here at Mount Hermon. It is fitting that we are permitted to meet in your midst this morning, in this school, the most cosmopolitan boys' school in the United States, (for here I meet boys from more parts of the world than in any other boys' school I visit) a school which has always given boys hard work to do, and which to my mind, therefore, is to be congratulated. In these days when there is so much tendency to luxury and softness in the schools as well as in the colleges of America, in this school it is fitting, I repeat, that this Movement which makes its appeal to the heroic, should here have its anniversary. Here in this school, always loyal to Jesus Christ and His plans, we meet; and I would pause to say to the boys who are students in this school those words of Archbishop Whateley: "If my faith be false, I ought to change it; whereas if it be true, I am bound to propagate it." If you have professed a falsehood in calling yourselves Christians, you have nothing more important to do than to change your faith and adopt some other religion; but if you have professed the truth—and I see boys here this morning who would die rather than give up their faith in Christ—then I say to you, do as many of your predecessors have done—be logical, be courageous, be honest, and dedicate your lives solemnly, on the twenty-fifth anniversary of this wonderful student missionary uprising, to the greatest work in the world, the work to which the founder of this school gave his life of unwearied, unselfish, and wonderful devotion, this great unselfish service of making Christ's Kingdom spread all over this world in our generation. And I say to all of the leaders of this and associated movements who are permitted to meet with you, let us hark back to the days of that conference, and let there be a fresh dedication on our part this morning to that devotion, that heroism, that obedience, and that vicariousness which filled the students at Mount Hermon in '86, that this Movement may be carried from strength to strength.

THE VISION OF THE STUDENT MISSIONARY PIONEERS REALIZED BY THE STUDENTS OF THE PRESENT GENERATION

ADDRESS GIVEN AT BRADFORD, MASSACHUSETTS
AT THE CENTENARY OF THE FOUNDING OF
THE AMERICAN BOARD OF COMMISSIONERS
FOR FOREIGN MISSIONS, OCTOBER 12, 1910

The great enterprise the centenary of which we commemorate here today began as a student movement. It has ever preserved a close and sympathetic touch with the student centers of America. It has to a wonderful degree commanded the loyal following and devotion of students. In its present-day policy it is doing possibly more than any other missionary agency to multiply the number of students in different lands and to relate them to the plans of the Kingdom. I deeply appreciate, therefore, the privilege of being present as the representative of the Student Movement. As I come from recent contact with the members of this large and growing Movement, and as I have studied afresh the achievements and spirit of the early bands of student missionary pioneers, I have been profoundly impressed with the fact that the spirit which animated the students in those days is still strong and conquering among the students of our day. I find among the students of this generation the same loyalty to the Church of Jesus Christ and the same confidence in the Church which characterized those of that first generation. I find among them the same intercollegiate spirit and conviction as to the importance of united action in advancing the missionary propaganda. I discover among them the same desire to secure the best possible preparation, that they may better discharge their responsibilities as missionary leaders at home and abroad. I find among them the same power of vision, the same responsiveness to their visions, and the same contagious heroism which constituted the glory of the early volunteers.

Those student missionary pioneers had visions which they sought to realize, but which they were unable to realize in their day—visions, however, which the students of our day are realizing.

The students of today are thus fulfilling the word of the writer of the Epistle to the Hebrews, "Apart from us they shall not be made perfect." In other words, the students of today are helping to usher in the full success of the students of those days. What are some of the visions of those early student missionary bands which are being realized by the students of today?

The students of those days had a vision of an intercollegiate missionary movement. In order to realize this vision they conducted a correspondence with students of different colleges. The students of various colleges exchanged visits. Some students left their own colleges and went to study in other colleges in order to spread their missionary ideas. Conditions, however, were not favorable then for the creation and development of such a movement. There were but few colleges, and, because of the poor means of communication, these were comparatively isolated. The intercollegiate consciousness as we understand it did not then exist. There was, generally speaking, a low state of religious life in the churches. The Christian forces were not highly and thoroughly organized. In contrast with such a situation, we have today in this and nearly every other land a well-developed Christian student movement touching profoundly the life of all the colleges. These national movements are bound together in the World's Student Christian Federation, which includes over 2,000 universities and colleges of more than thirty nations, and has a combined membership of 140,000 students and professors A strong and well-developed part of the work among students today is the Student Volunteer Movement. Think of that small devoted band of student missionary pioneers, who came to Bradford 100 years ago to appeal to the Church, and then think of the 4,000 delegates who came together in January 1910, at Rochester, in the Student Volunteer Convention, from over 700 colleges of North America, to consider how they could best serve the Church in extending Christ's Kingdom throughout the whole world in our day.

Think also of the fact that through correspondence and literature the Student Volunteer Movement last year reached over 1,000 different institutions; that more than 29,000 students were studying missions in voluntary mission study circles, under the leadership of an educational secretary set aside for that work; and that 450 different institutions were visited by student volunteer secretaries sent to them for the purpose of helping them to a fuller realization of their personal responsibility for the extension of Christ's Kingdom throughout the world.

Those student missionary pioneers had a vision of well-qualified students going forth in large numbers from the colleges and universities as missionaries to lands where Christ was not known. For example, the object of the Society of Brethren, of Williams College, as set forth in its rules, was to "effect in the persons of its members a mission or missions to the heathen." Only a part of the first little bands of New England students ever reached the mission fields to realize their vision; and at the end of the first full generation but a few scores of North American students had gone out as foreign missionaries. When we remember the ignorance which then prevailed as to the work to be done, the fact that there were so few missionary agencies in that period, the lack of missionary zeal and also of spirituality in the churches and the indifference of so many of the leaders of the Church to the sublime claims of Christian missions, it is not surprising that so few Christian students in those days reached the mission fields. Could Mills, Judson, Richards, and their associates be here today, what would they think as they contemplated the outreach of the Student Volunteer Movement of our generation? Let me remind you that within twenty-four years there have gone out to mission lands, under the auspices of the mission boards of North America, as a direct result of this Movement, nearly 5,000 student volunteers. In addition there have gone out from British universities some 2,000 more since the Student Volunteer Movement was transplanted to Britain. There should be added hundreds of others who have been recruited for foreign service and who have sailed from Australia, New Zealand, South Africa, Holland, Germany, Switzerland, France, and Scandinavia. Besides all this, the student volunteer idea has been transplanted to the schools and colleges of the Levant, India, Ceylon, China, and Japan, and their students are offering themselves in large numbers for the evangelization of their own people.

The student missionary pioneers of a century ago had a vision of the Christian forces of America united in a missionary agency of such scope and strength as would make possible the sending forth and maintaining in the non-Christian world of the missionary recruits of the colleges. They willed to accomplish this practical and important end, and it was done. The American Board, called into being as a result of their faith and consecration, has, through all the years, increasingly embodied their vision; but its largest result has been to influence by its example the development of the varied, extensive, and efficient missionary machinery of the North American churches. So today there are literally scores of mission boards in the United States and Canada which maintain, at an expenditure of $11,000,000 a year, thousands of missionaries in all parts of the world.

Those student pioneers for foreign missions had a vision of the speedy evangelization of the world. This vision also was not realized in their generation. Not until the present generation have Christians in any large numbers been able to rally with conviction under such a watchword as "The Evangelization of the World in This Generation!" But that is the inspiring battlecry of the Christian students of practically all Christendom. Why has God made the whole world known and accessible in our generation? Why has He provided such extensive and well-equipped missionary agencies in our day? Why has He placed such resources at the disposal of the Christian Church? Such vast preparations must have been made for some great and beneficent purpose. Everything is ready for a general and determined engagement of the forces of Christendom for the world-wide proclamation of Christ.

Thus the students of the present day are seeing realized the visions which so powerfully commanded the volunteers of that far-distant day. The churches listened to the students here at Bradford a century ago, and they gladly listen to the students of today. And what do the students of our time wish to say to the Church? They say to the Church: Enlarge your plans to embrace the whole world. The plans of the Church do not give the impression that it is the dominating purpose of Christian missions to make the Living Christ known to all living men in our day. The time has come when there can no longer be any reasonable excuse for not taking the whole world literally into our plan. A half generation hence it should not be possible to point to one unoccupied field. Even the citadels of the non-Christian world should be taken into the scope of the Church's missionary plan.

The students of today say to the Church: Make much larger and more heroic demands on the colleges. We are living in a time when things in the big make the greatest appeal to college men. The facts and forces of material civilization are just now presenting a colossal and dazzling appeal to the student class. There is no doubt whatever that the world plans of Christ can be so set forth that they will make a superior appeal to conscientious Christian college men. Let the Church show convincingly that she needs the students of our generation, and let her make confident demands on their sacrifice and devotion, and they will not be found wanting. But if she would move the strongest and most resolute natures among them, let her appeal to the heroic. The heroic appeal has ever won the heroic response.

Another message which discerning, thoughtful students bring to the Church is this: Help save the colleges themselves by enlisting them more largely in the effort to save the world. Some of the gravest perils of American colleges are the growing habits of luxury and extravagance, and the love of ease and transitory pleasures, a tendency to softness, and the allurements of our material civilization. Nothing less than vast and very difficult and exacting spiritual undertakings will counteract and overcome the spell of such perils and perilous tendencies. The sublime missionary movement can do more than any other one thing to call out and exercise the best energies of the minds and hearts of students.

Whatever communities we fail to cultivate and inspire for missions, let us not neglect to lead the students of our day to give expression to their religious convictions and feelings by relating themselves in practical ways to the missionary program of Jesus Christ. We continue to hear much about the need of the moral equivalent of war. The missionary enterprise best meets this evident need.

The students who in increasing numbers are dedicating their lives to the missionary career call upon the Church to afford them a better, a more specific preparation for their lifework. They believe that the time has come when the curricula of many of our theological seminaries and Christian colleges should be thoroughly and radically revised with reference to ensuring such preparation for intending missionaries. In far too many institutions the instruction and other facilities afforded are not calculated to give students that true and larger comprehension of the races to which they are to minister, of the religions or systems of belief which they must meet, of the present-day statement of Christian message which is to win its way most largely, of the imperial character of the missionary enterprise, of the growing science of the expansion of the Kingdom, of the resources at the disposal of Christ's ambassadors, and of the time in which we live and work—the time of all times. Never was there greater need of able leadership of the aggressive forces of Christianity. And we must admit with candor that our plans and means are not adequately adapted to ensuring such a leadership.

The Christian students of every name, today as never before, say to the Church: "Let us continue to work together." They press this point with deep conviction and strong feeling. They insist that they, representatives of all Christian communions which acknowledge the Divine Lordship of Christ, have lived together in the never-to-be-forgotten intimacies of school and college life; that they have learned not only to trust and love each other, but also to work together and to see that they are essential to each other. They wish to continue to work together. The students of this generation will not stand for disunion among Christians. They are ready to give themselves with enthusiasm and sacrifice to a great, united campaign.

The students, recognizing the great opportunities, crises, dangers, and duties of their day, say to the Church: "Help us to seek a new and greater accession of Divine power." They recognize that far more urgent and fundamental than the need of improved organization and methods, than the need of more comprehensive plans and wiser strategy, than the raising up of a multitude of devoted workers —deeper and more vital than all these—is the need of a larger discovery of God and of the conditions of the manifestation of His power, and the need of complying with these conditions. Then they believe we shall witness His wonder works. "Lo, these are but the outskirts of His ways; but the thunder of His mighty deeds who can understand?"

AMONG THE STUDENTS OF GREAT BRITAIN

ARTICLE BY JOHN R. MOTT
PUBLISHED IN *THE STUDENT VOLUNTEER*, 1894-5

Not long ago it was my privilege to spend several weeks at some of the leading student centers of the British Isles, making a special study of their Christian life and activity. My tour included Dublin University, Edinburgh University, Glasgow University, Oxford University, Cambridge University, the University of Wales, and Trevecca College. As the representative of the American Movement I received a most cordial and sincere welcome in every place. Everything which could be done, was done to put me in touch with the religious life and organizations of the colleges. Never shall I forget or lose the inspiration received from the conferences held in the rooms of office bearers and other prominent student workers at the different universities.

The organization which impressed me most was the Student Volunteer Missionary Union. Although it is the youngest, it seemed to be the most active, the most aggressive, and the most highly developed organization in the British colleges. It was practically the only inter-university student movement in any comprehensive sense. It had carried its work, within three years, into fifty-seven colleges and six missionary institutes and had enrolled fully 700 volunteers.

The British Volunteer Union is in advance of the American movement in several respects: (1) It has done a more thorough work among the women's colleges. During the last year two young women have been at work in such institutions in Great Britain, and the same will be the case this year. Last year we had no secretary at work in this important field; this year we shall have one. (2) The British Union has a stronger hold on medical students than we have in America. This was very noticeable in the great medical colleges of Edinburgh, Glasgow, and London. (3) The British Union has more volunteers in the foremost universities than has the American organization. For example, I found over twenty volunteers in residence at Oxford, and fifty-eight at Cambridge. We have no such showing at Harvard and Yale. It is no more than fair, however, to state that the great strength of the American movement is to be found chiefly in the 300 distinctively denominational colleges. And yet it has been a mighty achievement on the part of our sister organization to rekindle the missionary fires in the great universities of Duff, Burns, Wilson, Livingstone, Martyn, Hannington, Patteson, Mackay, and Keith-Falconer. (4) There is more *esprit de corps* among the volunteers in the British Isles than in the United States and Canada. This may be due in large measure to the fact that the American volunteers are so widely distributed, and to the comparatively small size of their bands. A further reason, however, may be found in the more conservative policy of enrolling volunteers pursued by the British Union from the beginning. (5) Over 10 per cent of the British volunteers have sailed, although their organization has been at work only about three years. Fully as large a percentage of the American volunteers have sailed, but our Movement is more than twice as old as the one in Great Britain. It is gratifying to recall the fact that more of our volunteers have gone to the field during the last three years than during the preceding five years and a half. A number of points might be given in which the American movement is in advance of the British Union but it will be more profitable for us to keep in mind the foregoing facts, and seek in the future, by the Spirit's guidance and power, to achieve equally favorable results on all these lines. From conversation with secretaries of the various British missionary societies I could see that the Volunteer Union has their complete confidence, just as our Movement has that of the American societies. A most practical illustration of this is seen in the fact that last year one of the Scottish societies made a donation from its regular funds toward the expenses of the Union.

A most remarkable student conference was held from July 30th to August 3d at Keswick, in the northern part of the wonderfully beautiful English Lake district. This was made possible by the conference of the Student Volunteer Missionary Union held in the same place the year preceding. The conference this year, it was said, constituted the first comprehensive inter-university student conference ever held in Great Britain. There were at least 250 students present from over thirty institutions. Practically every prominent institution in every part of the United Kingdom was represented. Edinburgh, with over thirty men, had the banner delegation. Oxford, Glasgow, Cambridge, and other universities had also large delegations. Germany sent two able representatives: Mockert who is so favorably remembered by American students, and who has done such an important work in promoting Bible study in the universities and gymnasia of Germany and Siemsen, a most brilliant and influential student from the University of Berlin. Two men came from France: Monnier who is at the head of the Fraternal Association of Protestant Students in the University of Paris and Vernier who has done so much to spread the missionary spirit among the French students. It was also a real inspiration to have present Hunter of South Africa, who has been so successfully extending the volunteer movement in that distant quarter of the globe. The program was carefully planned and carried out. At seven o'clock in the morning there was a prayer meeting; at nine, the missionary institute; at ten, the Bible class; at eleven, the conference on Christian work in colleges; at six o'clock in the evening, a meeting similar to the lifework conferences at our own summer schools; at seven, the public platform meeting; and at nine, the delegation meetings. The afternoons were spent in about the same way as at Northfield. In fact the whole conference reminded one constantly of Northfield and Lake Geneva. There was the same beautiful environment, the same blessed fellowship, the same frank and practical discussion of the problems of Christian work, the same reverent consideration of the Word of God, the same intense missionary spirit, the same heart-searching and inspiring addresses, the same soul and will struggles, the same depth and fervency of prayer life, the same glad obedience to heavenly visions, and the same eagerness and determination to attempt greater things for God. Certain it is that the Keswick Conference was not one whit behind Northfield in any essential respect. The only criticism which could be offered—and that came from all—was that it should have continued a few days longer. The Reverend F. B. Meyer and the Reverend Prebendary Webb-Peploe gave addresses abounding in spiritual life and truth. Canon Taylor Smith gave just such talks as we should like to have repeated all over the American student field. Professor Snape gave an address on the perils and temptations of college life which would be a godsend to every student who might hear it. Nothing was more impressive than the words and life of Bishop Tucker, who, after laboring forty-four years as a missionary in India and New Zealand, has just given up his bishopric in order to work as an ordinary missionary in Persia, because it is a more difficult and needy field. Speer conducted the daily Bible studies with consummate ability, and gave two addresses of remarkable spiritual power. In Keswick, as in American student gatherings, he was used by the Spirit in touching the very depths of the lives of many men. The most significant result of this conference was the real inauguration of the work of the Inter-university Christian Union.

This organization is to do a work in the British colleges corresponding to that which has been done in America by the Intercollegiate Young Men's Christian Association. It was decided to place a traveling secretary in the field. Largely as a result of the sacrifice of the students themselves, money enough was subscribed to meet the expenses of such a secretaryship for three years. It is proposed to employ also a corresponding secretary in conjunction with the Volunteer Union. There is a wonderful field before this new movement, both on the line of unifying and developing in the colleges the Christian organizations which already exist, and on the line of introducing organized Christian work in over 100 institutions of higher learning where practically nothing is now being done. It would be difficult to exaggerate the far-reaching importance of this new university union. Judging by what God has wrought through the corresponding agency in America, it constitutes the most signal development of recent years in the Christian life of the student world. The great success and power of the Keswick Conference and of the two movements represented there are traceable under God to a few young men: Fraser of Glasgow, who has been the very efficient traveling secretary of the Volunteer Union during the past year, and who made such a strong impression at Detroit; Anderson of Oxford, who directed the business of the Conference with such ability, and who has been so wisely chosen to be traveling secretary of the Volunteer Union for the present year; Bryde of Cambridge and Williams of London, who presided with such wisdom at the sessions of the Conference and who have sustained such a vital relation to the development of the Volunteer

Union; Maclean of Glasgow, whose farsighted judgment has affected so helpfully all interuniversity Christian efforts during the last six years; Learmouth and Williamson, of Edinburgh; Gairdner of Oxford; Butcher of Cambridge; Boyland of Dublin; Guinness of London; Burges of Wales; and others, whose intelligent, earnest, and unselfish work was so potent both at the conference and in their own universities. American students will recognize in the foregoing list the names of some whom they met at Northfield and Detroit with so much pleasure and blessing. Let us pray that the way may open for these and other leaders of the British student Christian forces to come over and help us, and also that their own work may be attended by the constant and marked presence of the Holy Ghost. May He continue to unite more and more closely the Christian students on both sides of the Atlantic for the speedy and complete evangelization of this world!

THE NATIONAL YOUNG MEN'S CHRISTIAN ASSOCIATION AND THE STUDENT VOLUNTEER MOVEMENT IN CHINA

ARTICLE PUBLISHED IN *THE STUDENT VOLUNTEER*
MARCH, 1897

On the occasion of my first visit to China, I was impressed by the fact that although in those days there were no organizations bringing them together, the students and teachers were very responsive to my suggestions as to the desirability of their coming into helpful relations to each other. They were deeply impressed by the messages of greeting which we conveyed to them from the students of other lands. In not a single institution did the students fail to favor the proposed plan of a national organization of their own. Accordingly, it was early decided to call a special conference to take steps toward the formation of such a national union.

This conference was held in Shanghai, November 3-5, 1896, at the close of our tour in China. Each Association was invited to send one delegate. Twenty-two out of the twenty-seven Associations did so. The conditions in China made it very desirable that the foundations of the national society should be laid by the leaders of the different colleges. It is an impressive fact that seventeen of the leading college presidents of the Empire left their work at the busiest season of the year and came to Shanghai, involving an expenditure of from five days to three weeks of time, in order to participate in launching this great work. We recall no movement which has been inaugurated under such favorable auspices. In addition to college presidents and other foreigners there were present several of the most influential Chinese Christian students and teachers.

The chairmanship of the conference was intrusted to me, and Mr. Lyon was elected Secretary. The first day was devoted to discussing thoroughly and adopting a national constitution. The next day was occupied in deciding Chinese terminology, in perfecting the permanent organization, and in determining several main points of policy to be followed by the movement. A strong national committee composed of fourteen men, one-half of whom are Chinese, was appointed. The executive of this committee includes some of the leading educationists of China. On the third day a special meeting was held with the National Committee, at which the policy of the coming year was outlined and discussed. It was decided to have a monthly paper devoted to the interests of the movement; to issue five pamphlet publications in English and three in Chinese; to hold a national convention, and also sectional conferences from time to time; to have Mr. Lyon, who has been sent out by the International Committee, serve also as general secretary of the National Committee to have the movement strongly represented at the convention of the World's Student Christian Federation.

Bishop Moule of Mid-China, Bishop Joyce of America, the college presidents, and other voting and visiting delegates, made speeches of warmest commendation and expressed their convictions as to the providential character of this movement. The unity of spirit which characterized a body representing so many sections, so many different classes of opinion as to the conduct of educational missions, and so many denominations was much commented upon. This new movement, which is called the College Young Men's Christian Association of China, will enable the Christian students of the Empire, for the first time, to know the strength of their numbers. It will make possible continuity and progression in their organized Christian work. It will enable each Association to profit by the experience of all the others. The strong will be able to help the weak. It will make possible communication with the great student world outside. The real significance of the movement is seen in the fact that old China is passing away; new China is coming on. The leaders of the new China are today being trained in those institutions which give the modern education. What shall that leadership be? This voluntary organization has been called into being to co-operate with the spiritual forces of educational missions in making that leadership truly Christian.

The Chinese Volunteer Movement. One of the most important developments of the tour in China was the extension of the Volunteer Movement to the students of the Empire. There are nearly 200 members of the British and American Volunteer Movements in China, about five-sixths of whom come from the United States and Canada. We met personally one-half of the whole number. Conversations with them, as well as with other missionaries, led us to think that steps should be taken at once toward definite organization of the Movement among the Chinese students.

A committee of old volunteers was appointed at two of the conferences to take the initial steps. This committee appeared before the convention which was held for forming the College Young Men's Christian Association of China. That convention, by unanimous vote, made the Student Volunteer Movement an organic department of its work. It appointed a committee of nine American and British volunteers to facilitate the development of this department. Among the members of this committee are such former leaders of the home movements as B. L. Livingstone Learmouth, D. Willard Lyon, and L. Herbert Roots. The members of the committee are scattered throughout the Empire.

We had two long sessions with this committee, going carefully into its work. Among the important actions taken were: the adoption of the form of declaration used by the Student Volunteer Movement of India and Ceylon—"It is my purpose, if God permit, to devote my life to direct work for Christ"; the provision for the organization of volunteer bands in the different colleges of China; the determination of lines of work to be pushed by Chinese volunteers; the introduction of a cycle of prayer; plans for conducting the missionary department of the monthly paper; the arranging for the preparation of a strong printed appeal to Chinese students to devote their lives to Christian work. Steps are also being taken toward the appointment of a similar committee of women volunteers to extend the Movement among the young women of China.

Great care will be taken in the development of the Volunteer Movement in China. The present seems to be a most providential time for its inauguration. The organization of the Association Movement has done much to prepare the way—by affording larger access to the Christian students; by affording a firm anchorage for the Volunteer Movement; by supplying favorable conditions for fostering the spiritual life of Chinese volunteers, and for training them in Christian work. The recent series of conferences has created a strong sentiment in favor of the Volunteer Movement. The fact that the college presidents of China with one mind voted to incorporate the Volunteer

Movement into the Association Movement as its missionary department is in itself one of the very strongest endorsements the Volunteer
Movement has ever received. The further striking fact that at two of
the conferences recently held not fewer than seventy-seven Chinese
young men decided to dedicate their lives to taking Christ to their
own countrymen, is another indication of the hand of God in the work.
And when we recall the awful spiritual crisis of China, involving one-
third of the human race, can we question that the volunteer idea has
been divinely planted in the Chinese student field?

THE STUDENT MISSIONARY UPRISING AND ITS
MESSAGE TO AUSTRALASIA

ADDRESS GIVEN AT
THE STUDENT CONFERENCE
MELBOURNE, AUSTRALIA, APRIL 10-12, 1903

We live in a time when students, as a class, do not apologize for
the great work of the extension of the Kingdom of Christ throughout
the world. The man who would apologize for the enterprise of world-
wide missions must be either ignorant or thoughtless. In doing so, he
apologizes for all enduring religion; for, as Max Müller says, "The
non-missionary religions are either dying or are dead." Manifestly,
therefore, he apologizes for Christianity, because Christianity is essentially a missionary religion. He apologizes for the Bible, because
missions constitute its central theme. He apologizes for the Apostles'
Creed, and for the Lord's Prayer; he need only repeat their familiar
phrases in order to realize how true this is. He apologizes for the
Fatherhood of God, and, at the same time, for the brotherhood of
man. If he is a Christian, he apologizes for every whit of spiritual
life that is in himself, and, worst of all, he apologizes for Jesus Christ,
who "is in the propitiation for our sins: and not for ours only, but also
for the sins of the whole world." Therefore, I repeat, the man who
would apologize for this sublime work of the world-wide extension of
Christ's Kingdom must be either ignorant or thoughtless.

Not only do students of today not apologize for world-wide missions, but they also believe in this enterprise to a degree not true of
any preceding generation of students. Of this there are many evidences. First of all, attention should be called to the development and
extension of an organized inter-university and intercollegiate missionary movement. This movement, taking its rise at a conference of
American and Canadian students, has spread from land to land, until

it has now assumed an organized form in Great Britain, Germany, the Scandinavian countries, Holland, France, Switzerland, Australasia and South Africa. Thus the Christian students of the northern and the southern hemispheres are united in the inspiring purpose of enthroning Jesus Christ as King among all nations and races of men. The fact that this missionary movement is regarded as one of the strongest departments in the more comprehensive Christian Union organization of most countries is in itself significant. It seems all the more remarkable when we remember that only a generation ago the missionary idea was not regarded with favor by students as a class. The World's Student Christian Federation, which unites over 1,500 Christian Unions in over forty countries, and which has a membership of over 80,000 students and professors, has as one of its three main objects the enlisting of students in the extension of the Kingdom of Christ throughout the world. Contrast this magnificent union of the Christian forces of the universities and colleges of the whole world with the isolation, ignorance, and lack of concerted effort which prevailed throughout the student world a generation ago.

Another indication of the growing missionary interest among the students of our day is seen in the remarkable student missionary conferences which have been held during recent years. These conferences have been the largest, most representative, most influential, most powerful, and most fruitful student gatherings ever held in the different countries. Take, for example, the Student Missionary Conference held in London during the first week of the year 1900. It was attended by some 1,600 delegates. Thirteen hundred of their number were students, of whom only a little over one-fourth were volunteers. Nearly fifty principals, professors, and teachers were in attendance, and also scores of missionaries and representatives of all the missionary societies of the British Isles. One hundred sixty-nine British institutions of higher learning were represented, and forty-five foreign universities and colleges. There were delegates present representing as many as twenty-six nations. Or look at the last conference of this kind held in North America about a year ago. It was convened in the city of Toronto, and was attended by nearly, if not quite, 3,000 delegates. Among their number were 2,300 students and 247 professors and teachers. Every important missionary society of the United States and Canada was officially represented, and over 100 missionaries from all parts of the world field participated in the sessions. Not less than 465 universities, colleges, and higher schools of North America sent delegates to the convention. Probably there has never been held a Christian gathering in that part of the world which has so deeply stirred the centers of learning or done more to stimulate the missionary zeal of the Church. We might also call attention to the similar conference held at Halle, in Germany, which was the greatest student religious conference ever held on the continent of Europe. From present indications, your own conference, convened today in Melbourne, and the one to be held a few weeks later at Christchurch, in New Zealand, bid fair not to be exceptions, but may prove to be the largest and most potent student gatherings ever held in this part of the world. Let us continue to associate our prayers and efforts, that they may likewise prove to be the most fruitful. Is it not striking that the missionary idea assembles in all parts of the world the strongest and most representative bodies of students, and arouses the most intense enthusiasm?

By far the largest sales of missionary literature, in proportion to the number of people involved, are to students. Is not this a further proof of the genuineness of the missionary interest among students? Leading publishers, both in America and Europe, have told me that their largest purchasers of missionary books are the students. One authority on missionary literature recently pointed out to me that the sales of the textbooks of the Student Volunteer Movement exceed those of all missionary books save two or three of a popular character. Several years ago students of but a few colleges and universities had access to the best missionary literature. Now, as a result of the work of the Student Unions, there are valuable collections of missionary books in hundreds of student communities. Moreover, I find that students are doing more than any other class of people to promote the circulation and reading of missionary literature. The students of one denomination in America have recently sold over 6,000 sets of carefully selected missionary books to as many congregations and Christian societies of young people. The Christian Union of one British college, in a short time, disposed of 22,000 copies of three telling missionary pamphlets.

One of the best evidences of the strength of the missionary spirit among students is the great development which has recently taken place in the scientific study of missions in the universities and colleges. Ten years ago an investigation showed that there were fewer than fifty groups of students in Christian nations who were carrying on in a progressive and thorough manner the subject of the study of missions, and that probably not more than 400 students were engaged in such studies. Last year over 6,000 students in some 400 classes and circles scattered throughout the various Christian nations were giving themselves to the study of mission fields, problems, and forces. The interest in these studies has become so keen that, for several years, the Volunteer Movement in North America has employed an educational secretary, a man of large experience and ability, to devote his whole time to guiding and developing this part of the work. The Volunteer Union in Great Britain has also, for several years, had an educational secretary. Under the leadership of these two secretaries, quite a large number of special textbooks on missions have been prepared, and cycles of mission studies reaching through a period of from two to four years have been arranged. The most notable recent addition to this list of textbooks specially prepared for use among students is *The Missionary Geography and Atlas,* issued by the American movement at the expense of over £1,400. There are bands of students not only for the study of foreign missions, but also for the study of the needs and methods of religious, philanthropic, and social reform work in the Christian nations.

That students are giving their money more largely than in times past towards missionary objects illustrates further the growth among them of the missionary spirit. One might call attention to the different university missions of Great Britain and North America, and to the various Christian university settlements in the cities which are supported in large measure by the gifts of present and past students. Most of these enterprises have sprung up within a generation. In every country which I visit I find various home and foreign missionary schemes financed by undergraduate and graduate students. Last year the students of the United States and Canada gave over £8,000 to foreign missions, and probably an even larger sum to various religious efforts which they are promoting on the home field. A large number of their unions are each supporting, wholly or in great part, their own missionary. Students of Princeton have for several years given about £200 a year to support Mr. Gailey, one of their alumni and, by the way, one of their famous football players and Christian leaders, in work among the students and other young men of North China. The students of Yale have contributed annually a like sum to support their representative in work among the students of Western India. Several of the Canadian colleges and schools have united their gifts from year to year to the extent of over £200 to support a representative at work among the students of Calcutta. Some of the theological colleges having fewer than 100 students each are giving from £100 to £200 to support a foreign missionary or a home missionary, as the case may be. In some instances this represents much self-sacrifice. To my mind, the great benefit resulting is not so much the amount of money set apart for missions as the effect of this object lesson on the lives of the students themselves. As they go forth from the colleges to become ministers and leading laymen in the various churches, they will have faith and courage to lead the churches likewise to support their own representatives on the mission field. The students are also doing much to increase the gifts of church members. A few Methodist students in Canada, as a result of working among the young people in their denomination during vacations, in a short time increased the missionary gifts by the sum of over £5,000. Fifty Congregational students in America, as a result of their visits in 200 churches, increased their gifts over 400 per cent.

Students today, more largely than ever before, are participating in Christian work in their own countries. Nothing is more encouraging than the growing concern among them for the moral, social, and religious welfare of the so-called Christian countries. In this connection I have in mind especially the interest shown among undergraduate students. Hundreds of Christian Unions of students are carrying on aggressive Christian work in the vicinity of the universities and colleges. They are seeking to spread the teachings and spirit of Christ among the neglected classes of people within the reach of their influence. The student Christian organization at Yale have erected a special building in one of the neediest parts of New Haven, where scores of undergraduates in the course of each week give a certain amount of time voluntarily to helping to improve the lives and social condition of the people in that dark part of the city. The Union at Harvard has enlisted the co-operation of hundreds of students in furthering various religious and philanthropic schemes in the neighboring city and outlying districts. These are but typical of what is being done by similar organizations of Christian students throughout the Christian nations. The undergraduates are also extending their activities to the vacation periods. A large number of Christian students in Canada devote their long vacations to Christian work in what you would call the backblocks of that country. Not a few of the earnest Christian students of the English and Scottish universities devote sections of their vacation to special services among children and other classes. In one state in America bands of students go out during the vacation to help to evangelize scores of villages and rural districts. I think of one band which, in one comparatively short vacation, succeeded in leading some 300 people to become Christians. While activities such as those described have been carried on by zealous groups of Christian students for many generations, it is without doubt true that, in the present generation, there is a vastly larger volume of such Christian endeavor than at any time in the past.

During the last two decades there has been an unprecedented offering of lives of students for the work of world-wide evangelization. The facts are not wanting to show that an encouraging proportion of students in a number of lands are entering Christian work on the home field. It is reported that the North American Student Movement has influenced, within a quarter of a century, 6,000 young men to enter the ministry. In different Christian lands students are offering themselves for the most difficult tasks in neglected and most discouraging fields in both cities and rural districts; but the number of students who have offered for foreign missions has been even more remarkable, when all the handicaps and obstacles are considered. Literally, thousands of young men and women in the universities and colleges have, within the past sixteen years, signed the Volunteer Declaration, saying, "It is my purpose, if God permit, to become a foreign missionary." Doubtless many of these will not be able to carry out their purpose, because of the fact that they lack the necessary qualifications to meet the requirements of the missionary societies, and for other reasons; but, after all allowances are made, a vast number of them will be enabled to carry out their declaration. Already, within sixteen years, not less than 2,100 of the volunteers of the United States and Canada have finished their preparation and gone out to the foreign mission fields under the auspices of the regular missionary societies. Over 600 of the volunteers of Great Britain have sailed to the mission field within about ten years. If we add to the numbers who have gone forth from North America and Great Britain, those who have been sent out from other Protestant Christian countries, we shall have a total of nearly, if not fully, 3,000 students who, within half a generation, have been thrust forth by the Holy Spirit from the student centers of Christendom to work among less favored lands and races in the non-Christian world. Over 100 percent more have gone forth within the last eight years than during the preceding eight years. This proves that the missionary movement is increasing in volume as well as in momentum. About one-third of the volunteers are women students. All faculties are represented. It is interesting to notice that, in Great Britain, about one-fourth of the volunteers who have been recruited are medical students. Some universities are furnishing a larger number of volunteers than others. One time I found at Edinburgh University as many as forty volunteers. I think of one university in America which has sent out over 200 missionaries. Anyone who has visited The Henry Martyn Memorial Hall at Cambridge must have been profoundly impressed with the wonderful missionary record of that university. His Grace, the late Archbishop of Canterbury, said to me at one time that few things inspired him with so much hope as the recent uprising of students for the evangelization of the world. An eminent Roman Catholic educator, in an article on the Student Volunteer Movement which appeared in an educational review of that Church, appealed to the Roman Catholic clergy and teachers to bestir themselves if Roman Catholicism is to take the same aggressive part in the conquest of the world which Protestantism is destined to take as a result of this Movement.

Those students who are to devote themselves to the so-called secular pursuits have come to recognize as no preceding generation of students that they are as much responsible for the world evangelization and betterment as their fellow students who give themselves to the work of the ministry at home or of foreign missions abroad. The result is that Christian students who will become teachers, doctors, barristers, editors, engineers, or business men are entering the churches of Christian nations to become lay leaders of laymen in this age of laymen. The active co-operation of this influential class will make possible far larger achievements on the part of the clergy and missionary force. It ensures the development of a stronger base of operations for the work both at home and abroad. It is doing much to bridge the chasm which unfortunately existed a while ago in many student communities between those who felt called to enter upon the work of missions abroad and those who considered themselves likewise called to work at home. This is most advantageous; for only by a strong union of the home and foreign missionary force, and by regarding the world field as a unit, can we hope to evangelize the whole world and establish the Kingdom of Jesus Christ.

The missionary idea has been transplanted within recent years to the student centers of non-Christian nations. It is specially strong in the colleges of India, Ceylon, Egypt, and China. In these countries alone there are now over 600 native student volunteers; that is, young men and women who have indicated their desire and purpose to turn from pursuits where they might receive larger salaries and spend their lives preaching and teaching Christ among their own countrymen. About one-fourth of this number have volunteered within the past two years. Eight years ago, when I visited a college up the Nile Valley in Egypt, a group of ten or twelve students decided to devote their lives to Christian work. They banded themselves together to influence other Christian students to do likewise. When Mr. Sallmon visited that college on his way home from Australia, he learned that the number of native volunteers had, during the intervening years, increased from ten or twelve to over threescore. About two years ago there was formed in Calcutta, by educated Christian Indians, what is known as the Indian Christian Workers' Band, which has for its object the leading of Indian Christians to devote themselves more fully to the evangelization of their own people. They took steps at their national convention, which I attended last winter, to extend the idea to other communities in India. The recent organization of the Jaffna Student Foreign Missionary Society in the northern part of the island of Ceylon is a most striking incident. This society is supported and controlled by Ceylonese students, and has sent one of its number to Southern India to work among the millions of Tamils. In Japan I found that the Christian students have come to feel a special burden of responsibility for the spread of the Kingdom of Christ in Formosa, Korea, and even China. In North China one of the Student Christian Associations for years supported a native Zulu worker among his own people in South Africa. Illustrations like these, which might be greatly multiplied, show that the missionary spirit is manifesting itself among the earnest bands of Christian students in heathen lands as at no time in the past. Nothing could be more significant, because, if these nations are ever to be evangelized, the larger part of the work must be performed by the native Christians themselves. We shall want a large number of the best men and women of Christendom to go forth to lead in the conquest; but the rank and file of the workers must come from the sons and daughters of the soil.

If any further proof were required to show that the students of our day are animated more largely than the students of other generations with the missionary spirit, attention might be called to the remarkable development and spread among them of what might be termed the cosmopolitan spirit. The students of today have taken the whole world into their view and plan. They have chosen as their watchword nothing less than "The Evangelization of the World in This Generation." What other generation in the history of the Church has adopted such a battle cry? Who can measure its power? Without doubt, it has enlarged the horizon of the Christian students of our day, it has strengthened their purpose, augmented their faith, inspired hopefulness, and intensified zeal. It has driven them to God in prayer. It has developed the spirit of heroism and self-sacrifice.

Why do the students of our generation believe so strongly in this enterprise of world-wide missions? One might answer in a sentence by saying, "Because they are students." In the first place, they are students of the Bible. They find it impossible to make a comprehensive and thorough study of the original documents of Christianity without discovering that it is the purpose of God that all mankind shall be given an adequate opportunity to know Jesus Christ, and to become His disciples. In the second place, they are students of the history of the Church of Christ. There they learn that the large majority of the leaders of world-wide missions have been students. From the days of St. Paul down to the recent wonderful missionary century, the moving spirits in the missionary enterprise have, with a few exceptions, come from the universities and colleges. They conclude that the students of our day, with larger outlook, larger opportunities, larger facilities, and therefore larger ability, must not be found wanting in performing this Christ-appointed task. They are also students of Christian sociology, or of the condition of mankind throughout the world, from the point of view of Jesus Christ. In the light of a conscientious, scientific, and sympathetic study of the facts concerning the moral and religious condition of heathen nations, they have formed the deep conviction that these nations, without Jesus Christ, are literally without hope. They are students of human nature; they are students of their own hearts as well. They have no shadow of doubt that they themselves need Christ. They argue therefore that, if they, having a Christian heredity, a Christian environment, and living under the influence of Christian ideas and ideals, need Christ, surely those who are without such favoring conditions stand in the deepest possible need of Him. Moreover, they are students of politics. In pondering the secret of the strength of Christian nations they have been profoundly impressed with the working of the law that the more a nation gives up of its best lives for the helping of more needy nations, the more its own religious life is purified and strengthened. They are students of Providence; therefore they cannot turn a deaf ear to the urgent appeals which are being made by the responsible leaders of the missionary forces at home and abroad for more students to devote themselves to the world's evangelization. Therefore, moreover, they recognize the wisdom of taking advantage of the rising spiritual tide which now characterizes the missionary movement in nearly all parts of the non-Christian world.

God grant that this convention, and the one soon to convene in Christchurch, the first of their kind in Australasia, may mark the beginning of a new epoch in the missionary life of the universities and colleges of this part of the world. The need of this is apparent. Students are needed to throw themselves into the troubled heart of the cities of Australasia in order to make them strongholds and propagating centers for pure and aggressive Christianity. Students are needed to extend the ministry of Christ to the back-block regions and all the rural communities, without which we cannot permanently hold the cities of the nation. Students are needed to evangelize the aboriginal and foreign populations in different parts of the countries who otherwise must be a menace to the nation. Above all, many students of ability are needed for the work of foreign missions. At present a much smaller proportion of the Christian students of Australasia are devoting themselves to missionary work than is the case in any other Anglo-Saxon country. Although the British and Dutch population of South Africa is much smaller than the Anglo-Saxon population of Australasia, over two times as many students in South Africa have dedicated themselves to the work of missions as is the case here. Canada, which has about the same number of Anglo-Saxon people as Australasia, has furnished severalfold more volunteers than Australasia. Britain and America have also yielded a larger proportional contingent for the world's evangelization. The fact should not be overlooked in this connection that all these other countries have a greater home mission population than is to be found here. Think, for example, of Canada with its over 1,000,000 French Canadians, not to speak of its Indians and Chinese. Think of the 10,000,000 and more Negroes in the Southern States; not to mention the great masses of foreign populations in American cities drawn from undesirable classes in Southern and Eastern Europe and the Levant. Think of the large numbers of natives who impinge upon the British and Dutch people in South Africa. The geographical position of Australia and New Zealand is also most favorable with reference to sending out foreign missionary influence. You hold the key to the situation in the Pacific island world, and also look into the very doors of the great mission fields of Southern and Eastern Asia. No Christian nation occupies a more strategic position. Manifestly, this is not without its message of duty and responsibility.

What should be accomplished? The delegates of this convention should give themselves with undiscourageable resolution to building up and perfecting the missionary organization and machinery of the Christian unions in all the universities and colleges. Students should be enlisted more largely in Christian and philanthropic work among neglected classes within the range of the influence of the unions. The number of students engaged in the study of missions should be greatly increased. The co-operation of Christian professors and teachers should be secured to ensure the better leadership of the mission study classes or circles. Far more students of ability and consecration should be led to devote their lives to the various forms of missionary work at home and abroad. The Union should stand for and promote the best possible preparation of those who enter these callings. Each generation of Christian students should be brought to face squarely and fairly the facts concerning the need of the whole world, and to place their lives where they will count most for the evangelization of the world and the establishment of Messiah's reign.

THE WATCHCRY OF THE STUDENT VOLUNTEER MOVEMENT

ARTICLE BY JOHN R. MOTT
REPRINTED FROM *THE STUDENT VOLUNTEER*
OF GREAT BRITAIN, JANUARY, 1895

1. The Meaning of the Watchcry. "The Evangelization of the World in This Generation" is the watchcry of the Student Volunteer Movement for Foreign Missions. It is emphatically a watchcry, not a prophecy. It states what the Movement will unswervingly and prayerfully strive to accomplish.

What is meant by "the evangelization of the world"? (1) Positively: It means for us to give every person in the world an opportunity to know Jesus Christ as a personal Saviour. (2) Negatively: It does not mean the conversion of the world, for the acceptance of Christ rests with the hearer, and not with the speaker. It does not mean the Christianization or the civilization of the world—important as both of these are. Nor must it be construed to mean an imperfect preaching of the gospel. Moreover, it must not be interpreted as in any way detracting from the real importance of any phase of missionary work which is being used by the Spirit. The Movement stands pre-eminently for the emphasis of the belief that by a great enlargement of the agencies employed by the missionary societies today, the gospel can and should be brought within the reach of every creature within the generation.

What is the meaning of "this generation"? As far as the activities and direct influence of the individual volunteer are concerned it means within his own lifetime. As far as the activities and direct influence of the Volunteer Movement as a whole at any given time are concerned, it means within a period commonly known as a generation from that time. It is of constant application to successive generations as long as the world remains unevangelized. Each generation of Christians must obviously evangelize its own generation of the unevangelized inhabitants of the world if they are to be evangelized at all.

2. Necessity of Evangelizing the World in This Generation. The Scriptures clearly teach that if men are to be saved they must be saved through Christ. Over half the inhabitants of the earth have never heard the gospel. Shall hundreds of millions go out of the world in this generation without having an opportunity to hear of Christ? If we know from experience that Christ is necessary for us, have we a right to assume that others do not need Him?

3. The Duty of Evangelizing the World in This Generation. It is a duty because it is a necessity. More than this, it is a duty because Christ has commanded it. It is impossible to interpret in any other way the last commission of Christ as given in Matthew, Mark, Luke, and Acts. It is also impossible to explain in any other way the interpretation which the Apostles unmistakably gave the commission. Christ's command has acquired tremendous momentum in eighteen centuries of invention, of opening the doors of nations, and of Christian organization.

4. The Possibility of Evangelizing the World in This Generation. What ought to be done, can be done. Christ never commands an impossible thing. Furthermore, it should never be forgotten that this is God's enterprise. In carrying it on we are absolutely sure of the constant presence and help of Him with whom resides all power in heaven and on earth. "Behold, I am the Lord, the God of all flesh: is there anything too hard for Me?" It will greatly strengthen a man's faith in the possibility of evangelizing the world in this generation, to consider thoughtfully and prayerfully the following examples of what has been done in the realm of Christian enterprise: what Christ accomplished in three years of preaching; what Paul accomplished as an evangelist and an organizer; the devotion of the Moravian Church to foreign missions (note the proportion of its members sent to the foreign field, and also the average amount of money given by each member to foreign missions) ; the achievements of the Gossner Missionary Society in one generation; the work carried on under the leadership of Pastor Harms; the labor of the English Wesleyans in the Fiji Islands; and the work of American missionaries in the Hawaiian Islands. The record of the Apostolic Church should be read with this point of possibility in mind. In contrast, recall the extent and resources of the Church today; her membership, her wealth, her organizations, her accumulated experience, and the wonderful facilities at her disposal. The power and influence of the native Church must also be taken into consideration. Above all, the Church today can avail herself of that which made possible the mighty works of the early Christians, "the Holy Ghost, whom God hath given to them that obey Him."

5. Favorable Opinions Concerning Speedy and World-wide Evangelization. Among many opinions which might be quoted only three are given.

At the General Conference of Protestant Missionaries of China held at Shanghai in 1877, attended by 126 missionaries, the report of the Committee on Appeal to the Churches, containing the following burning words, was adopted: "Ought we not to make an effort to save China in this generation? Is God's power limited? Is the efficacy of prayer limited? This grand achievement is in the hands of the Church. . . . We want China emancipated from the thraldom of sin in this generation. It is possible. Our Lord has said, 'According to your faith be it unto you.' The Church of God can do it, if she be only faithful to her great commission."

Again, at the conference held at Shanghai in 1890, attended by 427 regular missionaries, the following resolution, entitled "Of the Supreme Importance of Evangelistic Work," was adopted: *"Resolved: That, while we regard the educational and literary branches of our work as indispensable and likely to yield large fruits in the future, we nevertheless urge that in view of its paramount importance, the evangelistic work be pushed forward with increased vigor and earnestness, in order, if possible, to save the present generation."*

From the appeal "To the Secretaries of the Missionary Societies in Europe, America, Australasia, and Asia," sent by the Third Decennial Missionary Conference held at Bombay, 1892-1893, attended by over 600 missionaries, we quote the following: "In the name of Christ and of these unevangelized masses for whom He died, we appeal to you to send more laborers at once. . . . Face to face with 284,000,000 in this land, for whom in this generation you as well as we are responsible, we ask, Will you not speedily double the present number of laborers? The manifestation of Christ is greatest to those who keep His Commandments, and this is His Commandment: 'Go ye into all the world and preach the Gospel to every creature.' "

6. **Conditions Essential to the Realization of the Watchcry.** A thorough, honest, personal consideration of the claims of the enterprise of world-wide evangelization on the part of the Christian students of this generation; clear and settled convictions on the subject on the part of the volunteers themselves; volunteers thoroughly equipped, above all filled with the Holy Spirit, before they go forth to their fields of labor; giving commensurate with the project on the part of all Christians; a Church obedient to Christ's prayer command: "Pray ye therefore the Lord of the harvest, that He send forth laborers into His harvest."

7. **Advantages of the Watchcry.** Although the experience of the Student Volunteer Movement in the use of this watchcry has been comparatively limited, the results which have attended its use have abundantly justified its adoption. It is true that it has been misunderstood and misinterpreted by men both in and outside the Movement; but by no means as much as has been the case with the volunteer dec-

laration. The watchcry is gaining in favor year by year. It is a power in the lives of a hundred students today where it was in the life of one at the inception of the Movement. It puts the whole missionary enterprise in a more attractive form to many men in our colleges. It holds out a very definite end to be accomplished. It lends additional intensity to all one's missionary activity. It affords a new and powerful incentive. It gives the impetus to an individual which comes from realizing that he is a part of a mighty movement. It appeals to the heroic, the enterprising, and the self-sacrificing in a man's nature. Invariably it drives a man more to prayer, and leads him to rely more fully upon the Spirit of God.

THE OBLIGATION OF THIS GENERATION TO EVANGELIZE THE WORLD

ADDRESS GIVEN AT
THE ECUMENICAL MISSIONARY CONFERENCE
CARNEGIE HALL, NEW YORK CITY, APRIL, 28, 1900

There is a large and increasing number of Christians who believe not only that it is the duty of the Church to evangelize the world in this generation, but also that it is possible to accomplish the task. What is meant by the evangelization of the world in this generation? It means to give every person an adequate opportunity to know Jesus Christ as personal Saviour and Lord. We do not mean the conversion of the world in this generation. We do not imply a hasty or superficial preaching of the gospel. We do not use the expression as a prophecy. It calls attention to what may and ought to be done, not necessarily to what is actually going to occur. We do not minimize the importance of any method of missionary work which has been and is being used by the Spirit of God. We rather add emphasis to all the regular forms of missionary work, such as educational, medical, literary, and evangelistic. As Dr. Dennis says: "The evangelistic method must not be regarded as monopolizing the evangelistic aim, which should itself pervade all the other methods." The evangelization of the world in this generation should not be regarded as an end in itself. The Church will not have fulfilled her task when the gospel has been preached to all men. Such evangelization must be followed by baptism of the converts, by their organization into churches, by building them up in knowledge, faith, and character, and by training them for service. The great objective should be always kept in mind, namely, the planting and developing in all non-Christian lands of self-supporting, self-directing, and self-propagating Churches.

It is the obligation of the Church to evangelize the world in this generation. It is our duty because all men need Christ. The Scriptures clearly teach that if men are to be saved they must be saved through Christ. The burning question then is: Shall hundreds of millions of men now living, who need Christ, and who are capable of receiving help from Him, pass away without having even the opportunity to know Him? To have a knowledge of Christ is to incur a responsibility to every man who has not. We are trustees of the gospel, and in no sense sole proprietors. What a crime against mankind to keep a knowledge of the mission of Christ from two-thirds of the human race! It is our duty to evangelize the world in this generation, because of the missionary command of Christ. It seems impossible to explain the final commission of Christ as given in Matthew, Mark, Luke, and the Acts, as not implying that each generation of Christians should at least preach Christ to its own known and accessible world. This was obviously the interpretation placed upon the final commission by the Christians of the first generation.

Every reason for doing the work of evangelization at all, demands that it be done not only thoroughly, but also as speedily as possible. We are responsible for the present generation—for those who are living at the same time with ourselves. The Christians of the past generations could not reach them, neither can the Christians of succeeding generations. Obviously each generation of Christians must evangelize its own generation of non-Christians if they are ever to be evangelized. The present generation is one of unexampled crisis in all parts of the unevangelized world. Failure now will make the future task very much more difficult. It is also one of marvelous opportunity. The world is better known and more accessible, its needs more articulate and intelligible, and our ability to go into all the world with the gospel is greater than in any preceding generation. The forces of evil are not deferring their operations to the next generation, but with world-wide enterprise and ceaseless vigor they are seeking to accomplish their deadly work.

We do not ignore the difficulties in the way of making Christ known to the present generation—difficulties physical, political, social, intellectual, moral, and religious. It is well, however, to be on our guard against the tendency to magnify difficulties unduly, and to minimize the providential opportunities, the promises of God, and the resources of the witnesses and ambassadors of Jesus Christ.

It is possible to evangelize the world in this generation. It will help us to realize this possibility if we look at a number of considerations.

It is possible in view of the achievements of the Christians of the first generation. They did more to accomplish the evangelization of the world than has any succeeding generation. Their achievements are remarkable when viewed numerically, or when we consider how all classes of society were reached. The persecutions of the first and second centuries, the fierce literary attacks against Christianity, and the strong apologies in its defense, attest how vigorously the faith of Christ must have been propagated by the first disciples. These achievements seem very remarkable when we remember that at the time of the ascension of Christ the whole number of believers did not exceed a few hundreds. They seem all the more wonderful in the light of the fact that the early Christians had to meet practically every difficulty which confronts the Church today. As we recall the smallness of their number and the difficulties which beset their path, and on the other hand, remind ourselves not only of our obstacles, but also of the marvelous opportunities and resources of the Church today, shall we not agree with Dr. Storrs that the balance of advantage is with us of this generation? In studying the secret of what they accomplished one is led to the conclusion that they employed no vitally important method which can not be used today, and that they availed themselves of no power which we also can not utilize.

It is possible to evangelize the world in this generation in view of recent missionary achievements of the Church. Note the work of the Presbyterians in Korea; of the Russians, as well as of some of the Protestant Churches in Japan; of the Church Missionary Society, the Methodist Episcopal Church, and the American Board in the Fukien Province; of the London Missionary Society in Central China; of the China Inland Mission in the interior provinces of China; of the United Presbyterians of Scotland, and the Irish Presbyterians in Manchuria; of the American Board in the Sandwich Islands, the Wesleyans in the Fiji Islands, and of Dr. Paton in the New Hebrides; of the American Baptists among the Karens, and also among the Telugus; of the Gossner Mission among the Kols during its first twenty years; of the Church Missionary Society and the Society for the Propagation of the Gospel in Southern India; of the Methodist Episcopal Church in Northern India; of the Reformed Church in India, and also in Arabia; of the German Lutherans on the Island of Sumatra; of the London Mission and the Norwegian Lutherans in Madagascar; of the Church Missionary Society in Uganda, the Baptists on the Congo, the Southern Presbyterians at Luebo, and the United Presbyterians in the Nile Valley. Recall the medical work of Dr. Clark at Amritsar, Dr. Kerr at Canton, Dr. Post at Beirut, the Ranaghat Medical Mission in Bengal, the Tientsin Hospital, and of many other medical missionaries in all parts of the wide world-field. Think also of Duff College;

the Woman's College at Lucknow; the colleges of the Church Missionary Society and the American Board in Southern India; the Jaffna
College and the Oodooville Girls' School in Ceylon; the True Light
Seminary in Canton; the Anglo-Chinese College at Foochow; Dr.
Mateer's college at Tungchow; the Training Institute at Tungchow;
the early history of the Doshisha; the Women's College at Nagasaki;
the Euphrates College; the Syrian Protestant College; the College
at Asyut, Egypt; and many others.

Nor should we overlook the vital relation which literary work has
had and always will have to the evangelization of the world. The
patient and thorough work of the hundreds of missionaries who have
devoted themselves to the translation of the Scriptures and Christian
literature, the ceaseless activity of the scores of mission presses like
those at Beirut, Shanghai, and Calcutta, and the wonderful achievements of the Bible societies in all lands, which have multiplied the
power and influence of all other workers and agencies, and sown the
seed of the Kingdom far and wide. The most striking example of
achievement on the home field in the interest of foreign missions is
that of the Moravians. They have done more in proportion to their
ability than any other body of Christians. If the members of Protestant Churches in Great Britain and America gave in like proportion,
their missionary contributions would aggregate over $60,000,000, or
a fourfold increase. And if they went out as missionaries in corresponding numbers, we should have a force of nearly 400,000 foreign
workers, which is vastly more than the number of missionaries estimated as necessary to achieve the evangelization of the world in a generation. The practical question is, What has there been in connection
with the work already accomplished which is not reproducible? In
view of the extent to which the gospel has already been thoroughly
preached, whether with or without apparent results, by a comparatively small number of workers, it does seem reasonable to expect that by
a judicious increase and proper distribution of all missionary agencies
which have commended themselves to the Church, an adequate opportunity to know Christ as Saviour and Lord might be given to all people within our day.

It is possible to evangelize the world in this generation in view of
the opportunities and resources of the Church and the facilities at her
disposal. We must not measure the present ability of the Church by
the standards and practice of a Church in the past, only half awake to
her duty to the non-Christian world, and under far less favorable conditions for world-wide missionary operations. It hardly seems right
to call a thing impossible or impracticable which has not been at-
tempted. Livingstone said, "You don't know what you can do until

you try." The world-wide proclamation of the gospel awaits accomplishment by a generation which shall have the obedience and determination to attempt the task. For the first time in the history of the Church, practically the whole world is open. We are not justified in saying that there is a single country on the face of the earth where the Church, if she seriously desires, can not send ambassadors of Christ to proclaim His message.

The Church not only has an unexampled opportunity, but also possesses remarkable resources. Think of her membership! There are not less than 135,000,000 members of Protestant churches. In the British Isles, the United States, and Canada alone, there are over 25,000,000 communicants in evangelical Protestant churches. Contrast these with the few thousands constituting the small, unacknowledged, and despised sect which, on the day of Pentecost, began the evangelization of the then known and accessible world. As we recall the achievements of that infant Church, can we question the ability of the Christians of our day, were they unitedly to resolve to accomplish it, so to distribute within the present generation the gospel messengers and agencies that all mankind might have an opportunity to know Christ, the Saviour and Lord?

We have workers enough to send. It would take less than one-fiftieth of the Christian young men and women who will go out from Christian colleges in the United States and Canada within this generation to furnish a sufficient force of foreign workers to achieve the evangelization of the world in this generation. When we add the Christian students of Britain, the Continent, and Australasia, it will be seen that the Christian countries can well afford to spare the workers. Their going forth will quicken and strengthen, rather than weaken the entire Church.

The money power of the Church is enormous. If only one-fourth of the Protestants of Europe and America should give but one cent a day toward the evangelization of the world, it would yield a fund of over $100,000,000, as contrasted with the $19,000,000 given during the past year. Dr. Josiah Strong said twenty years ago: "There is money enough in the hands of church members to sow every acre of the earth with the seed of truth. . . . God has intrusted to His children power enough to give the gospel to every creature by the close of this century; but it is being misapplied. Indeed, the world would have been evangelized long ago if Christians had perceived the relation of money to the kingdom, and accepted their stewardship."

With over 500 missionary societies and auxiliaries there are, without doubt, missionary organizations and societies in sufficient number, and possessing sufficient strength and experience to guide an enterprise indefinitely larger than the present missionary operations of the Church.

The Bible societies, not fewer than eighty in number, have translated the Scriptures entirely or in part into 421 languages and dialects. If this work is properly promoted, before this generation closes, each African, each Pacific islander, and each inhabitant of Asia will be able to read or hear in his own tongue the wonderful works of God.

The organized Christian Student Movements constitute a factor characteristic of this generation. There are fourteen of these national or international Student Movements, comprising nearly 1,500 Christian Associations, with a membership of about 60,000 students and professors. They are seeking to make the universities and colleges strongholds and propagating centers for aggressive Christianity. Out of them has come the Student Volunteer Movement for Foreign Missions, which has in itself become a great factor in the world's evangelization. It has enrolled thousands of students as volunteers for foreign service. At least 2,000 of them have already reached the fields. The Church, in possessing this important recruiting and training agency, is equipped as in no preceding age for a world-embracing evangelistic campaign.

The various Christian young people's organizations which have been developed within the past two decades have added tremendously to the power of the Church. In North America alone these movements include fully 6,000,000 young people. These young people themselves, if properly educated and guided, are able to give and to raise each year a sum large enough to support all the foreign missionaries who would be required to accomplish the evangelization of the world.

The Sunday Schools constitute a large, undeveloped missionary resource. They contain over 20,000,000 scholars. If these were trained to give two cents each week it would yield an amount greater than the present total missionary gifts of Christendom.

The native Church is the human resource which affords largest promise for the evangelization of the world. It has 1,300,000 communicants and over 4,000,000 adherents. The character and activity of these Christians compares very favorably with that of church members in Christian lands. There are nearly 80,000 native workers, and their number and efficiency are rapidly increasing. There are 1,000,000 children and young people in the various mission schools and institutions. From the ranks of these students and their successors, during the next few years, are to come the hundreds of thousands of evangelists, Bible women, and other workers who will be needed to preach Christ to the unevangelized world. This emphasizes the importance of the Student Young Men's Christian Association movement in mission lands. In uniting the native Christian students, first, to lead their fellow students to Christ, and then, after their preparation is completed, to go forth to evangelize their own countrymen, it is doing much to solve the problem of the world's speedy and thorough evangelization.

In considering the Church's present power of achievement, we should take account not only of her resources, but also of the facilities at her disposal. Among these should be mentioned the work of the eighty-three geographical societies, which, through the investigations which they have encouraged, have done so much to make the whole world known.

Another help to the Church today is the intimate knowledge which she now possesses of the social, moral, and spiritual condition and need of all races of mankind.

The greatly enlarged and improved means of communication constitutes one of the chief facilities of which the Church of this generation can avail herself. Of the 400,000 miles of railway lines in the world, a considerable and growing mileage is already to be found in non-Christian lands. It is possible, for example, to go by rail to all parts of India and Japan. The greatest railway enterprises of the time are those now building or projected in non-Christian lands. When even a part of these materialize, as they will within a few years, more than one-third of the unevangelized world will be made much more accessible to missionaries. It took Judson eleven months to go from Salem to Calcutta. The trip can now be made in a month. Moffat was three months on the way from England to the Cape. Now the voyage lasts but two weeks. These developments mean an immense saving in time to the missionary force. The 170,000 miles of submarine cables which have cost at least $250,000,000, are also of great service to the missionary societies. They help the Church not only by promoting general intelligence, but also in facilitating the financial transactions and administrative work of missions. The thoroughly organized news agencies which, through the secular press, bring before the members of the Church facts regarding the most distant and needy nations, serve indirectly to awaken and foster interest in the inhabitants of less favored lands. The Universal Postal Union with its wonderful organization and its vast army of well-nigh 1,000,000 employees, immensely facilitates the work of foreign missions. Within a few years, doubtless, it will include within its sphere of action practically all those unevangelized parts of the world which have not already been brought within its reach. As a result of all these means of communication the world has become very small. They have, as it were, united the separate continents into one great nation. They have made the most remote parts of the inhabited world easily accessible. Ramsay points out that

"There are no stronger influences in education and administration than rapidity and ease of traveling, and the postal service. Paul, both by precept and example, impressed the importance of both on his churches."

The printing press has greatly multiplied the power of the Church to disseminate Christian truth. At the beginning of this century printing was done on hand presses, and only from one to two hundred impressions could be taken in an hour. Now there are presses which print, bind, and fold 100,000 papers in an hour. The linotype and many other improvements in printing have, to a remarkable degree, reduced the price of books. In past generations Bibles were expensive. Carey's first Bible sold at $20. A Bengali Bible can now be purchased for a few cents. So there is no mechanical difficulty in the way of giving the Bible to every family under heaven. The influence and protection of Christian governments is a decided help to missions. In no age could ambassadors of Christ carry on their work with such safety. Over one-third of the population of the unevangelized world are under the direct sway of Christian rulers. Moreover, the Protestant powers are in a position to exert an influence which will make possible the free preaching of the gospel to the remaining two-thirds of the people, who have not heard of Christ.

Why has God made the whole world known and accessible to our generation? Why has He provided us with such wonderful agencies? Not that the forces of evil might utilize them. Not that they be wasted or unused. Such vast preparations must have been made to further some mighty and beneficent purpose. Every one of these wonderful facilities has been intended primarily to serve as a handmaid to the sublime enterprise of extending and building up the kingdom of Jesus Christ in all the world. The hand of God, in opening door after door among the nations, and in bringing to light invention after invention, is beckoning the Church of our day to larger achievements.

The undertakings and achievements in the realm of secular and non-Christian enterprise should stimulate us to believe that it is possible for the Church to evangelize the world in its generation. Gold was discovered in the Klondike, and within a little over a year it is said that more than 100,000 men started over the difficult passes, at great risk and cost of life, to possess themselves of the riches of that region. Stanley wanted some twenty or thirty English helpers to accompany him on his last great African journey of exploration. He advertised the fact, and within a few days over 1,200 men responded, eager to face the deadly climate and other great perils involved in the expedition. It is reported that in the last presidential campaign one of the two great political parties, within a few weeks, placed two documents on the money question in the hands of practically every voter in the whole land. At the present time this country has about 50,000 soldiers in the Philippine Islands. This is not considered an extravagant number for the country to send to the ends of the earth to accomplish her purpose. It is noticeable that when the regiments return to the homeland they receive one continuous ovation from the time they enter the Golden Gate until they reach their homes.

There are now probably 200,000 soldiers in the British forces at the Cape. We have seen Canada send off contingent after contingent with cheers and with prayers. Similar scenes have taken place in the colonies of Australia and New Zealand. We have all been impressed by this exhibition of the unity, loyalty, and power of the British Empire. We have also been deeply moved by the example of the African republics, as we have seen not only the young men, but also the old men and boys going out to fight the battles of their country. It is looked upon as a matter of course that both of the contending parties should pour out without stint, the lives and substance of their people. And yet, when it is suggested that all Protestant Christendom unite in sending out 50,000 missionaries, more or less, it is impracticable and visionary. It would be too severe a strain on the resources of the Church. The naval budgets of at least three countries are from three to five times as great as the sum required to sustain the present missionary forces of the Church. The Mormon Church numbers only 250,000, but it has 1,700 missionaries at work in different parts of this and other lands. If they need more, it is said that their system would enable them to send out between 7,000 and 8,000. The little island of Ceylon has sent out multitudes of Buddhist missionaries to all parts of Asia. In the University of El Azhar, in Cairo, we found over 8,000 Mohammedan students coming from countries as widely separated as Morocco, the western provinces of China, and the East India islands. They were being prepared to go out as missionaries of the false Prophet. No human, secular, or non-Christian undertaking should surpass in enterprise, devotion, and aggressiveness the Church of Jesus Christ. Because of the magnitude of the task to which God has called us, because of the impending crisis and the urgency of the situation in all parts of the non-Christian world, because of the dangers of anything else than a great onward movement, because of the constraining memories of the cross of Christ, and the love wherewith He loved us, has not the generation come for the Church to put forth her strength and evangelize the whole world?

Notwithstanding the considerations upon which we have been dwelling, there are here and there to be found those who speak of the idea of the evangelization of the world in this generation as fantastic and visionary. And yet was it not Gordon Hall and Samuel Newell, who, in 1818, issued an appeal to Christians to evangelize the world

ADDRESSES AND PAPERS OF THE CHAIRMAN

within a generation? Did not the missionaries of the Sandwich Islands, in 1836, unite in a most impressive appeal to the Church to preach the Gospel to every creature within their generation? Did not the Shanghai Missionary Conference of 1877 express its desire to have China emancipated from the thraldom of sin in this generation, and its belief that it might be done? An increasing number of the most eminent and experienced missionaries of the world have expressed their strong belief in the possibility of the realization of this watchword. Secretaries of several of the leading mission boards of America and England have indorsed the idea without reservation. Editors, including that thorough missionary student, Dr. Robson of Scotland, have spoken of its reasonableness. The bishops of the Anglican Communion, at the last Lambeth Conference, expressed their gratification at the student missionary uprising which had taken as its watchword the evangelization of the world in this generation. Early in January of this year, at the great student convention in London, Alexander MacKennal, president of the Free Church Council, said, regarding the evangelization of the world in the generation, when the idea was put before him, "I felt first the audacity of the proposal, then the reasonableness of the proposal, and lastly that the confidence of young men and women would carry it into effect, I was sure. It seemed to me that the very finger of God was pointing the way, and the Spirit of God inspiring the endeavor." At the same convention the Archbishop of Canterbury said that "It is not an inconceivable thing that, as God has within the last generation opened the way, so within the present generation He may crown His works." It seems as if we who are now living, the young men among us who are now joining this very union, those who are now studying the great task to which the Lord has called them, shall, before they die, be able to say: "The whole race of mankind is not yet Christian, but, nevertheless, there is no nation upon earth where the Christian faith is not taught if men will accept it; there is no place upon the whole surface of the globe where man may not hear the message of God and the story of the cross." It is significant that during this great Ecumenical Conference it has not been the young men chiefly, but the veterans of the cross who have exhorted us to larger achievement. Was it not Bishop Thoburn who said that if this conference and those whom it represents will do their duty, within the first decade of the new century ten millions of souls might be gathered into the Church of Christ? Was it not Dr. Ashmore who expressed the belief that before the twentieth century closes Christianity would be the dominant religion among the multitudinous inhabitants of the Chinese Empire? And was it not Dr. Chamberlain who affirmed the possibility of bringing India under the sway of Christ within the lifetime of some, at least, in this assembly? If these great leaders are thus sanguine of victory, should those of us who are at home hesitate?

Let us not forget that the evangelization of the world is God's enterprise. Jesus Christ is its leader. He who is the same yesterday, today, yea, and forever, abides in those who go forth to preach Him. The Holy Spirit is able to shake whole communities. The Word of God is quick and powerful. Prayer can remove mountains. Faith is the victory that overcomes the world.

THE WATCHWORD AS A SPIRITUAL FORCE

ADDRESS GIVEN AT
THE STUDENT VOLUNTEER MISSIONARY UNION CONFERENCE
IN EDINBURGH, JANUARY, 1904

The watchword, "The Evangelization of the World in This Generation," is commonly understood to mean that in our day or generation an adequate opportunity should be given to all men to know and to accept Jesus Christ as their personal Saviour and Lord. This is the watchword of the Student Volunteer Missionary Union of Great Britain and Ireland, and likewise of four other movements in the World's Student Christian Federation. Three other movements stand practically on the threshold of adopting the same watchword. The remaining three movements in the Federation have been giving the matter their earnest consideration and are discussing what is involved in adopting it. Such a watchword is meaningless, however, unless it be made the watchword of individual members of the movement. This watchword has been much criticized. It has also been misunderstood, like every other good and great idea. People entertain conscientious objections to it; and yet it is gratifying to notice that as they are giving it more thorough study, and as they are coming to understand our use of terms, and what is involved in its acceptance, they are, in increasing numbers, accepting it as their personal watchword.

It is not the purpose of this hour to define the watchword, or to expound it, but to call attention to what a force it may be, and, as a matter of fact, is, in the life of the individual Christian who gives it right of way in his life, who makes it a dominating, controlling purpose in his life, and who takes it as the principle to govern his plans, purposes, and activities, and to guide him in the use of his powers and opportunities. If I shall say anything this morning that does not apply to our experiences while we have had this watchword, let us ask ourselves whether it may not be true that this is because we have so far failed to give it the right of way in our lives. In speaking of what a force this watchword may be in the life of the individual Christian, I shall limit myself strictly to its significance as a spiritual force.

The watchword, "The Evangelization of the World in This Generation," widens and enriches one's sympathies. It carries one's sympathies to the very ends of the earth, and embraces all mankind. It makes impossible national, racial, social, and religious barriers. It eliminates these more and more as the days come and go. It emancipates one from the selfish and the narrow, and how much of selfishness and narrowness creep into the lives of Christians! This watchword knows no home field, and it knows no foreign field. It sends the missionary out not to be a narrow missionary, and some of the narrowest people I have met in my travels are missionaries—men who could see only Japan, or a part of China, or a part of Africa. This watchword makes this impossible. It sends the student volunteer out to the front with the whole world in his view, in his prayers, and in his sympathies. The idea that the field is the world, that Christ is Lord of all, that His kingdom is to be co-extensive with the earth, are daily thoughts of those with such a watchword. Fox, the Friend, prayed that God might baptize him into a sense of all conditions, that so he might enter into the needs and sufferings of all. This is the spirit that pervades the watchword—that we may be baptized into a sense of the oneness of our common humanity, that we may enter more sympathetically into its sufferings and needs. Zinzendorf apparently was animated by the spirit of the same watchword, for when he was but a youth he formed a society known as the Order of the Mustard Seed, and wrote as the first article of its constitution that "The members of our society will love the whole human family."

This watchword stimulates and strengthens one's faith. Faith cannot grow strong without exercise. Difficulties are the great exercise-ground of faith. Where will one meet so many difficulties as in the pathway of the realization of a watchword such as this: to spread the knowledge of Jesus Christ throughout the inhabited earth in one's lifetime! This gives us a tremendous task. It is calculated to develop moral and spiritual muscle, to bring forth the best fiber of life. There is little danger that Christians of this generation will attempt things too large for God. The peril, on the contrary, is that we suffer atrophy because we attempt too little for Him. Any watchword, therefore, that summons men to the impossible, that reminds them necessarily of the Omnipotent, that calls out the best energies of mind and heart, that makes impossible slothfulness, idleness, and slackness, must be a spiritual benefit in a generation that needs such a corrective.

The watchword throws us back on our superhuman resources. The colossal magnitude of our task may well stagger us. The many difficulties in the way of its accomplishment may well baffle us. The first thought that comes to us is that these difficulties are so great, and the need of the world so real and awful, we are utterly helpless. Our next impulse is that we must give ourselves to prayer; for with men it is unmistakably impossible to evangelize the world in this generation, but with God all things are possible. One principal cause of the lack of spiritual life and power of Christians is the lack of prayer. As a rule, you cannot get a man to devote himself to prayer by telling him to do so. He must first realize the need for prayer. This watchword keeps vividly before him the extent of the need and the urgency of the task of meeting it. It was the knowledge of the terrible destitution of the Indian tribes that impelled David Brainerd to pour out his heart in the woods of New England and New Jersey. It was when Hudson Taylor began to prepare for publication a statement of the needs of China that he felt the horror of the situation, and prayed for twenty-four workers until he secured them. Not by an army, or by power—social, racial, political, financial—but by My Spirit the task will be performed. Therefore, anything which impels us to pray is a spiritual benefit.

The watchword does much to develop a life of reality. If one has such an idea as this before him—the evangelization of a whole world in a generation—how inconsistent it is if that man does not have a very genuine experience of the work of Jesus Christ in his own heart and life, if that man does not know Christ as his personal Saviour, if he is not being led in triumph day by day over his sins and temptations! I repeat, how presumptuous, how inconsistent, for him to be advocating an idea like this of taking a knowledge of our Saviour to a whole world! It brings a man in on himself, and leads him to realize and experience afresh and more constantly the real meaning of Jesus Christ to him. And involved in this, such a watchword is a test with which one may constantly judge his aims and motives. Day by day he may check himself; he may put himself alongside his great ideal. It will do much to correct his habits, his attitudes, his relationships, as I could mention from my own observation of students regarding the use of their time and money, and the determining of their studies and other work. We recognize quite generally the Saviourship of Jesus Christ, but are we not prone to put into the background in practice too much the Lordship of Jesus Christ? The watchword, which would enthrone him as Lord of all, reminds us in a very personal way, day by day, that if He is Lord of all, He has the mastership of our lives, and of all that is involved in them. The watchword constantly reminds the Christian that he must be a missionary here and now; that he is called to be a missionary from the moment that he heard God's voice —and no amount of missionary purpose and plans can take the place of present missionary activity. It means that every one, whether he is a volunteer or not—and here let me say that the watchword applies just as much to those who are not volunteers as to those who are volunteers, and I am glad to see that very many who are not volunteers are realizing that the message is for them—it means that the volunteer and the non-volunteer in the colleges will seek to lead their unbelieving fellow students to Jesus Christ; and that beyond the confines of the college, within the range of their influence, in their own families, amongst their friends and associates, amongst strangers whom God places in their path, they will likewise seek to spread the knowledge of the same Saviour. It was this spirit that was so constantly beating in the life of William Burns here in Scotland. While he longed to reach the foreign field, he waited not, but kept putting in the sickle here, and gleaned his thousands of converts before he was permitted to gather any in the Chinese Empire. So it is with some of the best volunteers that I have met on the foreign mission field. They were those who had had practice in soul winning on the home field. Our faith requires constant propagation to attest its genuineness, and one might add to preserve its genuineness, if we may trust Church history. Let students while they are preparing themselves for the mission field, give proof of their faith. It is a strong evidence to thoughtful, unbelieving men that there is reality in our faith. If we have professed the truth—and there are not a few here who would die for it—if we have professed the truth, let us be consistent, let us be logical, let us be genuine in dedicating ourselves and all that we have to the unwearied, undiscourageable propagation of the gospel, within the range of our influence, near and far. It is this note of genuineness, sounding forth from the watchword, that is its requirement of reality, which commends it increasingly to men as a practical factor and force.

The watchword lends intensity to the Christian life. We had better be tremendously in earnest, or take some other watchword. It means business. Therefore it makes impossible apathy, vacillation, drifting, indecision, and slothfulness, some of which are great perils in modern student life. We need some such powerful incentive to hold us to our great life purpose. This is true both of those who are volunteers, and of those who are not. I despair of certain volunteers ever reaching the foreign field, unless this watchword becomes a more real thing with them, unless they are holding on by every means, to the great objective to which Christ called them. I likewise despair of some good students I know who are planning to spend their lives at home ever leaving a very deep mark on their generation, unless they keep it vividly in their minds. Livingstone must have had some such watchword. His words, "I will go anywhere, provided it be forward," prove this. Again he said, when he was being urged by certain ones to defer the work that he was opening up, "I will go, no matter who opposes." It is the spirit of immediacy that rings out in the watchword, of reaching in one's day as many of the people of that day as possible, which adds intensity to it. Neesima, that splendid product of Christianity in Japan, must have had this watchword animating him. He said, "It is our humble purpose to save Japan." Not only did he say that, but to such as tried to dissuade him from this purpose, he answered, "I have a plough in my hands; I must work for my Lord." Again I revert to William Burns. If any man had the watchword of the S.V.M.U. he had it. "The longing of my heart would be," he said, "to go once all round the world before I die, and preach one gospel invitation in the ear of every creature." It must have been this spirit that impelled him, when he went out to China, to learn dialect after dialect, beginning in the extreme south, and reaching right up to Manchuria. He would labor in a place until he had learnt the dialect so that he might give the gospel to the people; he would work there until he saw the beginning of the dawning of the morning; and then he would leave to others the joy of the full sunrise, while he plunged again into some dark province, there to repeat his labors. Yes, the thought of *this generation* lends intensity. There is added a sense of urgency and immediacy, that one cannot escape from. This verse ringing in our consciousness: "I must work the works of Him that sent Me, while it is day, for the night cometh when no man can work," seems to gather up into itself the spirit of the same watchword.

> The work that centuries might have done
> Must crowd the hour of setting sun.

Scotland has given us another character that I always think must have been animated by the true spirit of this watchword. Remember the words of Bonar:

> Time worketh, let me work too.
> Time undoeth, let me do.
> Busy as Time my work I ply,
> Till I rest in the rest of eternity.
>
> Sin worketh, let me work too.
> Sin undoeth, let me do.
> Busy as Sin my work I ply,
> Till I rest in the rest of eternity.
>
> Death worketh, let me work too.
> Death undoeth, let me do.
> Busy as Death my work I ply,
> Till I rest in the rest of eternity.

The watchword helps to develop a life of self-sacrifice. Living under its spell the student is constantly asking himself, "How can I make the best use of my time, of my money, of my nervous energy, of my opportunities, of my influence, that none go to waste, that I may render a faithful account? My time being so short, how can I fill it to the best advantage?" Thus it leads one, in very practical ways, to the life of self-sacrifice. If a student is going to live the life of a Christian, he should begin during his student days. If he will not sacrifice in little things, he is not likely to do so in great things. And what are sacrifices today may cease to be so tomorrow. If we are to have a habit of self-sacrifice it will be developed in the pathway of repeated acts of self-sacrifice. It is the spirit of this watchword to cultivate more disregard for the things of this world, for the things which the world holds desirable and necessary, and to count all things but loss that we may know Christ and make Him known. When Von Welz found it impossible to move his church to give the gospel to the heathen, he gave up his title and his estates, and went out at his own charges to Dutch Guinea. Christian Frederick Schwartz lived on £50 a year in a single little room, spending and being spent. It is this spirit that literally overcomes the world. "Except a corn of wheat fall into the ground and die, it abideth by itself alone, but if it die, it bringeth forth much fruit." Such a watchword is needed that we may have more fully realized the expansive sacrifice that would sprinkle many nations with the best lives.

The watchword inspires men to lives of Christian heroism. The early Christians, I verily believe, had such a watchword as this. I find it impossible to explain their activity, and all they accomplished on any other hypothesis than this, that they set themselves before their death to make the knowledge of Christ readily accessible to all within the range of their influence. What did this involve? It meant in that day that they had to face the flame, the saber, the dungeon, and the arena. This watchword, let us have it clearly understood, does not call us to any easy or insignificant task. It appeals to the heroic in the men and women of our generation. I suppose that is one of the reasons why it has taken such a hold upon the strongest men. If we are to get a hold on the young men and women of heroic spirit, let us offer them some heroic, some masterful thing to do. It has been said that Christ never hid His scars to win a disciple. If the Student Volunteer Movement will act in the same way and not present the easy side of missions, but the difficult side—the loneliness, the isolation, the opposition, the temptations, the persecutions, the possibility perchance of martyrdom—we may not get so many volunteers, but the volunteers whom we do get will shake the world. The Moravians had this spirit of courage.

Did they not wish to go to the deadly climates, to the dangerous fields, to the unpopular places? There was no tribe so stolid or so apathetic, or so debased or so insignificant, that they did not look upon it as a chosen field. If that spirit pervaded the rest of Protestant Christendom, there would soon be not one unevangelized man or woman on this earth. Eugene Stock has said that Raymond Lull was one of the most heroic characters in the history of the Christian Church. A student at Montpelier and later a teacher, he said to his Lord one day: "I find scarcely anyone who out of love to Thee, is ready to suffer martyrdom as Thou hast suffered for us." And yet, that same Raymond Lull with his splendid equipment, with magnificent opportunities on the home field, went out to work among the Mohammedans with whom apostasy meant death, that people which for centuries has so bitterly resisted Christendom. Imprisoned in a dungeon a year and a half, twice banished from the shores of Africa, at last stoned to death outside the city wall by his persecutors, he exemplified the truth of his own word that "he that loves not lives not, and he that lives by the Life can never die."

I suppose the highest type of heroism that is going to be called for from most of us is not physical, but moral heroism. It takes moral heroism to have a watchword like this in some of our colleges today, to live an unworldly life in the midst of the crosscurrents of worldliness which prevail to such an extent in the centers of learning. It is going to take moral heroism, also, to go out to any mission field with which I am familiar. Your courage is going to be tested at a hundred points. It is not easy to keep up the standards of truth and holiness. Moreover, I would not disguise the fact that we are going to require a great deal of physical courage before this generation shall pass. There will probably not be another Indian mutiny, but Hinduism will not let loose its awful clutch without great convulsions, even to the costing of life. There may not be a repetition of the Macedonian massacres —though because of the inexplicable attitude of Christian powers, no one can say there will not—yet, believe me, before Mohammedanism yields to Jesus Christ, many a life will have to be surrendered, possibly the lives of some gathered here this morning. God grant that we may not have another Boxer catastrophe in our days, and yet any student of Chinese affairs knows full well that many a life will have to be laid down before Jesus Christ reigns in China. Each time I have been in China, I have gone to visit the grave of Stewart, who, if I mistake not, went out from one of the British universities, and laid down his life in martyrdom in China in 1895. And, by the way, in one of the Australian colleges, I found among the volunteers a son of Stewart, whose great aim it is to go back to the very mission field where his father died. My friend Pitkin of Yale, and later a secretary of the American Volunteer Movement, after defending the honor and the lives of two American women volunteers in North China in 1900, was beheaded by the Boxers. Knowing his impending fate, he said to a trusted Chinese servant, "Tell the mother of little Horace (his wife and son were in America) to tell Horace that his father's last wish was that he might, when twenty-five years of age, go out to China as a missionary." The spirit of martyrdom is in this movement, and it is the richest possession we have.

> They climbed the steep ascent of heaven
> Through peril, toil, and pain.
> O God, to us may grace be given
> To follow in their train.

The watchword gives men vision. How few comparatively there are among Christians who have a vision. That is, how few there are who are free, who are mounting up on wings as eagles. After all, is it not true that our visions are the strength of our lives, and that where there are no visions the people literally perish? Jesus Christ was the supreme visionary. Remember His word, "I, if I be lifted up, will draw all men unto Me." He looked down through the centuries, and gathered to Himself all mankind. Let us too be visionaries. May the vision of the need of the world, with its sin and shame and suffering, haunt us, and continue to move us. May we never become callous to it. Even more vivd and appealing may the vision of the cross of Christ ever be. Let us catch and become absorbed with the vision of a whole wide world evangelized, with the messengers of Christ so widely and wisely distributed, that before our eyes shall close in death, the knowledge of Christ shall be readily accessible to all people. Let us be under the spell of that sight beautiful on every mountain of those who proclaim good tidings and publish peace. Let us look also down through the centuries, far beyond this generation, till we see that "great multitude whom no man could number, of all nations and kindreds and people and tongues," standing "before the Throne and before the Lamb clothed with white robes, and palms in their hands," crying "with a loud voice, saying, Salvation to our God, which sitteth upon the throne, and unto the Lamb."

> But, lo! there breaks a yet more glorious day;
> The saints triumphant rise in bright array;
> The King of Glory passes on His way,
> Alleluia!

> From earth's wide bounds, from ocean's farthest coast,
> Through gates of pearl streams in the countless host,
> Singing to Father, Son, and Holy Ghost,
> Alleluia!

THE URGENCY AND CRISIS IN THE FAR EAST

ADDRESS GIVEN AT
THE STUDENT VOLUNTEER CONFERENCE
LIVERPOOL, ENGLAND, JANUARY 2-7, 1908

The present urgency and crisis in the Extreme Orient is unmatched by any other crisis and opportunity which has confronted the Christian Church. It involves the destiny of more than 500,000,000 people of Japan, Korea, China, Manchuria, and Mongolia. Among these multitudes massed around the Pacific Basin, the forces of youth and age, of radicalism and conservatism, of growth and decay, are seething and struggling for mastery. What religion shall dominate these changing people? Or shall there be no religion? Talk about crises is certainly overdone, but will anyone who is familiar with the facts question that the present is the time of times for the Far East?

Why is the present a time of urgent and supreme crisis in the Extreme Orient? Because of the recent remarkable triumphs of Christianity in the Far East, and the great importance of pressing the advantage which these triumphs afford. Think of Korea, and at once you think of a nation which is now being swept by a spiritual revival of national dimensions. The awakening in that country may well be likened to the Welsh Revival in point of pervasiveness, power, and transforming influence. There is one body of Christians in Korea which, during the year preceding the time I had the pleasure of visiting the country a few months ago, had nearly 10,000 accessions. Another Christian body had nearly as many. There comes vividly to my memory a scene which indicated the eagerness of the Korean peoples to hear the presentation of the gospel truth. It had been announced, when I visited Seoul recently, that in Independence Hall, located outside the city wall, commemorating a certain event in connection with the relations between Korea and China, there would be held a mass meeting of men of the gentry and other important classes. These were to be admitted by tickets. The tickets had been distributed with care through the city. The meeting was to convene at two o'clock. At nine o'clock in the morning of that weekday the men began to stream out beyond the city wall to this, the largest hall that could be obtained. By twelve o'clock every place in that hall, which would accommodate 2,500, was taken. When some of us, about two o'clock, drew near the place where the meeting was to be held, we noticed the landscape lined with Korean men. We wondered at it, because it was one of the bitter cold days of January. You know they do not reckon cold over there by so many degrees, but by so many coats. Well, this was a day when they were wearing five coats, and we could not understand why there were so many standing outside in the piercing cold. When we arrived we found the hall crowded with 2,500 men, and there were 3,500 more outside. We took possession of a Buddhist temple, which was soon crowded with as many as could enter; but the larger part of the great crowd had to stay outside in the open air, where they stood listening intently during the addresses of several speakers. The meeting in the hall lasted some three and a half hours. Never have I known greater eagerness in attending to the facts connected with the mission and the claims of Jesus Christ. Over 200 of those strong young men of Korea bowed their knees that day for the first time before Jesus Christ the Saviour.

This incident is indicative of the moving of the Spirit of God amongst the higher classes and the lower classes in north and central and southern Korea. The field is dead ripe! It is the last time for the Church to withhold her hand from thrusting in the sickle. One came away from Korea with the strong conviction that if the present attack of pure Christianity is adequately sustained, Korea will be the first non-Christian nation thoroughly evangelized in this modern foreign missionary epoch.

At the end of the first thirty-five years of missionary history in China there were six converts to Christianity. The Bishop of Mid-China told me, when I was in China for the first time about eleven years ago, that when he reached China there were only fifty Protestant Christian communicants, but that in that year (1896) there were 80,000. Now there are at least 180,000, and some maintain that the number is as high as 250,000. If we include the adherents to all Protestant bodies, the number would be swelled to nearly 1,000,000. Dr. Milne 100 years ago predicted that in 100 years there would be 1,000 communicants and adherents to Protestant Christianity in China. Think of 1,000,000, or 1,000 times as many as his prediction reached! Not only so, but there are great mass movements shaking parts of China today, and literally thousands of people are being held back from baptism because there are not a sufficient number of Christian teachers and preachers to follow them up properly, and therefore, to make it safe and wise to encourage their being baptized. This spiritual movement is touching not only the masses, but likewise the educated classes. Some of us had occasion last spring to notice the change coming over China in this respect. Six years ago it seemed to be impossible to get men of the *literati* and student class to attend evangelistic meetings or to go to hear apologetic addresses and lectures. But a few months ago we found that large halls and specially-constructed pavilions were invariably crowded to the doors by students and other influential classes of young men. This proved to be true in North China, in Mid-China, and South China. Some of the most remarkable ingatherings into the Kingdom of our Saviour have been in connection with the educated classes of China. Moreover, we have had evidence in recent years that not only numbers are being reached, but that the Holy Spirit is developing a type of Christian in China which commands the admiration of the Christians of the West. They have stood firm against every wind that blows, even against the fiercest blasts of cruel persecution. They are now developing a spirit of independence, initiative, and leadership which gives promise of wonderful advances in the years right before us. The prestige which Christianity has acquired in China in recent years as a result of the masterly work of medical missions, of educational missions, and of Christian reform movements is likewise not inconsiderable.

It seems incredible that within the lifetime of some people in this conference there were posted up in different parts of Japan official edicts, offering rewards of so many pieces of silver for revealing people found either professing or propagating the Christian faith; it is likewise almost incredible that there are now not less than 60,000 Protestant Christian communicants in Japan. What means much more than that is the fact that if you were to talk today to educated leaders of Japan about the religion of that country they would mention two religions, Buddhism and Christianity; but if they made any distinction between them it would be in favor of Christianity. The Japanese have developed a spirit of independent leadership which will compare favorably with that of the most aggressive and resourceful of the Christian nations of the West. Great spiritual movements have been in progress in that country within the past few years. Notable among them is what has been known as the Taikyo Dendo, a revival the like of which one has seldom, if ever, witnessed. This revival touched all strata of society, and swept throughout the Japanese islands. The most striking thing about it was that it was carried on so largely under Japanese leadership. There have been two events within the past few months that should in themselves startle us because of their significanve. One was the notable campaign waged amongst 750,000 Japanese soldiers. One of the oldest missionaries of Japan said to me that in his judgment the gospel was preached with fulness and power to more of the vigorous and aggressive classes of men of Japan over there on the Manchurian plains, during the Russian War, than during the same period by all the missionaries working in Japan. The other event was the World's Student Christian Federation Conference in April 1907, and the associated evangelistic campaign which have done so much to arrest the attention and awaken the spirit of inquiry among the educated and influential classes of the Japanese Empire. I am receiving constantly letters from the missionaries from different parts of Japan telling me that that united effort on the part of representatives of the universities of the Orient and Occident to present the claims of Christ has wonderfully opened the doors and hastened the solution of the problem of bringing Christ to bear upon the influential classes. God only knows the end of that great movement of His Spirit during those days. I do not think that that Chinese missionary exaggerated when he said that it was possibly the greatest single blow ever struck by united Christianity at the non-Christian world.

Let us bear in mind what the mighty work of God in Japan makes possible on the mainland of Asia. At the Student Volunteer Convention at Nashville in 1906, we received a cable message from the leaders of the Christian Student Movement of Japan, couched in this language: "Japan is leading the Orient, but whither?" It is a striking message. Certainly Japan is leading the Orient! She is doing it commercially, and it cannot be prevented. Only today one of your number was calling my attention to the statement in connection with the Peninsular and Oriental Steamship Company, that they have contemplated taking off the line of steamships sailing to Japan, giving as the main reason the fact that the Japanese have cut them out in that trade. They are doing the same with the American trade and with the German trade. They are leading the Orient politically. Japan has become the dominant political influence in Asia. She has been gifted with a wonderful international sense. She is leading the Orient educationally. At the present time there are not less than 1,000 Japanese teachers at work in all parts of China. While the Occident has been rubbing her eyes concerning this opportunity, Japan has seen it and seized it. Moreover, she has been welcoming within her doors the flower of Chinese youth. Our hearts have been touched by the appeal of Dr. Datta this evening concerning Indian students in Britain. But possibly we have not been aware of the fact there are also scores of Indian students in Tokyo. One day last spring when I was there, I was invited to attend a meeting of the Arya Somaj. There are nearly 700 Korean students there, also not a few students from the Philippines and Siam. There have been as many as 15,000 students there at one time from China. Without doubt Japan is leading the Orient educationally. She knows she is leading it, and she feels the burden of responsibility. I was reading the other day the translation of the titles of some articles in Japanese magazines. Note some of them: "Japan must take the leading place in developing Manchuria"; "Japan's safety lies in the regeneration of China"; "Japan's present position in China is the outcome of persevering effort during the past forty years"; "It is Japan's duty to free Korea from the misrule of the past and lead her toward modern enlightenment"; "Japan is the prophet of the Eastern World"; "Japan has a message for India." These are titles taken at random from some of the leading magazines appearing in Japan. They reveal the sense of responsibility that Japan feels toward the Eastern world.

When I returned from the Far East six years ago I could not say what I now can with great conviction, namely, that if some great catastrophe tomorrow made it necessary for all the missionaries to withdraw from Asia, Christianity is so securely planted in the lives of the Orientals that it would spread from them to all parts of the East; and were Christianity to die out in the Occident, in my judgment it has such propagating power in Asia that it would ultimately spread back to us. This is what we ought to expect if Christ is living in these Eastern peoples. It is inconceivable that He be pent up and not reach out until at last He encompass every man. Believe me, the spiritual tide is rising in the Far East, and it is always wise to take advantage of a rising tide.

It is a time of supreme crisis in the Far East, not only because of the triumphs of Christianity and the desirability of pressing the advantages which these triumphs afford, but also because of the stupendous changes now in progress in that Far Eastern world, especially on the mainland of Asia; and the great desirability of Christianity bringing its full influence to bear while the conditions are still plastic.

Japan is the most brilliant nation in the world. She has achieved greater progress in one generation than any other nation has achieved in two, if not in three, generations. She has gone to school to the whole world, and has learned her lessons with remarkable facility. Seldom does a man find himself upon an ocean steamship that he does not find among his fellow passengers one or more Japanese—not cruising about the world in search of pleasure, but journeying with serious intent to study some institution, some process, or some experience of some other nation or people, determined, in turn, to make this knowledge tributary to the national greatness of the nation they love with an almost insane patriotism. And they have not ceased to go to school. People thought that when they won their great victory over Russia they would lose their heads. I have formed the impression, in conversation with their leaders, that this victory has humbled and solemnized them. They have not ceased going to school; they have not relaxed their intensity of application to learn. The reason I say this now is to protest against the impression that prevails in some quarters that Japan at last is set; that it is too late to influence Japan; that the time of crisis for Japan has passed. It may have partially passed, but it has not wholly passed. Japan is still fairly vibrating with modern life. She has adjusted herself with great facility and rapidity to new ideas. It is not too late to change Japan. In face of the great peril of Japan —that of materialism—how urgently important it is that the Christian Church realize this fact. Japan is leading the Orient, but whither? Is it to be into paths of militarism, mercantilism, and gross materialism, or shall Christianity bring her full influence to bear upon Japan and cause Japan to exert a truly altruistic influence? The place to bring power to bear is at the point where power can be most widely distributed; and surely, so far as the Far East is concerned, Japan is that place.

I shall not linger upon the changes that are coming over Korea. Suffice it to ask, where are there ten millions of people in the world today upon whom the currents of modern life have been turned more abruptly, and with greater directness and power, than upon the Korean people since the Russian war? Since that war, railways have been stretched across the whole of Korea; there is being forced upon the people a system of modern education; the emperor is deposed; the government is being completely reorganized; a new system of finance introduced; countless social, political, and other changes are being effected. Has there been an instance in the history of nations where one country in so short a time has had to face and adjust herself to so much that is modern? The present is the time of times to impress Korea with Christian truth and spirit.

Next we come to China; and there we see the most marvelous changes. China has made greater progress in the last five years than any other country of the world. She has made a more radical adjustment to modern conditions than has any other nation in the same period of time. Those who have studied the great changes that came over Japan will remember that Japan made no such change in the first five years as China has made in her first five years of facing the West. Sir Robert Hart, that sagacious observer of things Chinese, in commenting on the recent changes in China, said: "During the first forty-five years of my residence in China, the country was like a closed room, without a breath of fresh air from the outside world. She was not in the least conscious of the existence of outside nations. During the past five years breezes from all parts of the world have been blowing through China." Dr. Griffith John, that Nestor of China missionaries, before he started back to China, said to me that if there had been associated with the changes in China the bloodshed which has characterized the recent changes in Russia, the eyes of the civilized world would have been focussed upon her, and nothing would keep back the nations from going to her relief. What are some of these changes? Eleven years ago I found 200 miles of railway in China. Now I am told there are 3,700, and, in addition, 1,600 miles building, and 4,000 miles more projected. Eleven years ago there were just a few telegraph wires; now a network covers all the provinces. Only a few years ago not one modern post office; now there are 2,500 post offices, and an average of one new one being added every day. Ten years ago, there was only one daily paper in Peking, the *Peking Gazette,* and it was devoted to publishing the edicts of the Imperial Government; now there are ten dailies there. One of them is a women's daily. Besides these there are papers published in the other cities throughout China, and they give news from all parts of the world. The printing presses, secular and religious, are not able to keep pace with the demand upon them in the printing of the translations of Western works about various phases of our civilization, development, and history. The anti-opium crusade is now being waged with vigor. The practice of foot-binding is being broken up. It has been decreed that China shall have constitutional government after a few years of preparatory work. These changes seem almost unthinkable when we pause to reflect on the constitution of the Chinese mind, on its unchanging attitude through centuries.

But the greatest changes in China are those pertaining to education. She has sent Imperial Commissions to Europe and America—not as a matter of courtesy, not as a matter of curiosity, but to learn with a view to going back to China to bring about changes. They have since shown by their works that they are carrying out their intention. Chinese students are being sent in increasing numbers to the Occident. I estimate that we now have possibly as many as 1,000 Chinese students in the universities of North America and Europe. I wish you would let the appeal of Dr. Datta, on behalf of the Indians, be widened to embrace all the Chinese students now studying in the West. When we recall what it has meant to Christianity that the first Japanese students who came to the Occident were befriended, we shall recognize the desirability of our making friends with every Chinese student who comes amongst us. Let us Christianize as many of them as possible; let us neutralize all the others—that is, so influence them that none of them will return to China antagonistic to Christianity. This will be highly multiplying work. Let me reiterate that China is also sending students to Japan. This has come about largely within the past two or three years. As recently as April there were 15,000 of them in Tokyo. It may interest you to know that 650 of that number came from the Szechwan Province of Western China, before the gates of Tibet. To go from there to Tokyo involves a journey of eight weeks, or the equivalent in time of going round the world to get to college! Fully 1,250 of them came from the exclusive province of

Hunan. That was the last province to let the missionaries in, and that within a decade. And more recently still, it was resisting the introduction of the telegraph. Yet now this most reactionary province is represented by a larger number of young men in Japan than is any other province in China. Think of it, 15,000 young men coming out of the proudest nation under heaven! the most secluded nation in the world, well called the Walled Kingdom, to sit at the feet of their conqueror! Is this not something absolutely unique? Where has there ever been a parallel? Is it not indicative of a most striking change?

Then we find the most wonderful of these educational changes has been the blotting out more than a year ago, by one stroke, of the old curriculum of studies, and the substitution of Western learning in the examinations for the Civil Service. This has been followed by the springing up, like mushrooms, all over China, of modern colleges and high schools. Yuan Shih-kai, Chang Chih-tung, and Tuan Fang, three of the most enlightened viceroys, have been leading off in this educational reform, and others have been following. In the province of Chihli alone there are already 3,000 modern schools, with over 30,000 students. This is a development of a few years. There are, literally, not hundreds, but thousands of these modern schools and colleges which have been started throughout China. Manifestly they are not being properly led. It is an interesting example of the blind leading the blind. They are doing exceedingly superficial work. Take their work in the English language. I had occasion to look into it, and in some places found that they are not teaching sentences but isolated words. Someone pointed out to us that, in one case, they were advertising they would teach English up to the letter G. Not only is this work superficial, but it is carried on without rigid and thorough discipline, and you know that would cause bad results in any country. Many mistakes will be made, much money will be wasted, and there will be many disappointments. But mark my word, this movement will never cease. China has determined to have the modern education. She has made up her mind to give her millions of youth Western advantages. Yes, there will be millions, literally. Japan now has over 5,500,000 of her youth in schools. The same proportion will some day give China over 50,000,000. The day is coming, and very soon, when China will have more students than any other nation of the world.

China is in the midst of an intellectual revolution. It is not yet a religious revolution; but it may become so. At present her education is purely utilitarian. Why does China want Western education? Solely that she may acquire the military, naval, industrial, and financial power of the West. That is her deliberate and practical purpose. May God help us to infuse China with Christian thought, Christian spirit, Christian influence! The next ten years are packed with possibilities. How we should strengthen the educational missionary establishment in China! How we should seek indirectly, as well as directly, to influence the character of the government and gentry schools! China and Korea are still in a fluid or plastic condition; they are not yet set or crystallized. It is for Christianity, largely, to say whether they shall set in Christian molds or materialistic molds. Japan sees it, whether we do or not; and, unhappily, her influence is going to be materialistic, excepting that of her Christian Church. I do not know how it impresses you, but I am overwhelmed as I think of this Chinese educational opportunity, and of the changes in China. When in the history of the human race have such vast numbers of people been undergoing such radical changes? I believe that we are going to see reproduced in China, during the next fifteen years, on a colossal scale what has actually taken place in Japan during the past thirty years. Religion is the most fundamental thing in civilization. If a race with the traits of the Chinese determine on a certain attitude toward religion, the danger is that they may not change again for a thousand years. The last thing about the Chinese is vacillation. I was talking to a leading Japanese delegate yesterday, and he agreed with me that what lent intense importance to the crisis was the fact that when the Chinese once settle this question they will not reopen it. The danger is that Christianity will not realize this sufficiently, and therefore will fail to pour in her full strength in time.

Why is it a time of supreme crisis in the Far East? Not only for the two reasons I have named, but also because of the rising spirit of nationalism and of race patriotism. Missions have had to reckon with this in Japan from the very beginning. May there not have been a Providence in it? For has it not made us wiser to deal with other races? May the lesson not be lost! We have heard most suggestive and convincing things concerning the rising national spirit in India. Allow me, as an outsider, to say that it is to the infinite credit of Britain that she has made possible the very development of that spirit. Some do not realize that in the Philippine Islands, and in Siam, the same national spirit has asserted itself. The spirit of nationalism is also moving in Korea, and the hopelessness of their situation lends an element of real pathos. But in China one finds the most marked example of growing consciousness of nationality, and of a desire to acquire national independence and power. Among the causes are the spread of railways, knitting the country together, and the work of Christian missions with their unifying influence. Other causes have been the last three wars in the Far East, and the return of the Chinese students from

Tokyo, with their hearts burning because of what they have learnt of the opium war with England, of the unjust exclusion acts of America and Australia, of the seizing of their territory by Russia, Germany, France, and Japan, and of the building in their own capital city of legations which remind one of great fortresses, stocked with munitions of war and manned with foreign troops. Put yourself in the place of an ambitious Chinese student, and under such conditions would not the national spirit assert itself in you? How do we find it exhibiting itself? In the many articles bearing on the subject which have been written by the Chinese; in frequent references to "our country" in periodicals and speeches; in the use of the Chinese flag on modern school-buildings; in the singing of patriotic songs in the schools—all this would have seemed incredible ten years ago in China outside the mission schools; in the societies organized to study how to prepare a national constitution; in the boycott against American and other foreign goods; in the anti-opium crusade; in the creation of a modern army—they have now under modern drill in two provinces 150,000 troops.

Speaking of the new army in China reminds me of an essay that a Chinese student wrote. In speaking of the growing military power of China, he said: "We are first going to conquer Japan; next we are going to conquer Russia; next we shall conquer the whole world, and then take our place as the Middle Kingdom." He was very much in earnest.

There is not only this rising national spirit, but also what I am pleased to call the spirit of racial patriotism. Lord Salisbury maintained that there is such a thing as race-patriotism. The cry is spreading over Asia: "Asia for the Asiatics!" We can no more resist, even if we would, this rising national and Oriental feeling, than we can resist the tides of the sea. But we would not resist it. We remember the nation and the race are as much the creation of God as is the family. We remember these mighty powers are to be allied with Christianity, and never placed in antagonism to it. What has it not meant in Japan that from the beginning patriotism was associated with Christianity? And what will it not mean in the other Eastern countries? We do not know when we may be put out of China. Even if we are not put out some of us believe that within ten years the Chinese Christians may take things into their own hands. Some of us believe that in twenty years there will not be a demand for many more new missionaries in China. We may be wrong, but unless the signs fail that one studies in Japan, and that one even now traces among the Chinese people, this is likely to be true. The next five years mean vastly more than the fifteen years which will follow the next five years. May Christendom assert herself in answer to the wishes of her Lord and evan-

336 ADDRESSES AND PAPERS OF JOHN R. MOTT

gelize, while there is yet time, the unevangelized parts of the mainland of Asia, and above all may we devote large attention to raising up, training, and energizing the native leadership of the Chinese Church!

If I were to mention another reason why this is a time of supreme crisis, it would be because of the grave and even disastrous reflex influence upon the Church in the West, of failure to improve the unparalleled opportunity in the East. I confess tonight that my anxiety is not lest there be a great awakening in the East, but lest there may not be a corresponding awakening of the Church in the West. I am burdened with the sense of solicitude lest the Western Christians may not see this door—this great and effectual door. You ask what will follow if they do not see and enter it? One result will be that we shall become callous and hardened, and unresponsive to the moving of the Living Spirit. It is a law of our nature that if we do not respond it becomes more difficult to move us the next time. What could God do, if it is not irreverent to ask that question, what could God do that would likely appeal to us more than what He is now doing in the East? There is something startling in the thought that we may pass into such a state that even the moving of the Living Spirit may not deeply touch us. Another serious result which will follow, will be widespread hypocrisy. To know duty and do it not is hypocrisy, and that is also sin. The startling thing about hypocrisy is that it not only damages our character and destroys confidence in our religion on the part of those outside the Church, but condemns to outer darkness millions who, but for our sham profession, would be ushered into His marvelous light. Another alarming consequence will be that, failing to become conductors of His truth, we shall cease to be conductors of His power. That will result in the grave peril that we shall become incapacitated for dealing strongly and effectively with the tasks at our own doors. May something move us! May someone move us, and save us from the perils of luxury, of selfishness, and of ease; call out the best energies of our minds and hearts, and stir us to act in line with the indication of the Holy Ghost!

What can we do to meet this supreme crisis in the Far East? There should be a masterly and united policy on the part of the missionary leaders of Europe and North America, with reference to facing this great question. The time has come—has it not?—when we should come together, not simply to congratulate and criticize one another, or to exhort one another, or to educate one another, but to face these great crises, to study how they are to be met, and how better to coordinate our forces and to introduce practical means of co-operation and federation. Our statesmanship should be characterized by comprehension. We should face the whole field, and not simply take it up in parts. We should face our whole generation, and not merely grapple with emergencies. We should face the whole range of missionary purpose. We should pay due regard to the principles of strategy with reference to places, to classes, to times, to methods.

There should be prompt and vigorous development of the great and comparatively latent resources of our western Churches, the laymen and the young people. Then we shall have all the money needed. Then we shall have faithful intercession on the part of many Christians. There is a striking Providence in the fact that, just as these wonderful doors have been opened in the Far East, the Holy Spirit has been calling into being the Young People's Missionary Movement and the Laymen's Missionary Movement. These two Movements constitute the complement to the Student Volunteer Movement. They are essential to it, and it is essential to them if this Eastern crisis is to be successfully met, and if the world is to be evangelized in our day. Our watchword—"The Evangelization of the World in This Generation"—should be made a commanding reality in the life of every Christian in this conference, and through us in the lives of Christians generally. I am glad to say that the leaders of the North American Student Volunteer Movement stand absolutely at one with the leaders of the British Movement, in their interpretation of this watchword; and our hope is that the leaders of the Continental student movements will soon join us in holding up this great ideal. We are united in repudiating the idea of reducing the realization of this great ideal to mere numerical terms. Let us keep it as an ideal; and let us translate it into terms of self-denial. For the watchword must be not only regarded as an ideal, but must also be worked out in action. This is a truth, not only to be contemplated, and to stir us, but also to be done. Whether or not the watchword is needed for any other part of the world, it is certainly needed for the Far East, because whatever we wish to do in the Far East must be done in this generation.

God help us so to work, and so to plan, not as though we had two or more generations in which to do the work, but as though we had but one; or, it may be, but part of one.

There must be far larger and more heroic dedication of lives to the work of evangelizing the world and establishing the Kingdom of Christ, if the crisis in the Extreme Orient is to be met. There is need, and that immediately and imperatively, of a great army of workers. Great as is the need for more young men of ability in our universities, to give themselves to the work of the Christian ministry, even greater is the need for a large number of the very best students of Europe and America to go as missionaries to the Far East. They are needed to press into unevangelized regions. They are needed to protect our present investment of lives, and to make them most highly productive. They are needed to dominate the educational standards of the East by sheer force of merit, efficiency, and spirituality. Above all, they are needed to enlist, train, lead, and inspire a host of native Christian preachers and teachers. But, let it be emphasized, they must be men and women of ability, as well as of courage, character, and consecration. This is vastly more important than numbers. We need those who will be statesmen. We need those with power to lead and inspire. We must have the pick of the universities, if they are to guide and mould the leaders of the new Far East. I do not forget that God will take some who are not thus conspicuously strong, and will use them to confound the mighty. Japan had killed, wounded, and diseased in the late war 457,000 men, in the supreme effort to preserve the balance in the Far East. The Japanese willingly laid down tens of thousands of lives to capture one position in the Liaotung Peninsula. "Thy people shall be willing in the day of Thy power." Is not this a day of His power? Is He not shaking the nations? At such a time can we withhold our co-operation?

God the Holy Ghost must be honored in this great enterprise. We must bow ourselves in reverence before Him. In our Creed we say: "I believe in God the Father Almighty . . . I believe in the Holy Ghost." Therefore let us be consistent, let us be logical, let us be genuine, and so work and speak, so pray and act, as those should who have professed faith in a superhuman religion. The ground of our hope and confidence in meeting this Eastern crisis rests not chiefly upon the strength and extent of the missionary establishment, not upon the number and power of the missionaries, not upon the methods and agencies evolved through generations of experience, not upon the brilliancy of the leadership of our forces, not upon the fulness of the treasury, not upon statesmanlike policies and plans, and the skill of our strategists, not upon watchwords and inspiring forward movements —not chiefly upon these things, but upon the fact that the great God is still pleased to visit men and women that are pure and humble and obedient with the Holy Ghost, Whom God hath given to them that *obey* Him. Therefore, let us turn from the crisis in the Far East, and face the crisis in our own lives. Are we willing to yield ourselves absolutely, unconditionally to the sway of Christ, to do His will and not our own? Each one of us has this infinitely potential, this awfully solemn power of choice. May we not be found wanting, but be true in the exercise of the highest office of the human will.

> Our wills are ours we know not how,
> Our wills are ours to make them Thine!

THE NEED OF A FORWARD EVANGELISTIC MOVEMENT

ADDRESS GIVEN AT
THE STUDENT VOLUNTEER CONVENTION
TORONTO, CANADA, 1902

There is need of a great forward evangelistic movement in the non-Christian world, because of the comparatively small number of people who are being won in those heathen and pagan regions to become disciples of Christ. When we compare the number being reached today with that of two generations ago, or one generation ago, or even ten years ago, there is much to encourage us. When we notice what has been accomplished recently in certain parts of the non-Christian world, for example, in Japan, Korea, Manchuria, the Fookien Province of China, and the Northwest Provinces of India, there is no ground for pessimism and discouragement. When we compare the number being won for Christ in the heathen world with the number being led to Christ in the so-called Christian countries, our hearts are filled with hope. But when we compare the number being reached now with the number who are not reached but who could be reached and therefore who should be reached, we recognize keenly and painfully the great need of an extraordinary evangelistic movement.

A forward movement of evangelization is needed because of the large numbers who are today within the range of the immediate influence of the foreign missionary enterprise. Think, for example, of the large number, reaching into millions, who are today being instructed in the schools and colleges of mission lands, of the multitude who are thronging the mission hospitals and dispensaries, of the vast number who are under the influence of the printed page as the truth is released and set at work in all parts of heathenism, of the yet larger number who come within range of the gospel in countless preaching places, or who are brought under the influence of Christian workers in the streets and shops and homes. One is impressed with the fact that there is a number, which in the aggregate must be enormous, of those who are inquirers or almost persuaded or secret disciples, and yet who have not the clearness of faith or the courage of conviction to come out and make open confession of Jesus Christ. We need this mighty spiritual movement in order that we may take advantage of the opportunities that we have in the fact that such multitudes are already more than halfway, are within the range of our influence, to whom we have abundant access, over whom we have special influence. We need the evangelistic spirit to carry them over the line into the Kingdom of our Lord and Saviour Jesus Christ.

The fearful onslaughts of the forces of evil suggest the need of a world-embracing evangelistic movement. The forces of the devil are at work in the great cities of this continent, but I know of no cities of North America which are such fierce vortices of temptation as the cities of the non-Christian world. Impurity is honeycombing all the non-Christian nations. Intemperance is making fearful ravages where it has the right of way, and I am ashamed to say that it has its way far more than it would, if Christianity were more aggressive. The opium curse is eating like gangrene into the best life of the strongest race of Asia. Gambling is casting its fascinating spell over the South American republics and other countries, and is leading not only to waste but to desperation, lawlessness, and suicide to a degree of which we know little in Christian lands. What shall I say of evils like the caste system and ancestor worship, of infidelity and agnosticism and of imported skepticism? Think of the magnitude of these forces of evil working in the non-Christian world! Think of their enterprise; it challenges one's admiration. Think of their ceaseless activity; they take no vacation. Think of their tireless energy. Think of their awful hatred and cruelty. They are after the life; they give no quarter; they want the best, and they will be satisfied with nothing less. Nothing but a mighty outpouring of the Spirit of the living God can turn back these great currents of sin and shame and darkness that are sweeping in and out among the non-Christian nations.

We need such an aggressive evangelistic movement in the non-Christian nations, because of that subtle and insidious spirit of criticism and unbelief which I regret to find working in every country which I have visited. One is specially pained to find this spirit manifesting itself in Christian countries and sometimes in Christian churches. There are people today who bear the name of Christ, who would try to give us the impression that we need some new gospel to meet the need of the world, as though we could have a new Jesus Christ. There are some who would have us believe that the methods of the Apostolic Church are obsolete. Something today is needed more than deliverances of conventions, more than articles and symposia in the press, more than public agitation of these questions. We need fresh evidences of the reality of the facts and forces which hold your life and mine. We need new demonstrations of the fact that the gospel is the power of God unto the salvation of every man that believeth, I care not how hardened or debased or depressed his condition may be. We need new proofs of the fact that the Holy Spirit is as able to shake mightily whole communities today in the most difficult non-Christian nations, as He was in the days of St. Peter and St. Paul. We need new demonstrations of the facts—I maintain that these are facts—that the power of prayer is not diminished, that it is able still to move the arm that moves the world and to achieve objectively wonderful works. We need new demonstrations of the fact that faith is literally the victory that overcomes the world. Evidences like these accumulating will banish skepticism and unbelief, and will nerve the Church to efforts commensurate with the peculiar opportunity of the present generation.

Then, we need this advance movement of evangelism because the work of winning men to Jesus Christ is incomparably the most important work which we have to do. After the bodies which we are seeking to heal have returned to the dust; after the knowledge which we are seeking to impart has been done away with because of restatements and enlargements of knowledge; after tongues which now so much divide the people of the world and stand as a great barrier to those of us who are to go to the front, detaining us so long from getting at the real problems—after these tongues have ceased, the souls of men will go on forever. Laying hold of men and relating them forever to Christ is therefore the most enduring and important work that we can do.

We need this forward movement for testimony and witness-bearing concerning Jesus Christ, because this is an intense age and because the non-Christian nations are intense nations. I know that this is not the common idea; I know that we have an idea that the only intense nations are the Western nations, and particularly those on this side of the Atlantic; but it is time that we were waking to the fact that there is a different form of intensity from that which manifests itself in great activity and feverish haste. An intense nation is one in which the people are absorbed. I have never visited a land in which a people were more absorbed in money-making than China. I have never visited a western country in which men were more earnest and self-denying in their ambition for political preferment and advancement than they are in China, India, and Japan. I have never been in a country where the masses are so fully occupied with what we fittingly call the struggle for existence as they are in India. I have never been in countries in the West where great evils were working with such fearful slaughter as impurity in Japan and as the opium curse in China. I have never been in any other country where any evil influence has so gripped those under its sway as the caste system does in India and ancestral worship in China. I think of no other part of the world where the political, commercial, and industrial influences and forces of Western nations are working with such tremendous energy to secure the attention of the people, as they are today doing in the Far East. The point I am making is simply this: If the Church of Christ is to arrest and hold the attention of men on the subject of personal religion, that Church must be tremendously in earnest. There must be such an outpouring of the Spirit of Pentecost as shall fill the Church and impel her to mighty deeds.

We need this movement, moreover, because our task is an urgent one. There is an element of immediacy about the command of Jesus Christ that has never adequately possessed a generation since the first generation of Christians. It is a simple proposition. The Christians now living must take Christ to the non-Christians now living, if they are ever to hear of Him. The Christians who are dead cannot do it; the Christians who are to come after us cannot do it. Obviously, I repeat, each generation of Christians must evangelize its own generation of non-Christians, if Christ is to see of the travail of his soul and be satisfied with reference to that particular generation. The forces of evil recognize this. Not one of them is deferring its operations. Lust says, "Let me go unbridled in the Turkish Empire in this generation." Rationalism says, "Let me have the right of way in the Indian universities for this generation, and I will not worry for the generations which are to follow." Materialism says, "Let me do as I will in Japan in this generation." We "must work the works of Him that sent us, while it is day, for the night cometh when no man can work."

If we want a further reason why this advance movement to make Christ known to all men is so much needed, I would indicate in this important consideration: that we may enter into the heritage which God has prepared for the Church in the non-Christian world, as a result of the working of His unchanging laws. Note some of these laws. There is the law of sowing and reaping. There has been an immense amount of sowing in the non-Christian world. I was impressed by this fact when I made my first journey around the world. And on my recent tour I was more impressed than before. I wish that all Christian workers in North America might witness the extent and the thoroughness of the seed-sowing and watering work as carried on by Christian workers in Asia, Africa, and other parts of the non-Christian world. There are no workers in the great harvest fields of God who have worked with more painstaking zeal, patience, and wisdom in the sowing process and in the watering process than have the laborers on the mission field. And wherever they have engaged in reaping work, they have done even better than we at home, considering the greater difficulties which confront them. But has not the time come for reaping on a larger scale than has at any time been possible in the past? I have found no part of the non-Christian world—and I suppose that I have been in some of the most difficult fields with the last six months— where, if the sickle be put in, I care not by whom, in the name of Jesus Christ and the power of the Holy Ghost, there were not sheaves that could be gleaned. The time has come to reap, to recognize that this law of God is certain in its working; that where there has been sowing and watering, there shall be reaping.

Then there is the law of prayer. It is well to think of it as a law. There is nothing like chance connected with it; it works with great certainty. Think of the prayer which has been focused upon different great non-Christian nations. Take North China for example. In vain is it, however, for all Christendom to pause and come to her knees and implore God to assert His power in North China, unless the Christians of the home Church and the Christians in North China itself, go forth to reap, recognizing that there is a heritage to be entered into as a result of this marvelous volume of real prayer.

Reflect also on that other law that has been working, the law of self-sacrifice. I am not one of those who believe that all of the sacrifice is being made in the non-Christian nations. There are individual Christians here and there among us who are really following Jesus Christ in self-denial. These are the salt of the home churches. Would that we had more! The law therefore is working in the Christian nations, but far more extensively, I am persuaded, is it working in the non-Christian nations. In the very act of leaving the home countries the missionaries deny themselves in a marked degree. Then they go to face misunderstanding, to meet opposition and loneliness; they go to subject themselves to a strain upon the sensibilities and the nervous organism, the like of which we know not in Christian countries. Think of the sacrifice of tears; and beneath and beyond all, think of the sacrifice of lives!

The most impressive experience of my life up to this time, was the one which God gave me a few months ago, of going, in response to the invitation of the missionaries, from my regular itinerary, to North China, where, in the old theater of the nephew of the Empress Dowager in Peking, now used as an American Board compound, we met the surviving leaders of the martyr Church. As I met there from day to day with some 400 Chinese Christians and was told that there was probably not one in the audience, who, in the recent fearful ordeal, had not lost relatives or friends or members of his immediate family by death or persecution, or who himself had not been through the siege or through worse persecution, I was thrilled to the center of my being; and as I heard some of their stories of suffering I was ashamed of the degree of Christianity which I myself possessed. Moreover, I formed a deeper conviction than ever as to the genuineness and thoroughness of the work which the missionaries have been doing. Think of the 15,000 Chinese Christians and the well nigh 200 missionaries and members of their families, who laid down their lives! It is one thing for Tertullian to say that the blood of the martyrs is the seed of the Church; it is another thing for the Christians of North America and other Protestant countries, and the Christians of North China and other persecuted mission fields, to rise up and enter into the heritage which these martyrdoms have made possible. The closing thought of the eleventh chapter of Hebrews, that apart from us those who have gone before shall not be made perfect, ought to move us. Those who have gone through the persecutions and martyrdoms of North China, will not be made perfect unless we do our duty. We therefore have a duty to the past, as well as to the present and future.

How may we promote this forward evangelistic movement? It is of fundamental importance that we recognize and realize the need of such a movement. It will take time to do this. I would like to put this point practically. My suggestion is that student delegates go back to the colleges, secretaries to the mission board rooms, missionaries to their fields, pastors to the churches, and that one and all stand in the presence of God and of the facts which have been poured in upon us in this convention, and which shall still come before us, and that we take time to realize the need. It will take time to make it vivid and commanding and real, so that it moves us. If we are to have prayer and action to change things, we must have conviction as to the need of prayer and action. If we are to have conviction, we must have vivid knowledge. Yet again let me repeat, it will take time to get that kind of knowledge. We become so accustomed to things as they are, so accustomed to the working of the forces of sin and evil, that their awfully sad side is lost sight of. Missionaries confessed to me on my recent tour, and time after time have Christians in the home countries done the same, that the facts of heathenism have ceased to move their spirits deeply, as they once did. If that is true of any of us here, we ought to be alarmed. It represents a lack of Christlikeness. It is impossible to read the life of Jesus Christ and discover that He ever became callous to the reality of the need of man. I have known students in certain colleges in the United States who have apologized for the missionary history of their college. Can these men have been pondering on the awful facts as Christ sees them? How a man could sit through a session like the one of last night and not be moved, is more than I can understand. Is he a real Christian, that is, does the spirit of Christ live in him?

How shall this need be made real? Not only by spending time in the presence of the facts, but by imagining what Jesus Christ would do were He in our place; by trying to see this need from the point of view of God and by trying to get a vision of these countries made new by the mighty Christ. Yes, there is going to be a new North China, a new Asia Minor, a new Uganda, a new Calcutta and Benares and Canton, as surely as God is God. There is coming a day when these habitations of darkness and cruelty shall be mountains from which shall flow down rivers of righteousness.

If we are to have this great spiritual awakening, we must not only realize the need, but as leaders in the work of Christ—and there are many here, who in His plan are leaders—we must strongly desire such an awakening. If we do not desire it so that it grips us and affects our life plans and ambitions, I despair of this world witnessing a great advance of the evangelistic movement.

It is essential that we have wise and comprehensive plans and a statesmanlike organization. At present we have the vision of the world. I believe that the day is coming before long, when the Church of Christ will take the whole world literally into her plan. It is what the Jesuits did centuries ago. There was a time when they had a chain of hundreds of colleges and seminaries stretching from Ireland to Japan. The day is coming when the Christian Church will map out the whole world, will wisely distribute the forces, will actually occupy the field; but until that time let every delegate in this convention plan with reference to the field within the range of his immediate influence. That will mean that in the colleges those of us who are students will begin as never before to evangelize; that others here will in their cities and villages on the home field propagate the gospel; that the missionaries will go back to their fields and go about the work of proclaiming Christ with renewed determination and under the larger sway of the power of the Spirit.

We ourselves as Christians must be mightily revived and awakened. Any world-wide movement for Christ must begin with the Christians. With what Christians? Not the indifferent Christians, not the inconsistent Christians, not the Christians in distant unevangelized countries, who do not have the opportunity to know so much about Christ and His work but those who are nearest Christ, who understand His purposes and desires best; with them it must begin. And I have come to believe, more than I at one time did, that the spiritual life in the non-Christian nations will not rise and stay permanently higher than it is in the Christian nations. This has a very vital meaning to the colleges, because Christian life in Canada and the United States will not stay higher permanently than it is in the institutions of higher learning. In the colleges we are being trained as the leaders of the forces of Christ in these countries. Therefore let us go back to the colleges, not to wait until next autumn, but to make the closing months of this year right up to commencement tell on the evangelization of our fellow students. In that way we shall be moving India and Africa and South America and China most effectively.

Prayer is indispensable to any widespread spiritual awakening.

Charles G. Finney, one of the three greatest evangelists of the last century, said that a great revival might be expected when there is definite prayer for a great revival. Prayer recognizes that we look to God as the source of the blessing. We are prone to magnify human agencies and human instrumentality. Our failure to prevail more largely with the non-Christian nations is due to our more fundamental failure to prevail with God in prayer. If I were to emphasize one thing about prayer more than another in this connection, it would be that there be concert or community of prayer among Christians. The greatest revival of recent years was the one that began in the churches of Japan last spring and still continues. That revival is traceable directly to the sinking of differences among Christians and uniting in prayer for this definite and great end.

We must also look to the Holy Spirit as the great Worker, and so honor Him. He is the author and the promoter of every spiritual movement. Why? Because He alone can convict men of sin; He alone can lead them to apprehend Christ as Lord; He alone can influence men to close in on Christ and relate themselves to Him; He alone can guide, empower, and embolden the Christian workers. A true awakening is the work of the Spirit of God. May He fall upon this convention in mighty power before we disperse to the ends of the earth.

In every way within our power we should seek to strengthen and to extend the Student Volunteer Movement for Foreign Missions. This Movement, in the plan of God, is striking at the heart of the great problem of the world's evangelization. It is this Movement which is raising up the workers who are to go out to the non-Christian nations in numbers sufficient to lead the forces of evangelism. And, in the second place, it is this Movement which must place the burden of responsibility upon the Christians going out from our colleges who are to work at home as ministers or as laymen so as to develop a base of operations adequate to sustain the great campaign at the front.

THE ENLARGEMENT OF THE NATIVE ARM OF THE SERVICE ESSENTIAL TO THE HIGHEST SUCCESS OF MISSIONS

ADDRESS GIVEN AT THE ANNUAL MEETING OF
THE AMERICAN BOARD OF COMMISSIONERS FOR FOREIGN MISSIONS
OBERLIN, OHIO, OCTOBER 16, 1902

There is need of strengthening greatly the native arm of the service throughout the mission fields of the world. The idea of evangelizing the world in this generation, apart from the raising up of a vast army of native workers, is at the best a vision which is not likely to be realized. We shall need during this generation several thousands of the choicest spirits which the colleges and the theological seminaries of North America, the British Isles, and other Protestant lands can furnish, to evangelize the heathen nations, to plant the Church, to guide and steady the Church, and to place at the disposal of native Christian agencies the acquired experience of Christendom. But for every thousand missionaries there will be needed not less than 10,000 native workers to serve as pastors, teachers, evangelists, catechists, and Bible women. This presents a stupendous problem, because if we are to flood the world with the knowledge and spirit of Jesus Christ and do the fair thing by our particular generation, we must have nothing less than an army of native workers.

The value and importance of raising up an adequate native force would seem to be evident. As a matter of economy and business sense it is desirable, because native agents can live and work in their own country at comparatively little expense. Moreover, the natives are already acclimatized, and can work at all seasons and without furloughs. They are in intimate association with their own people; they travel together, eat together, lodge together, live together. The foreigner, at the best, has exotic habits. Naturally, the natives have a more fluent command of the vocabulary and idioms of the language. They have an intimate acquaintance with the habitual trains of thought, the currents of feeling, and the springs of action. They understand the native character, and, other things being equal, are the best judges of the motives and sincerity of those among whom they work. They know the temptations, doubts, and soul-struggles of those with whom they are so closely associated. They have probably fought over the same battleground. They know the heart life of their fellows, and their fellows know that they know it. They are of the same blood. They will always have larger and more influential access to their own people. It took a German to lead the German Reformation. Wyclif did so in England. John Knox did so in Scotland. Americans have always most deeply moved this continent. And so it will ever be—the sons and daughters of the soil will leave the deepest mark on their own people and generation.

History teaches that the principal factor in the evangelization of non-Christian nations has been the native factor. There has never been an extensive region or nation thoroughly evangelized but by its own sons. It would seem to be the providential method. It is also the method which great missionaries have specially emphasized. Alexander Duff, that great missionary statesman—I class him among the great statesmen of the British Empire—said that "when the set time arrives, the real reformers of Hindustan will be qualified Hindus."

Joseph Neesima, after years of Christian work in Japan, said that "the best possible method to evangelize her people is to raise up a native agency." Mackay, of Uganda, a wiser missionary than his years gave promise of while he lived, but whose wisdom becomes more and more apparent as the missionary problem is grappled with in Africa, said that "the agency by which, and probably by which alone, we can Christianize Africa is the African himself." "But," he added, "he must first be trained for that work, and trained, too, by the European in Africa." Dr. Nevius, who was conceded to be one of the ablest missionaries in China, said that "the millions of China must be brought to Christ by Chinamen." Dr. Griffith John, the great Nestor of Chinese missionaries, wrote me some two years ago from the heart of China that the wonderful ingathering of the past few years in Fukien, Hupeh, Hunan, and Manchuria is attributable mainly, under God, to the efficiency, the earnestness, and the assiduity of the native workers. Dr. Goodrich wrote me about the same time, from North China, that whether we view this question politically, economically, historically, or sociologically, the only sound method of evangelizing a great nation is that of raising up and using the native agency.

There are difficulties in the way of securing and using native workers. It may be well to call attention to them. There is, for example, the contempt in which religious workers are held in the East. This is unlike what we find in America and Great Britain, where the ministry has dignity and prestige as a result of its honorable position and influence through centuries. All through Asia today, largely as a result of the corrupt lives of the Buddhist and other priests, religious callings are looked down upon, if not despised.

Unwillingness to incur the reproach which so often attaches to the native who is related to the foreigner, is another difficulty which keeps many from entering upon Christian service in these countries. They do not like to be called foreign hirelings, as a Japanese expressed it to me; or, as a group of Chinese put it, they do not want to be twitted with eating the foreigner's rice.

Then there is the question of status, which seems to stand in the way of some in India and in other lands; that is, the native workers feel that they are entitled to more power, liberty, and responsibility than they have; that they should receive larger recognition; that more confidence should be shown in them by the missionaries. It is admitted that in some instances they have good reasons for this opinion. But in more cases, I am persuaded, their attitude is due to a misconception of the motives and spirit of the missionaries. Nevertheless, this is a very real difficulty, and it is not easy to overcome it.

The opposition of parents and relatives is a very real hindrance.

Far more than at home, in lands where the Confucian ethics dominate, or where the system of caste exists, it is exceedingly difficult for young men to stand out against the expressed desire of parents, relatives, and friends.

The attractions presented by commercial pursuits, by government service, and by other so-called secular walks of life, is a principal reason, if not the principal reason, why it is so difficult today to get a sufficient number of strong native students to devote themselves to Christian work. The salaries paid in the secular callings range all the way from a little larger to thirty or more times larger than can be paid in Christian service. It is just as though the students of Oberlin and other colleges were offered five-thousand-dollar salaries to enter business or certain political positions. If this were done, it would be exceedingly difficult to get a sufficient number of men for the work of the ministry. Might it not prove to be a severe temptation to young men even in our theological seminaries? When one of my friends visited the Doshisha Seminary a few years ago, he found there eighty theological students. When I touched there the first time, five years ago, the number had fallen to less than a score. I was told by the professors that the chief cause of this decline in the number of ministerial candidates was the great inducements to money-making in connection with the recent commercial development of Japan. This is a real difficulty, and we should have sympathy with those subjected to such pressure, remembering that they have not, like ourselves, Christian heredity, Christian environment, and the dominance of Christian ideals to hold them to higher tasks.

A lack of spirituality should not be omitted among the causes making it difficult to get a sufficient number of men for Christian work. In these non-Christian lands many young men have a hold upon Christianity, but, generally speaking, Christianity does not have a powerful hold upon them. Wherever I found a native student upon whom the Spirit of God had laid His mighty hand, I found a student who was eager to enter upon the service of his fellow men, and, therefore, willing to face the hardships, opposition, and sacrifice involved.

If I may mention another reason why we are not raising up this army more rapidly and using it more extensively, I should say it is because of the lack of adequate efforts and measures to secure and to use more workers. Those boards and missions which have given most thought to this problem are the boards and missions which have raised up the largest number of effective agents. Those missionaries whom I have met in my travels, who have had the greatest burden upon them, that they might be used of God in enlisting young men and young women for this important service, are the missionaries who are leading or guiding the largest number of young men and young women into Christian work as a lifework.

What can be done to meet the difficulties to which attention has been called, and to raise up this army? In the first place there should be a comprehensive and thoroughgoing study of this question and a statesmanlike policy with reference to meeting the need. It should be comprehensive, in the sense of taking into the scheme, as the Jesuits have done, the whole world. It should be comprehensive in a second sense, that it embraces the generation for the serving of which God holds us responsible. Let the policy grapple with the whole generation, and not simply with emergencies. It should be a statesmanlike policy, in the sense that it takes account of all other forces in the Church of Christ at work on the mission field, thus avoiding duplicating or overlapping. We might wisely imitate the practice of the European powers, with reference to their naval programs. They adopt a policy which requires years to fulfill; for example, they plan to lay down so many battleships this year, to build so many torpedo boats and destroyers next year, to equip a certain coaling station and build a drydock a year later. So the Church should look down through the years, and so lay her plans as to bring up the forces to meet the needs of the world of our own generation.

A second thing which is exceedingly important is that we greatly enlarge and strengthen the educational missionary work. I have had the privilege of visiting nearly all the colleges of the American Board, some of them twice. In addition to that, I have visited scores, if not hundreds, of colleges and high schools of other boards of the North American and European societies. I would say here tonight what I have said concerning the American Board in the gathering of another denomination, that I know of no colleges which have had a larger fruitage in the respect of which we are speaking—that of furnishing the right kind of native agents—than the colleges of the American Board. It should be a distinct encouragement, and also an appeal that no one take our crown. I would add, also, a conviction that has not been formed hastily. There should be expended on these higher institutions of the American Board within the next five years not less than $1,000,000. I will not go into details explaining what this money should be used for: adding plants here, endowment there, strengthening the teaching force here, improving the equipment there. It seems like a reasonable proposition in a country like this, which has found it possible during the past year, in private gifts alone, to devote scores of millions of dollars to higher education. One bequest announced the other day for Princeton Theological Seminary is likely to amount to $1,500,000. The Protestant Episcopal Church has just issued an appeal for $1,000,000, to endow their work in their most recently entered field, the Philippines. I believe that men of large financial ability and large outlook will respond far more generously to a plan which seems adequate to do the work which God has assigned to our generation, than to one which is obviously insufficient to meet the need and opportunity.

But I am even more convinced that we should add to the force of workers in these colleges than that we should add to their material equipment. This is the last part of the foreign service that we should allow to be undermanned. It is poor economy to put up these large institutional plants and underman them to the point that we fall short of making them productive investments. It has seemed to me that the staff of workers was often so overburdened with the technical work of teaching, which ought, for the honor of the Church, to be kept up to scholarly standards, that they were not able to give the time that they desired to give to the most vital part, touching the lives of the students. We must add to the force of educational missionaries. They need not all necessarily be ordained men. Now and then an unordained man who has been well prepared for teaching, and who is a religious force among students at home, would be very successful in such work abroad.

We must add to this force to such an extent that in every mission college and school the educational missionary will have enough time to think, to grasp the problems, to pray, to do a lot of personal work, to impress the students deeply. I visited the college of Dr. Mateer in Shantung Province some years ago. He and Mrs. Mateer had started that Christian college about thirty years before the time of my visit. I learned that every graduate of that institution had become a Christian before graduation, and that the large majority of them had entered some form of Christian work as a lifework. Later, I found one or more of these graduates on the teaching staff of nearly every important mission college of China. When I asked Dr. Mateer the secret of the wonderful influence of the college, he replied: "My wife and I early came to the conclusion that we together could not deeply impress more than sixty students. And so we deliberately kept down the number of students." The yield that has followed would seem to prove the wisdom of their practice.

We should never cease to mention with gratitude the name of Miss Eliza Agnew, who within forty years sent out from her school in Ceylon 600 graduates as Christians, of whom over 200 entered what we would call distinctively Christian callings. She never let the number in the school become so large that she could not give personal attention to the individual student.

In India I met a man who made a profound impression upon me. Later, I learned that not infrequently he spent long hours—on one occasion, the whole night—in intercession for the native workers. A friend of mine went out from Oxford to India and became absorbed in executive work. He wrote me three or four years ago: "I have decided to change my method; I am going to spend a large section of my time this year with a little group of men." The size of the group, I may say, was twelve. I heard from him toward the close of the year that the fires of God were burning in the lives of those men. He was walking in the footsteps of Jesus Christ in this practice.

The greatest work of the missionary is the making of missionaries. In no other way can he so multiply himself. What a work was accomplished by the men who influenced for Christ such natives as Moses Kya of the Sandwich Islands; Tiyo Soga and Bishop Crowther of Africa; the great Sheshadri; the converted Brahmin, Banurji, of Calcutta; Chatterjea of the Punjab, and Pundita Ramabai of Western India; the Brothers Meng in North China and Pastor Shen, the worker of the London Missionary Society among the Chinese; Miyagawa of Osaka, and Honda and Uemura of Tokyo. Lives like these are not the product of foreign money and intellectual culture alone; they are the gift of God through the example, the training, and the spiritual nurture of Christian missionaries.

In the third place, if we are to have this army of workers, there must be a wise use of a large amount of money in raising up and sustaining such a native agency. I realize keenly the difficulty of the problem. Like every other important thing, it is beset with difficulties. But the fact of a difficulty should be a challenge rather than a hindrance to us. I believe there is a way to use money (and this has been proved again and again in the missions of the American Board) which will not hinder, but rather further, one of the great objects we have in view, namely, the stimulating and enlarging of self-support. It will not be easy. It will require the exercise of much patience and judgment, and call for much prayer. But there is no body of men in Christian work today who can be depended upon to make a wiser use of money for such a purpose than the men stationed in the key positions of the missionary societies of Great Britain and America.

Moreover, we should co-operate with the Christian Student Movement in the non-Christian countries. The Young Men's Christian Association Movement in the colleges of Asia and other non-Christian parts of the world is not a self-appointed task. It was planted in mission lands by the missionaries, and every one of the foreign secretaries engaged in developing and extending the movement in the heathen world has gone there at the call of the missionaries. It is the policy of this movement never to send a secretary to a non-Christian country until all the missionaries of all the responsible denominations at work in a given field unite in an appeal and take the initiative in asking for such a secretary. The thirty-one men now on the field have, without exception, gone in response to such calls. These men have already developed over 150 college Christian Associations. They are found not only in the Christian colleges, but also in many of the leading government institutions throughout Asia and in other parts of the world. These organizations and the secretaries are supervised by national committees, the principal members of which are missionaries: such men as Dr. Davis on the National Committee of Japan, and Dr. Sheffield on the National Committee of China. The object of this Christian movement is to help evangelize the students, and then lay upon them the burden of evangelizing their own people. Thus it is, in a true sense, a Student Volunteer Movement for Home Missions. And herein lies the reason why the missionaries believe in this work so strongly wherever it has been well established and supervised.

The methods employed by this movement are those which have been most fruitful in the colleges of the West. The devotional, thorough study of the Bible is much emphasized. Already, from one-fourth to one-half of the Christian students in the colleges with associations have been drawn into voluntary Bible classes. Among other methods promoted are personal work, evangelistic campaigns in the neighborhood, and the development of missionary interest. Special stress is laid on influencing strong students to devote their lives to Christian work as a lifework. About 500 students in China, India, Ceylon, and the Levant have already become volunteers. Of this number, over one-fourth volunteered during the past year. The means employed by the national committees to develop this movement are: conferences for the deepening of the spiritual life and for training voluntary workers; the preparation and use of literature designed to help in the formation of right habits for the cultivation of the spiritual life, and to stimulate Christian effort; the visits of expert secretaries, necessary even in a country like the United States, if the fires are to be kept burning and if the work is to be co-ordinated and brought into vital connection with similar movements of other countries. By means of the World's Student Christian Federation the Christian student movements of non-Christian lands are organically related to the Christian organizations of students all over the world. Over 80,000 Christian students and professors in forty different nations are bound together in this worldwide movement for the evangelization of the world and the complete establishment of Messiah's Kingdom. I have just come from Denmark, where I met in conference the representatives of twenty-nine of these national student movements. There native Christian Japanese, Chinese, and Indian delegates sat with the leaders of the work in Christian lands and helped to shape the policy for the work of Christ among the students of the world. It was decided that the next conference of the World's Student Christian Federation be held in Japan—the first world's conference, either secular or religious, that has ever gone to Asia. What may it not mean to the great government student centers in Japan, and to missionary colleges and schools in Korea, Japan, and China?

Above all, there is need of far more prayer for the raising up and the thrusting forth of the army of native workers. This means is necessary to make all the other means effective. It is necessary to make them most largely productive. It is the means and the only means on which Christ has placed stress in connection with getting laborers. Any plan which neglects this factor is exceedingly superficial. Why leave unappropriated and unapplied the greatest force for the raising up and energizing of laborers and for calling into being and energizing spiritual movements?

What we do to solve this great problem, and every other problem which has come before us during these days, we must do quickly. Too many organizations and individual Christians today are acting and planning as though they had two or three generations to do the work for which God is going to hold them responsible. We need to revise our method in this respect and to focus our energies upon the task at hand. While it is true that we should build for the future generations and for eternity, the best way to do it is to serve our own generation by the will of God. The only way that this world is ever going to be evangelized is going to be by each generation of Christians resolving to evangelize its own generation of non-Christians. The Christian world today can evangelize the unevangelized now living; the Christians of the last generation and the Christians who are to come after us cannot do it. I repeat it: We must evangelize our own generation of unevangelized if they are ever to know and obey Jesus Christ. There is an element of urgency and immediacy in the command of Jesus Christ that we are prone to overlook. The dominant impression made on me during my last tour around the world was that every mission field is ripe, yes, dead ripe, and that the time has come to reap. In my judgment, if we rise to our opportunity, the next ten years will witness an unprecedented ingathering into the kingdom of Christ in all the great mission fields.

WINNING THE NEW GENERATION

ADDRESS TO STUDENTS IN GREAT BRITAIN, 1930

One of the most disconcerting impressions borne in upon me along the pathway of my journeys in Europe and America was that the youth now thronging the universities and colleges, and likewise those who have graduated from these institutions during the last decade, have by no means been won to the missionary cause. There has been a marked falling off in the number of volunteers for missions, also in the number of undergraduates devoting themselves to the thorough study of missionary questions. The situation is more critical than facts like these imply. Not only do large numbers of students and professors criticize the technique of missions, but there is also on their part a sincere and sharp challenge of some of the most fundamental assumptions: for example, the existence of a personal God, the authority of a moral law, the absolute character of Christian truth. This springs largely from the controlling influence of science and mechanistic scientific conceptions over all thought, and especially in the field of psychology. Thus the total motive and the goal of Christian missions are meaningless to wide ranges of student life. I am not unmindful of exceptions in individual universities here and there. Nor do I overlook the significant fact that students today, possibly more largely than ever before, are identifying themselves with other forms of altruistic interest and service. Moreover, the signs are not wanting in certain parts of the student field, both in America and in Britain, indicating a turn in the tide. When all of a reassuring character is said, however, which can be said, the serious fact remains that this generation, to which are coming heavier burdens than to any preceding generation, must still be won to intelligent and whole-souled allegiance to the world mission of the Christian religion.

While there may not be, and probably will not be, a demand during the next two or three decades for anywhere nearly as many students of the West to become missionaries as during the past two or three decades, there is today clamant need of a larger number of the ablest young men and women than the universities can furnish. As I have tried to point out to selected companies of the very flower of the student bodies on both sides of the Atlantic, they are needed to fill important gaps in the missionary ranks. It is solemnizing to see how many posts of major importance are unfilled, and this at the last time when such should be the case. Many more are needed who will put themselves in preparation to provide a worthy succession to faithful workers who, as a result of age and failing strength, must all too soon hand over their great trusts to younger men and women. Others are needed right now to supersede relatively incompetent workers who, with commendable devotion, are holding positions of large importance simply because there are not enough of front-line ability and equipment to assume the responsibility. Then, as my journeys in mission fields have shown me in an unforgettable way, we soon must have highly competent reinforcements to avert the breakdown of many a willing and overburdened missionary who is now carrying an impossible load.

On virtually every field there should be additions to the staff in order to make much more highly productive the work of the missionaries already there. I did not visit a hospital, or a Christian college, or a field open to evangelism which I considered adequately manned. One came away believing that an addition and proper placement, in the near future, of possibly ten per cent in the number of well-qualified missionaries might well yield 100 per cent increase in results. Then, as we think of the growing complexity of the missionary program, calling for higher specialization in function and, therefore, in preparation, we see at a glance the demand for special reinforcements. The reason that in so many fields there are baffling and unsolved problems lies, in part at least, in the want of more new missionaries of the highest qualifications. It is well also to remind ourselves that there are still many totally unoccupied fields, having in them in the aggregate tens of millions of inhabitants, which stand in need of all that we associate with the Christian gospel. Is there anything, therefore, which has a claim upon the leaders of the Christian forces prior to that of praying, planning, and persevering in well-directed efforts to win for the world program of Christ more young men and women of power, of vision, of strength, of personality shown in gifts of initiative and willingness to accept and discharge responsibility, of capacity to grow, and determination to continue to grow all their lives, of willingness to go into training and stay in training longer than their predecessors, of social and ethical passion and concern, of the spirit of adventure and ability to endure hardness, of genuine personal experience of Christ?

Wherever I have gone in my recent visits in the universities of the West, students have raised the question, "Granted that we may be needed on the mission field, are we wanted there, especially by the nationals or natives of the country?" Before my last round-the-world journey, I had discovered that this was one of the most important unanswered questions in the minds of students, and, therefore, along the way I made it the subect of special inquiry. I was able to bring back the significant report that not in a majority of areas but in them all, including fields occupied by three-quarters of the inhabitants of the non-Christian world, the native Christian leaders without exception authorized me to state that they both need and want more missionaries from the West; but in all instances they specified that these must be from the ablest and best furnished that the student communities of Europe and America can provide.

I will not dwell upon the reasons which have militated against the winning of the new generation to deep conviction in favor of the world mission and life commitment to it. The point just mentioned has had its influence. Deeper still has been a fundamental doubt as to whether Christ is absolutely essential to the followers of non-Christian faiths. The widespread spirit and philosophy of secularism has had a benumbing effect. The many and often worthy opportunities for unselfish service nearer home or in so-called secular pursuits abroad are deflecting not a few among the abler youth. The money-making pursuits absorb a vastly disproportionate number. Too often the advice and pressure of relatives and friends are exerted in directions quite different from that of the missionary career. In the main, however, I became convinced in the light of very many contacts with present-day and gone-down students that the reason why more of the ablest are not dedicating themselves to this greatest work in the world lies in the lack of exposure to adequate appeals, in inconclusive thinking on appeals which they have heard or read, and in a want of spirituality.

How meet this basic need? As I have said again and again, it behooves us to become alarmed, for what calamity could be greater than to fail at this point—the point of ensuring an adequate leadership of the missionary forces of tomorrow? Then let us act as though we regarded this as the most important single thing we have to do. Without such conviction we shall not pay the prices necessary to ensure the desired result. With the help of the ablest apologetic voices and pens we must help youth to answer their fundamental questions pertaining to faith and life. They must be exposed to the most dynamic personalities among the returned missionaries and visiting Christian nationals. The hands of the Volunteer Movement, and the Christian Student Movement in general, should be strengthened in every way in our power. In some fields I was pained to find that as a result of uncertainty as to its message, lack of sense of direction and mission as to its objectives, and resultant divided counsels, this Movement has ceased to be the world power that it had been in earlier years. No sign encountered afforded more hope for the future than the unmistakable evidences among Student Movement leaders of honest searchings of heart, humbling confession, and prayerful determination to provide the intellectual and spiritual causes which have invariably been the precursor of every marked advance in the Kingdom of Christ.

THE PLACE OF PRAYER IN THE STUDENT VOLUNTEER
MOVEMENT

ARTICLE IN *THE STUDENT VOLUNTEER*
OCTOBER, 1894

The Student Volunteer Movement owes everything to prayer. It was conceived in days and nights of prayer at Mount Hermon. The missionary enthusiasm which it called forth all over the student field had its springs in prayer. Its secretaries were all chosen under the clear guidance of the Holy Spirit in answer to persevering prayer. They went about their intense and deeply spiritual work, creating, molding, and promoting the student missionary activities of a continent, in the power of prayer. The generous gifts of money which made possible the extension of the Movement came from prayerful men and women as a result of believing prayer. It was in a series of three prayer meetings that the permanency of the Movement was ensured by effecting its wise organization. It was in prayer in a little boat on Lake Geneva that the idea of the memorable and fruitful Cleveland Convention was suggested. The secret of the spiritual power of the wonderful Detroit Convention was in the fact that all the plans were wrought out in months of prayer, and that while the convention itself was in session over 400 missionaries, in all parts of the foreign field, were uniting in prayer for it day by day. *The Student Volunteer* was called into being by the prayer of faith of one man. The missionary institutes and the newly created educational department had a common prayer origin. The new declaration, which has done so much to intensify the Movement, was adopted in a joint prayer meeting of the Executive Committees of the British and American organizations. The watchcry, with all its depth and range of meaning, was most emphatically the product of prayer. Thus prayer—definite, fervent, importunate—has marked every important step in the development of the Movement from its origin down to the opening of the wonderful doors of opportunity of the present college year.

If prayer has had a large place in the life of the Movement in the past, it should be a still more prominent factor from this time forth. Consider the vital things pertaining to the Movement which hinge on prayer.

The most delicate, critical, and important work of leading students to volunteer for foreign missions surely calls for much prayer, not only on the part of those who undertake this responsible work and of those to whom they go, but also on the part of all those who are in a position to realize the difficulty and the great possibilities of this work. If decisions are to be reached which shall stand, there must be increasing prayer that students who hear the calls to volunteer "may be filled with a knowledge of His will."

The spiritual equipment of the volunteers for their lifework should be a burden on the hearts of all prayerful people who sincerely desire to see the central purpose of the Movement realized. To evangelize the world in this generation requires something more than for 20,000 students to go out to mission fields, and to work there the rest of their lives. To accomplish this mighty enterprise it is absolutely essential that the volunteers be Spirit-filled men and women. When should they receive this indispensable part of their equipment? For every reason, before they leave their native land. Therefore, now, as in the days of the early Church, definite and constant prayer should be made, that the volunteers may go forth in the power of the Holy Ghost.

If the money is to be forthcoming to enable the missionary societies to send the steadily growing number of intending missionaries, the intimate relation which exists between the prayer life of the Church and abundant offerings of money must be more fully recognized. The experience of the Church Missionary Society at times of financial depression, and that of the church of Dr. A. J. Gordon in Boston in its missionary giving last year suggests clearly that prayer is the true secret of the solution of the financial problem of missions. In this connection there are some words by Hudson Taylor which each volunteer should ponder again and again: "How important, therefore, to learn before leaving England to move man, through God, by prayer alone."

If the volunteers are to go out to their lifework in the right way (*i.e.,* with the consciousness that they are sent by God) there must be a far more implicit compliance on the part of Christians with that wonderful condition involved in the command of Christ: "Pray ye therefore the Lord of the harvest, that He send forth laborers into His harvest." Some people have criticized the Movement at times because more of its members have not already sailed. What the Movement needs is not such unavailing criticism but more prevailing prayer. Granted a great volume of earnest, sincere, constant, intercessory prayer, and the volunteers would be thrust forth at the right time, into the right places, with the right equipment, to make possible an abundant realization of the watchcry of the Movement.

Our prayers for the Movement should not cease with influencing it in the foregoing critical stages. We should remember with faithfulness the increasing number of volunteers scattered throughout the whole foreign field. Now, as they stand in the very midst of the conflict, they need our spiritual support even more than ever before. It is this, as Livingstone was wont to urge, that the missionary most prizes.

Paul's request to the Thessalonians is the request of every missionary, coming to us today: "Brethren, pray for us, that the Word of the Lord may run and be glorified, even as also it is with you." Some of the mightiest spiritual achievements of missions are waiting on our full and glad obedience to the prayer requests of the volunteers at the front. And, let it be reiterated, this world will not be evangelized in this generation if Christians continue to ignore that which is at once their chief obligation and their most transcendent privilege.

What may we as members and friends of this Movement do to meet its greatest need? There are a few definite things which might be done, and which, if well done, may mark an epoch in its life:

See that the Day of Prayer for the Movement is faithfully observed. By following the plan for the monthly misisonary meeting outlined in this number of *The Student Volunteer* the importance of this whole subject may be brought home forcibly to thousands of Christian students and professors.

Ensure a very wide circulation of the pamphlet, *Prayer and Missions,* by Mr. Robert E. Speer. A student, a band, or an association can do no greater good for missions than to have on hand a supply of this remarkably trenchant and spiritual paper, and to give it out wisely to students, professors, ministers, association secretaries, and leaders of Christian societies of young people.

As volunteers, make our own prayer life more real, practical, and powerful. To this end might we not in our daily devotional Bible study during the next six months specialize on the subject of prayer, bringing to bear the incentives, helps, conditions, promises, examples upon our personal lives? Along with this Bible study, much help would be derived from a thoughtful reading of Murray's *With Christ in the School of Prayer,* Moule's *Secret Prayer,* Phelps's *Still Hour,* and the *Memoirs of David Brainard.*

By wise personal work seek to enlist others to pray regularly for the Movement, and, more than that, to become intercessors on behalf of the great missionary enterprise as a whole. To what further-reaching work, to what deeper joy, to what more exalted privilege can we invite them?

Let every volunteer and friend of the Movement obtain a copy of the *Cycle of Prayer of the Student Volunteer Movement,* and introduce the plan into his own prayer life. This *Cycle,* which has just appeared, has been prepared with great care, and is issued in a very attractive form. It is not intended for general circulation, but only for those who desire to undertake to pray daily and intelligently for world-wide missions. The opening pages contain the "Calls to Prayer,"

"Incentives to Prayer," "Conditions of Prevailing Prayer," and "Assurances for the Prayerful." Then follows the Cycle of Prayer proper which provides three objects for prayer for each day of the month. It is left open in several places so that other requests on foreign or home missions may be introduced. The closing pages contain invaluable suggestions on the use of the Cycle. It may be obtained from the office of the Movement for five cents. No one should send for it who does not fully intend to employ it. It will be far better to have a few hundreds of students using the Cycle conscientiously, than to have tens of thousands of copies sent broadcast over the student field. May God use this agency in helping to raise up that number which Spurgeon pleaded for in such burning words: "Oh, for some 500 Elijahs, each one upon his Carmel, crying unto God! and we should soon have the clouds bursting with showers. . . . Oh, for more prayer—more constant, incessant mention of the mission cause in prayer! and then the blessing will be sure to come."

PRAYER AND THE MISSIONARY ENTERPRISE

ADDRESS GIVEN AT
THE STUDENT VOLUNTEER CONVENTION
TORONTO, CANADA, FEBRUARY 26 - MARCH 2, 1902

Prayer and missions are as inseparable as faith and works; in fact prayer and missions *are* faith and works. Jesus Christ, by precept, by command, and by example, has shown with great clearness that He recognizes the greatest need of the enterprise of world-wide evangelization to be need of prayer. Before "give" and before "go" comes "pray." This is the divine order. Anything that reverses or alters it inevitably leads to loss or disaster. This is strikingly illustrated also in the wonderful achievements of the early Christians, which were made possible by their constant employment of the irresistible, hidden forces of the prayer kingdom. They ushered in Pentecost by prayer. When they wanted laborers they prayed. When the time came to send forth laborers the Church was called together to pray. Their great foreign missionary enterprise, which carried forward its work so rapidly through the Roman Empire, began in prayer. One of the two reasons for establishing the order of deacons was that the apostles, that is the leaders of the Church, might give themselves to prayer. When persecutions came, the Christians nerved and braced themselves by prayer. Every undertaking was begun, continued, and ended in prayer. In this we find the secret of those marvelous triumphs of the early Christian Church which never fail to move Christians.

As I traveled up and down the non-Christian world, making a comparative study of the progress of Christ's Kingdom in different sections of the great harvest field, the conviction became clear and strong that those missions for which the most real prayer has been offered, are the missions which have had the largest and apparently the most enduring spiritual success. This explains why some missions and organizations have had larger and more spiritual results than others, even though they have been at work in more difficult fields and in the midst of more adverse conditions and circumstances.

The source of the spiritual vitality and power of any Christian movement is prayer. Our hope and confidence in this sublime enterprise of world-wide missions that has engrossed our attention these five days is placed, not in the extent and strength of the missionary organization; it is not placed in the number and power of the missionary force; not in the fulness of the treasury and in well-appointed material equipment; not in the achievements of the past, even those of a spiritual character; not in the experience acquired in a long century of Christian missions; not in the methods and agencies which have been devised; not in the brilliancy and popularity of the leaders of the missionary movement at home and abroad; not in statesmanlike and far-sighted policies and plans; not in enthusiastic forward movements and inspiring watchwords:—"not by might, nor by power, but by my Spirit, saith the Lord of hosts." In the last analysis the source of the power of any spiritual movement is God, and the energies of God are released in answer to prayer.

Everything vital to the missionary enterprise hinges upon prayer. The opening of the difficult fields depends upon prayer. Some one has said that China was opened at the point of the lancet, but that is a very superficial observation. Any one who has studied the history of the pioneer missionaries of China and the cause of their going to lay siege to that great Empire, knows that prayer was the great unlocking force. Not many years ago it was said that the zenanas could not be opened to missionaries in India and in other parts of the Far East. It was the subject of much discussion. But while the discussion was in progress, God swung the doors ajar in answer to the fervent and faithful prayer of those who believed on Him.

Moreover, to batter down the walls of opposition, persecution, and peril, prayer is as essential as it is sufficient. There has been no more heartening example of the reality of intercession than we have had in that marvelous group of facts connected with the raising of the siege of Peking. At a time when rationalists in Europe and in our own country have been loudly asserting that prayer does not have achieving power, that it does not bring things to pass objectively, that it has simply a reflex influence, this experience has been an inspiring evidence in the eyes of the world, which has challenged attention and has banished much of skepticism upon this subject.

Are more workers needed? This is the secret of securing them. It is not by organizations, not by fervent appeals, not by multiplying the secretaries of the Student Volunteer Movement, that we are going to get all the workers needed. The one method which Jesus Christ emphasized for obtaining laborers is prayer, and He went to the center of every problem. "Pray ye the Lord of the harvest that He send forth laborers into His harvest." It never ceases to move me to wonder, that God has conditioned the going forth of the laborers upon the faithfulness or the faithlessness of His own disciples in prayer.

In 1872 the Church Missionary Society adopted the plan of a day of intercession in order that they might obtain more workers. In the five years preceding 1872 they sent out fifty-one missionaries; in the five years following that year, during which years they observed this day of special intercession, they sent out 112 missionaries. Dr. Scofield, after winning $7,500 in prizes in the British colleges and achieving a reputation as one of the most brilliant students in those universities, went out as a medical missionary to China in 1881. He died in 1884 after putting in three years of useful service. He had a great burden on his heart that God would thrust forth more university men into the foreign mission field, and he gave himself much to prayer for this purpose. His wife has borne testimony since his death, that time after time she heard him praying in his study that God would separate from the English universities more students unto missionary work. The year after his death the Cambridge Seven went forth. One is now Bishop of West China, another is assistant general director of the China Inland Mission, one was a pioneer missionary in Tibet, another we are honored in having with us in this convention. All of them have been useful workers in the harvest field. And I can testify, after traveling widely among the universities for well-nigh fourteen years, that the example of the Cambridge Seven has influenced scores of the strongest university men of North America and Europe to devote their lives to missionary service.

In 1886 the China Inland Mission had 200 missionaries. A number of them met that year for an eight days' conference for Bible study and also for united prayer. While they were together they were led by a great grip of faith to unite in prayer that God would thrust forth into that mission during the year 100 additional missionaries; and before the conference closed one of them suggested that they have a praise meeting to thank God for answering the prayer, because he said, "We shall not all of us be able to come together for that purpose a year hence." They did so. Within the following year there were 600 who applied to be sent out; the Mission selected and sent out 100 of them.

Is it money that we need? If so, here again I find the deepest secret. Take the illustration I have just given, the sending out of 100 missionaries by the China Inland Mission. It required an increase in their budget from $100,000 to $150,000. Hudson Taylor and some of his co-workers have called attention to the fact that they were led to offer this definite prayer, that, if it be the will of God, the $50,000 needed might be received in large amounts. Within a year, in eleven gifts ranging from $2,500 to over $12,000, the whole sum came in. Dr. A. J. Gordon, of sainted memory, had a church which, some of us know, was by no means one of the wealthy city churches of America. It was giving $5,000 to foreign missions. That was regarded as very generous by all who knew the church. And yet Dr. Gordon was not satisfied. He said, "We ought to do better than this," and so one day he said from his pulpit: "We are going to change our method this year. Let us continue to use all the plans and agencies which have been successful in the past. But in addition to these, let us this year in the Sunday school, in the young people's societies, in the missionary organizations, at the family altar, in secret and in the public service, pray more for this great cause, that God may lead us to devise more liberal things for His kingdom." When they came to take the offering a year later, they received not $5,000 but over $10,000.

When I was in Kyoto, Japan, I heard an incident that impressed me much in this connection. Dr. Gulick and his wife wanted to assist some Japanese students to secure money for a Young Men's Christian Association building in connection with one of the government colleges in that city. They wanted only $2,000. They wrote a letter to *The Evangelist* in New York, describing their need. That copy fell into the hands of a certain business man in New York State. He read it and was vexed by it. He thought that there were enough regular appeals for financial help without having special appeals made. He put the paper away, but could not leave it. The matter kept troubling him. Finally he took up the paper, read the article again, and dictated a letter to *The Evangelist* asking whether they had received the $2,000 needed. They replied that none of it had come in. He then wrote that he would give four instalments of $500 each that the building might be erected. Dr. and Mrs. Gulick and a group of Japanese students had been uniting daily in prayer for this definite object.

We need greater efficiency in all the missionary agencies and among all the various influences that are being exercised. There are being poured upon this world each year in Bible and in Christian literature, in preaching and teaching, far more Christian truth than was proclaimed and disseminated in the Roman Empire in many long years in the early history of Christianity. If the truth is not achieving as large results proportionately as it did in those days, it is not the fault of the missionaries, I am persuaded, so much as it is the fault of those of us who are Christians at home for not backing up their efforts that there may be added the help of the Holy Spirit in the use of this truth. The truth does not convert men. It is the Spirit of God using the truth and using us who convicts men of sin and leads them to close in upon Christ as their Saviour; and the Holy Spirit works in answer to prayer.

Thinking about the efficiency of agencies leads me with deep sympathy to enter a plea for more prayer for the missionaries. I have met in my travels nearly 2,000 missionaries representing about 100 different missionary organizations, and they presented to me one unbroken appeal for more prayer on the part of home Christians. Louder than their cry, "Brethren, come over and help us," there rang in my ears, as I journeyed through the mission fields, the cry, "Brethren, pray for us." The day upon which you think the missionaries need your prayers least, they may need them most. Might I be pardoned for a personal illustration? Before I started on my recent journey I sent out to not a few of the delegates of this convention, as well as to earnest Christians in different lands, a prayer card, and on that card were the dates of my different engagements in Japan, China, Ceylon, and India. On that card October 28-29 was put down for the voyage between Nagasaki and Shanghai. When I reached Japan I received an appeal from missionaries in North China urging me to visit that region. It was made plain to me that I ought to respond favorably to the invitation. The two days I was put down to be on the sea, when some of you might have thought that I needed your prayers very little, turned out to be the very days when I had a responsible part in connection with a conference of the Christians who had come up from the martyr Church of North China; when, if for any two days in this whole journey I in my soul craved the prayers of friends it was at that time.

We know not when the missionary stands before his greatest opportunity. We know not when fierce temptation may sweep in upon him like a flood. We know the devices of the adversary. Let the Scripture warning ring in our souls, "God forbid that I should sin against the Lord in ceasing to pray for you." I sin against myself in ceasing to do so, for such neglect makes me that much more selfish and unsympathetic. I sin against you in ceasing to pray for you, because I reduce your working power. But the serious and awfully sad side of the subject is that I sin against the Lord in ceasing to pray for you. Therefore let us be faithful in praying for those who are not within the range of our vision; who are in fields of great difficulty and peril and trial and loneliness, and who without our prayers cannot do their largest and best work.

Let us not forget to pray for the native Christians. Remember that they have come up out of sin, superstition, and degradation. Remember how weak they are in many cases. Remember how fiercely they are tempted. Above all, remember that from the ranks of the native Church are to come by far the larger part of the laborers who are to evangelize the world in our generation, if it is to be done. I think of that Pastor Hsi whose life has been written so interestingly and inspiringly by Mrs. Howard Taylor in the book entitled, *One of China's Scholars*. That pastor in his lifetime founded and set in motion many Christian and benevolent institutions, and by work and life directly and indirectly was the means of the conversion of hundreds of Chinese. Let it not be forgotten that his conversion was traceable to the prayers of David Hill, that saint and scholar; and, by the way, the life of David Hill is another biography which should be read along with the life of this Chinese scholar. We could multiply many, many fold the evangelizing power of the missionary agencies, if we would set apart more time from day to day to pray for the native Church.

Do we desire to witness spiritual awakenings on the mission field? This is pre-eminently the secret. It ought to be reiterated in every missionary convention. Take the great Telugu revival in which, as the result of the prayers of a few who did not become discouraged, nearly 10,000 were baptized within less than a year. That great movement in Northern India, in connection with which tens of thousands of people are being born into the Kingdom of Jesus Christ, its leaders persist in telling us, is a definite product of prayer. When I was visiting a college in Ceylon, one morning before daybreak I heard singing. I did not know what it meant, but later I was told that some of the students were up having a before-daybreak prayer meeting that the Spirit of God might strengthen them to lead their fellow students to Christ. I was not surprised to find that before night that day they had led several of their fellow students to Christ.

Speaking of Ceylon reminds one of that mother of a thousand daughters, Miss Agnew. In connection with her labor by her words and life, it is said that during her career fully 1,000 of the girls who attended her school were led to become Christians. It has been pointed out since her death that she had the habit, in addition to all her administrative and teaching work, of setting aside literally hours each week to pray for these girls by name.

In 1883 a wave of rationalism and skepticism swept over the Doshisha, the leading Christian college of Japan, and it became very cold spiritually. Dr. Davis, one of the missionaries there, recognized the truth of what we have been speaking of tonight and wrote back to over twenty colleges and theological seminaries of America, asking the students to unite in prayer for the Doshisha. Not a few Christian students heeded the request. On the night that the American students united in prayer the Doshisha students in different rooms, without any direct human influence being brought to bear upon them, were led to fall into conversation on the subject of personal religion and to give themselves to prayer. A revival began that very night and spread through the college. It resulted in the conversion of a large number of the students. Every forward movement, if we could get at the facts, would be traceable to hidden places where we should find some Paul or Zinzendorf or Carey or George Müller or Hudson Taylor giving himself to prayer. The streams that turn the machinery of the world rise in solitary places.

Prayer is the greatest force that we can wield. It is the greatest talent which God has given us. He has given it to every person here. There is a democracy in this matter. We may differ among ourselves as to our wealth, as to our social position, as to our educational equipment, as to our native ability, as to our inherited characteristics; but in this matter of exercising the greatest force that is at work in the world today, we are on the same footing. It is possible for the most obscure person in this great convention, if that one's heart is right toward God, to exercise as much power for the evangelization of this world, as it is for those who stand in the most prominent positions but do not use this talent. Therefore is not the greatest sin which we can commit the sin of omitting to pray? Think of the blessing that we are withholding, not only from ourselves, but also from our colleges, from our missionaries, from the distant mission fields. What right have we to leave unappropriated or unapplied the greatest force which God has ordained for the salvation and transformation of men and for the inauguration and energizing of Christian movements? May the wish of Spurgeon be ours—the wish that there might be 500 Elijahs, each one upon his Mount Carmel, making incessant mention of the mission cause in prayer. Then that little cloud, which is no larger than a man's hand, would spread and spread until it darkened the heavens, and the windows above would open, and the showers would come down upon this thirsty earth.

When I went through Palestine I was deeply moved with the reflection, that if the little hill back of Nazareth could disclose its secret, if the Galilean lake could tell all that has taken place there, if the desert places round about Jerusalem could unfold their story, if the olive trees could reveal what they have witnessed, they would fill in the silent places of the Gospels and would tell us chiefly about the prayer life of our Lord. They would tell us of the range of His prayer life, of its unselfishness, of its intensity, of its unceasingness, of its fervor and of its irresistible power because of the godly fear behind it. Does there not take possession of us a stronger ambition than ever to be men and women of prayer? And shall we not in the quiet of the closing of this convention resolve that whatever else we do or do not do, we will form the undiscourageable resolution to be more faithful in prayer, to follow in the footsteps of Jesus Christ our exemplar in prayer? May His Spirit actually energize our wills now, both to will this thing and then to do it, in a way that pleases Him.

THE VOLUNTEER AS A SPIRITUAL FORCE

ARTICLE IN *THE STUDENT VOLUNTEER*
FEBRUARY, 1893

Each volunteer should be a center of power. By virtue of his consecration and his clearly defined life purpose, he is in a position to exert a mightier influence for missions than any other man. In what ways should the energy of each volunteer—from the weakest and most obscure to the strongest and most prominent—make itself felt?

Each volunteer should be an educational force. In the college or seminary, in the association or the missionary society, in the church, and in the young people's organization he should have the reputation of being well informed on missions; and, more than that, of being able to present the subject in an interesting and forcible manner. By public address, by conversation, by pen, and by the circulation of literature, he should spread the most telling missionary facts, and make known the great principles of missions. All this involves diligent, continuous, and progressive study. Some volunteers of very ordinary ability have aroused entire institutions and communities on missions as a result of giving themselves to this work with determination and enthusiasm.

There is need today for each volunteer to become a financial force. In no other direction will his efforts be more useful to his missionary board. Many colleges, seminaries, and churches have been led to support a missionary because of the persevering work of a few volunteers. One volunteer in one summer vacation influenced the churches where he spoke to increase their contributions over $5,000. Very few volunteers are using their opportunities for doing this important work. What a field presents itself in the religious societies of young people in the various churches. They include in the aggregate 3,000,000 members. Only a small portion of their number are giving systematically to missions. If even a majority of them were influenced to do so, the financial problem would soon be solved. Who can appeal to these young people with anything like the force of the sincere, earnest, and intelligent volunteer? A volunteer should aim to secure a financial constituency, and so to cultivate it as to insure his own support on the foreign field.

The greatest responsibility resting upon the volunteer is that he be a praying force. If he would exert a marked influence on educational and financial lines he must have behind his words and efforts a momentum born of spending hours and hours in prayer. If he would preserve and strengthen his missionary purpose against the many and insidious influences which tend to weaken it he must "pray always with all prayer." If he would see the obstacles removed which prevent volunteers from hastening to the open places of the world he must obey the command of Christ and "pray the Lord of the harvest that He thrust forth laborers into His harvest."

While absorbed with the great interests which concern his future work in regions thousands of miles beyond, the volunteer should also strive to be a missionary force today in the field just at hand. He should be one of the most constant personal workers in his college as well as a moving spirit in country or city missions. Let it not be said of him, whose lifework is to be that of soul-winning, that he has spent from three to seven years in intellectual preparation but has never led a man to commit his life to Jesus Christ. Mr. Moody's question is a searching one: "If you cannot win souls in your own college or your own town, how can you expect to win souls in Africa or India?"

It is essential that each volunteer be a self-perpetuating force. He should enroll other volunteers among his fellow students to take his place when he leaves. Nothing will so strengthen his own convictions. In no way can he to such an extent multiply his own influence. A volunteer in a western college, who afterward attended an eastern seminary, enlisted during his student days 108 volunteers, some of whom have already sailed. Upon such efforts put forth by individual volunteers depends not only the permanency of the Movement but its very life.

The volunteer must not lose sight of the fact that he belongs to a Student Volunteer Movement; that it is a Movement for foreign missions; moreover, that it has for the execution of its work a time limit—the present generation. The only victory which will take this world for Christ will be an active, unwavering, ever-growing faith in the watchcry: "The Evangelization of the World in This Generation." This should be the pervading purpose, the controlling idea, the only sufficient reason for the existence of such a Movement. Each volunteer therefore should keep before him as his first ambition and as his final ambition—the Pauline ambition: to be an evangelizing force where Christ has not been named.

THE SPRINGS OF POWER

ARTICLE IN *THE INTERCOLLEGIAN*
FEBRUARY, 1920

The Volunteer Movement at the end of thirty-three years is strong and vital and was never more so. Why has it gone from strength to strength all these years and what has been the secret of its productive power? The true answer to this penetrating question will point the way to the larger achievements which lie before the student missionary uprising. In the first place, its personnel has been made up of those who are young and vigorous, whose minds are educated and whose lives are consecrated to the service of God and man. Its members have been fired with undying enthusiasm and have ever been responsive to new and larger visions and plans. Their eyes have been fixed on the coming day and they have never lost the first flush of optimistic hope.

Vigilant and constant supervision has been one of the prices paid for the growing fruitfulness of the Movement. Only one year was it left without administrative direction and in that short time it broke into parts and its impact on the college life of the continent was greatly weakened. The lesson, however, was learned and ever since, the Movement has had the benefit of wise guidance. In this connection attention should be called to the mutual benefits which have been obtained from the close organic relation which has ever existed between the Volunteer Movement on the one hand and the Young Men's Christian Association and the Young Women's Christian Association of the United States and Canada on the other. Throughout the whole generation they have acted and reacted most helpfully upon each other. Moreover, the Movement has had the invaluable counsel of trusted leaders of the Foreign Mission Boards of the churches. It has regarded itself as their servant and has never lost touch with them. Now that so many of the boards have candidate secretaries or departments closely articulated with the Movement, and now that so many of their administrative officers are men or women who were once volunteers or whose early lives were profoundly influenced by the Movement, this relationship has become closer than ever.

Through all the years the Movement has focused its energies on its distinctive work, that of recruiting men and women for the missionary career. It has furnished a splendid example of undeflected energy. Time after time efforts have been made to induce it to interest itself in other objects or to broaden or weaken its purpose but it has held without wavering to its objective and has continued to find its strength in the appeal for life.

The Student Volunteer Movement has kept a continuous human stream flowing out from the American and Canadian universities to the nations of the earth. This has made possible the preservation of its reality, its contagious enthusiasm, and its world-conquering power. Had it not thus preserved its crusading character, it would, like so many other organizations, have stagnated and passed away.

The path of boldness is the path of growth. The Student Volunteer Movement addressed itself to a colossal task which made an heroic appeal. In undertaking to give all people now living an adequate opportunity to know the Living Christ, and in adopting the audacious program of making the reign of Christ co-extensive with the inhabited earth, it confronted the students of the world with a challenge great and bold enough to call out their latent capacities and to command their extreme devotion.

The realization of the watchword of the Movement has necessitated its traveling by the way of the Cross. In those colleges and seminaries and in those countries where its leaders have recognized this most clearly, the spirit of the Movement has been preserved in greatest purity and in truly world-conquering power. The program of the Movement might well be characterized as a campaign of unselfishness. It has never sought to develop into a permanent organization or to become an end in itself. In a sense it has violated all canons of building up a strong organization in that every year of its life it has pushed out to foreign lands nearly all of its leaders. Its ambition has been not to perfect an organization but to lose itself in the world's greatest cause. Thus it has expressed itself through many Christian communions and through countless Christian organizations and agencies. It has decreased; they have increased. It is this deep, sacrificial strain running through all its activities which explains its multiplying power. "Except a grain of wheat fall into the ground and die it abideth by itself alone; but if it die it bringeth forth much fruit."

The true source of the vital energy of the Movement has been its relation, through the exercise of prayer, to the Source of all life and power. The streams that turn the machinery of the world rise in solitary places. The origins of this incomparable offering of life lie in secret places—in the lives of individual students in communion with the Living God. The Movement assumed visible, corporate expression in the never-to-be-forgotten gatherings for united prayer of the undergraduates at Mount Hermon. Every onward impulse in its career was generated in prayer. Everything vital or essential to its trimphant progress among the nations—the separating of workers, the thrusting them forth as God-sent men, the overcoming of apparently insuperable obstacles, the coming upon them of accessions of superhuman power, the manifesting through them of the Spirit of Christ, the fountain of all the real beauty that is in the world, the laying of the foundations and raising of the walls of the Kingdom of Christ among the nations—these and everything else bearing the divine marks are traceable to prayer. Jesus Christ is at once the attractive and the impelling force of the Movement. It is occupied with His program. It acknowledges Him as its divine leader. In so far as it humbles itself and yields itself to His sway, He will continue to be its productive power. "A body of free men who love God with all their might, and yet know how to cling together, could conquer this modern world of ours."

PART FOUR

RESOLUTIONS OF THE EXECUTIVE COMMITTEE OF THE STUDENT VOLUNTEER MOVEMENT IN APPRECIATION OF THE SERVICES OF DR. JOHN R. MOTT AS CHAIRMAN OF THE EXECUTIVE COMMITTEE, PASSED JUNE 5, 1920

RESOLUTIONS OF THE EXECUTIVE COMMITTEE OF THE STUDENT VOLUNTEER MOVEMENT IN APPRECIATION OF THE SERVICES OF DR. JOHN R. MOTT AS CHAIRMAN OF THE EXECUTIVE COMMITTEE, PASSED JUNE 5, 1920

⁂⁂⁂

THE REALIZATION of the magnitude of the debt that the Student Volunteer Movement for Foreign Missions owes to Dr. Mott, and our gratitude to God for all that Dr. Mott has meant to the Movement, make it impossible to formulate resolutions that will adequately express our appreciation.

Dr. Mott was one of those hundred men who in 1886, kneeling together in that historic room at Mount Hermon, gave birth to the Student Volunteer Movement. From that day to this Dr. Mott has been, under God, one of the most potent factors in the history of this Movement. He has built his life into it so that it has come to hold a central place in his heart.

In 1888 Dr. Mott became chairman of the Executive Committee of the Movement, which position he has held continuously for thirty-three years.

His work with the International Committee of the Young Men's Christian Association, serving the interests of the students of North America, gave to him a place of commanding leadership. He was one of the founders, in 1895, of the World's Student Christian Federation, and its first General Secretary. In 1895-1897 he made an extensive tour of the world, at which time he helped to found the student movements of India, China, Japan, and Australasia.

Important national and international honors and responsibilities have come to Dr. Mott with the passing of the years, but to the Student Volunteer Movement he has continued to give a large share of his time. To this Movement he has contributed a deep personal interest and a close and wise supervision. The ideals and watchword of the Movement, "The Evangelization of the World in This Generation," have completely dominated his life in all its relationships.

Dr. Mott's books, *The Strategic Points in the World's Conquest*, *The Evangelization of the World in This Generation*, *The Pastor and Modern Missions*, *The Future Leadership of the Church*, and *The Present World Situation,* have enabled him to present the challenge of the world-wide foreign missionary movement in a convincing and powerful manner to Anglo-Saxon Christendom, and have greatly helped to extend the influence of the Student Volunteer Movement throughout North America. Especially is this true of the book *The Evangelization of the World in This Generation,* which is an explanation and defense of the watchword of the Movement. By his clear and convincing presentation of the watchword in this book thousands of pastors, missionaries, and missionary administrators have come to believe in it and have accepted the evangelization of the world in this generation as a permanent working ideal for their own lives. There are hundreds of missionaries and missionary administrators who owe to this book the inspiration for their lifework in Kingdom service.

From the early days when the budget was only a few thousand dollars, Dr. Mott has always borne a large share of the financial burden. The manner in which this increasingly large budget has been raised through these years is evidence of God's blessing upon the methods and ideals of the Movement under Dr. Mott's leadership.

The quadrennial conventions, which for the past generation have held such a unique place in the religious and missionary life of the educational institutions of the United States and Canada, were made possible largely through Dr. Mott's great administrative ability. All who are at all familiar with the history of these conventions connect them invariably with Dr. Mott's name and personality. His quiet and forceful dignity made him a master of great assemblies so that he guided these conventions, where were gathered the choicest lives in our American colleges, so that great spiritual resources for the enrichment and healing of the whole world were released at Cleveland, Detroit, Toronto, Nashville, Rochester, Kansas City, and Des Moines. His wonderful addresses at these and other student conferences and assemblies the world over have lifted men to high unselfish endeavors and won numbers to acknowledge Jesus Christ as Lord and Master.

The Movement owes much of its present influence and prestige to Dr. Mott's national and international reputation. But greater than all this has been the depth and power of his personality. It has been his missionary passion and the quiet strength of religious life with its constant emphasis upon the great spiritual fundamentals of the Christian faith that have enabled this Movement to remain true to the great formative ideals so that it is today recognized as an outstanding spiritual force in the life of our churches and in the colleges of North America.

It was the unanimous wish of the Nominating Committee of the Executive Committee that Dr. Mott continue his leadership of this Movement. It is therefore only with great reluctance, and a keen sense of individual and personal loss, that his resignation has been accepted. In recognition of these thirty-three years of service, it is resolved that we incorporate in the records of the Student Volunteer Movement for Foreign Missions our high appreciation of this wise, able, and efficient leadership throughout a generation.

Dr. Mott's continued interest and helpful counsel in the future of the Movement is assured. He loves the Student Volunteer Movement and we love and honor him. Our friendship, our best wishes, our prayers, will continue to follow him in the wide service to which he so unselfishly gives his life.

INDEX

Intercollegiate Young Men's Christian Association, 34, 35, 56, 291
See also: College Young Men's Christian Association, Student Young Men's Christian Association
Intercollegiate Young Women's Christian Association, 34, 35, 56
See also: College Young Women's Christian Association, Student Young Women's Christian Association
International Committee of the Young Men's Christian Associations, 9, 26, 274, 293, 375
International Committee of the Young Women's Christian Associations, 9, 26
International Health Board of the Rockefeller Foundation, 220
International Labor Office, 219, 263
International Missionary Council, 227, 231, 240, 256, 267, 268, 269
International relations, Christianizing, 195-197
Interracial Commission of the Young Men's Christian Association, 226
Interseminary Missionary Alliance, American, 8, 9, 26, 29, 34, 35, 56
Iowa, 16, 31, 36, 206, 275
Ireland, 62, 186, 266, 318
Islam (Mohammedanism) 52, 154, 155, 156, 166, 249, 324
Italy, 12, 32, 206

Jaffna College, 311
Jaffna Student Foreign Missionary Society, 302
Japan, 5, 12, 24, 32, 83, 92, 98, 108, 109, 122, 138, 139, 151, 152, 156, 166, 175, 186, 192, 206, 215, 221, 232, 249, 254, 260, 261, 263, 282, 285, 302, 310, 313, 322, 326,, 328, 329, 330, 331, 332, 333, 334, 335, 338, 339, 341, 342, 346, 348, 349, 353, 354, 364, 365, 375
Jenks, Jeremiah, 254
Jerusalem, 227, 231, 238, 239, 240, 258, 267, 368
Jesuits, 350
Jesus Christ and World Evangelization, 257
Jews, 214, 252
John, Griffith, 331, 348
Jones, Stanley, 239
Joyce, Bishop, 293
Judson, Adoniram, 3, 285, 314

Kagawa, Toyohiko, 235, 260

Kansas, 16, 31, 36
Kansas City, 141, 172, 175, 184, 203, 210, 235, 376
Kant, Immanuel, 206
Keith-Falconer, 51, 289
Keller, F. A., 36, 37
Kellogg, S. H., 78
Kemmerer, ———, 254
Kennedy, ———, 36
Kennedy School of Missions, 178
Kentucky, 16, 30, 36
Kerr, Dr. ———, 310
Keswick, 290, 291
Kidd, Benjamin, 102, 179
Kinsinger, ———, 36
Klondike, 315
Knotts, J. E., 57, 74
Knox, John, 347
Kobe College, 249
Korea, 12, 32, 98, 122, 175, 186, 206, 249, 254, 302, 310, 326, 327, 329, 330, 331, 334, 339, 354
Kraemer, Dr. H., 249
Kya, Moses, 352

Laidlaw, Sir Robert, 254
Lake Geneva, Wisconsin, 76, 211, 290, 358
Lake Mohonk, New York, 156
Lambeth Conference, 71, 111, 317
Laos, 12, 32, 98, 122
Larsen, L. P., 249
Latin America, 119, 135, 139, 166, 167, 192, 196, 214, 224, 227, 232, 235, 246, 254, 256, 258, 261, 264
Latin Church countries of Europe, 98, 123, 175
Lawrence, E. A., 78
Laymen's Missionary Movement, 129-130, 135, 148, 179, 189, 227, 281, 337
Laymen's Missionary Movement (Australasia), 154
Lea, Bishop, 249
Leadership, indigenous, development in mission lands of, 190-191
Leadership of the Student Volunteer Movement; early lack of, 7, 25, 25-26; training of the, 11, 76
Leadership needed by Christian missions, characteristics of the, 242-247, 357
League of Nations, 218, 219, 221
Learmouth, B. L. Livingstone, 292, 294
Leavitt, G. W., 75
Lee, E. J., 75
Levant, 109, 186, 285, 304, 353
Lewis, R. E., 57